Catching Up
and
Falling Behind

Post-Communist Transformation
in Historical Perspective

David A Dyker
University of Sussex, UK

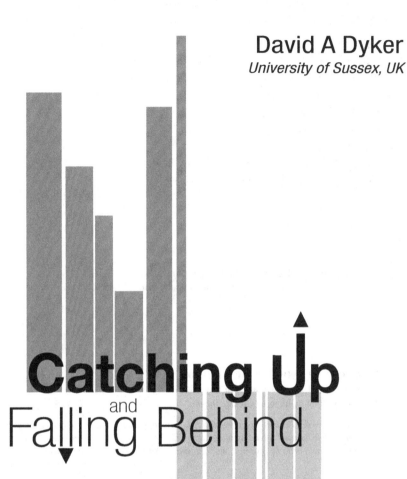

Catching Up
and
Falling Behind

Post-Communist Transformation
in Historical Perspective

Imperial College Press

ICP

Published by

Imperial College Press
57 Shelton Street
Covent Garden
London WC2H 9HE

Distributed by

World Scientific Publishing Co. Pte. Ltd.
5 Toh Tuck Link, Singapore 596224
USA office: 27 Warren Street, Suite 401-402, Hackensack, NJ 07601
UK office: 57 Shelton Street, Covent Garden, London WC2H 9HE

British Library Cataloguing-in-Publication Data
A catalogue record for this book is available from the British Library.

ISBN-13 978-1-86094-434-5
ISBN-10 1-86094-434-5

Typeset by Stallion Press
Email: enquiries@stallionpress.com

Printed in Singapore

Acknowledgements

The majority of the articles contained in this book were originally published in various journals. "*Nomenklatura* nationalism: The key to an understanding of the new East European politics?" was published in the *Australian Journal of Politics and History*, Vol. 41, No. 1, 1995. "The structural origins of the Russian economic crisis" was published in *Post-Communist Economies*, Vol. 12, No. 1, 2000. "Technology and structure in the Polish economy under transition and globalisation" first saw the light of day in *Economic Systems*, Vol. 24, No. 1, 2000; and "Trade policy for the countries of the FSU: what can the developed industrial countries do to help?" first appeared in *Ritsumeikan Journal of International Relations and Area Studies*, Vol. 28, No. 2, 2002. "The dynamic impact on the Central-East European countries of accession to the European Union" was first published in *Europe-Asia Studies*, Vol. 53, No. 7, 2001, and "'East'-'West' networks and their alignment: Industrial networks in Hungary and Slovenia" in *Technovation*, Vol. 23, 2003. "Key actors in the process of innovation and technology transfer in the context of economic transition" and "Economic performance in the transition countries: A comparative perspective" both originally came out in

Science and Public Policy (Vol. 25, No. 4, 1998 and Vol. 27, No. 3, 2000). "The Russian R&D system and the foreign business sector" was originally published in *Research Policy*, Vol. 30, 2001, and "Building the knowledge-based economy in countries in transition — from concepts to policies" in the *Journal of Interdisciplinary Economics*, Vol. 12, No. 1, 2000. "Building social capability for economic catch-up: The experience and prospects of the post-socialist countries" was published in *Innovation*, Vol. 14, No. 3, 2001. "What transition has learned from Economics — and what Economics has learned from transition" was first published in *The Current State of Economic Science*, Vol. 5, edited by SB Dahiya and published by Spellbound Press. Finally, I have to thank my co-authors — Stanislaw Kubielas of the Department of Economics, University of Warsaw for Chapter 4, Slavo Radošević of the School of Slavonic and East European Studies, University College London, for Chapters 10 and 12; and Agnes Nagy (Kopint-Datorg, Budapest), Hedvika Spilek and Peter Stanovnik of the Institute of Economic Research, Ljubljana, Jeffrey Turk of the Slovenian Academy of Sciences and Peter Vince (Institute of Economics, Hungarian Academy of Sciences, Budapest) for Chapter 7. Their contribution was in each case invaluable.

David A. Dyker
December 2003

Contents

Part I

Introduction

Introduction

Chapter 1

Transforming The Post-Socialist Economies: Patterns and Paradoxes

Capitalism is by nature and form a method of economic change, and not only never is but never can be stationary. And this evolutionary character of the capitalist process is not merely due to the fact that economic life goes on in a social and natural environment which changes and by its change alters the data of economic action... The fundamental impulse that sets and keeps the capitalist engine in motion comes from the new consumers' goods, the new methods of production or transportation, the new markets, the new forms of industrial organisation that capitalist enterprise creates.

Joseph Schumpeter, *Capitalism, Socialism and Democracy*, Chapter VII

It would be odd, indeed, if the economic experience of the countries of Central-East Europe (CEE), the Balkans and the former Soviet Union in the period since the collapse of communism were significantly different from that of other groups of economies in dynamic phases of development. It would be particularly odd if countries that had gone through a sustained and increasingly profound structural crisis in the last decades of communism did not encounter equally profound structural challenges in the initial period of transition. And it

3

Chart 1.   The antonyms of transformation.

Fall in production	Increase in production
Falling behind	Catching up
Poverty	Prosperity
Strengthening the state	Strengthening the market
Debureaucratisation	Institution-building
Distrust	Trust
Cultural confrontation	Cultural congruence
Forgetting	Learning
Polarisation	Equalisation
Peripheralisation	Integration
Fragmentation	Integration
Exclusion	Integration

would be scarcely credible that these challenges could be met without engendering a whole gamut of tensions and contradictions, economic, social and political. That, in a nutshell, is the theme of this book — the pain and the gain from transformation, and the complex pattern of interaction between them.

So what have the main tensions and contradictions of transformation been? Chart 1 presents a set of pairs of antonyms which bring out the key paradoxes of the process. Some of these paradoxes are easy

Fall in production/ growth in production

enough to resolve. It is hardly surprising that there was an initial fall in output in all the transition countries, following by renewed growth from the mid-1990s onwards, as the countries concerned made preliminary, painful adjustments, and "stepped back so as to be able to jump further". More puzzling is why some economies, notably those of the former Soviet Union, took so long to start growing again. Most disturbingly, some countries had, by the late 1990s, fallen into renewed recession, following an initial recovery.

Catching up and falling behind

These patterns are analysed in detail in Chapter 11. The issue of catching up and falling behind, which is, indeed, a central theme of the book as a whole, is first broached in Chapter 4 and further developed in Chapter 6. Finally, in Chapter 12, we try to provide a synthesis of the arguments involved. Chapters 6 and 12 likewise highlight the question of poverty, while at the same time trying *Poverty and prosperity* to plot the likely pathway to general prosperity, in some of the sub-regions of the transition area, if not necessarily all of them.

The contradiction between the goals of strengthening the state and strengthening the market is, again, more apparent than real. As Margaret Thatcher showed in Great Britain in the late 1970s and early 1980s, you can roll back the state and strengthen it at the same time. It takes a strong — and honest — state to collect taxes and keep big companies in order, and in the absence of such a *Strengthening the state and strengthening the market* state the basic conditions for level-playing field market activity will not be met. But in the post-socialist countries there are paradoxes within paradoxes here, as evinced by the analysis presented in Chapters 2 and 3. The typical transition state of the 1990s was weak and dishonest, unable to collect taxes except through corrupt deals with regional and sectoral power-brokers, more interested in selling favours than in levelling the playing field. And indeed any strengthening of the *nomenklatura* nationalist/feudal-bureaucratic regimes (see Chapters 2 and 3 for definitions) of that period would likely have generated as many new abuses as it removed old ones. But there is a sea-change here in the late 1990s and early 2000s. In the Balkans, the election defeat of Slobodan Milošević in October 2000 spelled the end of a classic *nomenklatura* nationalist regime. The death of Croatian president Franjo Tudjman in December 1999 and the subsequent election victory of the leftist-reformists in Croatia put that country firmly on the political road of the "clean-break" countries of CEE. The resignation of President Boris Yeltsin from the Russian presidency at the end of 1999 and the succession to that post of Vladimir Putin seemed to many to be more of a "consensual coup" than a democratic transition. But while President Putin's background is clearly *nomenklatura*, and while his policies on Chechnya, and on the freedom of the press, have posed big question marks over his democratic credentials, economic policy in Russia under Putin has done much to level the playing field. The effectiveness and probity of the tax collection system has improved greatly, and there has been some rationalisation of the political division of labour between centre and periphery. The Russian state is still weak and dishonest, but it is stronger and more honest that it was a few years ago, and the general impact of this on the Russian economy has been good.

In the CEECs and the Baltic countries the late 1990s witnessed a gradual improvement in the legislative thrust and executive power of the state. By the late 1990s, however, the situation in these countries with respect to the role of the state had been revolutionised by the prospect of accession to the European Union (EU). That prospect offered the candidate countries a ready-made system of governance, in the form of the *acquis communautaire*, covering many (not all) areas of economic policy, plus a number of related policy areas. Indeed, the EU went further than that, in *insisting* that all candidate countries adopt the chapters of the *acquis communautaire*, as a *prior condition* of accession. Thus the candidate countries were, in a sense, forced to accept the "free gift" of a fairly comprehensive system of economic regulation. As we shall see in Chapters 6 and 12, there are serious questions to be asked about the gaps in the *acquis*, and on the suitability of some of the elements of the *acquis* for catch-up countries. But it is beyond doubt that the assimilation of the *acquis* by the candidate countries has resulted in a significant strengthening of the capacity of the states involved.

In the economically least developed parts of the transition region — the Caucasus and Central Asia — there has been much less evolution in the political situation. In Georgia, Azerbaijan, Kazakhstan, Turkmenistan and Uzbekistan, the *nomenklatura* nationalist leaders

Debureaucratisation and institution building

who took power at the beginning of transition are still in power. Certainly, the nationalist element here is measured and low-key, with none of the rabid xenophobia of the Milošević regime. And significant progress has been made in building the executive capacity of the state, notably in Kazakhstan. But corruption is still a huge problem throughout these sub-regions. And when the governments of Central Asia and the Caucasus seek to develop proactive economy policy, they often seem to fall back into the style and pattern of Soviet "state capitalism". Here, then, we can probably say that states remain weak and ineffectual — and it is better that they should so remain.

It is within the state sector that we see the drama of institution-building against a background of debureaucratisation played out in its starkest form. The old socialist systems were bureaucratic systems *par excellence*, and it has been a huge challenge for the transition countries to build modern civil services to replace the old communist apparatuses. Getting rid of the "petty tutelage" of communism has certainly allowed for large-scale rationalisations of public sector employment. But the task of building the administrative and legal services necessary for a market economy has been a daunting one — even the *acquis communautaire* is of little use if you do not have a system of courts and a cadre of legal officers to implement its provisions. It is hardly surprising that, in the face of this challenge, that some transition countries have seen the total number of people employed in state administration rising rather than falling.

Yet it is in the new private sector, rather than the new public sector, that the greatest challenges of institution-building present themselves. The old *enterprises* of the socialist order were also essentially bureaucratic formations. The new *firms* of the post-socialist order are market-oriented, or are, at least, meant to be. But firms are not made overnight; still less are socialist enter-   ***Distrust and trust*** prises transformed into firms overnight.

Much of this book is taken up with the process of firm-building in the transition region (see, in particular, Chapters 7 and 9). I believe that this is the most important aspect of institution-building in the transition countries. As the following chapters show, the process is already well advanced in the CEECs. Elsewhere in the transition region it is still at an early stage. It goes without saying that transition to a mature market economy is ultimately not possible unless the country in question possesses an adequate network of mature firms, capable of operating profitably in a competitive and technologically dynamic environment (see Chapter 12).

Firms do not exist in a cultural and ethical vacuum. While the market imposes the parameters that channel the activity of firms, the precise way in which particular firms react to those parameters, outside the limited area of perfectly competitive commodity production, is conditioned by a mass of behavioural factors (see Chapter 7). Where there are significant network elements in supply relationships, involving the partial internalisation of transactions going outside the boundaries of the firm as such, trust is indispensable. Yet trust was also indispensable in the communist world, a world characterised by generalised distrust. Here we encounter a mass of apparent contradictions, which can only be resolved by digging deeper into the functional patterns of communism, on the one hand, and the market mechanism on the other. Under communism, the absence of elementary democratic rights and functions, and the poverty of civil society, meant that trust between strangers was impossible. Trust existed between friends and family members — and between the members of political "families" within the *nomenklatura*. To a degree, these patterns of trust within the old political elite survived the shock of the collapse of the communist system. But, as we shall see in Chapters 2 and 3, this continuity of trust must be rated a largely negative aspect of early transition. The kinds of trust which are both inputs into and outputs of a mature market system are of a wholly different kind. They are based on *experience and learning*. So while they are often between friends, they may be between strangers. They are also *institution-based*. As we shall see in Chapter 7, trust is no substitute for contractual commitments. Rather the two are seen, in a market context, as complementary. Good contracts make for trust, and trust helps to give contracts the flexibility they need to have in a technologically dynamic world.

But trust is not indivisible within the capitalist world. Trust seems to come easier between some combinations of cultural/national groups than between others. Let us take, for instance, the dimension of foreign direct investment (FDI), a crucial vehicle of technology transfer and productivity enhancement for post-socialist countries (see Chapter 8). The bulk of the FDI in the transition region originates from a small number of leading capitalist countries, notably the USA, Germany and Italy. It is clear, in this context, that, for instance, German companies are more comfortable investing in neighbouring countries with close cultural and historical links, like the Czech Republic, than, say, in Uzbekistan. And here the ethical/cultural notion of trust seems to refocus as something more concrete and production oriented. In Chapter 4 we will introduce and develop the concept of "technological congruence" in an attempt to give this refocusing a more precise analytical content.

As always, however, there is a flipside to this discourse of trust and congruence. If some of the outstanding successes of FDI in the transition region have been built on cultural congruence, other promising avenues have been cut off by cultural confrontation. FDI in Russia's manufacturing sector has been largely blocked *Cultural congruence and cultural confrontion* by the reluctance of Russian partners to adapt to the corporate and technological culture of their would-be partners from the West (Ahrend, 2000). Full normalisation of economic (and indeed political) relations between Serbia and Montenegro and the EU and the US continues to be hampered by residual bitterness over the Kosovo war, and the unresolved status of Kosovo today. And the general reluctance of Japanese firms to invest in the transition region (there are some outstanding exceptions, as we shall see later on) has reflected a lack of confidence on the part of those firms in their ability to impose their corporate and technological culture in the countries concerned.

Thus the paths of self-improvement that transition societies have to traverse are conditioned and constrained by the cultural and technological limitations of the organisations that would teach them. It is not just a matter of coming to grips with higher levels of management of innovation, quality and marketing, of building the "knowledge-based economy" (see Chapter 10). It is also a matter of coming to terms with Germanness or Japaneseness, and with the blindspots which appear on the corporate vision of the most advanced and far-sighted companies. So the learning that transition involves can be on a grand scale, or it can be petty. Something similar can be said of forgetting. There is much about the communist past that is best wiped from human memory altogether — the arbitrariness and ethical nihilism of the one-party system, the contempt for the consumer, the principle that "they pretend to pay us, we pretend to work". But communist societies were among *Forgetting and learning* the best educated in the world. Not all of the education was of the highest quality, and what passed for Economics in most communist countries, for example, was fit for nothing except the rubbish bin (Poland and Hungary were striking exceptions). But the knowledge base in areas like theoretical physics and mechanical engineering was sturdy and serviceable.

Almost as soon as the old system collapsed, many of the countries of the region began to experience the phenomenon of the "forgetting curve". It was particularly noticeable in the West Balkans, as a direct and indirect result of the post-Yugoslav conflict. Thus in FR Yugoslavia ("rump" Yugoslavia), which was subjected to sanctions through much of the 1990s, sanctions which, *inter alia*, barred Yugoslav airliners from landing at foreign airports, Yugoslav pilots effectively forgot how to fly.[1] Even in more normal conditions, in the successor states of the Soviet Union, the machine-tool industry collapsed so dramatically that the capability to make machine tools seems to have been largely lost — completely lost as far as computer-controlled machine tools are concerned (Gubanov, 2000). And these phenomena should not be seen as some bizarre outcome of the collapse of a dysfunctional system. Forgetting curves are well known in the development literature (Bell, 1997). The inability to sustain learning curves is, indeed, one of the central features of economic backwardness. By the same token, getting rid of forgetting curves is one of the essential conditions of sustainable growth.

Not all the transition countries have suffered from the forgetting curve problem. The CEECs have generally managed to forget the bad bits and hang on to the good bits. And in so doing, they have reinforced the gap between themselves and the other transition countries, a gap which has, indeed, tended to increase on nearly every key development indicator since transformation began. And the tendency to greater inequality can be seen on virtually every dimension as well. The gap between the richer and the poorer transition countries has increased. The gap between the rich and poor among the populations of the transition countries has increased in every case. The gap between the richer and poorer regions of virtually every transition country has increased. And the gap between the post-socialist countries as a whole and the developed industrial world has increased.

---

[1] I am indebted to Professor Ljubo Madžar for pointing this out.

These tendencies are not set in stone. Indeed over the past couple of years the post-socialist world has caught up a little with a faltering EU/US economy, while most of the countries of the FSU have been reporting growth rates of GDP higher than those of the CEECs (see Chapter 11). But it is too soon to say whether there has been any change of underlying trend. And the trend in personal inequality is unremit- *Polarisation and equalisation* ting. These patterns have to be set in the context of world trends. At the global level, too, the tendency is for the gap between the richest and the poorest countries to increase, for the distribution of income to become less equal, certainly among the OECD countries, and for regional disparities within countries to increase. So what is different and special about the transition countries? That is, indeed, a question that we have to ask repeatedly in relation to the role and position of the post-socialist region within the world at large.

One of the recurrent themes of the studies contained in this book is the key role of foreign investment, specifically foreign direct invest-ment in the process of transition. We noted above how issues of cultural congruence and confrontation can modify the impact of FDI. But we must be careful not to overparticularise the analysis of this central variable. In in-depth interviews carried out within the frame-work of a number of projects, one of the dominant themes has been the essentially global strategic vision of most multinational compa-nies. We hear the most straightforward arguments on this dimension from international oil companies, for example in justifying their investments in the former Soviet Union — we are global players, we are in every region of the world, and that is part of our competitive advantage, so when a new region opens up, we have to get in there. But while the argument is simple enough in relation to a natural-resource-based sector in which international prices are very volatile, it is less obvious, but no less compelling, in relation to engineering-based sectors. Here, the implicit argument is that, in Dunning's terms (see Chapter 4), you maximise your firm-specific advantages by being global — and therefore you maximise your scope for technology transfer by being global. In the language of the business executive, if you are not world-class, you will not become world-class by investing in Eastern Europe. Thus it is crucially important not to assume that a German firm investing in the Czech Republic is pursuing a purely regional strategy. If you do, you risk misunderstanding the nature of the technology transfer process involved, and therefore the pattern of productivity enhancement. Most seriously, you risk misunderstanding the pattern of supply networking that may flow from the initial investment, and therefore the pattern of productivity spillovers. It is not only lead firms that have global strategies. First-tier suppliers (see Chapter 4 for definition) may also think of themselves as global players, seeking to build production complexes in particular regions (e.g. CEE), but with *global* objectives in view. If you only ask such firms questions about their relations with *local* firms (including foreign-owned local firms), you may come away with the (completely mistaken) idea that they are not interested in network-building.

Does that mean that the firms and economies of the transition region are condemned to an essentially peripheral role in the game of global economic development? Have they simply

Peripheralisation and integration

exchanged the old hub-and-spoke pattern of the Soviet-dominated CMEA (Council for Mutual Economic Assistance) system for a new hub-and-spoke pattern centred on the EU and, more generally on the OECD area? If we look only at the main lead investments of key multinationals we may be inclined to say "no". Volkswagen-Škoda in the Czech Republic, the Audi Engine Plant in Hungary, Magyar Suzuki in the same country, to mention just a few, have succeeded in establishing highly complex operations in the region, operations founded on advanced technology and high productivity, and reporting satisfactory levels of profitability.

But the picture is clouded when we go beyond the lead investments. As we shall see in detail on subsequent chapters, even the most advanced transition economies have struggled to generate locally-owned supply industries to serve the great international projects and ensure that the gains in productivity and financial strength those projects produce are disseminated throughout the economy. International companies nearly always have serious problems with their local suppliers. But while the multinationals are anxious enough to resolve these problems, they do not generally take active measures to that end. They do not integrate their suppliers into their own, within-company training and technology transfer programmes, which play a key role in raising human capital endowment, and ultimately productivity, within the lead project. To a degree, multinationals seek to solve local supply problems indirectly — by operating with a much smaller number of first-tier suppliers than would be normal within Western Europe, and thus effectively devolving the problem of productivity and quality control to a limited number of first-tier suppliers. More directly, some companies follow an active policy of helping local suppliers to find foreign partners. The implication is that firms from transition countries are simply not capable of achieving the status of first-tier supplier on their own. Thus the top firms in the FDI business do not have many ideas about raising the game of local suppliers in transition countries beyond helping them to sell out to other foreign firms, so the whole cycle stays within the ambit of FDI. The key issue of linkages and spillovers *outside* the area of FDI remains unresolved. And it is that issue which is crucial in terms of the balance of deep and superficial integration within the region as a whole.

With peripheralisation goes fragmentation. Firms that are unable to integrate into international supply networks will find it difficult to develop their *domestic* supply linkages, difficult to grow in accordance with the underlying scope of markets and production possibilities. But the *Fragmentation and integration* theme of fragmentation is played out not only on the dimension of firms. At the level of civil society, and indeed of the state itself, the break-up of the communist monolith has created a new tension between the forces of dispersion and reintegration. The break-up in the immediate aftermath of the collapse of communism of the Soviet Union, the old Yugoslavia and Czechoslovakia, produced a pattern of Balkanisation that stretched from the Adriatic to Central Asia. If we factor out the Russian giant, the population of the average transition state is just 10 m. That in turn means that, in terms of GDP, most transition countries are substantially smaller than Portugal or Denmark or Finland. There is no reason why small states should not be efficient states, but the smaller the typical state in a particular region, the more time the government of that state will have to spend on the management of its relations with its neighbours — on border agreements, trade agreements, visa agreements, etc. The *reductio ad absurdum* of fragmentation is presented by the case of Bosnia, where a country of not many more than four million inhabitants is in turn divided into two "entities" — the Serb-dominated *Republika Srpska* and the Croat-Muslim confederation, with the latter in turn sub-divided into Croat and Muslim sections. The result is a political and economic nonsense, a "country" virtually incapable of exporting, totally dependent on foreign aid and racked by the corruption which that inevitably brings. But fragmentation has produced other paradoxes. Kazakhstan, a country with rich hydrocarbon reserves and the highest levels of GDP per head in Central Asia, finds itself nevertheless in a peculiarly isolated situation. Still heavily dependent on Russia for, e.g. oil pipeline transit, it now has to resolve any problems that arise therefrom through international negotiation rather than domestic consultation. Russian remains effectively the only *lingua franca* of Kazakhstan, and the teaching of English has made less progress than in Russia itself. The situation is similar in the other countries of Central Asia. These problems are clearly essentially transitional, but in this case the transition seems destined to take anything up to a generation to resolve. And normal patterns of economic intercourse across that region, and between it and the rest of the world, will not be established until they have been.

Political fragmentation is, of course, no obstacle to rational international cooperation as long as effective frameworks for such cooperation exist. Thus fragmentation is not so much the antithesis as the complement to integration or re-integration. But, as the experience of the EU in Western Europe has shown, effective international cooperation does not come of its own accord. It is built slowly, and with difficulty, through the acceptance by sovereign states of binding treaties involving onerous commitments and clear-cut loss of sovereignty. The countries of Central-East Europe and the Baltic region have been lucky to be able to "piggy-back" on the EU as an existing institution of integration with a record of success in terms of creating a genuine single market and moving Europe towards ever more ambitious levels of concerted action. The countries of the CIS (Commonwealth of Independent States — the former Soviet Union minus the Baltic Countries) are largely excluded from that theatre of integration, and their own attempts to create some kind of single market within post-Soviet economic space have been a dismal failure. The countries of the Balkans constitute an uneasy inter-mediate group in this respect, with the prospect of accession to the EU held out, but not guaranteed. The issue of fragmentation and inte-gration leads us on, therefore, to a consideration of the last of our key antonyms of transition — exclusion and integration.

Exclusion of particular countries or groups of countries can occur on different dimensions. In the present context, the key exclusion issue is clearly exclusion from the European Union. But there is at least one other major exclusion issue affecting transition countries — exclusion from the World *Exclusion and* Trading Organisation (WTO). At the time *integration* of writing, Russia, Ukraine, Kazakhstan, Uzbekistan and Serbia/ Montenegro all remained outside the WTO, in addition to a number of smaller West Balkan and CIS countries. Thus more than half the population of the transition region remains outside an organisation which can claim virtually universal membership in every other major region of the world. But let us set the WTO issue aside for the moment, and concentrate on the key exclusion issue — who will end up inside and who outside the European Union, and what difference it will make. The main conclusions to emerge from the research that has been done on this subject are as follows:

1. When macroeconomic and liberalisation effects are taken into account, the net aggregate impact of enlargement of the EU on the non-applicant countries is not unequivocally negative — indeed it may well be positive (Fidrmuc, 1999; Frandsen *et al.*, 2000; ECE, 2003).
2. Even where the general impacts of enlargement are clearly positive, the overall *distributional* effects of enlargement are, however, very likely to be negative (Manzocchi & Ottaviano, 2000).
3. Cross-border issues are of *critical* importance to the non-applicant countries on account of historical peculiarities of border configu-ration. For that reason visa regime issues have an unusually strong bearing on trade issues.

4. While there is good reason to be optimistic about the overall impact of enlargement on the economic development of the non-applicant countries, it must be recognised that there are particular problem areas, where the impact *could* be significantly negative. These include Kaliningrad, and the less developed countries of the former Yugoslavia. Irrespective of the actual outcome of enlargement for Kaliningrad, the Kaliningrad problem is likely to become a major diplomatic issue between the EU and Russia, which could affect the mediation of other enlargement issues.

5. There are some very specific areas like energy and energy goods transit which figure prominently in the diplomacy of non-accession, but where the prospects for resolving outstanding problems are relatively good, assuming that other enlargement issues do not encroach on the negotiation process.

6. Non-applicant countries which have not joined the WTO by the time the CEECs have joined the EU may be faced with special difficulties *vis-à-vis* trade regimes. Specifically, countries facing "double exclusion" may find themselves exposed to increased application of 'trade remedies' (anti-dumping, etc.) in relation to sensitive sectors, while still unable to turn to the WTO for protection against the unreasonable application of such measures.

7. The most important "empty box" in relation to non-accession is investment. It is investment impacts that will ultimately determine whether the net impact of enlargement on the non-applicant countries is negative or positive, and whether enlargement will tend to disrupt the developmental evolution of particular economies.

Let us briefly amplify one or two of these points.

Cross-border Trade/Kaliningrad

This is where the issue of fragmentation intersects with that of exclusion. As discussed in detail in Chapter 5, many of the non-applicant transition countries have very tortuous or economically arbitrary - borders with countries due to join the EU in 2004, or possibly joining in 2007. Because cross-border trade, often in the form of *shuttle trade* (see Chapter 5 for detailed discussion) is so important for the economies of these border areas, visa regimes can have a greater bearing on trade flows than trade regimes. The extreme example is Kaliningrad, the Russian "exclave" on the Baltic Sea. Part of the old East Prussia, Kaliningrad is not connected by land to any part of Russia proper, and shares land frontiers only with Poland and Lithuania, both due to join the EU in May 2004. Until recently, the inhabitants of Kaliningrad (numbering rather less than 1 m) could still travel across those borders on the basis of just identity cards. From October 2003 they required visas. Many Kaliningraders live from shuttle trade, and the impact of the new visa regime on their livelihoods could be serious.

Energy

Russia is a major supplier of oil and natural gas to Western, Central and Central-East Europe, and this poses a number of problems for the Russian government, and for the Russian oil and gas industries, viz.:

a. It is the general policy line of the EU (though not always adhered to by Mr Prodi, the Commission Chairman) that long-term contracts for energy supply should be avoided. The Russian standpoint is that, particularly with relation to gas, long-term contracts are vital if the risks of gas field development are to be kept within reasonable limits. This is a general problem in EU-Russia relations.[2] It will be exacerbated by enlargement because Russia stands to lose the existing long-term contracts it has with the CEECs. It must be stressed that it is unclear how actual this issue this, since the European Commission has no direct powers to prescribe contractual principles to private gas companies.

b. CEECs, which, for historical reasons, rely almost exclusively on Russia and other countries of the former Soviet Union for their gas supplies, are under pressure from the EU to diversify those supplies, which would obviously be to the detriment of the

---

[2]T.D.Adams, *EU-Russian Energy Relationships*, DTI presentation, 19 June 2001, p. 6.

Russian gas industry. Diversification is facilitated by the EU policy of seeking to remove destination clauses (which specify end-users) from gas contracts.

c. Russian gas supply and pipeline service contracts in CEE are generally composed of a mixture of cash and barter elements. Implicit "real" prices are difficult to ascertain, but prices as invoiced tend to be low. Once the CEEC countries are inside the EU, the barter element will have to be removed, as contracts are standardised to the norms of EU commercial law, and prices of gas and pipeline services will be brought up to EU levels. There is some anxiety on the Russian side that prices of pipeline services (paid *by* Russian organisations) may be "normalised" more rapidly than prices of gas (paid *to* Russian organisations).[3]

d. EU standards of pipeline safety (affecting gas and oil pipelines) are generally higher than those of the CEECs. After accession, these standards will be imposed in CEE, and the burden of meeting the extra costs of upgrading the pipelines will fall mainly on the supplier, i.e., in most cases Russia.

It is impossible to quantify the likely impact of these problems. In some cases, they may turn out to have been groundless fears. The rule that no EU member country should rely on a single source of energy for more than 30% of its total energy supply is a rule of thumb rather than a regulation, and Russian sources claim that the European Commission has stated that it will not apply the rule to Russian oil and gas (Ivanov, 2002, p. 12). In some cases, issues may be resolved by negotiations going on under headings other than EU enlargement. But energy trade problems currently have a serious effect on the atmosphere of EU-Russia relations, and must have a secondary impact on the crucial dimension of investor confidence *vis-à-vis* the hydrocarbon resources of the countries of the former Soviet Union.

---

[3]Talks between Gazprom and the Polish Oil and Gas Company (PGNiG) on a wide range of energy issues, including volumes and delivery schedules for gas and cooperation on construction of the Yamal-Europe gas pipeline, ended on 4 April 2002 without agreement on any of the issues discussed.

Investment

As discussed in detail in Chapter 6, EU enlargement will certainly improve the perception of the investment possibilities of the acceding countries, if to what exact extent is unclear. Thus the *relative* perception of investment possibilities in the non-applicant countries will, other things being equal, worsen. That is only a problem for the non-applicant countries if the total international investment "budget" for the transition countries is in some way constrained. In that case, there would be a real danger of the non-applicant countries being "crowded out". But it is not clear that there is any good reason to believe that such constraints exist, at least in a hard form. Total investment expenditures, whether globally or within particular countries, vary sharply between different time periods and between firms, depending on a whole range of variables, including current profitability, the stage in the business cycle, the state of business confidence, the rate of interest, etc. In the case of the CIS countries, the international price of oil and likely future trends in that price, are of particular importance in relation to investment decisions, by foreign and domestic firms alike. It is not clear that any of this is likely to be significantly affected by enlargement. It would certainly be dangerous to ignore the possibility of crowding out of investment in non-applicant countries. But there are no strong *a priori* reasons for placing special stress on this issue. A more serious danger is that non-applicant countries may, as a result of exclusion, become stuck at the bottom of the "technological ladder", as exclusion keeps capability levels and wages in those countries low. Alan Smith writes:

> A "vicious cycle" may occur. Economies that fail to restructure industry … may fail to attract foreign investment and fail to develop a skilled labour force … Low returns on investment … may also result in low domestic saving rates and low investment ratios, which further hinder investment in human capital. … In these economies, there is the potential for a vicious circle of relative, and possibly even absolute, decline as investment is attracted to more successful regions which generate external economies while the unrestructured economies remain dependent on

exports of labour-intensive and resource-intensive goods that embody relatively low levels of technology.[4]

VADE MECUM

In the papers that follow, we shall return repeatedly to these points, these tensions and contradictions inherent in the transformation process. But the book does not pretend to offer a comprehensive survey of the transition process. It is a collection of papers written at different times, and the coverage essentially reflects my judgement on what were the burning issues of transition at those different times. I have made no systematic effort to update the papers, except for Chapter 11. In one case (Chapter 3) I have added a short postscript. Generally, however, arguments have been left to stand on their merits, and in their own time frame. Thus Chapter 2 must be read as an exegesis of the early politics of the transition period, while Chapter 4 seeks to present a structural "photograph" of the Polish economy in the mid-late 1990s. These two papers are, I believe, valuable, because they look at key issues in crucial periods. They are in no sense "status reports" on the politics or economic structure of the transition region as a whole, or of any of the countries of that region specifically. What I have tried to update as much as possible in all the papers is straightforward facts. Wherever I could revise a table or any other form of data or information set without disrupting the line of argument I have done so. Facts speak for themselves. I trust that the arguments will be equally eloquent.

REFERENCES

Ahrend, R (2000). Foreign direct investment into Russia — Pain without Gain? A Survey of Foreign Direct Investors. New Economic School, VIII Conference, *Transforming Government in Economies in Transition*, Moscow, 2–4 November.

---

[4]A. Smith, *The Emergence of New Divisions in Europe? An Analysis of Changes in the Structure of Trade Relations Between Central and South-East Europe and the EU Between 1995–98*, School of Slavonic Studies, UCL, mimeo (not dated).

Bell, M (1997). Technology transfer to transition countries: Are there lessons from the experience of the post-war industrializing countries? In *The Technology of Transition*, DA Dyker (ed.). Budapest: Central European University Press.

Economic Commission for Europe (ECE). *Economic Survey of Europe 2003 No. 1*, Chapter 6.

Fidrmuc, J (1999). Trade diversion in "left-outs" in eastward enlargement of the European Union: The case of Slovakia. *Europe-Asia Studies*, 51(4), 633–45.

Frandsen, SE, HG Jensen and DM Vanzetti (2000). Expanding "Fortress Europe": Agricultural trade and welfare implications of European enlargement for non-member regions. *World Economy*, 23(3), 309–29.

Gubanov, S (2000). Stankostroenie: Usloviya konkurentosposobnosti. *Ekonomist*, 9.

Ivanov, ID (2002). *The Impact of the Enlargement of the European Union on a Non-Applicant Country in Transition: Case Study of the Russian Federation with References to Other Countries Concerned*. United Nations, Economic and Social Council, Economic Commission for Europe, Coordinating Unit for Operational Activities, 10 May.

Manzocchi, S and GIP Ottaviano (2000). *Outsiders in Economic Integration: The Case of a Transition Economy*. CEPR Discussion Paper, No. 2385, February.

Part II

The Political Economy of Transition

Chapter 2

Nomenklatura Nationalism — The Key to an Understanding of the New East European Politics?

Nationalism is the last phase of communism. It represents the final attempt by the old ideology to find support within society for dictatorship... At the same time, it is an expression of opposition to communism.

Adam Michnik, 1990, p. 13

Patriotism is the last resort of the scoundrel.

John Wilkes

Who, the reader may ask, is an economist to pose, and to pretend to answer, such a wide-ranging, and essentially political question? How, the author might respond, is an economist to make sense of the "new" political economy of Eastern Europe without some kind of compass to guide him on the purely political side? Economists and political scientists alike have been struck by specific elements of continuity between, for instance, the political economies of the old Yugoslavia and the successor states. East Europe specialists of every discipline have found themselves wrestling with the interpretation

of new economic phenomena across the region which seem to have
their roots in the pattern of realignment of political forces following
the demise of the old communist party structures. To make sense
of these — often bizarre — patterns, it seemed necessary to go back
into the history of the communist systems, and in particular of
the *nomenklatura* and of the way the *nomenklatura* impinged on
the economic sphere, to try to pin-point roots and key principles. The
results are tentative, but, I believe, revealing. Before proceeding with
the analysis, however, we must pause over a question of definition.
Strictly speaking, the communist *nomenklatura* system was a system
of political control over key appointments, meritocratic within the
limitations of the one-party system. There were two lists — a list of
key jobs, and a list of party members considered fit to hold them.
Here we use the term *nomenklatura* in the more general sense in
which it is now used among the populations of Eastern Europe —
simply to describe the top elite of the old system.

The propositions that we seek to demonstrate are as follows:

1. That the main function of nationalism in Eastern Europe over the
   last decade or so (i.e., going back well before the collapse of communism), from the point of view of those in power or aspiring to
   power, has been to provide a new rationalisation and legitimisation
   of the old, but threatened power of the apparatus. This essentially
   manipulative, top-down dimension of the nationalist revival has, of
   course, struck a deep chord with the bottom-up, mass dimension
   of that same revival. Perhaps I should just make the obvious point
   that without the meeting-in-the-middle, *nomenklatura* nationalism
   would never have worked as a way of holding on to power.
2. That continuity between communist-*nomenklatura* and *nomenklatura*-nationalist eras is firmly based on an essentially *territorial*,
   even *seigniorial* view of authority and management. To quote
   President Leonid Kravchuk of Ukraine, "everything on Ukrainian
   soil is Ukrainian property" [i.e., the property of the Ukrainian
   government] (*Russkoe televidenie*, 1993): In this sense we can use
   the term "bastard feudalism" (cf. the declining years of both
   Russian and Turkish Empires) to describe both late-communist
   and post-communist periods.

3. Related to 2, the notion of the "license to print money" as an essential prerogative of power comes through strongly from pre- to post-collapse periods, rendering the very idea of macro-economic policy as we understand it in the West essentially meaningless. It is intriguing, in this context, to note that the term used by bankers and economists in the West to describe the income the central authorities derive from the emission of currency is *seigniorage*.

4. Again flowing from 2, the way that *nomenklatura* nationalists view the market mechanism is grossly distorted in a way that rules out even slow progress towards a Western-type economy, viz., it is seen as a mechanism based on *monopoly*, not on *competition*.

But first a bit of potted history.

From Apparatchik to Nomenklatura Nationalist: The Evolution of a Ruling Group

The professional apparatus of the Soviet Communist Party, and of its clones in Eastern Europe, was always organised on a territorial basis. From the early Stalin period onwards, the key actors were the party secretaries at province and city level, who tended to dominate Communist Party Central Committees, the nearest to parliaments that the old one-party systems of the region ever got. These *apparatchiki* played a key *economic* role as trouble-shooters, oiling the wheels of creaky centrally planned systems, and generally making a system that was on paper unworkable (just about and less and less as time went on) workable. This gave them enormous effective power, *vis-à-vis* centre and local populations alike. It was as systems became increasingly corrupt, from the 1960s onwards, that the system of territorial party organisation degenerated into the pattern of *feudal-bureaucratic power and privilege*. And because the final stages of the communist period saw a particularly rapid degeneration of state administrations (Åslund, 1993), those final stages actually saw a general tendency for the power of the fief-holders to increase.

This helps us, for example, to understand why Gorbachev, a genuine enough reformer, came up with the (to Western eyes) rather bizarre idea of setting up the more economically advanced and forward-thinking regions of the Soviet Union as independent, self-financing business units — what we might dub the Estonia/Latvia/Lithuania plc model, as he strove to reform the communist system without doing away with it altogether. Just as the *apparatchik* mind instinctively views administration in territorial terms, so equally instinctively, however illogically, it tends to see the decentralisation of administration in territorial terms. It is significant in this context that the first major economic reform in Soviet economic history, Khrushchev's *sovnarkhoz* reform of 1957, which signalled a strikingly early recognition that all was not well in the Soviet socialist economy, was based on the creation of a network of regional economic councils territorially identical with existing provincial/city/republican units, i.e., identical with the territorial profile of the top party elite. In political terms this was, to use a favourite Soviet/Russian phrase, "not accidental". Khrushchev was at the time locked in a life-and-death struggle with the so-called "Anti-Party Group", and was only able to emerge from that struggle on the basis of maximal mobilisation of the Communist Party apparatus. As First Secretary of the party Khrushchev was, among other things, the president of the apparatus, and it was perfectly natural — in political terms — that he should seek to strengthen the position of his constituents through his economic policies. That Khrushchev's *sovnarkhoz* reform was a complete failure from the economic point of view was largely a function of its failure to strengthen in any way the market principle within the Soviet economic system, and of the fact that, in enhancing the role of local political elites, it merely exacerbated perennial weaknesses of that system, notably the tendency to organisational autarky (taking, under the *sovnarkhoz* reform, an explicitly territorial form) (Dyker, 1991). Gorbachev had by 1987 progressed as far as recognising that there can be no effective decentralisation without a dominant place for the market. He seems to have completely failed to recognise that in the Western international economy the spatial identity of large business organisations — which on any interpretation are key players in contemporary international affairs — is nearly always defined in terms of *lines of communication*, rather than of a well-defined, compact territory.

The history of the old Yugoslavia offers a somewhat different, but equally fascinating story of interaction between *nomenklatura* politics, nationalism and the economic sphere. The uniqueness of the Yugoslav case derives from the fact that the Tito regime had already introduced a form of market socialism at a time when economic Stalinism still reigned in the rest of Eastern Europe, and from the genuine federalism of the Yugoslav state that emerged from the confrontation with Stalin. The former means that we are able in the Yugoslav case to obtain a very clear picture of some dimensions of *nomenklatura* behaviour that are obscure in the cases of the more conventional communist systems — because, for instance, market socialism brings with it the reintroduction of *active* money. The latter reflects the fact that from a very early stage Tito was concerned to take the heat out of a political situation that was fraught with ethnic and economico-territorial tensions derived from the bloody intercommunal strife of the war years and the extreme regional inequalities of the Yugoslav area.

But the compromises of the 1950s, while providing a perfectly serviceable base for rapid initial economic growth, did not offer a permanent, stable solution either to the economico-systemic issues initially raised during the ideological reappraisal of the early 1950s, or to the underlying socio-political problems of Yugoslavia. Indeed by the 1960s these two dimensions were beginning to interact in a very volatile way. Sustained economic growth demanded a shift towards a more full-blooded version of market socialism, involving the marketisation of the two main areas of the economy which up to then had been kept within the centralised, administrative purview of the state — investment finance and foreign trade. But the reforms of 1961–65, which sought to implement such a shift, opened up a Pandora's Box of national tensions, as different nationalities, and in particular the Croats, began to argue over the way that this further marketisation was affecting flows of resources between republics. In Croatia the crisis took on an overtly politico-cultural dimension in 1967, with the *Declaration on the Croatian Literary Language*.

In 1971, with the very existence of Yugoslavia coming under threat, Tito decided that enough was enough. Initially taking a classically

Leninist line, he purged the Croatian League of Communists drastically, to rid it of nationalist elements. But the purge was not confined to the problem republic, and in Serbia, for instance, there were mass expulsions of "liberal" elements. At the same time, however (and here we see Tito's unique approach to consensus-building coming out again), the Yugoslav president sought to provide a new safety value for nationalist pressures by allowing the formal structure of the Yugoslav state to move further in the direction of federative polity. Indeed the new constitution of 1974 in some respects converted Yugoslavia into a confederation, with republics devolving powers to the federation rather than the other way round. What Tito was counting on was that a re-Leninised League of Communists would provide the cement to hold the new system together, and ensure that republican governments used their new powers to advance the national interests of Yugoslavia, rather than just regional or sectional interests.

Tito's compromise of 1971–74 was a short-term triumph but a medium-term disaster.

> The new key to political legitimacy was — and remains to this day — the special national interests of the Yugoslav peoples, *as represented and defended by the republican power elites.* Yugoslav communism, which after the successful resistance to the pressures of the Cominform [i.e., of Stalin's attempt to blockade Yugoslavia and unseat Tito] had become "national communism" ... now became "communist nationalism" ... The regime adopted nationalism as a key part of its own identity, a part which would later become the whole (Teokarević, 1991, pp. 55–2, emphasis added).

At the more mundane level, Communist Party cadres at republican level seized the opportunity to reassert their political dominance, but did so through the establishment of regional webs of nepotism, corruption and economic privilege. Politicians used their power over key appointments to turn republican banks into paymasters to the *nomenklatura*, thus arrogating to themselves the "license to print money" in a uniquely explicit way. They also used their veto power in the counsels of the Yugoslav Federation to block any attempts to implement the principle of the "unity of the Yugoslav market". In this way they were able to "deliver" monopoly positions to big regional firms. The license to print money syndrome soon went beyond the purely domestic sphere, as the National Bank of Yugoslavia became increasingly powerless to protect the national balance of payments. Lured by the blandishments of private transnational banks seeking desperately to recycle petro-dollars, the republics, especially the poorer ones, went on an international borrowing spree which paved the way for the external debt-service crisis of 1982–3 (Dyker, 1990).

Yugoslavia probably did not provide the first confirmed sighting of the *genus nomenklatura* nationalist. That honour should almost certainly go to what was then Soviet Central Asia, with the sighting as early as the late 1950s. There, the political compromises of the Khrushchev reforms combined with a local ethnic pattern that made each *sovnarkhoz* identical with a national group ruled by a local *nomenklatura* composed largely of members of that same national group. The result was a level of economic autarkism that can hardly be explained purely in terms of the operational weaknesses of central planning (Dyker, 1983, esp. Chapter 2). While the post-Khrushchev Soviet government abolished the *sovnarkhozy* in 1965, it was unable to reverse the powerful trend towards increased political corruption, strongly correlated with vigorous growth in the second economy, in the region (Lubin, 1984, esp. Chapter 6). But all of this happened within the context of what was still a centrally planned economy and a one-party state. Those features could not prevent the emergence of *nomenklatura* nationalism, but they could constrain it, and keep it, in a sense, *sub rosa*. It was in Yugoslavia, with its semi-market economy and overt federalism, that we see the emergence of the *nomenklatura* nationalist as, for the first time, the *dominant* element in a notionally communist political system. A more fully fledged version of the market economy would, of course, have blown these Yugoslav *nomenklatura* nationalists away, since it would have deprived them of the basis for trading-in-favours. We should bear this in mind when we come, in a moment, to a consideration of post-communist transitional systems.

A Provisional Anatomy of Nomenklatura Nationalism

On the basis of the foregoing, and extrapolating into the post-communist period, we would expect to be able to identify *nomenklatura* nationalist regimes, on the economic plane, by the following characteristics:

1. "Weak" macroeconomic policy, uncontrolled monetary expansion, tending toward hyperinflation.
2. A tendency to nationalise rather than privatise, or indeed to nationalise while pretending to privatise.
3. A tendency to autarky in foreign trade policy.
4. Notwithstanding 3, a search for "strategic alliances" in the international field.

These criteria are most obviously useful in determining what are *not* *nomenklatura* nationalist regimes. With all their weaknesses, the economic policy platforms of the post-communist governments of Poland, the Czech Republic and Hungary have, at least, made a real attempt to keep the money supply under control, to implement meaningful privatisation policies, and (subject to externally imposed constraints) to enter into the international division of labour in an open way. Ukraine, by contrast, is a country already suffering from hyperinflation, having recorded a budget deficit of, however improbably, over 40 per cent of national income in 1992. It has, to date, made virtually no progress with privatisation beyond general pronouncements, and its foreign trade policies have been dominated, hitherto unsuccessful attempts to do a long-term oil deal with Russia apart, by one-off deals with other classic *nomenklatura* nationalist regimes like Tatarstan (oil equipment for oil) and Turkmenistan (various industrial and agricultural products for gas and cotton), and regimes like Iran (gas pipeline construction, and possibly arms for oil and gas), which might also be described as a *sui generis nomenklatura* nationalist regime. It is worth adding that the only major controversy over the political antecedents of President Kravchuk of the Ukraine, formerly ideology secretary (i.e., hitman-in-chief) of the Ukrainian Communist Party, is whether he left the Communist Party at the time of the 1991 *putsch*[1] or immediately afterwards.[2] Meciar's Slovakia initially seemed very much to fit the Ukrainian pattern. By mid-1993, however, Slovakia seemed to be wobbling towards something more like a clean-break stance, at least as far as economic policy is concerned. It may be significant that Meciar, although an old communist, was in fact *never a member of the nomenklatura as such*.

But it is again the former Yugoslavia which offers the richest material in terms of filling out the profile of the *nomenklatura* nationalist. We concentrate here on Serbia and Croatia, the two major successor states of the old Yugoslavia. In the case of Serbia, the direct political evidence on Milošević's status as a prime *nomenklatura* nationalist is as strong as the circumstantial evidence. President Franjo Tudjman of Croatia is a more complex case. A former communist, army general and close associate of Tito, Tudjman went into dissidence in the 1970s, and spent some time in jail on that count. He claims[3] to be a "born-again" nationalist, so that we will have to look at the policy evidence with particular care in his case.

Let us start with macroeconomic policy. It is important to remember that the final collapse of Yugoslavia was preceded by a brief Indian summer of rational (in our terms) economic policy, under the premiership of Ante Marković. By the end of 1989 the inflation rate in Yugoslavia had, under the impact of money supply policies now firmly under the control of regional *nomenklaturas*, reached 2,500 per cent. From the beginning of 1990, Marković implemented a Polish-style shock-therapy package, which brought the inflation rate down to under zero within five months under a tough new money supply policy stance. But Marković was politically weak, and indeed could only survive by seeking to accommodate powerful republican leaders, in particular Slobodan Milošević of Serbia, who had taken over the leadership of the Serbian League of Communists in 1987. (Later on

---

[1]When Communist Party conservatives briefly kidnapped Mikhail Gorbachev and his wife, in an attempt to reverse the *perestroika* reforms; the unsuccessful *putsch* merely hastened the demise of the Soviet system, and of the Soviet Union itself.

[2]Kravchuk was replaced as president by Leonid Kuchma in 1994.

[3]Franjo Tudjman died in December 1999.

Milošević would be elected president of Serbia.) And it was Milošević who, in December 1990, effectively scuppered the Marković plan, and Yugoslavia's last chance of a civilised transition to post-communist society, when he connived at a *démarche* which became known as the Great Bank Robbery. In brief, the Serbian National Bank, notionally subordinate to the Yugoslav National Bank, illegally rediscounted a huge volume of commercial bank loans to enterprises and the Serbian government. This enabled Milošević to pay state salaries and pensions for the first time for months, and to keep big, but loss-making, operators in the economy afloat. It surely helped him to win his first democratic election, which took place a few days later.

Since the break-up of Yugoslavia the macroeconomic trend in Serbia/Montenegro has been inexorably in the direction of hyperinflation. By early 1992 the monthly inflation rate was already in the region of 80 per cent, and by March 1993 to have had reached 225.8 per cent (Bojičić & Dyker, 1993). At present the state budget is almost wholly financed by *selective* primary monetary emissions (Pejović, 1993). The force of the "selective" is that the National Bank increases the money supply by rediscounting loans to specified sectors of the state or economy — as was always the practice (if more constrained) in communist Yugoslavia, thus giving Milošević wide scope to finance his strategic alliances within Serbia/Montenegro itself. In Croatia, the trend has been less dramatic, but since independence and the launching of the independent Croatian dinar inflation has risen steadily to a rate, at time of writing, of 25 per cent per month, i.e., over 1000 per cent per annum. Not unconnected are the facts that the National Bank controls only 40 per cent of the money supply (one must presume, though I have seen no explicit confirmation of this, that the other 60 per cent is accounted for by ear-marked selective credits), and that only 50 per cent of assessed taxation is actually collected (Bićanić, 1993).

In these ways, *nomenklatura* nationalist regimes are able to pre-empt staggeringly large volumes of resources — in the Serbian/Montenegrin case, for instance, public expenditure accounts for 70 per cent of national income, most of it, as we have seen, financed by the printing press, and most of it going on military expenditure

and social security (Pejović, 1993) — i.e., rewarding Milošević's supporters. (Note that Milošević's industrial supporters are rewarded
through soft "selective" credits rather than direct transfers as such.)
Most strikingly of all, perhaps, Serbia/Montenegro was still managing to transfer 20 per cent of its national income to the Serbs in
Croatia and Bosnia in 1993 (Shields, 1993).

When we look at the microeconomic policies of the Tudjman and
Milošević regimes, we find a similar pattern. Privatisation policies
have tended effectively to the *nationalisation* rather than the privatisation of commercial and industrial property formerly socially owned
under the self-management system. In both Croatia and Serbia the
principle has been established that the proceeds of privatisation
should go largely into republican development or restructuring
funds, and that companies not privatised by a certain date should
automatically become the property of restructuring agencies
(Kalodjera, 1991; Bogdanović & Lakićević, 1991; Petrović, 1992;
Dumezić, 1992; "Privatizacija", 1992; Boarov, 1993).

The flavour of these privatisation programmes can perhaps best be
appreciated through the medium of case studies. Trepča, for instance,
the biggest lead, silver and zinc mine in the world, located in the
Albanian-majority region of Kosovo, was "restructured" by the Serbian
government at the end of 1992. Perhaps inevitably, 63.6 per cent of
the shares in Trepča have ended up in the hands of the Republican
Development Fund. Among the other thirteen shareholders are num-
bered Jugobanka, Geneks, Beobanka, Progres — all "restructured and
financially consolidated" [i.e., effectively nationalised] enterprises. The
Trepča mine is in fact currently operating at only 20 per cent of capacity, and it labours under a burden of debt equivalent to 60 per cent of
estimated total capital. Only massive investment, including a hard currency element, will put it on its feet again, and there is no prospect of
the funds being raised under this new "mixed ownership" package. So
why was the Serbian state so eager to step in? To stop, so the reports
run, the Berlin Grafikohandels firm, supported by a "wealthy
American-Albanian lobby", from buying up Trepča lock, stock and
barrel — and more generally to save Trepča from "Albanian saboteurs
and loafers" (Ursić, 1992).

A rather different light on Serbian/Croatian "restructuring" policies is shed by the case of the Croatian newspapers. The imposition of so-called "management committees" on a number of opposition newspapers in Croatia at the end of 1992 signalled their effective nationalisation. The Agency for Restructuring and Development said that it was a matter of financial regularisation. The opposition said that it was an attempt to muzzle the press ("Štampa", 1992). A similar case was reported from Serbia around the same time. The only three independent pharmacies in Serbia (one in Belgrade, one in Novi Sad, one in Niš), were nationalised in the summer of 1992. This was presented at the time as a temporary move, pending the introduction of a government programme for the reprivatisation of the health sector as a whole. But by the end of the year nothing further had been done. In an interview, Branko Radović, general director of the Belgrade Pharmacy, said that at the time of the original action he had himself been in favour of temporary nationalisation, as a basis for solving technical real estate problems. But by the time of interview (December 1992) he was clear that they had been tricked, and that the government had no intention of proceeding with reprivatisation. Under the "temporary" arrangement, the council of the pharmacy was dominated by government nominees. Radović was worried that the pharmacy, which under the existing regime did not have a free hand to restructure and reorganise, would go bankrupt because it was grossly overmanned. Then it would be bought up for a song by someone from the old *nomenklatura*. Radović believed that a clearly-defined plot to this end has been laid by governing circles (Dukanac, 1992).

It goes without saying that commercial intercourse between Croatia and Serbia has now largely ceased. More telling, perhaps, is the fact that trade between Croatia and Slovenia, two countries at peace with each other, and sharing a general antipathy towards Belgrade, has been seriously hampered by something approaching the dimensions of a trade war. Against a background of disputes over the common border, over territorial waters, and over fishing rights, Croatia, in the middle of 1992, decided to impose emergency duties on imports from Slovenia *and* restrictions on exports to that country ("Zatezanje", 1992). A few months later Slovenia imposed new import duties on goods coming from Croatia (Furtinger, 1992; "Vesti", 1992). The autarkic mentality is beautifully summed up in the remark by the then Croatian trade minister, Branko Mikša, to the effect that "exporting tree trunks and hides and importing mineral water and toilet paper is no basis for international exchange". ("Zatezanje", 1992). No, the non-*nomenklatura*, non-nationalist economist might reply, but at least it's a start.

These case studies bring out a whole range of themes. The idea of a particular enterprise as part of the national patrimony, which must be defended at all costs against foreigners; the link between seigniorial economic policies and the suppression of democracy on the political front; the link between *nomenklatura* nationalists and *nomenklatura* capitalists; the penchant for autarky; above all, the insistence on the *prerogative* of regimes, ultimately to dispose of the property "of the people" as they see fit. But how universal are these themes?

The Problem of Generalisation

There is a powerful argument to the effect that Tudjman and Milošević are simply Tweedledum and Tweedledee, both bastard clones of a corrupt and degenerate political system. As we have already seen, the argument seems to hold up pretty well in relation to Kravchuk's Ukraine, and to most of the Central Asian republics. The Romania of President Ion Iliescu, too, appears to exhibit most the critical features of *nomenklatura* nationalism. ("I will not say that it is only the government coalition [in Romania] that is using nationalism. Unfortunately, some of the opposition parties are using the same instrument, even if they are more discreet" (NCA/Mort von Duyke, 1993).) But what happens when we try to generalise to the level of Eastern Europe as a whole?

To repeat our earlier conclusion, the regimes in Poland, the Czech Republic and Hungary do not fit the pattern, in economic terms, at all. But this is not surprising, since these are precisely the three countries of Eastern Europe in which there was a genuine revolution, dramatic in the case of Poland, velvet in the two other cases. So if we find no traces of *nomenklatura* nationalism in Warsaw, Prague and Budapest, it only serves to verify our hypothesis. Interestingly, the early days of the Solidarity government in Poland were marked by considerable concern on the part of the new regime about the activities of *nomenklatura* capitalists. But while peculiarly East European forms of insider dealing did, certainly, flourish in Poland at that time, *nomenklatura* capitalism did not develop into a permanent political problem, simply because the Polish *nomenklatura* capitalists — mainly survivors from the old governmental-industrial hierarchy — were unable to forge strategic alliances with opposite numbers in the political sphere. There is no evidence, it should be added, to suggest that there are any significant *nomenklatura* nationalist elements in the reformed communist party which emerged triumphant in the parliamentary elections in Poland in late 1993.

The Russia of Boris Yeltsin, too, is, whatever its problems and weaknesses, no *nomenklatura* nationalist regime — though Yeltsin is indisputably of the old *nomenklatura*, and also in some sense a nationalist. It is equally clear, however, that the pre-October 1993 Russian "opposition" — if the anti-government elements in the old Supreme Soviet were worthy of that name — was a *nomenklatura* nationalist opposition. In the Congress of People's Deputies we saw the same pattern of alliance between erstwhile Communist Party *apparatchiki*, beleaguered heavy-industrial interests and rabid nationalism that we see in Serbia. To the extent that the Congress of People's Deputies was able to influence economic policy it did so in the direction of gross permissiveness in Central Bank credit policy, which was a major source of inflation in Russia 1992–3 (Åslund, 1993). It is too early to hazard an assessment of how *nomenklatura* nationalists fared in the December 1993 elections in Russia, though it seems probable that they are fairly strongly represented in the new upper house — the Council of the Federation.[4] In the lower house, the Duma, it is, of course, the "clean-break" nationalism of Vladimir Zhirinovskii which has caught the public eye. It seems, however,

---

[4]Subsequent developments confirmed that guess.

likely that under Yeltsin's new constitution the Council of the
Federation will be the more important body.[5] Once again, then, the
Russian case provides, on close examination, confirmation of our
hypothesis rather than the opposite. A similar pattern is evident in
Kyrgyzstan, the most go-ahead of the Central Asian republics. When
President Askar Akaev asked his Supreme Soviet to pass a law permitting private and corporate ownership of land and natural resources,
the parliament refused, and instead decreed that all land and natural
resources in the republic should be the property of the state (ITAR-
TASS, 1993a). In so doing they explicitly legislated a feudal-bureaucratic prerogative which is usually left implicit by *nomenklatura*
nationalist formations.

But there are plenty of other cases which do not fit neatly into the
pattern. President Milan Kučan of Slovenia, a communist finding
refuge in nationalism if ever there was one, has yet shown few of the
characteristics of the classic *nomenklatura* nationalist. The silly trade
war with Croatia apart, Slovenian economic policy has been sensible,
and cautious to a fault. Inflation is only 2–3 per cent per month
("Janez Drnovšek", 1993). Radical economists have, indeed, perceived in the slow pace of privatisation signs of a plot by the old elites
to keep control over the industrial capital stock (Grličkov, 1992;
"Koncept", 1992). Prime minister Janez Drnovšek, on the other
hand, himself a survivor of the old system, promised that 1993 would
be a critical year for privatisation, following on the passage of a law on
transformation of ownership at the end of 1992 ("Janez Drnovšek",
1993). In practice, progress with privatisation in Slovenia remains
slow.[6] The fact is, however, that, if we look at Poland, Hungary and
the Czech Republic again, it is clear that reasonably tight monetary
policy, rather than breakneck speed on privatisation, has been the critical indicator of a "clean" regime. (The Czech Republic, with its
voucher-based privatisation scheme, is a partial exception to that
generalisation.) Macedonia, too, is headed by an ex-communist

---

[5]This prediction proved to be less accurate.
[6]And continued to be slow right up to the early 2000s.

president — Kiro Gligorov.[7] Gligorov, like Kučan, has certainly found political refuge in nationalism. But Macedonian economic policy has, on the whole, followed the Slovenian pattern of cautious conservatism (Nikolić, 1993) — in much more difficult conditions, it must be added, than those prevailing in the more northerly republic. And both Kučan and Gligorov have conspicuously avoided the kind of ethnic sectarian rhetoric that is the trade mark of *nomenklatura* nationalist leaders like Milošević and Tudjman. The nationalism of the Serbo-Croat-speaking Muslims of Bosnia is, almost by definition, "clean-break" nationalism, as exemplified in the person of Bosnian president Alija Izetbegović, a former dissident.[8] But there are *nomenklatura* nationalist elements within the Izetbegović regime, notably Fikret Abdić, a member of the Bosnian presidency, boss of the Agrokomerc agricultural combine of Bihać, and effective warlord of the Bihać Pocket. Abdić was jailed for two years in 1987, in connection with the "Agrokomerc Scandal", a classic episode of corrupt and inefficient business management, bolstered by a subservient local banking network which effectively printed money to cover losses being made at that time by the agricultural combine, all under the protection of powerful regional League of Communists interests (Williams, 1993).

But it is when we look at the former Soviet Union as a whole, including the regions and localities of Russia, that the *nomenklatura* nationalism hypothesis comes under greatest pressure, *at least if we insist that ethnic sectarianism is a characteristic symptom of nomenklatura nationalism*. Even Ukrainian president Leonid Kravchuk himself, so archetypically *nomenklatura* nationalist in many respects, remains free of any taint of ethnic sectarianism. Indeed his attitudes and policies towards the Russian minority within Ukraine, and towards the difficult issue of the Crimea, have been positively statesmanlike. One might grudge the same soubriquet to President Shevardnadze of Georgia. But in terms of domestic policy there has been nothing that would justify lumping Shevardnadze in with the

---

[7]The current president is Boris Trajkovski.
[8]Izetbegović resigned as president in 2000. Bosnia now has a rotating presidency.

likes of Milošević and Tudjman. (It is, certainly, a little difficult to assess Georgian economic policy. With industrial output at mid-1993 down to under 20 per cent of pre-independence levels and agriculture in even worse case (Barraclough, 1993), there is little economy left to form the subject of policy-making. By the same token there is probably little short-term alternative to the massive budget deficits that have accumulated.) In the Baltic republics, "clean break" regimes have pursued generally sensible economic policies, but have verged on ethnic sectarianism in their policies towards minorities (mainly Russian). In Lithuania, the "clean" nationalist regime of Vytautas Landsbergis was replaced in 1992 by a reformed communist government led by Algirdas Brazauskas. On economic performance, Brazauskas has been just about as bad as Landsbergis was (rather worse on inflation after big increases in public sector salaries and pensions — see Girnius, 1993), but he has been more diplomatic on relations with other nationalities.

In many respects the most interesting of the post-Soviet republics in the present context is Azerbaijan. The first post-Soviet president of Azerbaijan — Ayaz Mutalibov, a classic *nomenklatura* nationalist, was removed in 1992, and ultimately replaced by Abulfaz Elcibey, a "clean-break" nationalist, with a background of historical-literary and political studies, who refused even to speak Russian when being interviewed for Russian television. But he was in turn effectively replaced in July 1993 by Geidar Aliev, previously president of the parliament of Nakhichevan (the Azeri enclave tucked in between Armenia, Turkey and Iran, and currently under blockade by the first of those), a former chief of the Azerbaijan KGB, Communist Party First Secretary in the republic, and member of the Politburo of the CPSU under Andropov. Then in August 1993, Alikram Gumbatov, former CPSU member and Azerbaijani deputy defence minister, proclaimed himself president of the Republic of Talysh, covering the territory of the Farsi-speaking minority in southern Azerbaijan, and demanded the return of Mutalibov to the presidency in Baku. Government forces reasserted control of the region almost immediately.[9]

---

[9]Geidar Aliev was still president in 2003.

It is difficult to discern any clear-cut differences in style and policy between different Azerbaijani leaders. Of course all Azeri politicians, whatever their antecedents, are obliged to be wholly committed to victory on the issue of Gorno-Karabakh,[10] and indeed Elcibey's fall from grace was largely a function of his failure to resolve that issue. Geidar Aliev has not done much better. Under Elcibey, Azerbaijan introduced its own currency (the manat) side by side with the rouble. While privatisation proceeded slowly under Elcibey, relations with Western companies were good, as witness the major BP/Statoil investment in Caspian oil development. Aliev's ouster of Elcibey was widely interpreted as representing the victory of the pro-Russian party against the pro-Western party within Azerbaijan. Yet BP and Statoil subsequently successfully re-negotiating their contracts with the new government, and have since committed billions of dollars to the development of the oil-fields of Azerbaijan. *Nomenklatura* nationalist and clean-break nationalist leaders have, then, generally pursued the same *weak* policies on both military and economic matters in Azerbaijan. The Gumbatov episode does, however, seem to indicate that the *dynamic* in Azeri politics is a fragmentatory interaction between old *nomenklatura* members and ethnic-linguistic consciousness.

Within the Russian Federation, one striking example of *nomenklatura* nationalist regime is in another Turkic-speaking area — Tatarstan. Russian and Tatar opposition groups in the Volga republic, divided on so many issues, are agreed that the government of Tatarstan is firmly in the hands of a communist "clan". The clan, it is alleged, originally put Mintimer Shaimiyev into the top position of republic First Secretary of the Tatarstan Communist Party. When the clan switched its allegiance from communism to nationalism, it switched Shaimiyev to the presidency of the new "sovereign" republic. The members of the organisational committee of the new Tatarstan Unity and Progress Party "are all from the *nomenklatura*, they all had

---

[10]Nagorno-Karabakh is a mountainous area of Azerbaijan with a predominantly Armenian population. It was occupied by Armenian insurgents at the end of the Soviet period. At 2003, the matter remained unresolved.

jobs with the old provincial committee of the CPSU — there are still a few economists, journalists, and even doctors among them ... In their draft programme ... the central concept is the *sovereignty* [emphasis added] of the Republic of Tatarstan" (Stogova, 1993). Shaimiyev does not try to deny the charge of *nomenklatura* nationalism, and says, simply, "if it were not for the *nomenklatura* the situation would not be nearly so stable in Tatarstan" (Gray, 1993).[11]

Here and elsewhere in the ethnic minority areas of Russia, we find quite sharply delineated *nomenklatura* nationalist patterns and a characteristic obsession with the notion of sovereignty. This is, of course, in the first instance a political issue — if outright independence is out of the question, as it is for Tatarstan or Bashkirtostan because they are enclaves within Russia, then sovereignty, however vaguely defined, is the next best thing. But on the economic side, sovereignty is actually quite clearly defined, and in terms which are pure *nomenklatura* nationalist. Sovereignty means ownership of the natural resources located on national territory. Nearly all the ethnic minority areas of Russia do have significant natural riches — oil in Tatarstan, Bashkirtostan, Chechnya and Komi, diamonds and non-ferrous metals, including gold, in Sakha (formerly Yakutia), etc. By asserting sovereignty on behalf of the "nation", *nomenklatura* nationalist groups effectively seek to arrogate to themselves, or rather preserve, feudal-bureaucratic rights over those resources. It is once again not accidental that when in mid-1993 chairmen of supreme soviets of eleven out of nineteen autonomous republics of the Russian Federation rejected President Yeltsin's draft new constitution, the chairmen of the supreme soviets of Adygei, Altai, Komi, Marii El, Sakha, Tuva, Udmurtiya and Khakassia issued a joint statement criticising the draft for failing to confirm the status of the autonomous republics as sovereign states, and for emphasising human rights and freedoms *to the detriment of the rights of nations* (Interfax, 1993).

A number of these republics have issued their own currencies. More correctly, they have issued their own *quasi-currencies*, often initially in the form of ration coupons, which subsequently become

---

[11]Shaimiyev was still president in 2003.

interchangeable with roubles as a means of payment. This is a clever trick, which was also played by the Ukrainians until the Russian Central Bank caught up with them, and still is being played by the Uzbeks. Whether the Azeris are playing it, and if so whether they know they are playing it, is not clear. The cleverness resides in the fact that by printing *coupons* (let us use the Ukrainian term as a general term for quasi-currency), a republican government arrogates to itself the license to print money, thus giving it a powerful instrument for the diversion of real resources *within* the republic — while at the same time preserving very substantial scope for diverting real resources from *outside* the republic — principally from metropolitan Russia — through the use of roubles. For the *nomenklatura* nationalist, to have control of the printing press, *and* to have a license to run balance of payments deficits within very wide limits is a privileged position indeed. In a Western world of hard currencies, political leaders, whatever their background, can be expected to place substantial emphasis on the accumulation of hard-currency reserves — and that means running a reasonably tight monetary policy, as a way of ensuring that the balance of payments stays at least in balance, if not in surplus. But in the feudal, anti-mercantilist world of the *nomenklatura* nationalist, everything is turned upside down. The only thing that matters is control over *real* resources, and a mixture of coupons and roubles is nicely calculated to maximise the extent of that control.

So far so good. But the neatness of the picture is seriously disturbed when we start to look at Russia as a whole. The kinds of patterns we have been describing are, in fact, prevalent in many of the regions of Russia which have no significant non-Russian populations. And that is not really surprising, if we refer back to the earlier discussion of the composition of the Russian "opposition" in the old Supreme Soviet. They were mostly *nomenklatura* nationalists, mostly with the same territorial power base that they had under the Soviet regime. Therefore they perceived their self-interest in the same, feudal-bureaucratic terms, and pursued it on the basis of the same macroeconomic dodges. The old party elites have, furthermore, demonstrated an impressive capacity to come back and win democratic elections in the ethnically predominantly Russian regions of

Russia. A striking example is Egor Stroev, formerly First Party Secretary in Orel province, and member of the Politburo and the Secretariat of the CPSU. In April 1993 Stroev was returned as head of the administration of Orel province on a platform of "partnership, professionalism and social guarantees" (ITAR-TASS, 1993b). That last phrase is, of course, a standard codeword for national, even nationalist solidarism. It seems likely that there are many Stroevs in the new Council of the Federation.

In some ways even more interesting than the Orel case is the case of St. Petersburg. The old imperial capital, with its imperial name restored, has acquired a reputation, perhaps somewhat exaggerated, for municipal and entrepreneurial dynamism in the period since the collapse of the Soviet Union. Under the leadership of mayor Anatolii Sobchak, it has always been a staunch supporter of President Yeltsin, and this came through again in the referendum of April 1993. Over 70 per cent of voters gave the president the vote of confidence he asked for, and something under 70 per cent supported Yeltsin's economic policies. But around three quarters of voters gave a positive response to one of the extra questions that Sobchak had inserted into the referendum in "his" territory — Should St. Petersburg be elevated to the status of an autonomous republic within the Russian Federation? (NCA/ITAR-TASS, 1993c). Now no one can question Sobchak's credentials as a genuine, market-oriented reformer, and a genuine supporter of Yeltsin. Rather the St. Petersburg result — and more importantly, in the present context, the fact that Sobchak asked the question about autonomy in the first place, reflects the fact that, against the background of a weak, and weakening central power in Russia, *every* regional leader with any clout at all, irrespective of whether he is a *nomenklatura* nationalist or a born-again liberal, is seeking greater independence from Moscow. Indeed by mid-1993 the governments of no less than five other provinces of Russia — Amur, Maritime, Kaliningrad, Sverdlovsk (Yeltsin's home base) and Vologda — none of them with significant ethnic minorities, had announced their intention of going for autonomous-republic status. Of course this process of weakening of the centre has, arguably, been largely a function of the obstructive tactics of the *nomenklatura*-nationalist "opposition" as it coalesced in the old Supreme Soviet, of the "party of bureaucratic revanchism, of state monopolism" (Latsis, 1993). But it is clear that, while the phenomenon of *nomenklatura* nationalism can thus be called up to explain the pattern of politics in *Moscow*, it is not, by itself, adequate to explain the enormously complex pattern of politics in the *regions of Russia*, whether they have significant non-Russian populations or not. In emphasising the essentially territorial mentality of *nomenklatura* survivors it does, nonetheless, provide an essential element in any full explanation of Russian regionalism.

Conclusion: Does It Hold? Does It Matter?

As a way of describing the Croatian and Serbian regimes, the *nomenklatura* nationalist hypothesis seems to be comprehensively appropriate. The further we get away from the former Yugoslavia, or rather from the Serbo-Croat-speaking core of the former Yugoslavia, the less consistently applicable it seems to be. If we factor out ethnic sectarianism as such, which certainly has no direct link with the political economy of *nomenklatura* nationalism except to the extent that it links up with autarky, then we increase the number of "perfect" *nomenklatura* nationalists to include at least Kravchuk of Ukraine. Romania, too, and the Central Asian states, are more or less close approximations to the "ideal". Beyond that, we encounter a whole mass of case studies for which the idea of *nomenklatura* nationalism is helpful without being comprehensively explanatory.

In the end, *nomenklatura* nationalism should be seen, perhaps, as (*hoffentlich!*) an insight, rather than as a theory. It sheds light on a whole range of aspects of a process of political fragmentation which has overtaken the entire region, but which we characterise *en masse* as "nationalist"/"liberal democratic" or "progressive"/"retrogressive" at our peril. Rather than trying to squeeze too much mileage out of the notion of *nomenklatura* nationalism as theory, then, we finish by asking the question: if it is accepted that the phenomenon is widespread, at least as a tendency, an element, does it really matter?

Certainly all politicians have to come from somewhere. Certainly the nastiest East European nationalist to date, after Milošević, was

Gamsakhurdia of Georgia, a poet and ex-dissident. Certainly there is more than a suspicion that Geidar Aliev replaced Abulfaz Elcibei in Azerbaijan simply because he is seen as an effective leader — the same reason, no doubt, why Stroev was able to make his dramatic comeback in Orel and Sobchak to obtain such a resounding vote of confidence in St. Petersburg. There are still grounds for arguing, however, that *nomenklatura* nationalist attitudes are a systematic obstacle to good economic policy-making, however able the particular leader is, and however varied specific goals might be. "They all want different things, [but] they are all communists because they are all the same in the question of how to do it: crude persuasion, command, force, restriction, ban, confiscation, expropriation. They don't know any other technology" (Efron, 1993). The obstacles to good economic policy-making, furthermore, go well beyond the definitional penchants for inflationary financing, continued state ownership and autarky. The *nomenklatura* nationalist (a stylised figure, if you like) is certainly likely to be corrupt, but that is because he is ex-*nomenklatura*, not because he is a nationalist. More specifically, his autarkic prejudices spell death to any more sophisticated notion of international or inter-regional division of labour — extending, for instance, to international technology transfer — a disastrous result in the context of general territorial fragmentation. On a more philosophical level, but still on the technology theme, feudal-bureaucratic attitudes tend to produce a systematic overestimation of the importance of land and natural resources, and/or of labour as an undifferentiated factor of production, and a systematic underestimation of the importance of human capital in the prospective development of the countries of the region. This latter tendency is particularly harmful in times when the pressures of economic restructuring make it very difficult for firms to look beyond the very short term. It is striking, for instance, that in Croatia the government does not appear to *comprehend* the importance of trying to limit the wastage of human capital as firms cut back staff in order to retrench financially (Radošević, 1993a). This in turn means an inevitable loss in technological momentum, including technology transfer (something the communist systems were bad enough at), again in an environment where the short-term imperatives of restructuring at firm level mean that government has to play a *greater* rather than a *lesser* role in relation to technology and innovation issues (Radošević, 1993b). In its crudest forms, *nomenklatura* nationalism simply makes a nonsense of any notion of credible economy policy.

Finally, *nomenklatura* nationalism lets the racist genie out of the bottle. In the words of one Belgrade political scientist who speaks from personal experience, "it is possible to instrumentalise nationalism only in the short term" (Teokarević, 1991). At the time of writing, overt ethnic sectarianism is still largely a post-Yugoslav phenomenon. But *nomenklatura* nationalism does at minimum leave the region deeply vulnerable to a process of general "Yugoslavisation" which hardly bears thinking of.

REFERENCES

Åslund, A (1993). *Systemic Change and Stabilisation in Russia*. Royal Institute of International Affairs, *Post-Soviet Business Forum*. London: Chatham House.

Barraclough, C (1993). Georgia's instability unravels economy. *Christian Science Monitor*, 20 July.

Boarov, D (1993). Od imovine do kapitala. *Ekonomska Politika*, 8 February, p. 23.

Bićanić, I (1993). The Croatian economy: Achievements and prospects. *RFE/RL Research Report*.

Bogdanović, S and M Lakićević (1991). Država odumira jačajući. *Ekonomska Politika*, 15 April, pp. 10–11.

Bojičić, V and DA Dyker (1993). *Sanctions on Serbia: Sledgehammer or Scalpel?* Sussex European Institute Working Paper, University of Sussex.

Dukanac, V (1992). Konfiskacija: Jeste ili nije? *Ekonomska Politika*, 28 December, pp. 22–24.

Dumezić, T (1992). Kovači lažnih deonica. *Ekonomska Politika*, 15 June, pp. 17–18.

Dyker, DA (1983). *The Process of Investment in the Soviet Union*. Cambridge University Press.

———— (1990). *Yugoslavia. Socialism, Development and Debt*. London: Routledge.

Efron, S (1993). Communists find life as born-again bureaucrats. *Los Angeles Times*, 25 August. (The quote is from S.A. Arutiunov of the Russian Academy of Sciences.)

Furtinger, J (1992). Kako razmršiti čvorove. *Ekonomska Politika*, 19 October, p. 22.

Gray, J (1993). Republic shakes, disintegration looms. *The Toronto Globe*, 22 April.

Grličkov, V (1992). Zamke svojinskih promena. *Ekonomska Politika*, 14 October, pp. 20–1.

Girnius, S (1993). Establishing currencies in the Baltic states. *RFE/RL Research Report*, Vol. 2, No. 22, 28 May.

Interfax (1993). Presidential constitution draft rejected by Supreme Soviet chairmen of 11 autonomies. 17 May.

ITAR-TASS Daily News (1993a). Konstitutsiya Kyrgyzstana ob"yavila zemlyu gosudarstvennoi sobstvennost'yu. 13 April.

——— (1993b). Egor Stroev zaregistrirovan glavoi administratsii orlovskoi oblasti. 13 April.

"Janez Drnovšek: Reforme jos nisu realizovane" (1993). *Ekonomska Politika*, 10 May, p. 37.

Kalodjera, D (1991). Nedopustiva avantura. *Ekonomska Politika*, 15 April, pp. 12–13.

"Koncept Korze-Mencinger-Simoneti" (1992). *Ekonomska Politika*, 16 March, pp. 24–5.

Latsis, O (1993). Verkhovnyi sovet Rossii: Sessiya pechal'nykh rekordov. *Izvestiya*, 27 July, p. 2.

Lubin, N (1984). *Labour and Nationality in Soviet Central Asia*. London: Macmillan, in association with St Antony's College, Oxford.

Michnik, A (1990). Natsionalizm: Chudovishche probuzhdaetsya. *Vek XX i Mir* (Moscow), No. 10.

NCA/ITAR-TASS (1993). Strong support for Yeltsin reported from St. Petersburg. *291/RTR/RUS/SVC/Rezunkov*.

NCA/Mort von Duyke (1993). New form of nationalism seen among emerging democracies. 28 April.

Nikolić, D (1993). Obavljen rat inflaciji. *Ekonomska Politika*, 8 February, pp. 17–18.

Pejović, S (1993). Život sa blokadom. *Ekonomska Politika*, 15 March, pp. 12–13.

Petrović, S (1992). Institucionalno vlasništvo — stara logika. *Ekonomska Politika*, 6 April, pp. 31–2.

"Privatizacija — završni krug" (1992). *Ekonomska Politika*, 21 December, pp. 18–19.

Radošević, S (1993a). *The Generic Problems of Competitiveness on Company Level in the Former Socialist Countries: The Case of Slovenia*. Science Policy Research Unit, University of Sussex.

——— (1993b) *A Visit to Hungary and Slovenia*. Science Policy Research Unit, University of Sussex.

Russkoe Televidenie (1993). **News bulletin**, 14 April, 14.00 hours.

Shields, M (1993). No quick breakthrough seen for Yugoslav sanctions. *Reuters*, 26 April 1993.

"Štampa na valovima podržavljenja" (1992). *Ekonomska Politika*, 12 October, pp. 21–2.

Stogova, N (1993). Report on Informatsionno-Analiticheskaya Programma. *Radio Rossii*, 14 August, 22:00.

Teokarević, J (1991). Jugoslavia i Istočna Evropa. In Raspada Jugoslavije, R Nakarada, L Bašta-Posavec and S Samardžić (eds.). Produžetak ili Kraj Agonije, Belgrade, Institut za evropske studije.

Ursić, P (1992). Dogodilo se neizbežno. *Ekonomska Politika*, 19 October, p. 15.

"Vesti iz Slovenije" (1992). *Ekonomska Politika*, 19 October, p. 23.

Williams, CJ (1993). Drive to carve up Bosnia splits leadership. *Los Angeles Times*, 24 July.

"Zatezanje užeta" (1992). *Ekonomska Politika*, 20 July, p. 18.

Chapter 3

The Structural Origins of the
Russian Economic Crisis

INTRODUCTION

Why did the Russian economy fail to follow the pattern of the Central and East European countries, in rediscovering economic growth after just a few years of sharp recession in the early transition period? Why were Russian budget deficits so recalcitrant prior to the sharp increase in international oil prices through 1999? (Table 1). Why does Russia have such difficulty in servicing its foreign debt even when the balance of payments is in surplus? Why was the domestic commercial banking system in Russia so devastated by the use of a perfectly normal policy instrument like devaluation in the course of the financial crisis of August-September 1998? The argument developed in this paper is that behind the stagnation in production levels and the financial dramas which were the main features of the Russian economy in the 1990s lay a range of deep-seated structural factors, the origin of some of which goes back long before the beginnings of transition in Russia. In the opening sections of the paper we seek essentially to map the phenomenon of structural inertia as it has affected key sectors of the Russian economy. We start by looking at factors and issues

Table 1.   The Russian economy in transition: Basic statistics.

	1992	1993	1994	1995	1996	1997	1998	1999	2000	2001
GDP (% change)	-14.5	-8.7	-12.7	-4.2	-3.5	0.8	-4.9	5.4	9.0	5.0
Gross fixed investment (% change)	-45.0	-25.8	-26.0	-7.5	-18.5	-5.0	-6.7	-14.8	19.7	19.0
National savings ratio (% of GDP)	29.0	29.4	27.9	24.8	25.4	21.9	16.4	27.5	36.5	33.4
Budgetary balance (% of GDP)	-10.3	-7.0	-9.8	-5.4	-7.9	-7.1	-4.2	-1.2	2.4	2.9
Balance of trade ($b)	5.5	10.8	17.8	20.8	23.1	17.5	16.9	36.1	60.7	49.4
Balance of payments, current account ($b)	4.2	6.4	8.9	7.9	12.0	3.6	0.7	24.7	46.4	35.1
Rate of inflation (annual average)	1,353.0	876.0	307.4	197.4	47.6	14.6	27.7	85.7	20.8	21.6

Source: Economist Intelligence Unit, *Country Forecast Russia*, various numbers; (balance of trade and payments figures) *Rossiiskii Statisticheskii Ezhegodnik*, Goskomstat, Moscow, various editions; *Rossiya v Tsifrakh*, various editions, Goskomstat, Moscow.

relating to the structure of production. We then go on to a consideration of technological structure and the structure of the financial sector before examining the possibility that foreign investment might have been able to compensate for some of the rigidities found within the domestic Russian economy. In the subsequent sections of the paper we look for explanations of the patterns revealed, on both international and domestic dimensions, before trying to draw some conclusions, and to reflect on the implications of the analysis for current Russian economic prospects. While the early sections of the paper deal essentially with facts, the latter are inevitably somewhat speculative in nature, dealing, as they do, with a number of hypotheses which cannot be formally tested.

STRUCTURAL CHANGE IN PRODUCTION

Let us start at the broadest level. Table 2 shows that the breakdown of officially reported GDP between the four major sectors of the economy (industry, agriculture, construction and services) changed surprisingly little through the 1990s. There is a huge increase in the weight of services within GDP in 1992. (The increase is slightly less dramatic if "estimated financial intermediation services" are netted out against services, but the basic trend is unaffected.) What is even more striking is that there was no further systematic increase after that. Again, if we net out "estimated financial intermediation services" we see an upward tendency through the middle 1990s, but too slight to qualify as a real trend. And from 1998 the trend in services as a proportion of GDP is clearly downwards, leaving the share of that sector significantly lower in 2001 than it had been in 1992. So the structural change in favour of services should more properly be attributed to the impact of *perestroika* than to that of transformation. The pattern for agriculture and construction presents a mirror image of that of services, with sharp falls in 1992 and relative stability thereafter. Industry is the one sector where there does appear to be a clear downward trend from 1992. Even here, however, there is some doubt about the validity of the inference. The figures presented in the table for individual sectors are all net of the bulk of indirect taxes and

Table 2.   The structure of the Russian economy by main sector (GDP).

	1990	1991	1992	1993	1994	1995	1996	1997	1998	1999	2000	2001
Industry	35.4	37.6	34.5	32.4	31.5	28.7	27.5	25.7	27.3	27.6	28.4	25.6
Agriculture	15.4	13.7	7.2	7.4	5.8	7.1	6.7	6.5	5.1	6.8	5.9	6.1
Construction	8.9	9.3	6.4	7.5	8.7	8.2	7.6	7.9	6.5	5.5	6.4	7.3
Services	32.6	36.7	52.7	46.3	49.3	48.6	49.7	50.5	51.8	49.3	48.1	49.5
Estimated financial intermediation services	−0.5	−2.2	−4.0	−3.5	−3.9	−1.0	−0.2	−0.3	−0.2	−0.2	−0.8	−1.3
Other sectors	1.3	1.3	1.4	0.7	0.7	0.8	0.9	0.9	0.8	0.6	0.6	0.6
Sales taxes net of subsidies	6.9	3.7	1.8	9.1	7.8	7.6	7.7	8.8	8.7	10.4	11.4	12.2
Total GDP	100	100	100	100	100	100	100	100	100	100	100	100

Source: Rossiiskii Statisticheskii Ezhegodnik 1998, pp. 50–57; *Rossiiskii Statisticheskii Ezhegodnik 2002*, pp. 284–91.

Note: Calculated on the basis of output data in current prices; figures may not add up exactly to 100 because of rounding; inclusion of the (negative) item "estimated financial intermediation services" seems to represent an attempt to remove an element of double-counting from the "services" item.

subsidies,[1] and there is a separate row for "sales taxes net of subsidies". It is clear that the burden of indirect taxation in Russia falls mainly on industry. To what extent these taxes are absorbed rather than passed on is less clear. Subsidies are shared between industry and agriculture, but again the proportions of the share-out are unclear. If we make the most simplifying assumption and attribute all net sales taxes to industry, the break in trend in 1992 shows up much more sharply, with industry's share of GDP in that year standing at 36.3 per cent, compared to 41.3 per cent in 1991. But the clear subsequent downward trend disappears, with the share of industry in 1997 standing at 34.5 per cent, just 1.8 percentage points below of the 1992 level. And when net sales taxes are included, there is a well delineated recovery in the relative importance of industrial production in the period 1998–2001, with the combined proportion standing at 37.8 per cent in the end year of that sub-period.

It must certainly be borne in mind in all this that the second economy, estimated to account for around one-third of "true" GDP, is probably dominated by services to an even greater extent than official GDP, so that the structure of "true" GDP may be different from that presented in Table 1. But this will affect *trends* in structure only if the size of the second economy relative to "true" GDP is changing. Available evidence suggests that increases in the relative weight of the second economy may, indeed, help to explain why the share of services in official GDP actually falls in 1993, and why it had still not regained the 1992 level by 1997.[2] Overall, however, available statistics and "guestimates" provide no clear evidence of any structural dynamic in

---

[1]Reference to the tables in the *Statisticheskii Ezhegodnik* for sectoral breakdown of GDP by income shows that a small proportion of total net taxes are included in value added.

[2]Goskomstat surmises a steady increase in the share of the second economy in GDP from 20% in 1995 to 25% in 1997 and 30% in 1999 (*Vek*, No. 36, September 1999). The Institute of Mass Socioeconomic Problems estimates that the share of the second economy in GDP rose sharply between 1993 and 1996 (from 27% to 46%), and has been stable at around 50% since then. See P. Goble, "The long shadow of the second economy", *RFE/RL Newsline, Vol. 3, No. 188, Part 1, September 1999.*

the Russian economy through the 1990s at the level of output of main sectors. The distribution of investment by main sector was also relatively stable 1992–2000, notably for industry and construction. The share of fixed capital formation in the services sector was fairly constant up to the mid-1990s, when it started to rise on account of (relative) increases of investment in transport and communications. Agriculture is the only odd-man-out here, with investment collapsing after 1991 (*Rossiiskii Statisticheskii Ezhegodnik 1998*, p. 698).

Perhaps we should not expect too much from statistics at such a high level of aggregation. What about the internal structure of each sector? Let us take each in turn.

Agriculture

Crop and husbandry patterns are largely determined by geography and the tastes of the population, and while the eccentricities of Soviet planning and Soviet biology did produce bizarre attempts to defy the laws of nature by, for instance, growing maize inside the Arctic Circle (see Strauss, 1969, pp. 175–8), the scheme of agricultural activity inherited by Russia from the Soviet Union was not seriously distorted. Rather, the problem with Soviet agriculture was a level of labour and capital productivity that was both appallingly low and stagnant, and an aggregate level of production which showed no growth trend after 1973 (Dyker, 1992, p. 104). The reasons for such poor performance were manifold, but by common consent the major one was the peculiarly distorted (even by communist standards) organisational structure in the sector. The great bulk of the stock of agricultural land was held by huge and hugely inefficient collective and state farms, which were run by their chairmen and directors on a feudal-authoritarian basis which effectively excluded high productivity by definition. Every collective and state farm peasant, plus large numbers of non-agricultural rural dwellers and even some town dwellers, were permitted to hold "subsidiary private plots" of an acre or so. These were intended mainly for purposes of auto-consumption, but in fact provided large proportions of the marketed output of some basic agricultural goods, notably eggs. In

1979 the private subsidiary sector accounted for 26.5 per cent of total Soviet agricultural output (Shmelev, 1981, p. 69), this reflecting levels of labour and land productivity many times higher than those on the socialist sector of agriculture. A succession of attempts in the 1960s and 1970s to defeudalise the collective and state farms by permitting the formation of financially independent work-teams within their frameworks were invariably wrecked by conservative Communist Party *apparatchiki*. Gorbachev was still struggling with the problem when the Soviet Union collapsed in 1991.

The organisational structure of agriculture remains, today, much as it was in Soviet times. The majority of collective and state farms have been converted, in formal legal terms, into joint-stock companies or cooperatives, but they continue to be run on essentially Soviet lines. The private subsidiary sector increased its aggregate land holdings by around 30 per cent 1991–1999, but still holds only about 4 per cent of total agricultural land. The new private farmer sector increased its land holdings rapidly up to 1993, but only marginally thereafter, and holds only some 6 per cent of the total land stock today. The collective/state/joint-stock/cooperative sector still holds more than 80 per cent of total agricultural land. And this pattern of preservation of Soviet-era organisational patterns is exactly matched by trends on the production side. Output from the collective and state farms and their successors has continued to fall steadily, and while there has been some downward trend in the agricultural workforce, medium-term productivity trends also continue to be sharply negative. The private subsidiary sector now contributes a rather larger share of total agricultural output than it did in Soviet times.

Industry

Soviet industry was dominated by heavy industry, including the defence industry, and by hydrocarbons. The consumer sectors were poorly developed, and specialist component supplier sectors hardly existed. Repeated, if half-hearted and/or misconceived, attempts to restructure Soviet industry from the 1960s onwards produced no results, with fuel and energy increasing its share of total investment steadily from the mid-1970s to the mid-1980s, and consumer goods, chemicals and building materials losing out (Dyker, 1992, p. 173). Increases in the share of investment going to hydrocarbons were no doubt inevitable, in the face of rising extraction costs in the Soviet oil and gas industries. In practice, however, the increased investment was used to increase *gross* output of oil and gas, but at the cost of reducing *net* output of the same, because the energy requirements of producing additional hydrocarbons exceeded the energy equivalent of those additional hydrocarbons (Aksenov, 1989). Thus structural sclerosis[3] led to value-subtraction, and this was undoubtedly one of the main reasons for the collapse of the Soviet planned socialist economy.

The pattern changed remarkably little through the 1990s (Table 3). While aggregate levels of fixed investment in industry plummeted, industry's share of total investment showed a striking degree of stability,[4] while the pattern of investment by branch remained uncannily similar to that reported for the Soviet Union over the last couple of decades of its existence. The share of the energy and fuels sectors taken together continued to rise inexorably, as did that of metallurgy. The shares of chemicals and the food industry stagnated (there was a temporary fillip to investment in the latter 1998–1999 on account of import substitution after the August 1998 crisis), while those of machine building and the timber industry fell sharply. Investment in light industry and the building materials industry virtually ceased.[5] Within the general picture of continued structural sclerosis in industry, some positive structural trends could be detected. Thus, within the hydrocarbon sector, the share of oil-processing increased.

---

[3]Here, and *passim*, we use the world sclerosis in the sense of "morbid hardening, as of arteries" (*Chambers's Twentieth Century Dictionary*).

[4]Note that the significant increase in the share of total industrial investment in aggregate investment in the early 2000s was almost wholly on account of increases in investment in the oil extraction sector.

[5]In the former case largely due to the foreign competition that liberalisation of the Russian economy has brought. One may still wonder why domestic Russian consumer goods enterprises proved so utterly unable to stand that competition, given their advantages in terms of cheap labour.

Table 3.   The structure of fixed capital formation in industry 1990–2001 (% of total for whole economy).

	1990	1991	1992	1993	1994	1995	1996	1997	1998	1999	2000	2001
Electricity	2.4	2.7	4.9	5.0	4.7	5.2	6.0	6.9	6.1	4.5	3.7	4.1
Fuel	11.6	11.1	16.8	15.6	13.0	14.4	14.9	15.4	12.1	14.0	18.5	22.1
Oil extraction	7.6	8.0	12.3	10.6	8.0	8.4	8.0	8.5	7.3	8.8	11.6	14.4
Oil processing	7.6	0.2	0.4	1.2	1.3	1.4	1.2	0.9	1.1	0.8	1.8	2.1
Gas	2.9	1.5	2.0	2.1	2.1	2.9	4.0	4.3	2.5	3.4	4.3	4.7
Coal	1.1	1.4	2.1	1.8	1.6	1.7	1.7	1.6	1.2	1.0	0.8	0.9
Metallurgy	2.9	3.2	4.6	4.0	3.6	3.9	3.4	3.5	3.6	4.4	4.8	5.5
Chemicals	1.7	1.7	2.3	1.7	1.5	1.6	1.7	1.7	1.6	1.6	1.6	1.8
Machine building	8.3	6.9	4.9	4.5	3.6	3.1	3.4	3.1	3.2	3.6	2.9	3.0
Timber	1.7	1.9	1.6	0.8	1.0	1.3	1.0	0.9	1.0	1.6	1.5	1.2
Building materials	1.4	1.7	1.6	0.9	1.1	1.0	0.8	0.7	0.5	0.6	0.7	0.7
Light industry	1.2	1.2	1.0	0.6	0.5	0.3	0.3	0.2	0.3	0.3	0.2	0.2
Food industry	2.9	3.1	2.7	3.0	2.6	2.7	2.7	3.1	4.1	5.9	3.6	3.2
Total industry	35.9	34.7	41.3	37.0	32.3	34.4	34.8	36.4	33.3	37.3	38.5	42.6
Total economy	100.0	100.0	100.0	100.0	100.0	100.0	100.0	100.0	100.0	100.0	100.0	100.0

Source: Rossiiskii Statisticheskii Ezhegodnik 1998, p. 698; Rossiiskii Statisticheskii Ezhegodnik 2002, p. 578.

The share of gas also increased, while that of oil fell, which would appear to be structurally progressive given how much cheaper it is to extract Russian gas than to extract Russian oil. In the light of the legacy of wasteful investment in gas as outlined above, however, this can hardly be taken for granted. In any case, the trend was reversed in the early 2000s. Business reports from the two main hydrocarbon branches indicate critical problems of underinvestment, especially in pipeline networks, and it seems clear that as of the late 1990s there were serious problems of allocation of oil and gas investment.

We should bear in mind in all this that these shares are shares in a total which fell by over 75 per cent 1991–1999. It is nevertheless clear that what industrial investment was being done in Russia was largely in the sectors which enjoyed priority under the Soviet system, and that investment trends within those sectors were, on balance, structurally reactionary. It is noteworthy that the one sector which had priority status in Soviet times but which lost out heavily in investment terms after 1991 is machine-building — of all the sectors of traditional priority the one with the highest concentrations of human capital. We return to this point later.

So much for production. But what about selling, in what was now, after all, a kind of market economy? Specifically, what about selling to the outside world? There has, of course, been a major directional restructuring of Russian trade, away from the rest of the former Soviet Union and the CMEA towards Western markets. But in terms of what is actually exported to those markets, there was, once again, remarkably little sign of structural evolution through the 1990s. Table 4 depicts the broad tendencies in Russia's export pattern to 2000. It shows hydrocarbons (listed against minerals in the table) continuing to dominate exports, though falling slightly in terms of share of total exports in the mid-90s (note that the absolute value of hydrocarbon exports continued to grow steadily in that period). Exports of metals and precious stones as a share of total exports grew rapidly to 1997, and then fell away slightly. Shares of chemicals and wood and paper grew a little through the mid-90s, but there is no clear upward trend. The position of the machine-building sectors remained largely unchanged, but with a slight downward trend.

Table 4.   The structure of exports* 1992–2000 (%).

	1992	1994	1997	2000
Machinery & equipment	8.9	8.3	8.3	7.5
Minerals	52.1	45.1	47.1	54.5
Metals and precious stones	16.4	26.4	28.0	23.5
Chemicals	6.1	8.2	8.2	6.7
Wood & paper	3.7	3.9	4.7	4.5
Textiles	0.6	2.0	0.9	0.6
Leather & fur	0.2	0.6	0.5	0.3
Food	3.9	4.2	1.5	1.0
Other	8.1	1.3	0.8	1.4
Total	100.0	100.0	100.0	100.0

*Based on data in current prices. Trade with CIS countries not included.
Source: As for Table 3.

Textile exports grew in relative importance up to 1994, but then fell away sharply, remaining at a nugatory level in 2000.

The main structural shift in Russian exporting during the 1990s, therefore, was in terms of the sharp increase in the exports of metals and precious stones. That would appear, *a priori*, to represent a retrogressive structural shift, and microeconomic evidence confirms this impression. The increases in metal exports came largely in the form of increases in exports of commodity metals. In the case of aluminium, the world market was swamped in the early-mid-1990s by supplies of Russian metal, as domestic demand from the Soviet military-industrial complex collapsed, and the European Commission was persuaded by the European aluminium producers to impose in August 1993 an anti-dumping quota on imports into the Community of unwrought aluminium from Russia. At around the same time the European Commission imposed anti-dumping duties on imports of hematite pig iron from Russia, and initiated anti-dumping proceedings in relation to unwrought magnesium from Russia. The year before Russia had been forced into a voluntary export restraint in relation to uranium by the US government (Dyker, 1994, pp. 49–50; ECE, 1994, pp. 154–5). While anti-dumping actions and the like may be poor indications of genuine dumping behaviour (in the sense of selling abroad at less than the domestic price or selling abroad below cost), they are very good indications that the goods involved were undifferentiated commodities facing low price and income elasticity of demand. (There were, it must be added, some interesting exceptions, which we will discuss later on.)

The picture is the same in chemicals. Increases in Russian exports during the 1990s were largely in the area of bulk, commodity chemicals, and this is again confirmed by the incidence of contingent protection measures against them. Increases in exports of timber products came largely in the form of rough-hewn logs, timber for papermaking, etc. Russian exports of machinery and equipment were dominated by traditional Soviet strengths like aircraft, military equipment, ships and railway equipment. There was some structural dynamic within the aviation sector, with a number of joint ventures formed between Russian and Western aviation companies (Dyker, 1998). And the 1990s witnessed the appearance on world markets, for the first time, of high-tech sub-sectors like lasers and space-launching, previously buried beneath the secrecy of the Soviet military-industrial complex. While Russian laser exports are no more than an interesting cameo, Russia has managed to break into the world commercial space-launching market to a significant extent (Bzhilianskaya, 1999). Still, none of this was on a scale that would herald the arrival of Russia as a major exporter of manufactures.

Thus consideration of export trends largely reinforces the picture that comes through from the production and investment figures. During the 1990s Russia continued to export the things it exported in Soviet times. Where there were significant structural changes within total exports, they tended to reinforce Russia's status as a raw material producer. Structural rigidity in exporting, in the context of highly volatile international prices for hydrocarbons and metals, meant an ever-present danger of the (fundamentally strong) balance of trade suddenly worsening, with critical implications for external debt-servicing, etc.

Some new high-tech/knowledge-intensive sub-sectors did emerge on the export scene, but not on such a scale as to affect the overall picture. Why should this be? In a country with such a huge "knowledge industry", why did knowledge as a factor of production not have more of an impact, now that it was no longer the prisoner of the military-industrial complex? Why did the technological capabilities of the Russian population have so little visible impact in terms of upgrading existing sectors or introducing new? We try to answer this question in the next section.

STRUCTURAL CHANGE IN THE SCIENCE AND TECHNOLOGY SYSTEM

Russia inherited from the Soviet Union one of the biggest science and technology (*S&T*) complexes in the world (see Table 5). It was a complex dominated at the level of basic science by the Academy of Sciences of the USSR and its numerous specialist institutes and in the sphere of applied R&D by the design[6]/testing/production networks of the

Table 5.   The Russian *S&T* complex.

	1991	1994	1997	2000
Total number of *S&T* organisations	4564	3968	4137	4099
Of which:				
R&D organisations	1831	2166	2528	2686
Design (*konstruktor*) bureaux	930	545	438	318
Design (*proekt*) and exploration organisations	559	297	135	85
Experimental factories	15	19	30	33
Higher educational institutions	450	400	405	390
Industrial enterprises	400	276	299	284
Others	379	265	302	303
Total *S&T* personnel ('000s)	1677.8	1106.3	934.6	887.7
Total R&D expenditure as a percentage of GDP	1.43	0.84	0.99	1.16

Source: *Nauka Rossii*, 1998, pp. 10, 28 & 42; *Rossiiskii Statisticheskii Ezhegodnik 2002*, Goskomstat, Moscow, pp. 511, 513, 520.

---

[6]In the limited Soviet Russian sense of *konstruktorskaya rabota* — literally constructing prototypes. The Western notion of design as a synthesising element running through the whole matrix of R&D does not appear in Russia, or in the Russian language, until the word *dizain* is coined in the 1990s.

Soviet military-industrial complex. There was also a network of civilian industrial branch R&D institutes under the aegis of the various industrial ministries, while individual enterprises would normally have some kind of R&D unit in-house. But outside the military-industrial complex the linkages between R&D and production were weak. The dominant conceptualisation of the R&D process was in terms of crude science-push. In practice, science did precious little pushing. The institutes of the Academy of Sciences did not see it as their job to help enterprises develop new products and processes. In any case, the system of central planning on the basis of output indicators which continued to operate in the Soviet Union until its collapse in 1991 gave the enterprises themselves little enough incentive to look for new ways of doing things (Dyker, 1992, Chapters 1 and 2). The best of the industrial branch institutes had substantial R&D potential, but they, too, were caught up in a bureaucratic system which offered no rewards for original thinking. In a word, the whole notion of *innovation* was essentially foreign to the Soviet system, and to the Soviet mind-set. And the negative aspects of the *S&T* complex seemed to predominate more and more as the country entered the late Brezhnev/*perestroika* period, with the effective level of creativity of the system, as measured by the incidence of patenting in the US, falling sharply through the 1980s (see Table 6).[7] While it would be reckless to posit a simple cause-and-effect relationship between these R&D trends and trends in total productivity in the Soviet economy, it is striking that it is in the 1970s that rates of growth of total productivity go negative, heralding the end of the Soviet economy as a self-sustaining system (Dyker, 1992, p. 43).

Russia, therefore, inherited an *S&T* system from the Soviet Union which was better at spending money than at making money, which had a deserved international reputation in certain areas of basic science, materials science and defence-oriented and dual-purpose technology,

---

[7]The collapse of patenting in the US may well have been exacerbated by other factors. Research institutes, for instance, may have become increasingly reluctant to finance the process as budgets tightened against a background of economic stagnation. But the strength of the underlying trend, which was common to all the communist countries, can hardly be explained without reference to deep-seated systemic factors.

Table 6.   Number of Soviet patents registered in the US 1975–93.

1975	1980	1985	1989	1990	1991	1992	1993
421	463	148	161	176	178	69	59

Source: Computer Horizon Inc.

but which was run by people with no understanding of the notion of innovation and little sympathy, outside the military sphere, with the idea that R&D should be client-driven.

Since the collapse of the old system, Russian *S&T* has been going through a prolonged crisis, the end of which is not yet in sight. As Table 5 shows, expenditures on R&D as a proportion of GDP were cut by nearly 45 per cent 1991–97. In the context of persistently negative rates of growth of GDP, the cuts have been much sharper in real terms, and the apparent modest recovery in the mid-late 1990s illusory. There was a more genuine, but still modest, recovery 1997–2000. Total *S&T* personnel fell by some 45 per cent 1991–97, and by a further 5 per cent 1997–2000.

Yet the real problem in the Russian *S&T* system is not the cuts, but rather the fact that, against the background of these cuts, structural trends within the system have been such as to *reinforce* its essentially Soviet profile. While the total number of personnel has fallen, the number of R&D organisations has actually *risen*. And that increase has been to a substantial extent concentrated in the Academy of Sciences, with the total number of Academy institutes increasing from 586 to 804 between 1991 and 1997 (*Nauka Rossii*, 1998, p. 13). The hardest hit units within the *S&T* system have been the design organisations of various kinds (Table 5) which, with all their shortcomings, did provide the most client-oriented elements within the Soviet *S&T* complex. The result by 2000 was a Russian *S&T* system dominated by the elements best equipped to survive in what remained an essentially bureaucratic system — and that means the elements that were already surviving best under the old system.[8] The

[8]For an excellent discussion of the same phenomenon in Poland, see Kozlowski and Ircha (1999).

well-organised and politically well-connected Academy of Sciences came out of the crisis best, if at the cost of a good deal of fragmentation and dilution, as new institutes were spun-off to maximise leverage on funding authorities, and core funding spread as thinly as possible to maximise the rate of survival of old institutes. The industrial branch institutes suffered most, with the abolition, in most cases, of their hierarchical superiors and patrons under the old system, the industrial ministries. Levels of R&D activity at enterprise level, never high, fell even lower. Partly as a result of all this, basic research actually increased as a proportion of total R&D at the cost of applied research during the period 1991–97, and the downward trend in US patents continued through the period 1994–96 (Radošević & Kutlača, 1999, p. 99).[9] Under pressure of shortage of money, both institutes and individuals turned to "moonlighting" as a means of survival. Where this moonlighting involved the provision of R&D services to market-oriented clients, the structural implications were positive. In many cases, however, the moonlighting diverted R&D organisations and workers from their core business. The favourite institutional money-making scheme was to rent out part of one's building to a commercial company. And institute employees often made ends meet by doing ancillary work which might require specialist knowledge — and access to institute equipment — but which had no R&D content as such. Whether moonlighting is on balance structurally positive or negative is difficult to say. What can be said with confidence is that it tended to reinforce the pattern of bare survival at the cost of dilution and fragmentation which dominated the "official" institutional world.

In the case of one or two individual, big companies, like Gazprom, there was some movement towards the typical Western and East Asian pattern, whereby large concentrations of R&D activity are nested within the hierarchies of the commercial sector. The general trend, certainly as far as Russian-owned companies are concerned, was, however, in the opposite direction. What was left of the Russian

---

[9]Note, however, that *total* Russian external patents did start to rise again in the late 1990s (private communication from the OECD).

S&T system was more heavily concentrated in the "ivory towers" of the Academy of Sciences than ever before. Institutional sclerosis was mirrored and reinforced by attitudinal rigidities. Many Russian *S&T* leaders and managers openly expressed the view that the old system was best, and should ideally be reestablished — meaning effectively that the *existing* system should be preserved, but should be funded at a much higher level. Under the economic circumstances of the time this was, of course, pure fantasy. But it does demonstrate that the actors on the Russian *S&T* stage continued to await restructuring, and the fruits of restructuring, from another quarter, rather than considering how they themselves might contribute to that restructuring.

THE BANKING SYSTEM

If there is one sector of the Russian economy where there certainly has been restructuring, it is the banking sector. The Soviet monobank system, under which the State Bank (Gosbank) doubled as central bank and commercial bank for all of Soviet industry, with a sister Investment Bank (Stroibank) handling long-term finance of planned projects, survived intact until the break-up of the Soviet Union. The first government of independent Russia created a new *Central Bank*, which was to operate strictly as a central bank on the Western model. New legislation paved the way for the formation of new, privately owned, commercial banks. In the event, private banks sprang up like mushrooms, and by September 1994 there were 2500 of them. But while this represented a major new structural element in the Russian economy, it generated little of the restructuring impetus *vis-à-vis* the rest of the economy normally expected of banks. The new Russian commercial banks were poor mobilisers of savings, with a large proportion of total savings going either abroad or under the mattress. Total capital flight 1991–2000 is estimated at $160 b. The stock of dollar savings kept in cash at home in the late 1990s is estimated at $30–50 b. It must be added that many Russian banks were not particularly interested in mobilising savings. It is estimated that at 1994 some one-third of Russian banks were "zerobanks" — in which the owners, the main depositors and the main customers are all the same people. The purpose of the zero-bank is, of course, essentially fraudulent — to keep ailing enterprises going on the basis of "funny money" in the form of unbacked credits from the bank, with a view ultimately to creating a situation where it will be politically very difficult for the authorities not to bail out ailing enterprise and zero-bank alike. This does, of course, ultimately amount to a form of "looting",[10] which is further discussed below. Even where banks did not engage in fraudulent activity as such, it should be added, they generally lacked the branch structures necessary to mobilise savings on a large scale — and indeed the equally indispensable trust of the saving population.

Russian banks were equally ineffectual at the other end of the business — channelling funds into new business developments. Zero-banks were by definition uninterested in doing any such thing, but again even the (more or less) honest banks tended to find easier ways of making money. As long as inflation stayed above 100 per cent (up to the end of the 1995) the banks were generally happy to play the inflation game, exploiting high nominal interest rates and the numerous opportunities for arbitrage on foreign exchange markets. With inflation rates coming down from 1996 the banks found themselves under increasing pressure to look for investments in the real economy. But the pressure of the Russian budget deficit started to push up interest rates on government stock from late 1997, once again offering the banks an easy alternative to looking for good investments in the business sector (Schröder, 1999, pp. 964–66), and an irresistible temptation to borrow in hard currency in order to increase the take-up of these easy budgetary pickings. The banks were punished for their laziness when the Russian government devalued and defaulted on some of its rouble-denominated debt in August 1998. Strikingly, however, they refused to mend their ways. Thus the new money which the Central Bank pumped into the commercial banking system after the default to help the banks meet their commitments to customers and stop the economy going into a downwards spiral was, in fact, in the main diverted into foreign exchange speculation.

---

[10]The ploy is familiar, if limited in scope, in Western banking systems. See Akerlof and Romer (1993).

It would be wrong to put all the blame for the weaknesses of the banking system on the banks themselves. Where banks tried to operate as strategic investors (like Oneksimbank), they often met with stern resistance from powerful insider groups within the companies concerned (see discussion of portfolio investment, below). The fact is, however, that, on the whole, the new Russian commercial banking sector failed to mobilise savings on an adequate scale, and failed to channel what savings it did mobilise into the development of new production lines and new technologies. In an environment dominated by rigidities and inertia, we looked in vain to the new banks to provide impetus and enterprise.

THE STRUCTURAL IMPACT OF FOREIGN INVESTMENT

On paper at least, foreign investment could have come in to compensate for each of the structural rigidities we have identified. Foreign *direct* investment can help to refashion the structure of production and the science and technology system. Purely financial investments can help to supplement aggregate investible funds. And portfolio investment can in principle do both. In practice, foreign investment was able to play none of these roles in a satisfactory way.

While there is a considerable degree of uncertainty about the exact size of foreign investment flows into Russia, Table 7 presents a tolerably clear picture of the overall situation through the 1990s, on the basis of which we can venture the following generalisations:

- Overall levels of foreign investment were relatively very low, and showed no sustained upward trend, with a substantially negative figure for (net) total foreign investment reported by the UN ECE for 1999.
- Foreign direct investment (FDI) was low throughout the period, with net FDI falling to nugatory levels by 1999.
- To the extent that imperfect data permits analysis, portfolio investment seems to have been low throughout the period, with the relatively high estimated figure reported by the ECE for 1997

Table 7.   Net foreign investment in Russia by main category, 1995–99 (US$ b).

	1995			1997			1999		
	FIPC	ECE	EBRD	FIPC	ECE	EBRD	FIPC	ECE	EBRD
Direct	1.88	1.71	1.71	3.36	3.62	3.75	1.8[†]	0.8	1.1
Portfolio	0.03	0.88	—	0.19	15.70*	1.00	—	—	—
Other	0.89	1.20	—	8.22	13.83	31.00	—	—	—
Total	2.80	3.79		10.50		35.75		−16.0	

*Jan–Sept
[†]FIPC give only a figure for gross inflow. I have subtracted from that figure the ECE figure for
outflow, to produce a figure for net inflow.
Key: FIPC = Foreign Investment Promotion Centre, Ministry of Economics of the Russian
Federation; ECE = Economic Commission for Europe, United Nations; EBRD = European
Bank for Reconstruction and Development.
Source: Dyker, 1998; ECE, 2000, p. 143; ECE, 2001, p. 156; EBRD, 2000, p. 205; EBRD,
2002, p. 193; FIPC website.

probably reflecting some definitional quirk (cf. the EBRD
figures).
• The big increases in foreign investment in 1997 appear largely to
have reflected increases in financial investment, which dried up
after the August 1998 crash.

Thus FDI never amounted to more than 5–6 per cent of total
investment in Russia during the 1990s. This compares to corresponding figures for over 20 per cent for Hungary in 1997 and nearly
20 per cent for Poland and Romania in the same year (Hunya, 1998,
p. 6). Given the generally low levels of investment in Russia over the
transition period, it is clear, therefore, that FDI has hardly achieved
critical mass in purely quantitative terms. In more qualitative terms, it
has made a big impact on general levels of management and "soft"
(organisational) technology. It has also served as a vehicle for the
transfer of hard technology to key sectors like oil, e.g. in relation to
the refurbishment of old wells. The continued reluctance of the
Russian parliament to pass satisfactory production-sharing legislation
has, however, ensured that overall levels of FDI in hydrocarbons are
way below what they might be. Hydrocarbons apart, most of the FDI

has gone into food processing and commerce and catering. While we should not underestimate the impact of investment by e.g. MacDonald's and Coca-Cola in terms of transfer of soft technology, the structural impact of investments like these is minimal. Where foreign companies have sought to invest in more human-capital intensive sectors, the hard-technology transfer has sometimes been more from East to West than from West to East, e.g. in the case of space-launching (Bzhilianskaya, 1999). In cases like the motor-car industry, the scope for structural impact has been sharply constrained by continued dominance of insider interests (see discussion below), and by the poor environment for building up supply chains (Richet & Bourassa, 1998). In other words, and to run ahead of the argument somewhat, the very factors that block domestically initiated structural change operate to ensure that foreign direct investment cannot come to the rescue. In Central and Eastern Europe, by contrast, wholly-owned subsidiaries of major automotive multinationals have made substantial, if uneven, progress in building up supply chains that are themselves substantially internationalised in character (Havas, 1997; Martin, 1998).

But it is not only the difficulties of the Russian business environment that have inhibited the structural impact of FDI in Russia. Investing companies, especially German ones, have in many cases been prepared to take a long view of their investments in Russia, happy to plough back what profits they make in the short-to-medium term. While cases of restrictiveness in relation to transfer of technology to Russian partners are by no means uncommon, they are the exception rather than the rule (Barz, 1999). But the general pattern throughout the transition region is for FDI to create "shallow" rather than "deep" integration, with investments in human-capital- and knowledge-intensive activities largely limited to lower-level design activities (adaptation of standard designs for local markets, etc.) and "Bangalore" activities (e.g. employing Russian programmers to develop software for global systems) (Inzelt, 1999; Urem, 1999; Dyker, 1996). And there is no *a priori* reason to believe that shallow integration will automatically "grow" in deep integration (Dyker & Radošević, 1999). To the extent that we view the problem of what to do with the existing human-capital stock, specifically how to use it as a base for developing a knowledge-based economy, as the underlying structural issue in Russia, this pattern is profoundly negative.

What about direct investment in the beleaguered Russian banking sector? This is one of the few areas, outside hydrocarbons (see above) and the defence industry proper, where Russian law places severe constraints on foreign direct investment. Foreign banks are, in fact, not allowed to own, in aggregate, more than 12 per cent of the total capital of the banking sector. In practice, however, the limitation is not an onerous one, with foreign banks, up to now, staying well within the 12 per cent limit. Thus there are no immediate prospects of foreign-owned banks playing a big role in the mobilisation and allocation of savings in Russia.

Portfolio investment has been a particularly problematic area in Russia. It has been extremely difficult for foreign shareholders to exercise their rights (Hanson, 1997). (It must be added that, here again, the differences in the situations facing foreign and domestic investors have not been so great, with Russian "strategic investors" often finding it as difficult to impose control over incumbent managers as foreign investors.) But perhaps the distinction between FDI and portfolio investment is a little artificial when we are talking about foreign investment in manufacturing. Many such investments are in the form of joint ventures, i.e., involving less than 100 per cent foreign ownership. And any portfolio investment that amounts to more than 10 per cent of the total equity of the given company is, according to internationally accepted methodology, counted as FDI. The problem of entrenched insiders affects all foreign ventures that are not wholly-owned subsidiaries. The problem of poor environment for building supply chains affects *all* foreign investment that is not purely financial in character.

Financial investment has, as noted above, been the dominant element in foreign investment into Russia. Vigorous inward flows of financial investment are not, in themselves, bad things for emerging economies. In principle, they make extra resources available for investment. In practice, in the Russian case, they were, up to 2000, used largely to cover budget deficits. And because they encouraged governments at all levels to run bigger deficits than they otherwise might, they did not free up domestic resources for real investment. Worst of all, it was precisely the excessive dependence on foreign finance to cover budget deficits that precipitated the rouble crisis of 1998, with all its negative effects on flows of real investment, domestic and foreign. In the Russian case, therefore, the strength of inflows of financial investment through the 1990s must be viewed as an essentially negative factor in structural terms.

STRUCTURAL SCLEROSIS: A CHRONIC AND TERMINAL DISEASE?

The inability to implement structural change in response to changing patterns of demand and technological parameters was widely perceived as a key reason for the collapse of the Soviet system, not only in the Soviet Union itself, but also in the communist countries of Central and Eastern Europe (CEEC). Since transition began, the rate of structural evolution in the CEECs has certainly been uneven. But the Polish and Hungarian economies stand out as examples of genuine structural dynamism in a transition context (though exhibiting that dynamism in very different ways) (Dyker, 1999). We cannot, therefore, seek an explanation for Russia's peculiarly oppressive structural problems, and the extraordinary degree of continuity between the structural problems of the Soviet economy and those of the Russian economy in transition, in terms of general factors of transition. Structural change is always painful, the communist structural heritage sits heavily on the shoulders of the young democracies of the former communist world, and the installation of democratic regimes makes it in some ways more difficult for (often inexperienced) governments to resist the pressures and blandishments of sectoral lobbies. But this is true across the macro-region. What is different and special about Russia?

External Factors: The Role of Western Trade Policy

As noted earlier, Russia has suffered at the hands of the European Commission and the US government in terms of the imposition of contingent protection measures on commodity exports. In this respect, Russia is no different from any other transition country. And however unjust some of those measures may have been, their structural impact must have been positive, in that they have provided one more argument for the former communist countries to move away from commodity production. What is special about Russia is the fact that she has the capability to manufacture to export standards technologically sophisticated military and dual-use equipment. And here, the structural impact of Western trade restrictions has been less clear-cut. Attempts to curtail Russian exports of military aircraft and nuclear technology have certainly made it difficult for Russia to develop lines of obvious comparative advantage in high-tech areas. Restrictions on Russian commercial space-launching written into successive US-Russia trade agreements have had the same effect (Bzhilianskaya, 1999). But these facts have to be interpreted with care. Where the output of the former Soviet military-industrial complex is switched to new, export markets (and bear in mind that the Soviet Union was a major arms exporter), we can certainly identify a process of globalisation. Whether we can identify a parallel process of restructuring is less clear. And in the space-launching case, Western trade restrictions have had the secondary effect of encouraging the formation of joint Western-Russian ventures in the field. These have helped Russia to export existing technologies, but have also permitted them to upgrade those technologies through assimilation of complementary technologies (often in the field of "soft", organisational and management technology) from Western partners, thus strengthening their competitive advantage. If Western restrictions on the export of Russian manufactures have been inimical to the cause of restructuring the Russian economy, it has been at most to a marginal extent. If we want to understand what is special and different about Russia in the present context, therefore we have to focus primarily on the domestic dimension.

Internal Factors: Insiders and Inaction

We have seen that Russian industry is predominantly owned and controlled by insiders. It is equally clear that this preeminence on the part of insiders should be seen as an integral part of the Soviet legacy.

> The insider-dominated transactions, the bureaucratised corruption, and the importance of accumulating political power in order to wield economic clout all had their roots in Soviet times (Johnson, 1997, p. 360).

But why are Russian insiders so opposed to structural change in the first place? Research on the CEECs confirms that outsiders are better strategic managers than insiders (Frydman *et al.*, 1997). But insiders have nevertheless played an important role in the restructuring of particular sectors and enterprises in the CEECs, notably in Poland and Slovenia, and there is a powerful argument to the effect that if you want to implement radical, sometimes painful, structural policies, you have to be prepared to "do deals" with insider interests (Aghion & Blanchard, 1998). More specifically, the "*nomenklatura* capitalists", who have used money and contacts accumulated during tenure of key positions in the communist period to build up strong business positions in the transition period, have often been a force for structural change in the CEECs. Thus the experience of the more advanced transition countries suggests that as long as insiders and outsiders share the same basic goal — to make money, and are not too far apart on their time horizons, there is no reason why deals between outsiders and insiders should not stick.

What is special and deeply damaging to the cause of restructuring in the Russian case is the peculiar combination of paternalistic and feudal attitudes among insiders which ensures that they are *not* primarily interested in making money, in the sense of maximising profit as a flow. It is extraordinary that a survey conducted in 1997 by the Russian Federal Bankruptcy Administration found that only 4 per cent of the managers interviewed could be described as "market-oriented". (RIIA, 1998, p. 64). Lying behind such extraordinary facts is the tendency for Russian *nomenklatura* capitalists to treat their employees as "their people" in a manner reminiscent of the serfdom of imperial Russia as much as of the Soviet system.[11] That may involve a degree of

---

[11] Andrei Kuznetsov notes that, under the Soviet system, "management had the privilege of utilising the labour of enterprise employees for purposes other than their contractual obligations" (Kuznetsov, 1994, p. 965). Thus the labour-power of workers could be redeployed by managers directly, e.g. to help build their dachas, or lent to local farms at harvest time, in a way extraordinarily similar to the *corvée* system of classic feudalism.

genuine philanthropic paternalism, as insider bosses strive to keep the basic social fabric of the factory together, even if they cannot pay wages. Perhaps more fundamentally, it reflects a tendency to see employees as a form of personal *wealth*, rather than as an independent factor of production. Not surprisingly, perhaps, attitudes to real estate are similar, with many farm bosses preferring to "sit" on large tracts of uncultivated land rather than selling it off to "new" private farmers. Thus while the total stock of land under the *control* of agricultural organisations increased from 651.0 m hectares in 1992 to 699.9 m hectares in 1997 and that under the control of new private farms fell from 54.8 m hectares to 29.5 m hectares, total land *cultivated* by state farms, collective farms and cooperatives fell from 162.8 m hectares to 149.2 m hectares over the same period (Rossiiskii, 1998, pp. 441 & 451). In relation to natural resources, too, many Russian insiders are, it seems, inclined to "keep" deposits to themselves, rather than share them with the outsiders who may hold the key to effective commercial exploitation (Humphreys, 1995). And even obsolescent machinery in rustbelt factories may be viewed in terms of the principle that "at least it's mine". Just as it would be wrong to see these *nomenklatura* capitalists as totally uncaring for those beneath them, so it would be misleading to think of them, or at least all of them, simply as warlords, caring not a jot for country or state. But to the extent that they think of obligations *vis-à-vis* the state, they tend to think in terms of a *debt of service*, rather than in financial terms. Just as they do not pursue those that owe them money, so they see nothing wrong in not paying their taxes. Thus insider control not only reinforces structural sclerosis, thus eroding the tax *base*, it also makes it virtually impossible for the government to use that tax base effectively for fiscal purposes. Budget deficits, excessive borrowing and recurrent financial crisis are the inevitable outcome.

The result is a society, or at least an elite, obsessed with *stocks* to the exclusion of *flows*, but at the same time little interested in increasing or upgrading those stocks through new investment and or the introduction of new technologies — because the process of defining or redefining "bourgeois" property rights over those stocks is still far from complete.

As in Western Europe a thousand years ago, so in the Russia of today the borders between private and public in many cases are blurred or do not even exist ... Just as it was one thousand years ago, property and power are closely intertwined, and it is often impossible to separate them from each other. Just as royal emissaries turned their districts into private fiefdoms instead of using them to serve the king, Russian officials have tended to do the same with their positions in the hierarchy. In modern Russia, bureaucrats at all levels use their political power to exercise control over property, while rich people exchange money for power in order to control political decisions (Shlapentokh, 1996, pp. 393–4).

The extent of income inequality in Russia, reflected in a ratio of top to bottom deciles in the overall income distribution in the region of 13:1, testifies, however, that while Russian *nomenklatura* capitalists may not be profit maximisers, they certainly manage, in many cases, to be (relatively) extremely rich. What this in turn reflects is the degree of *monopoly advantage* that most of them enjoy, whether on the basis of outright monopoly or of collusion with fellow *nomenklatura* capitalists. Again, the Soviet legacy is critically important.

During the Soviet era giants of all kinds were created, natural and artificial monopolies. It is only natural that these monopolistic tendencies still continue to exist today with the beginning of the transition to market relations. That is how we arrived at a situation where ten or fifteen very big businessmen control the production of more than half of the gross national product (Interview with Vladimir Potanin, head of Oneksimbank and former first deputy prime minister, 1998, quoted in Schröder, p. 974).

Only a monopolist can afford to be a "satisficer", (i.e., a businessman who aims to attain an adequate level of profits, as defined by himself, rather than seeking to maximise profits) only a monopolist can afford the luxury of playing the feudal lord. So in the Russian case the issue of balance (or rather lack of balance) between outsiders and insiders is not only a question of capacity for strategic management. It is also a question of contesting markets. Outsiders are generally the only ones that can bring competition and thus *force* a change in behaviour. Otherwise, the only hope is that the insiders will change by themselves. We return to this theme in our conclusions.

Internal Factors: Fraud and Looting

As noted above, the process of establishment of property rights is still going on in Russia. Thus while markets may not generally be contested, property rights certainly are. The distinction between contest and expropriation is, however, difficult to maintain, and such difficulties of distinction plague the whole business of "modelling" the pattern of bureaucratic feudalism in the post-Soviet world. While most *nomenklatura* capitalists are rich monopolists/satisficers, the lion's share of the enterprises they control actually make losses.[12] So much of the wholesale abuse of monopoly power that has characterised transition Russia has probably been outright looting (i.e., the illegal appropriation of part of the capital stock) rather than just rent-extraction. Once again, we see, this time in a peculiarly negative way, the obsession with stocks rather than flows. And the proceeds of the looting have, of course, fuelled the stream of capital flight which has deprived Russia of investible funds as well as tax revenue, and weakened the balance of payments, sometimes to a critical extent. The Russian *nomenklatura* do not generally maintain private armies in the manner of the great landowning aristocrats of the past. Rather they create zero banks and do deals with organised criminals, conniving at mafia looting in exchange for such "security" services as they require, thus ensuring that a large part of the economy will remain imprisoned within a corrupt and exploitative sub-system in which there can be no accumulation and no innovation, because there can be no trust. All of this is more reminiscent of a contemporary African kleptocracy than a mediaeval European feudalism. Feudalism does not exclude trust.

---

[12]In 1997, 50.1 per cent of all the enterprises in Russia were making losses (*Rossiiskii Statisticheskii Ezhegodnik 1998*, p. 669).

Kleptocracy does, because using political and social power as a basis for theft is by definition an abuse of trust. *Ergo*, feudalism can grow into something different; kleptocracy cannot. The Western economic systems that have grown out of the old feudal systems of Western Europe continue to suffer from a whole range of fraud problems, especially in banking (see fn. 9). But these problems do remain the exception rather than the rule. In Russia, by contrast, fraudulent dealing is a universal characteristic of the economic system. How can such a system possibly engender structural change?

CONCLUSIONS

Bringing all the foregoing together, and to a degree reversing the sequence of argument, we can list our main conclusions as follows:

- Patterns of mind-set and behaviour among Russian business elites have conspired to reduce the profitability of Russian business, to despoil the existing capital stock of the nation, and to block the flow of resources into new investment, and into the state budget.
- The weakness of the banking system has exacerbated these underlying problems because banks have failed to mobilise alternative sources of finance or to channel finance into investment in the real economy, preferring to feed off the budget deficit, and in the worst case operating as instruments of looting.
- The weakness of the Russian R&D system has meant that, where companies have implemented new investment, they have not been able to count on support from an effective "national innovation system" to ensure that the technologies embodied in that investment are appropriate.
- In the absence of significant levels of investment in areas with growth potential, the Russian economy has failed to develop any real dynamic on the structural dimension, and in many cases continues to suffer from structural defects inherited from the Soviet period.
- Lack of structural change at the production level has left the Russian balance of payments heavily dependent on exports of oil

and gas, and therefore vulnerable to changes in world prices of energy materials. Capital flight has created serious problems of hard-currency liquidity for the Central Bank. The combined operation of these two factors meant that the "real" balance of payments, in terms of the Central Bank's ability to meet external obligations, was at best delicately poised, at worst in hopeless deficit, throughout the 1990s.

- In combination, these structural factors ensured that production levels in Russia would stagnate throughout the 1990s, and that that stagnation would be punctuated by recurrent crises of domestic (budgetary) and external (debt service) balances. Of course other factors reinforced these trends. But the role of structural factors was absolutely central.
- The role of the international dimension in all of this has been at most marginal. Foreign direct investment has eased structural rigidities to only a minor extent. The structural impact of purely financial investment from abroad has probably been negative. Barriers to trade have imposed an additional rigidity on the Russian economy, but it has not been a critical one.

What of the future? The metaphoric use of the term *sclerosis* to describe the structural rigidities that have defined the Russian economy over the past few decades is graphic and useful. But it should not be taken too far. In human beings, sclerosis is a terminal illness. We should never imagine that Russia, as a society, is somehow bound for ever, as if by some biological law, in its sclerosis. No, full recovery is perfectly possible. But how? Internal factors are clearly central, and among them "mind-set" factors are clearly the most important subset. The most optimistic element in our diagnosis is the identification of feudal-bureaucratic attitudes to property as a key obstacle to structural change. For those attitudes are primarily a feature of the older generation of *nomenklatura* capitalists, men schooled and formed by the Soviet system, and locked inside the Russian language, with all its richness and all its limitations. The younger generation of Russian businessmen, carrying much less baggage from the Soviet period, speaking English actively, and in many cases trained or re-trained in Western style business schools, are less paternalistic, less feudal, in a word, much more conventional in their attitude to property and factors of production. But are they more *honest*? Are they less tempted to loot, less inclined to stow away their savings in foreign banks, less inclined to do deals with gangsters? If the answer is "no", and if we are inclined to stress the kleptocratic features of contemporary Russia as much as the feudal, then the future for Russia, whether in connection with structural change or anything else, is bleak indeed.

POSTSCRIPT

How have these factors developed through the early 2000s, in the years since this article was written? There is good news on a number of counts. As foreseen in the original conclusions, generational change in Russian business management, reinforced by institutional reforms implemented under the Putin presidency, has weakened feudal-bureaucratic attitudes. Consistent buoyancy in the price of oil in the period since 1999, backed up by tax reform and significant improvements in the effectiveness of tax collection, have seen Russian budget deficits transformed into surpluses. After a decade of stagnation, Russian GDP has started to grow modestly but steadily. On the downside, capital flight continues unabated. More fundamentally, the improvement in the macroeconomic performance of the Russian economy seems to have flowed purely from the improvement in Russia's terms of trade. There are few signs of any accelerated structural shift. The Russian economy remains largely dependent on raw-material extraction, and the performance of the human-capital-based sectors continues to be disappointing. At mid-2003, the rate of growth of Russian GDP seemed to be slowing. With the international price of oil forecast to fall sharply in 2004 and then stabilise at around $20 per barrel (as compared to an average of around $25 for the period 2000–2003), the weaknesses of the political economy of Russia, as discussed in this article, are likely to reemerge as critical factors of Russian economic performance.

REFERENCES

Aghion, P and O Blanchard (1998). On privatisation methods in Eastern Europe and their implications. *Economics of Transition*, 6(1).

Akerlof, GA and PM Romer (1993). Looting: The economic underworld of bankruptcy for profit. *Brookings Papers on Economic Activity*, 2, 1–73.

Aksenov, D (1989). Strategiya "chistoi" energii. *Ekonomicheskaya Gazeta*, 16, p. 5.

Barz, M (1999). British and German MNCs in Russia and the FSU — Evidence from the Western side. In *Foreign Direct Investment and Technology Transfer in the Former Soviet Union*, DA Dyker (ed.). Cheltenham: Edward Elgar.

Bzhilianskaya, L (1999). Foreign direct investment in the science-based industries of Russia. In *Foreign Direct Investment and Technology Transfer in the Former Soviet Union*, DA Dyker (ed.). Cheltenham: Edward Elgar.

Dyker, DA (1992). *Restructuring the Soviet Economy*. London: Routledge.

——— (1994). Russian perceptions of economic security. *Tokyo Papers*, 7, pp. 33–65.

——— (1996). The computer and software industries in the East European economies — a bridgehead to the global economy? *Europe-Asia Studies*, 48(6), 915–30.

——— (1998). R&D Collaboration and the Foreign Business Sector in Russia. Paper presented to OECD conference, Moscow.

——— (1999). The transition economies — why has performance been so variable? In *The European Economy*, 2nd Ed., DA Dyker (ed.). Longman: Harlow.

Dyker, DA and S Radošević (1999). *Building the Knowledge-Based Economy in Countries in Transition — from Concepts to Policies*. SPRU, University of Sussex, mimeo.

Economic Commission for Europe (ECE) (1994). *Economic Survey of Europe in 1993–1994*. United Nations, New York and Geneva.

——— (2000). *Economic Survey of Europe 2000 No. 1*. United Nations, New York and Geneva.

——— (2001). *Economic Survey of Europe 2001 No. 1*. United Nations, New York and Geneva.

European Bank for Reconstruction and Development (EBRD) (2000). *Transition Report 2000*. London.

Frydman, R, C Gray, M Hessel, and A Rapaczynski (1997). *Private Ownership and Corporate Performance: Evidence from Transition Economies*. EBRD Working Paper No. 26 (December).

Hanson, Philip (1997). What sort of capitalism is developing in Russia? *Communist Economies & Economic Transformation*, 9(1), 27–42.

Havas, A (1997). Foreign direct investment and intra-industry trade: The case of the automotive industry in Central Europe. In *The Technology of Transition. Science and Technology Policy for Transition Countries*, DA Dyker (ed.). Budapest: Central European University Press.

Humphreys, D (1995). Mining and metals in the CIS; between autarky and integration. In *Investment Opportunities in Russia and the CIS*, DA Dyker (ed.). Washington: Royal Institute of International Affairs and Brookings Institute.

Hunya, G (1998). *Integration of CEEC Manufacturing into European Corporate Structures by Direct Investments*. The Vienna Institute for International Economic Studies, mimeo.

Inzelt, A-M (1999). The transformation role of FDI in R&D: Analysis based on material from a databank. In *Quantitative Studies for Science and Technology Policy in the Countries of Central and Eastern Europe*, DA Dyker and S Radošević (eds.). NATO, Brussels: Kluwer.

Johnson, J (1997). Russia's emerging financial-industrial groups. *Post-Soviet Affairs*, 13(4), 333–65.

Kozlowski, J and D Ircha (1999). The structure of disciplinary comparative advantage in post-communist countries. In *Quantitative Studies for Science and Technology Policy in the Countries of Central and Eastern Europe*, DA Dyker and S Radošević (eds.). NATO, Brussels: Kluwer.

Kuznetsov, A (1994). Economic reforms in Russia: Enterprise behaviour as an impediment to change. *Europe-Asia Studies*, 46(6), 955–70.

Martin, R (1998). Central and Eastern Europe and the international economy: The limits to globalisation. *Europe-Asia Studies*, 50(1), 7–26.

Nauka Rossii v Tsifrakh 1998 (1998). CSRS, Ministry of Science and Technology. Moscow: Russian Academy of Sciences.

Radošević, S and D Kutlača (1999). Technological "catching-up" potential of Central and Eastern Europe: An analysis based on US foreign patenting data. *Technology Analysis and Strategic Management*, 11(1), 95–111.

Richet, X and F Bourassa (1998). *Restructuring of the East European Car Industry*. Final Report, TSER Workshop on Restructuring and Reintegration of Science and Technology Systems in Economies in Transition, Berlin, June.

Rossiiskii Statisticheskii Ezhegodnik, various editions. Goskomstat, Moscow.

Royal Institute of International Affairs (RIIA) (1998). *Scenarios for Russian Medium and Long Term Development*. The Russia and Eurasia Programme, January.

Schröder, H-H (1999). El'stin and the oligarchs: The role of financial groups in Russian politics between 1993 and July 1998. *Europe-Asia Studies*, 51(6), 957–988.

Shlapentokh, V (1996). Early feudalism — the best parallel for contemporary Russia. *Europe-Asia Studies*, 48(3), 393–411.

Shmelev, I (1981). Obshchestvennoe proizvodstvo i lichnoe podsobnoe khozyaistvo. *Voprosy Ekonomiki*, 5.

Strauss, E (1969). *Soviet Agriculture in Perspective*. London: Unwin.

Urem, B (1999). R&D behaviour of firms in transition economies: An analysis of the key determinants. In *Quantitative Studies for Science and Technology Policy in the Countries of Central and Eastern Europe*, DA Dyker and S Radošević (eds.). NATO, Brussels: Kluwer.

Part III

Transition and the Global Economy

Chapter 4

Technology and Structure in the Polish Economy Under Transition and Globalisation[1]

INTRODUCTION

The technology factor is increasingly recognised as a crucial determinant of structural upgrading and economic growth in open developing economies. Modern trade and growth theories have illuminated the role of technology diffusion for global trade and capital flows in general. To date, however, little systematic research has been done on the process of technological integration of the economies of Central-East Europe (hereafter CEEC) into the European and global trading systems. This paper represents an attempt to fill this gap on the basis of Polish empirical material — both aggregate statistics and selected case studies.

Increasing globalisation and the growing complexity of state-of-the-art technologies have conspired to give international production ever greater prominence among channels of technology diffusion. This trend is confirmed at the global level by the fact that growth

---

[1]This paper was prepared within the framework of ACE project 94-0660-R, *EU Enlargement and the World Trading System: The Case of Poland.*

rates of internationalised production have been much higher than growth rates of international trade in commodities or arm's length trade in technology.[2] It is also observable that rates of growth of FDI into CEEC have, since opening-up, been consistently higher than those of aggregate trade volumes, or of direct trade in technology (which have actually decreased) (United Nations, 1996, pp. 111 and 150). There is good reason, therefore, to study the technological transformation of the transition countries through the prism of trends in FDI and its impact on their trade performance since liberalisation. The problem with this approach is that we cannot directly observe the technological content of FDI, or its role in "technological accumulation" within the host countries. So we need a theory of international production, and we need to be able to rank industries in relation to technology, to fashion a theoretical framework within which we can establish interrelationships between FDI flows and revealed comparative advantage (RCA) in terms of a ranking of industrial activities by technological content. Once we have done that, we should be able to analyse the Polish data in such a way as to highlight that country's position in the technological chain of industrial activities on a global, or at least macro-regional level.

CONCEPTUAL AND THEORETICAL FRAMEWORK

The Basic Model

The eclectic paradigm of international production developed by J. Dunning (1988) specifies most comprehensively the conditions necessary for the emergence of multinational enterprise. These conditions flow from the specificity of economic assets (resources able to generate a future income stream), and from the optimal modes of utilisation and trading of these assets. The assets may be mobile or immobile,

---

[2]From 1983 to 1989, FDI by OECD countries grew at an annual average growth rate of 31.4%, nearly three times faster than trade (11.0%) and gross fixed capital formation (11.9%) within the OECD, and over three times as fast as GDP (10.4%). See OECD, STIID Database, September 1991.

transferable or non-transferable between countries. They may be natural or man-made; the latter can be further divided into tangible and intangible assets. Firms and countries differ in asset endowments, since firm-specific assets constitute ownership-specific advantages (appropriated by particular firms), while country-specific assets (available to all firms in a given country) are by definition locational advantages. Due to structural and transactional market failures, these asset endowments, and the streams of services they provide, cannot be traded freely without serious efficiency loss. They are better used under a common hierarchical governance, i.e., under a regime of internalisation.

In the simplest case, a firm located in a particular country, and endowed with a mobile and intangible asset, chooses a production location in another country which disposes of assets that are natural and immobile — on the condition that the internalisation of the new production facility generates a more efficient outcome than would an arm's length transaction. But while this simplest case may also be the most typical, one can imagine a whole series of combinations of ownership and locational advantages that can provide a rationale for international production. In most cases where the advantage is based on a created asset, it is in fact the superior technology of the investing firm, in the face of a strong internalisation effect (usually traceable to the low appropriability of "tacit" knowledge and/or weak absorptive capabilities in the host country) that is the main driving force behind international production.

So much for the static framework. In a dynamic world the pattern of both ownership and locational advantages may change, and with them the conditions for international production and trade. *Natural assets* may be depleted or exhausted. *Created assets* may be accumulated, transferred or acquired. Thus locational advantages may be *dissipated* or *upgraded*. The same is true of ownership advantages, where those are based on natural or created assets. Thus the pattern of comparative advantage itself may change in function of the process of transnational investment, to the extent that that involves transfer of created (especially intangible) assets (technology and associated spillover effects), or through depletion of natural assets. Such dynamic tendencies affect home and host countries alike.

These considerations suggest that we can distinguish between two contrasting models of foreign investment:

- FDI oriented towards the *absorption* of the existing assets in the host country, as a basis for exploiting the locational advantages of that country, whether created or natural.
- FDI which transfers new technologies and *creates* new assets in the host country, drawing mainly on the ownership advantage differential between the two countries.

The *a priori* supposition must be that *asset-absorbing* FDI should, like ordinary trade, more or less follow the RCA pattern, whether defined in Ricardian (productivity differentials) or Heckscher-Ohlin (differences in factor endowments) terms, of the host country. It will tend to reinforce existing RCA patterns, and, by the same token, the differential in ownership advantages between home country and host country firms. This in turn will tend to result in a further divergence of patterns of RCA in home and host countries. *Asset-creating* investment, by contrast, will tend to run against the RCA pattern of the host country, and the strength of the flow of such investment should, *ceteris paribus*, be a direct function of the extent of the ownership advantage differential between home and host countries. Asset-creating investment should visibly change the RCA pattern of the host country. In consequence, the ownership advantage differential will diminish, and RCA patterns in the two countries converge.

Of course in practice the bulk of FDI flows exhibit features of both asset absorption and asset creation. But where asset absorption predominates, FDI will tend to concentrate on the domestic market of the host country, sometimes crowding out domestic production. After a temporary improvement, the overall RCA pattern may even deteriorate, because asset-absorbing investment tends to push up the prices of the assets absorbed, resulting in a loss of international competitiveness; and to weaken rather than strengthen local sourcing networks, in the extreme case setting the host economy onto an "unlearning curve" (Bell, 1997, p. 74). Thus the balance of asset absorption and asset creation emerges as a key issue in the analysis of the dynamic impact of FDI.

The Cross-sectoral Approach to Asset Absorption and Asset Creation: Two Taxonomies

We will examine how the dichotomy of asset absorption and asset creation develops in conditions of inflow of FDI by introducing two overlapping but contrasting industrial taxonomies. The first is based on *factor mix*, following Neven (1994, pp. 22–26), the second on *technology sourcing/use/appropriation*, following Pavitt (1984, pp. 343–75) and Bell and Pavitt (1993, pp. 177–82).

Neven classifies industrial sectors according to their factor intensities (in the West), using these variables: the share of wages in value added, investment as a percentage of value added, average wages, and the proportion of white-collar workers in total employment. A high rate of investment is taken to represent high physical capital intensity, and a low average wage combined with a high share of wages in value added, high labour intensity. Where average wages are high, the share of labour in value added is high, and the weight of white-collar workers within the work force is also high, high human-capital intensity is inferred. This mode of analysis generates two key criteria — physical-capital intensity and human-capital intensity — and Neven proceeds, at the NACE three-digit level, to classify 120 sectors of manufacturing industry into five clusters — the four corresponding to the four possible combinations of high and low physical- and human-capital intensity, plus an extra one featuring very high human-capital intensity.

Table 1. Neven's industry groups by factor mix.

Factor Intensity	Share of White-collar Workers	Average Wage	Wage Bill/ Value Added	Investment/ Value Added
1 very high human capital	very high	very high	high	high
2 high human, low physical	high	high	high	low
3 low human, low physical	low	low	very high	low
4 low human, high physical	low	low	intermediate	high
5 high human, high physical	high	high	low	very high

Source: Adapted from Neven (1994, pp. 22–23).

We shall use this taxonomy to analyse the sectoral patterns of inward FDI and RCA for the Polish economy in the period 1989–97, in order to ascertain to what extent foreign investment in that period was oriented towards exploiting locational advantages in terms of factor abundance, as demonstrated by the RCAs of the various groups. To the extent that it turns out that FDI inflow has reinforced the existing RCA pattern, a relatively high incidence of asset absorption will be inferred. To the extent that the opposite pattern is observed, an increasing degree of *factor incongruity*, possibly rectified through inflow and creation of complementary assets, may be inferred.

In the second taxonomy, Pavitt identified four basic types of industry, on the basis of a combination of indicators reflecting sources of technology, technology user requirements and the means by which technology is appropriated. In decreasing order of potential for technological dynamism, they are: the science-based sector, specialised suppliers, the scale-intensive sector, and the supplier-dominated (traditional) sector. For our purposes it is clearly important to distinguish natural-resource-based activities — which Pavitt did not do because natural-resource orientation is not important for technological ranking. So we split the scale-intensive cluster into two sub-clusters: technology-based scale-intensive and resource-based scale-intensive.

Table 2.   Pavitt's industry groups by patterns of technology sourcing/use/appropriation.

	Sector	Factor Intensity	Main Product Characteristics
1	science-based	very high human capital	Schumpeterian
2	specialised suppliers	high human, low physical	Schumpeterian, Smithian[a] differentiated
3	supplier-dominated	low human, low physical	Heckscher-Ohlin, Ricardian
4	technology-based, scale-intensive	low human, high physical	
5	resource-based, scale-intensive	high human, high physical	Smithian non-differentiated, Smithian differentiated

Source: Adapted from Bell and Pavitt (1993).
[a]Heterogeneous products developed through extensive division of labour.

We end up, then, with five clusters which bear some resemblance to Neven's five clusters. It is obvious that science-based industries and specialised suppliers must be more human-capital-intensive than traditional industries, and that scale-intensive sectors require relatively more physical capital than, for example, specialised suppliers.

Utilisation of the modified Pavitt taxonomy can provide a basis for measuring the relative importance of asset-absorbing and asset-creating effects along the axis of technology sourcing/use/appropriation. In applying the asset-absorbing and -creating categories to FDI in terms of the Pavitt taxonomy, we will actually be looking at the skill-absorbing and -creating effects of foreign investments. Where FDI inflow reinforces the existing RCA pattern in terms of the Pavitt taxonomy, a high degree of skill absorption prevails. In the opposite case we should infer a tendency to skill creation through intensive technology transfer.

DATA SOURCES AND METHODOLOGY

Our analysis is based on two sorts of statistical data on trade and FDI, and on a wide range of case studies. The trade data cover Polish trade with the EU in 120 manufacturing industries at the three-digit NACE classification for the period 1988–96, and were obtained from the Eurostat COMEXT trade data base, 1997 edition. The FDI data cover inward direct investment in Poland in the same manufacturing industries, grouped in accordance with the same NACE classification, over the period 1989–97. This data was obtained from the Polish Central Statistical Office (*Glowny Urzad Statystyczny*). The three-digit classification was used mainly to aggregate each set of data in line with the Neven and Pavitt taxonomies. Further analysis proceeded exclusively on the basis of the five clusters in each taxonomy, for both trade and FDI. Correlations were examined at the level of clusters rather than at that of individual industries because the aim of the analysis was to analyse technological content in the context of transformation and globalisation rather than detailed branch characteristics.

The decision to limit analysis to European trade was taken partly on grounds of convenience. But the decision is not difficult to defend on substantive grounds. The structure of Poland's trade with the EU can be regarded as representative, since that trade accounts for 65–70 per cent of total Polish external trade. And it is surely reasonable to assess Poland's pattern of comparative advantage by reference to the yardstick of the EU's trade with the rest of the world (extra-EU trade).

Our analysis focuses on broadly-defined clusters characterised by specific factor-mix or pattern of technology sourcing/use/acquisition. It is therefore by definition oriented to inter-industry (more accurately inter-cluster) rather than intra-industry trade. There is, accordingly, no systematic treatment of intra-industry trade in the paper. But the analysis does throw up specific insights on intra-industry trade, and these will be noted in the course of the discussion.

Since our trade analysis is limited for data reasons to trade in manufactured goods, we were also constrained in the aggregate statistical part of our FDI study to limit the range of the analysis to manufacturing tradables, which do, indeed, account for more than two-thirds of FDI inflow into Poland. In our case studies, we do, however, present material on the software industry, which straddles the manufacturing and services sectors. Again, we did not distinguish between joint ventures, minority or majority holdings, simply because the data available is not comprehensive enough to make such a disaggregation at the three-digit level.[3] In all cases the FDI data reflect actual investment, not planned, approved, or committed flows.

TECHNOLOGY AND TRADE

The Factor Proportions Axis

Despite a fourfold increase in Polish exports to the EU in 1988–96, and a complete reorientation of trade away from the old CMEA area towards Western markets, the dominant export and import trends in

---

[3]Inzelt's (1999) analysis based on a unique Hungarian government data base demonstrates a (statistically weak) positive relationship between size of foreign stake and expenditure on R&D in firms hosting foreign investment. This suggests that the higher the foreign stake, the stronger the chance of asset creation. It would be fascinating to test this hypothesis using Polish data.

Table 3.   Polish and EU manufacturing exports as percentages of total exports:
Neven's industrial clusters 1988–96.

	1988 (%)	1989 (%)	1990 (%)	1991 (%)	1992 (%)	1993 (%)	1994 (%)	1995 (%)	1996 (%)
Poland									
Sector N1	5.7	5.7	5.9	5.9	4.9	5.0	5.0	5.9	6.5
Sector N2	6.1	6.3	7.4	7.5	7.3	6.7	6.6	6.6	7.7
Sector N3	19.1	17.2	19.1	23.6	26.8	31.7	29.3	27.5	28.9
Sector N4	32.4	30.7	28.9	29.2	32.9	32.2	35.5	36.3	34.8
Sector N5	6.7	8.4	7.8	7.4	6.5	6.0	5.9	5.5	5.4
% of total	70.1	68.2	69.1	73.6	78.4	81.6	82.2	81.8	83.2
EU									
Sector N1	16.6	16.7	16.7	18.0	18.9	20.4	20.4	20.6	21.2
Sector N2	20.1	20.2	21.1	21.3	21.4	21.1	20.9	21.6	22.4
Sector N3	9.8	9.8	10.0	10.1	10.0	9.4	9.3	9.0	9.2
Sector N4	31.2	30.5	29.6	28.7	28.4	30.0	30.3	30.2	29.0
Sector N5	4.5	4.6	4.5	4.5	4.7	4.6	4.5	5.2	4.8
% of total	82.2	81.7	81.9	82.7	83.3	85.4	85.5	86.6	86.6

Source: Eurostat COMEXT databank and authors' calculations.

terms of factor intensities have remained relatively stable for Poland. The most significant overall change is the 13 percentage-point increase in the share of manufactures in total Polish exports to the EU, which can largely be accounted for by the increase in the share of Sector N3 goods by 10 percentage points.

The two sectors which Neven classifies as of low human-capital intensity (N3 and N4) were, by 1996, together accounting for around two-thirds of total Polish exports of manufactures to the EU. This trend may be interpreted as generally consistent with Heckscher-Ohlin predictions for an economy with relatively abundant and inexpensive labour. However the penchant for labour-intensive and capital-saving exports seems to be much less pronounced than might have been expected, in particular when we consider that Sector N4 is physical-capital- as well as labour-intensive. Sector N4 trends can, of course, be easily explained in terms of technologically conditioned low elasticity of substitution between labour and capital in that sector.

The other three sectors (N1, N2 and N5), all characterised by high human-capital intensity, have accounted for much lower shares in total exports to the EU, and these shares have remained remarkably stable, at a level, taken together, of about one-third of labour-intensive exports.

Perhaps the most striking general conclusion to be drawn here is that there was a remarkable tendency, through the globalisation-transition period, to trade labour for human capital, in the context of general similar levels of physical-capital intensity of exports and imports. Note, for instance, the roughly similar export and import shares of physical-capital-intensive sectors N4 and N5 (Tables 1 and 2). The declining import shares of Sectors N1 and N2 seem to run against the proposed generalisation, but note also the rapid increase of Sector N4 imports (Table 4), which, though physical-capital-intensive, may have compensated for falling imports in Sectors N1 and N2. Thus we may hypothesise that where intermediate goods have in the past been directly imported on

Table 4.   Polish and EU manufacturing imports as percentages of total imports: Neven's industrial clusters 1988–96.

	1988 (%)	1989 (%)	1990 (%)	1991 (%)	1992 (%)	1993 (%)	1994 (%)	1995 (%)	1996 (%)
Poland									
Sector N1	17.5	13.9	15.0	15.6	16.9	17.0	16.5	15.4	15.5
Sector N2	25.9	25.5	28.2	21.1	21.2	19.6	20.4	20.6	20.9
Sector N3	5.3	6.5	7.0	10.9	7.4	7.0	7.7	8.0	8.8
Sector N4	19.9	20.6	19.4	23.2	24.9	28.2	28.8	30.8	31.0
Sector N5	5.2	5.3	3.9	4.8	3.9	3.7	3.7	5.0	3.8
% of total	73.8	71.8	73.4	75.5	74.5	75.5	77.0	79.7	79.9
EU									
Sector N1	17.9	18.5	18.2	19.2	19.1	20.8	20.8	21.5	22.2
Sector N2	11.8	11.8	12.0	12.2	12.4	12.3	12.5	12.7	12.8
Sector N3	8.0	7.9	8.5	9.7	10.2	11.0	10.4	10.3	10.5
Sector N4	25.0	24.0	23.0	22.8	24.0	25.9	26.0	25.1	23.3
Sector N5	5.6	5.5	5.3	4.9	4.9	4.5	4.7	3.5	3.1
% of total	68.4	67.7	66.9	68.8	70.6	74.4	74.5	73.1	71.9

Source: Eurostat COMEXT databank and authors' calculations.

account of the absence at home of the human capital necessary to make them, Poland now tends to import inputs within the context of Sector N4 (which includes the vehicle industry) intra-industry trade. In any case, both Sectors N1 and N2 run huge deficits throughout all the period, which surely finally validates our conclusion. Looking ahead briefly to our analysis of the Pavitt classification, we may note that an identical pattern can plausibly be suggested for Sectors P2 and P4, where, in conditions of highly developed intra-industry trade, the output of specialised suppliers often constitutes intermediate inputs for scale-intensive production in Sector P4.

When we compare the structure of Polish exports to the EU with that of EU extra-bloc exports, we find, again, that the main point of contrast is in terms of specialisation between human-capital-intensive and labour-intensive goods, rather than between physical-capital-intensive and labour-intensive. With Sector N4 (physical-capital-intensive) exports taking more or less the same proportion (in the range of 30–35 per cent) of total manufacturing exports in both cases, the really striking difference between Poland and the EU in terms of export structure is the relative share of Sectors N1 and N2 taken together (respectively 14 per cent and 43 per cent) and of Sector N3 (29 per cent and 9 per cent respectively). With import patterns differing little, it is these contrasting export patterns that really determine trends in RCA for the Neven sectors.

Analysis in terms of RCAs measured as the difference between export and import shares shows clearly that the pattern of advantaged and disadvantaged industries, in terms of factor mix, did not change in ranking over the transition period (Fig. 1). The dominant, labour-intensive, Sector N3 improved its position steadily, peaking in 1993, while the position of the physical-capital-intensive Sector N5 fluctuated around zero and that of Sector N4 deteriorated while remaining just positive. Human-capital-intensive Sectors N1 and N2 remained clearly negative throughout, but slightly improving, though with no clear-cut upward trend in the case of N1. The decreasing RCA in Sector N4 and the slight improvement in the RCA of Sector N2 may reflect the trend hypothesised above, whereby imports of intermediate capital goods (N2) are substituted by intra-industry trade in

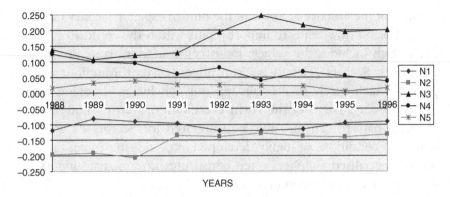

Fig. 1. RCA in Poland: Neven's clusters 1988–96.

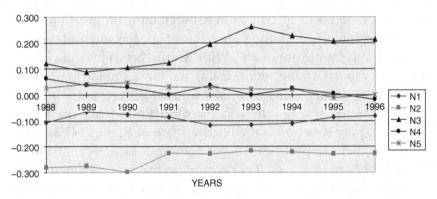

Fig. 2. RCA convergence between Poland and the EU in terms of Neven's clusters 1988–96.

components (N4).[4] Thus the overall Polish RCA pattern is simply the EU pattern in reverse, but with a much broader dispersion.

If we look at the differences in RCA by sector between Poland and the EU (Fig. 2), we see a general upward shift in Poland's favour, mainly due to the improvements in Sectors N2 and N3, without any marked changes in the pecking order of sectors. This tends to the conclusion of a general upgrading in the competitiveness of Polish

---

[4]RCAs based on exports only (calculated as the ratio of the share of a given industry in total Polish exports to the corresponding share in the EU) indicate a remarkable improvement in Sector N4 and a negligible change in Sector N2. Thus the observed effect is mainly due to the relative decrease in N2 imports and increasing imports, presumably largely of components, to Sector N4.

industry. Though negative differences in relation to human-capital intensive Sectors N1 and N2 fell only slightly over the period reviewed, the positive differential in favour of labour-intensive Sector N3 increased substantially, while the position of the physical-capital-intensive sectors remained unchanged, or, in the case of Sector N4, actually deteriorated 1988–96. Thus, leaving Sector N3 (the most labour-intensive) to one side, we can see a clear tendency for convergence rather than divergence of RCA patterns in the course of globalisation.

The Technology Sourcing Axis

Pavitt's taxonomy is obviously more precise in its technological ranking of particular industries than is the pure factor-mix principle of classification. It should, therefore, give us clearer idea of the existing pattern of technological gaps and help us to visualise the impact of globalisation on a latecomer country. To make the ranking even more transparent, we can imagine a technological ladder, with Sectors P1 and P2 (Schumpeterian goods) at the top, Sectors P4 and P5 (Smithian) in the middle, and Sector P3 (traditional Ricardo goods) at the bottom. Moving up or down this ladder means raising or lowering the technological position of the given country in the global division of labour.

Table 5 shows that the structure of Polish exports, as compared to that of the EU, is characterised by a strong bias towards low-tech industries. The share of Schumpeterian goods (Sectors P1 and P2) in total exports started from the extremely low level of 5.2 per cent at the beginning of the period and only managed to crawl up to 11.3 per cent over eight years of transition. The corresponding figures for the EU were 31.5 per cent and 38 per cent. At the same time supplier-dominated traditional industries (Sector P3), which consistently account for less than 19 per cent of EU exports, increased their share of total Polish exports from 23.3 per cent to 36 per cent. It is also noteworthy that of the two scale-intensive sectors, Sector P5 (resource-based) generally took between two to five times as big a percentage of total Polish exports as Sector P4 (technology-based), with the gap widening over the first three years of transition and then easing back again to a level similar to what it had been in 1988.

Table 5.   Polish and EU manufacturing exports as percentages of total exports: Pavitt's industrial clusters 1988–96.

	1988 (%)	1989 (%)	1990 (%)	1991 (%)	1992 (%)	1993 (%)	1994 (%)	1995 (%)	1996 (%)
Poland									
Sector P1	1.6	1.5	1.5	1.6	1.6	2.9	2.5	2.8	3.2
Sector P2	3.6	4.4	5.4	4.5	4.4	5.0	5.6	6.6	8.1
Sector P3	23.3	22.7	25.9	29.9	32.6	35.8	36.5	34.8	35.7
Sector P4	8.4	5.8	4.0	3.9	6.8	10.8	8.8	9.5	11.4
Sector P5	17.9	20.8	21.5	20.2	18.6	15.4	17.0	18.1	16.4
% of total	54.8	55.2	58.3	60.1	64.0	70.0	70.3	71.7	74.8
EU									
Sector P1	14.8	14.9	15.0	16.1	16.7	18.6	18.4	18.9	18.9
Sector P2	16.7	16.8	17.9	18.1	18.3	18.2	18.0	18.6	19.2
Sector P3	18.5	19.0	19.0	18.4	18.2	17.7	18.0	17.3	17.4
Sector P4	13.0	12.3	12.9	12.3	12.5	12.7	13.1	13.1	13.2
Sector P5	16.8	16.9	16.1	16.1	16.0	16.6	16.3	16.5	16.3
% of total	79.8	79.9	80.9	81.0	81.8	83.8	83.8	84.4	85.0

Source: Eurostat COMEXT databank and authors' calculations.

It seems, then, that trade liberalisation has focused the technological capabilities of the Polish economy towards the bottom end of the technological ladder. This view finds support in the trends on the import side (Table 6). There is a striking and sudden increase of 8 per cent in the share of traditional goods in total imports, presumably reflecting growth in the outward processing trade, while the share of specialised suppliers intermediate goods (Sector P2) falls. This latter trend corresponds closely to an opposite trend in imports of more highly-processed, technology-based, scale-intensive products. As we saw earlier, increases in P4 imports may reflect an intensification of intra-industry trade within that sector. In general, however, the pattern of import linkages into the Polish economy also seems to cluster very much at the bottom end of the ladder. As a result, the huge deficit in the trade in Schumpeterian goods has been covered by exports of traditional goods, rather than by exports of scale-intensive manufactures.

Table 6. Polish and EU manufacturing imports as percentages of total imports: Pavitt's industrial clusters 1988–96.

	1988 (%)	1989 (%)	1990 (%)	1991 (%)	1992 (%)	1993 (%)	1994 (%)	1995 (%)	1996 (%)
Poland									
Sector P1	14.9	12.0	12.0	12.9	15.2	15.0	14.8	14.3	14.3
Sector P2	20.0	19.0	19.7	15.0	16.0	15.4	16.5	16.8	17.4
Sector P3	13.9	14.7	19.6	19.1	20.7	20.8	22.3	20.6	19.0
Sector P4	5.6	7.8	8.7	18.7	10.6	12.9	11.0	12.4	15.3
Sector P5	18.7	17.6	14.2	15.5	14.0	12.8	13.2	15.6	13.6
% of total	73.1	71.1	74.2	81.1	76.5	77.0	77.8	79.6	79.6
EU									
Sector P1	15.2	15.9	15.6	16.6	16.6	18.4	18.4	19.4	19.6
Sector P2	9.3	9.4	9.6	9.8	10.1	10.4	10.9	10.9	11.1
Sector P3	16.1	16.2	16.7	17.3	18.1	19.3	19.2	18.6	18.5
Sector P4	7.6	7.3	7.6	8.2	8.4	8.2	7.5	6.6	6.8
Sector P5	14.2	14.7	14.4	13.5	13.2	13.0	13.4	11.8	10.7
% of total	62.3	63.5	63.9	65.4	66.4	69.3	69.4	67.4	66.7

Source: Eurostat COMEXT databank and authors' calculations.

The picture becomes clearer still when we compare the RCA patterns of Poland and the EU. While the EU enjoys RCA in nearly all sectors, with specialised suppliers and technologically-based scale-intensive sectors at the top of the pile, Poland shows a pattern of ranking that is just the inverse of the EU's. Here only two sectors — traditional industries and the resource-based scale-intensive sector — come through with positive RCA, while the other three sectors — science-based, specialised suppliers and technology-based scale-intensive — reveal comparative disadvantage throughout the period (Fig. 3). Liberalisation seems to have reinforced rather than moderated the trend, with a substantial increase over time in the RCA coefficient for traditional industries and an intensification of the degree of comparative disadvantage revealed for technology-based scale-intensive industries.

Looking at the differences between Poland and the EU in terms of the RCAs of particular sectors (Fig. 4), we can detect a trend towards *increasing specialisation along the technological axis*, with Sector P3

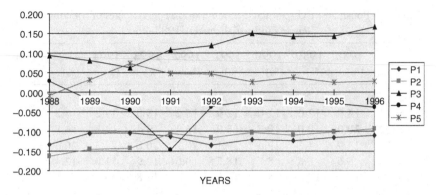

Fig. 3. RCA in Poland: Pavitt's clusters 1988–96.

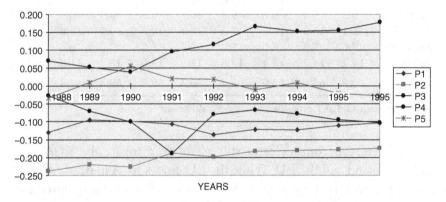

Fig. 4. RCA convergence between Poland and the EU in terms of Pavitt's clusters 1988–96.

exhibiting initial RCA, and then reinforcing its advantage, and the other sectors either falling further behind or remaining relatively stagnant.

These initial results of the liberalisation process should not surprise us, because upgrading technological capabilities, which is the basis of moving up the technological ladder, hinges upon raising the level of *absolute* advantage, i.e., the ability to do things which (at least some) trading competitors simply cannot do at all. This a much more management- and time-intensive process than the improvement of "mere" comparative advantage in particular industries through the optimisation of factor inputs and the adjustment of trade structure. There is nothing like a factor price equalisation mechanism to guide the process. It involves learning new activities and learning to be *good* at those new activities. As such, it is a process of asset creation rather than absorption, a process that can only unfold once the initial stage of factor absorption has been completed. Note that the negative shock of opening-up looks much more spectacular in terms of the shift down the technological ladder than in those of adjustment of factor intensities in the production of tradable goods. This reflects the fact that autarky created much more severe distortions within manufacturing in relation to technological capabilities than in relation to factor proportions. Thus globalisation may be expected to push the Polish economy towards a higher degree of technological specialisation, as reflected in a wider spread of RCAs by P-sector.

TECHNOLOGY PATTERNS IN FDI

Perhaps the most significant single dimension of the globalisation of the Polish economy after the opening-up was the liberalisation of the FDI regime. Levels of FDI were nugatory during the communist period, which was much more autarkic in terms of capital flows than in relation to trade. The aggregate stock of FDI rose from $67 m in 1989 to about $6.9 b at the end of 1995 and an estimated $20 b at the end of 1997. Thus we cannot talk about differences in FDI patterns between pre- and post-reform periods because there was effectively no FDI under the old regime. By the same token it is not surprising that the sectoral pattern of FDI inflow (Table 7) was very unstable over the first three years after liberalisation.

Factor Mix in Sectors Targeted for FDI

The most obvious thing to emerge from Table 7 is the initial dominance of Sector N2 within (an admittedly very small) total FDI. In 1990, there was a sudden diversion of funds into the labour-intensive Sector N3. But this lasted only one year — as if it took foreign

Table 7.   Structure of stock of inward FDI (cumulated): Neven's industrial
clusters 1989–97.

Sector	1989 (%)	1990 (%)	1991 (%)	1992 (%)	1993 (%)	1994 (%)	1995 (%)	1996 (%)	1997 (%)
Sector N1	6.9	1.9	15.3	12.8	12.6	21.5	18.4	16.6	16.9
Sector N2	43.3	8.5	19.2	14.9	11.8	14.1	17.4	15.8	16.0
Sector N3	18.0	64.4	22.2	17.0	11.8	11.5	12.5	12.3	11.7
Sector N4	9.1	6.3	30.2	21.5	37.1	35.3	30.5	34.3	33.8
Sector N5	22.6	19.0	13.1	33.7	26.7	17.6	21.2	20.9	21.7
Total	100.0	100.0	100.0	100.0	100.0	100.0	100.0	100.0	100.0

Source: Polish *Central Statistical Office* databank and authors' calculations.

investors just one year to find out that cheap labour was not the factor to look for in their investments in Poland. Subsequent trends revealed a clear-cut preference on the part of foreign companies for investment in the physical-capital-intensive Sectors N4 and N5, which were together accounting for 55–60 per cent of total foreign capital stock from 1992 onwards. But it is Sector N4, characterised by high levels of both labour intensity and physical-capital intensity, that has exhibited the most buoyant FDI trends, taking about one third of the total at the end of the period. The exclusively human-capital-intensive sectors N1 and N2 dominated the (nugatory) inflow of FDI in the first year of the period, and then nose-dived in 1990, as labour-intensive investments took over, to stage a steady subsequent recovery which saw them together take almost 36 per cent of total FDI by 1994, a level largely maintained over the following years. Thus foreign investment has generally brought into Poland mobile physical capital or absorbed the (largely) immobile human capital available in the country. These trends confirm a conclusion that emerges from virtually every study of FDI in the transition countries — that accessing cheap labour is hardly ever a key consideration (Sharp & Barz, 1997).

The crucial question that remains to be answered is: in focusing on human-capital- and physical-capital-intensive sectors, has FDI followed the pattern of RCA or gone against it? The data show clearly that it was only in the first years after liberalisation — when FDI was still at a generally very low level — that FDI inflow (primarily into Sectors N3 and N5) was clearly correlated with the RCA levels of recipient industries. In subsequent years, the FDI stream turned, apparently at random, to one more or less disadvantaged sector or another. There does, however, seem to be a kind of *gravity pull* between similarly comparatively advantaged sectors in home and host countries. Thus sectors N4 and N5, with the highest levels of similarity in RCA patterns between Poland and the EU, receive the largest shares of total FDI. Sectors N2 and N3, by contrast, show the biggest differences in RCAs, and the smallest rate of FDI inflow. The tendency for FDI to look for host industries of more or less similar factor mix to the "mother" industries has been observed in East Asia (Ozawa, 1979; Wells, 1983). Our analysis suggests that this evolutionary pattern may be repeated in the transition countries.

Technology Clusters in Sectors Targeted for FDI

In Pavitt's more specific taxonomy we can trace the evolution of FDI flows up and down the ladder of technological rankings. Here again, the FDI patterns of 1989 were completely reversed in subsequent years. The most dramatic change occurred in relation to Sector P2 (specialised suppliers), which dominated the small total for 1989, but had declined to 3 per cent by 1995. Sector P4 (technology-based, scale-intensive), in contrast, barely registered in 1989; a few years later, however, it was accounting for more than one-fifth of the total stock of FDI. Resource-based scale-intensive industries (Sector P5) have received a consistently large share, rising from 22.9 per cent of the total stock of FDI in 1989 to 51.8 per cent in 1990, before easing back to 38.5 per cent in 1997. Traditional industries have shown a similar pattern, claiming 22.2 per cent of total FDI stock in 1989 and 43.3 per cent in 1991, with their share then declining to 24.9 per cent in 1997. The science-based sector (P1) — obviously the most advanced technologically — received only 5 per cent in 1989, but had pushed its share up to nearly 20 per cent by 1994 (due to foreign takeovers of telecom equipment manufacturing companies), finishing on 11.7 per cent in 1997.

Table 8.   Structure of stock of inward FDI (cumulated): Pavitt's industrial clusters 1989–97.

Sector	1989 (%)	1990 (%)	1991 (%)	1992 (%)	1993 (%)	1994 (%)	1995 (%)	1996 (%)	1997 (%)
Sector P1	5.0	4.6	9.4	12.4	10.4	19.9	16.1	12.1	11.5
Sector P2	49.1	17.5	4.6	5.1	3.3	3.4	3.0	3.1	3.5
Sector P3	22.2	23.1	43.0	31.8	26.1	25.3	26.5	25.9	24.9
Sector P4	0.8	3.0	18.3	7.4	22.9	22.3	19.1	22.4	21.5
Sector P5	22.9	51.8	24.6	43.3	37.2	29.2	35.2	36.5	38.5
Total	100.0	100.0	100.0	100.0	100.0	100.0	100.0	100.0	100.0

Source: Polish *Central Statistical Office* databank and authors' calculations.

The pattern in terms of Pavitt's taxonomy, as it stabilised after 1993, was thus characterised by a clear dominance of scale-intensive industries (Sectors P4 and P5), which consistently captured a share of over 55 per cent in total FDI stock. Within the scale-intensive cluster there was a palpable shift from resource-based to technology-based industries. At the same time, there was a stabilisation of FDI inflow into traditional industries at a relatively high level, roughly a quarter of total FDI, and a moderate expansion of FDI into science-based industries. These trends clearly reflect some improvement over time in the technological level of FDI. But it is still dominated by traditional and resource-based scale-intensive industries, and the failure to maintain the early momentum of FDI in specialised suppliers is disturbing.

What does a comparison of FDI and RCA trends tell us about the determinants of these trends? We found stronger, more consistent and more significant relationships between FDI shares and the pattern of RCA in terms of Pavitt's taxonomy than we did in relation to the factor-mix breakdown. Here, the sectoral distribution of FDI follows RCA patterns, so that comparatively advantaged sectors have received relatively larger shares of foreign investment, which signals the asset-absorbing type of FDI. And the narrower the technological gap between given industries in Poland and the EU, as reflected in RCA, the higher the FDI flow. FDI flows appear to respond to relatively high levels of RCA in host industries, and to technological closeness between those industries and the corresponding industries in the EU. The extreme cases are specialised suppliers and the resource-based, scale-intensive sectors. The former, it would seem, receives a small share of FDI because it has a low level of RCA relative to other sectors of the Polish economy, and because its RCA coefficient lags furthest behind the corresponding EU RCA. The latter does well in terms of share of FDI because it has a high RCA ranking within Poland and shows very similar levels of RCA to the EU.

These results point clearly to the key role of the *technological congruence/proximity effect* as a determinant of the pattern of joint production activities between integrating economies. Technological proximity and factor-mix proximity may, indeed, be mutually reinforcing in this regard.

CASE STUDIES

The original research project on which this article is based included a dozen or so case-studies of Polish firms, all operating in science-based and specialised supplier industries in terms of Pavitt's taxonomy. Detailed discussion of the individual case studies can be found in Dyker (1996) and Kubielas (1996, 1997). Since then the authors have been involved in a number of other projects which have generated relevant case-studies, including in technology-based scale-intensive industries, both in Poland and more widely across the transition region. In this section we look across the whole gamut of these case studies, to see how the patterns that emerge at firm level correspond to the picture shown by the aggregate trade and FDI data. We note in particular the following points:

- The case-study material from the science-based and specialised supplier sectors in Poland fleshes out the skeleton of sectors P1 and P2 provided by the aggregate statistical data. Here are sectors heavily dependent on imports, but which have at the same time played a significant import-substituting role throughout the transition period in terms of "downstream" products. This is reflected in fairly stable shares of P1 and P2 imports into Poland throughout the period analysed, with exports remaining at a very low level, though rising over time as a proportion of total exports. FDI has not been a critical factor of development except in telecommunications, the sub-sector which dominates the FDI trends for sector P1. Rather licensing, franchising and other forms of disembodied technology transfer have provided the crucial technological platforms, especially in software.

- The software industry provides a particularly good illustration of how a P2 sector can serve as a vehicle for a process of continuous improvement in general levels of organisational efficiency in a catch-up economy. Software firms mainly sell complex networking systems, and their main customers for these are other firms. Because standard licensed software packages always have to be customised for particular countries, and often for particular firms, these software firms play a unique role as a bridgehead for the transfer of state-of-the-art office technology into the host economy. In practice, furthermore, customising usually involves a degree of upgrading, and sometimes these upgrades are incorporated back into the basic licensing package. So Polish software companies become part of a cumulative process of technological change and learning, and therefore of asset creation, which impacts directly on the general level of efficiency of the Polish business sector. That, as we have seen, has been the major dynamic variable in the evolution of Poland's interface with the global economy. But FDI does not play a key role in the process.
- The Polish shipbuilding industry provides a graphic illustration of commercial and technological upgrading in a technology-based, scale-intensive industry in which there has been relatively little FDI. An outstanding individual example is that of the Szczecin Shipyard. The key factors in the successful turning round of this part of the communist industrial legacy can be listed as follows (Bitzer & von Hirschhausen, 1998a,b):

1. Sharp cut-backs in the work force (by more than 50 per cent 1991–98).
2. Intensive integration into the global shipbuilding supply network and rebuilding of supply networks within Poland.
3. Successful capture of a niche — in this case construction of container ships, a rapidly growing and innovative segment of the global shipbuilding market.

4. Reorientation of production towards the export market (2/3 of output is sold to Germany).
5. Wholesale import of computer hardware and software for Management Information Systems and design purposes.

Thus the Szczecin Shipyard has become profitable again by reorganising its activities into a market-oriented assembly operation, organised through contemporary computerised management systems (in this case imported), sourced from all over the world (not excluding Poland), and manned by a relatively small number of workers in Szczecin itself.

Wage costs are an important variable for the Szczecin Shipyard, as they are generally in technology-based, scale-intensive industries, while there are huge differences in real wages between Poland and its competitors in the industry. Polish shipyards can, nevertheless, compete against Chinese, just as Korean and Japanese can against Polish. So the key to success in shipbuilding does not seem to be cheap labour. Rather it seems to be *efficient general organisation* (including organisation of the work-force and the supply network) and a flexible approach to the development of specific in-house capabilities relating (in this case) to the construction of container ships, which lower-cost competitors do not (as yet) possess. Thus while the Szczecin Shipyard has its own design department, that department works mainly on the basis of standard designs from abroad. Just as in the software case, therefore, the crucial input from abroad is basic technology, not FDI, and this basic technology serves as a springboard for upgrading capabilities and therefore asset creation.

• The motor vehicle industry offers a contrasting case study within the technology-based, scale-intensive sector. Here there has been substantial FDI (notably from Fiat, Ford, General Motors and Daewoo),[5] and foreign investment has in this case provided the main impetus for the general improvements in managerial efficiency that have been a feature in this sub-sector. A key feature of

---

[5]In 1997 the stock of FDI in the Polish car industry was 200 times the stock in the shipbuilding industry.

organisational upgrading has been reconstruction of the supply network. But while in shipbuilding the redevelopment of supply networks proceeded along international and national axes right from the start, in the automotive industry it was initially largely limited to the former. Traditional first-tier suppliers[6] from Poland, and from other former CMEA countries, have been largely cut out, and investing companies have put pressure on their own suppliers from EU countries to set up production inside Poland (Havas, 1997). But local second- and third-tier suppliers are used. This must largely represent asset absorption, because learning effects are very limited where supply networking does not include design elements. Daewoo's acquisition of FSO's entire second-tier supply network and subsequent integration of that network into its own supply system is clearly an exception here, involving significant elements of asset creation. Thus the foreign-owned car industry in Poland has operated as something of an enclave, with real integration largely limited to areas of obvious preexisting technological congruence. The extent of asset creation has been far from maximised, while there are have been definite elements of asset-depleting absorption. Once again, however, there has been a big impact on general levels of X-efficiency.

- While the shipbuilding case indicates that the specialised supplier sector is not universally weak in Poland, the motor vehicle case confirms the general case, as reflected in the aggregate trade statistics. A sourcing strategy based largely on imports and transplants provides no incentives at all for the development of the local specialist suppliers who would be expected to equip local component manufacturers, and may even tend to inhibit imports of specialist supplier goods too. The seriousness of this situation comes out clearly if we compare Poland with other transition countries in this regard. Strengthening of the RCA position of specialised supplier industries is one of the key indicators of success in transition, with

---

[6]Supplying complex car parts like engines or gear boxes involving a significant level of design inputs; *second-tier suppliers* provide advanced single components to first-tier and *third-tier suppliers* simple components to second-tier suppliers.

Czechoslovakia/the Czech Republic and Hungary showing big improvements in RCA indicators for this sector 1988–95. Indeed by 1995 Hungary was actually running a trade surplus in specialist supplier goods. The Soviet Union/former Soviet Union, by contrast, shows stagnation — at a very low level — in specialist supplier RCA over the same period. The corresponding RCA for Poland increases 1988–95, but only slightly, leaving that country midway between the former Soviet Union on the one hand, and the Czech Republic and Hungary on the other, in terms of level of specialist supplier RCA in 1995 (Kubielas, 1999). The reasons for Poland's weakness in this area are partly historical. The Polish engineering industry before 1989 was less developed than its counterparts in Czechoslovakia and Hungary, and its human capital stock significantly weaker in terms of engineering capabilities. But the gap has widened since then, and there is no sign of a reversal in that trend. The failure of the market mechanism to correct this weakness is clearly a major factor limiting the scope for asset creation in Poland.

• Case study material confirms that FDI into Poland has generated significant streams of asset creation. But it also confirms that FDI is neither a necessary nor a sufficient condition of asset creation, and that where FDI does create assets, it tends to do so only weakly. Finally, it gives strong support to the proposition that, whether FDI is present or not, the most important variable affecting competitive advantage is general business efficiency. Thus at the most general level the case-study material provides striking corroboration of the results of our aggregate, statistical investigations.

SUMMARY AND CONCLUSIONS

The general tendency since the beginning of reform has been for Poland to *trade labour for human capital*, with the traditionally central role of physical capital intensity tending to be marginalised as physical capital becomes an increasingly mobile factor in the course of globalisation. In the context of that process, there has been a general upgrading of competitiveness, in sectors intensively using immobile factors of production. Existing patterns of comparative advantage have generally been reinforced, and marked by increased specialisation, in particular in terms of the technology content of traded goods, but with no major changes in the pecking order of RCA by sector.

The underlying pattern of globalisation has been essentially *Schumpeterian rather than Heckscher-Ohlin;* thus the legacy of autarky and the command economy appears to weigh more heavily in terms of lagging technological capabilities than in terms of factor intensities of manufactured and traded output. On the technological axis, this Schumpeterian pattern is revealed as tending to polarisation, with Poland increasingly specialising in low-tech products in international trade, despite the general technological upgrading visible in the Polish domestic economy. The clear implication is that if globalisation is to generate factor creation, rather than just factor absorption, it must go beyond competitiveness as such. Internationally, as domestically, the key to the future lies in technological upgrading, which means learning to do things that have not been done in the past.

To the extent that Western firms have invested in Poland since liberalisation, they have tended to do so in firms exhibiting similar characteristics to themselves in terms of factor mix and technological level. On both factor-mix and technological-orientation dimensions, therefore, FDI has tended to act merely as a corrective to pure trading trends.

FDI has shown a tendency to *complementary asset creation* as far as factor proportions are concerned, and to *asset absorption rather than asset creation* in terms of the technological ranking of industries.[7] Thus while the impact of FDI in terms of general levels of X-efficiency has been impressive, FDI has done relatively little to create new blocks of assets as such.

---

[7]For similar observations see Hoekman and Djankov (1997), who found inflows of foreign direct investment into Poland to be positively associated with measures of RCA at the two-digit NACE level for 1990–95. In this respect Poland is shown to be at odds with the other four CEE countries researched, for which a negative correlation was found. Note that in our more detailed study this conclusion applies to the ranking on the Pavitt taxonomy, but not to the ranking on the factor-mix taxonomy.

The globalisation process has so far not had much impact on the pattern of trade at the general level. But it has tended to pull it more into line with the pattern of RCAs, following an evolutionary path marked by complementary or asset-absorbing FDI.

REFERENCES

Bell, M (1997). Technology transfer to transition countries: Are there lessons from the experience of the post-war industrializing countries? In *The Technology of Transition: Science and Technology Policies for Transition Countries*, DA Dyker (ed.). Budapest: Central European University Press.

Bell, M and K Pavitt (1993). Technological accumulation and industrial growth: Contrasts between developed and developing countries. *Industrial and Corporate Change*, 2(2), 157–210.

Bitzer, J and C von Hirschhausen (1998a). Case study Poland: Restructuring and integration in international networks: The case of the Szczecin Shipyard, 1990–98. TSER programme "Restructuring and Reintegration of Science and Technology Systems in Economies in Transition", draft. Berlin: DIW, June.

———— (1998b). *The Shipbuilding Industry in Eastern Europe: A Sector Survey*. TSER programme "Restructuring and Reintegration of Science and Technology Systems in Economies in Transition", draft. Berlin: DIW, June.

Cantwell, J (1991). The theory of technological competence and its application to international production. In *Foreign Investment, Technology and Economic Growth*, Donald McFetridge (ed.). Calgary: University of Calgary Press.

Dunning, JH (1988). The eclectic paradigm of international production: A restatement and some possible extensions. *Journal of International Business Studies*, 19(1), 1–31.

Dyker, DA (1996). The computer and software industries in the East European economies — a bridgehead to the global economy? *Europe-Asia Studies*, 48(6), 915–30.

Havas, A (1997). Foreign direct investment and intra-industry trade: The case of the automotive industry in Central Europe. In *The Technology of Transition: Science and Technology Policies for Transition countries*, DA Dyker (ed.). Budapest: Central European University Press.

Hoekman, B and S Djankov (1997). Determinants of the export structure of countries in Central and Eastern Europe. *The World Bank Economic Review*, 11(3), 471–87.

Inzelt, A (1999). The transformation role of FDI in R&D: Analysis based on material from a data bank. In *Innovation and Structural Change in Post-Socialist Countries: A Quantitative Approach*, DA Dyker and S Radošević (eds.). Dordrecht: Kluwer.

Kubielas, S (1996). International co-operative agreements in Poland in the mid 1990s: Evolution, organisational forms and industry characteristics. Part I: Country Industrial Report, draft paper for ACE project *Technology Transfer or Blockaded Entry: International Co-operative Agreements in the Central European Economies in Transition* (PL 95-2071-R). University of Warsaw, Faculty of Economic Science.

——— (1997). As above, Part II: Case Studies.

——— (1999). Transformation of technology patterns of trade in the post-socialist economies. In *Innovation and Structural Change in Post-Socialist Countries: A Quantitative Approach*, DA Dyker and S Radošević (eds.). Dordrecht: Kluwer.

Neven, D (1994). Trade liberalization with eastern nations. how sensitive? *CEPR Discussion Paper*, No. 1000. London: Centre for Economic Policy Research.

Ozawa, T (1979). *Multinationalism, Japanese Style*. Princeton: Princeton University Press.

Pavitt, K (1984). Sectoral patterns of technical change: Towards a taxonomy and a theory. *Research Policy*, 13(6), 343–73.

Sharp, M and M Barz (1997). Multinational companies and the transfer and diffusion of new technological capabilities in Central and Eastern Europe and the former Soviet Union. In *The Technology of Transition: Science and Technology Policies for Transition Countries*, DA Dyker (ed.). Budapest: Central European University Press.

United Nations (1996). *Economic Survey of Europe in 1995–1996*. New York and Geneva.

Wells, LT (1983). *Third World Multinationals*. Cambridge, Mass.: MIT Press.

Chapter 5

Trade Policy for the Countries of the Former Soviet Union (FSU): What Can the Advanced Industrial Countries Do to Help?*

INTRODUCTION

Essential Factors of Trade in the Region of the FSU

In examining the evolution of international trade in the FSU, it is useful to distinguish between three types of trade — Heckscher-Ohlin trade, intra-industry trade and local cross-border trade, including shuttle trade. Let us start by identifying *Heckscher-Ohlin trade* (HOT), which is driven by differences between economies in endowments of factors of production, broadly defined. In FSU terms, this means relative endowment in natural resources, primarily hydrocarbons but also metals, including gold, in land well suited for the cultivation of particular crops, e.g. grain in the Black Earth region of Russia and Ukraine and cotton in Central Asia, and differences in capital availability and real wage rates. *Vis-à-vis* the rest of the world, the CIS derives Heckscher-Ohlin-based comparative advantage from

---

*This article is based on a study originally commissioned by the UK Department for International Development.

its natural resources and low wage rates, but suffers relative shortage of capital.

The next category is that of *intra-industry trade* (IIT), which extends the principle of comparative advantage to include fine differences in endowments of specific sub-factors of production, usually based on elements of human capital or technological capability that derive from micro-specialisation. Trade between developed industrial economies is dominated by IIT. In trade between LDCs, by contrast, it is of minor importance. On *a priori* grounds we might expect the overall FSU pattern to lie somewhere in between those extremes, but with substantial differences between countries stemming from differences in levels of industrialisation.

The third category is *local cross-border trade* (LCT). LCT may be driven by fine distinctions of comparative advantage, or simply by convenience in terms of how frontiers and communications networks relate to each other. Thus any rational pattern of transport logistics for the populous and fertile Fergana Valley would involve crossing borders between Uzbekistan, Tajikistan and Kyrgyzstan continually. In the Caucasus, the Nakhichevan region of Azerbaijan is cut off from the rest of that country, and road and rail transport between Nakhichevan and the rest of Azerbaijan has to go across Armenia, or through Iran. We would, therefore, expect to find a relatively high incidence of LCT between CIS countries. On the old Soviet border with the rest of the world, where in Soviet times LCT was largely forbidden, we would expect such trade to grow rapidly, at least in the initial stages of transition, and this expectation is borne out by the case of Ukraine and Poland.

Extra dynamism has been injected into the post-Soviet development of local cross-border trade by the peculiar phenomenon of *shuttle trade*. Because distribution was so undeveloped in Soviet times, CIS countries are generally poorly endowed with efficient import-export organisations, especially with regard to consumer goods. This gap has been to a remarkable extent filled, over the early years of transition, by a new breed of traders called shuttlers, who go back and forward across frontiers, perhaps several times a day, with suitcases full of goods to be sold on. At its crudest level, shuttling is simply an exercise in arbitrage and/or tax evasion. It can, however, play a role in terms of low-level IIT, especially where trade in electronic components is involved. Either way, it is by definition an ephemeral phenomenon.

It is particularly important in the context of former centrally planned economies to stress that comparative advantage does not always translate into *competitive advantage*. Gross mismanagement of traditional export sectors like agriculture, and poor marketing across all sectors, meant that many sectors and sub-sectors of the Soviet economy with obvious strengths in terms of factor endowment contributed little or nothing to exports. Because competitive advantage is embedded in particular firms, it is built slowly and with difficulty, even in mature market economies. It is not built at all in economies in which there are no firms. In the context of the hesitant transition which has been characteristic of most of the CIS countries over the past decade, it would be unrealistic to expect the process of rebuilding competitive advantage in international markets to have progressed very far.

The Historical Background

The Soviet Union was effectively the Old Russian Empire under a new name. But Russia did not subject the peripheral areas of the Union to crude exploitation. Thus while, under the system of central planning, Central Asia had to supply cotton to metropolitan Russia, it was more than compensated for this by deliveries of Russian oil. There was, however, no systematic industrialization of the peripheral areas. Where, as in Ukraine, Belarus and Azerbaijan, there was an existing industrial base inherited from the Tsarist period, it developed that base further. Where, as in Georgia or Central Asia, pre-revolutionary economies were basically agrarian, they remained so, though with some uneven, sometimes ill-conceived, industrialisation at the local level. Partly as a corollary of that, the peripheral areas of the Union remained significantly poorer than the central areas, despite substantial transfers from the latter to the former.

The allied victory of 1945 left the Red Army in control of most of Central-East Europe (CEE), and allowed the Soviet Union to form an "outer empire". Post-war economic relationships between these inner and outer empires were mediated through the Council for Mutual Economic Assistance (CMEA). Within the CMEA, the Soviet Union tried to develop a "socialist division of labour" which would take advantage of the substantial human capital endowments of the CEECs as well as of their natural resources. In this it was only partially successful. As in relation to the peripheral areas of the USSR itself, Russia found itself basically playing the role of supplier of cheap energy materials to its "satellites" in CEE, obtaining in return a wide range of manufactures which, however, rarely came up to world standards in terms of quality and technology. These problems were a source of continual tension within the CMEA.

The CMEA and the Soviet Union broke up in 1991 because the major players on those stages no longer wanted to play the old game. Russia had had enough of supplying cheap energy materials to all the others; the CEECs (and also the Baltic republics within the USSR) had had enough of being locked into the Eastern market, and wanted to reorient their economies to Western markets. There was a general recognition among all the major political forces in these countries that socialist planning — and the one-party system of government — had broken down, and would have to be replaced by some kind of package of parliamentary democracy and market-based economic system.

The other republics of the FSU were largely onlookers in relation to this process. The leaders of Ukraine and Belarus conspired with Boris Yeltsin in late 1991 to liquidate the Soviet Union. But this political manoeuvre was not accompanied, in Ukraine and Belarus, by any serious moves in the direction of economic reform. The "Commonwealth of Independent States" (CIS) proclaimed by the leaders of the three Slav states as the successor to the Soviet Union initially contained only these three states, and there is no evidence to suggest that Yeltsin, Kravchuk and Matskevich had any plans to bring the others in.

In the event, the others (the Baltic countries apart) asked to be allowed in. In the case of the Central Asian countries, this was not generally accompanied by any significant political reforms, and most of those countries are now ruled by the men who filled the posts of First Secretary of the Communist Party in each republic when it was still part of the Soviet Union (Kyrgyzstan is an exception). While, furthermore, the Central Asian countries have moved, at differing speeds, in the direction of economic reform (again, Kyrgyzstan has been a front-runner), they generally retain many of the characteristics of centrally planned economies, with the state still dominating the ownership of industrial assets. Transcaucasia is a mixed bag in this respect, with Azerbaijan tending to the Central Asian "model", on both economic and political dimensions, and Georgia and Armenia rather following the pattern of Russia.

The key point to emerge from all this is that, of all the countries currently members of the CIS, Russia was the only one to come out of the break-up of the Soviet Union with a clear agenda in terms of changing trade patterns. The Yeltsin governments of the early 1990s were steadfast in their determination to stop subsidising neighbouring economies with cheap oil and gas. The new principle that all Russian oil and gas had to be paid for at world prices was almost universally supported within Russia, however difficult it may have been to apply it consistently in all cases. The role of the other FSU countries in this drama has, inevitably, been an essentially reactive one.

The break-up of the Soviet Union has also highlighted the extent to which the countries of the South Caucasus and Central Asia remain underdeveloped, predominantly agrarian societies. Hydrocarbon-rich Kazakhstan apart, none have levels of GDP per head above $1000, and some are well below $500 on that indicator. None possess significant concentrations of manufacturing capability. The countries of the post-Soviet South all bear the marks of the misconceived Soviet approach to industrialisation, and indeed to the excesses of Soviet agricultural policies, which, in Uzbekistan have created an environmentally disastrous pattern of cotton monoculture. But they are basically LDCs, and global trade policies *vis-à-vis* these countries must be based firmly on recognition of that fact.

KEY POLICY ISSUES

The Impact of EU Enlargement

EU enlargement may affect trade between acceding countries and the countries of the FSU on account of:

- The imposition of the common tariff on trade between the CIS and acceding countries;
- The introduction of the Common Agricultural Policy (CAP) in the acceding countries;
- The imposition of the EU regime of contingent protection (anti-dumping, etc.) on trade between the acceding countries and the countries of the FSU;
- The introduction in the acceding countries of EU regulations on environmental issues and transit issues relating to safety, etc.; and
- The introduction of the EU visa regime on the borders between acceding countries and CIS countries.

In fact, enlargement is likely to affect individual CIS countries on only some of these counts, and some of the 12 countries may not be affected at all. HOT and IIT between the (former) Soviet Union and CEE largely ceased with the break-up of the CMEA in 1991, and has not been revived to a significant extent. EU enlargement will therefore have little or no impact on this type of trade.

What has survived and indeed developed since 1991 is LCT between CIS and CEE countries. But by definition this only applies to CIS countries with common borders with CEE countries. That means, in the first instance, Ukraine *vis-à-vis* Poland. There is a substantial amount of LCT, including shuttle trade, across those two countries' common frontier, which stretches for several hundred miles through an economically relatively well developed part of Eastern Europe in which transport is relatively easy. LCT is facilitated by the fact the Ukrainian citizens do not require visas to enter

Poland. The total number of visits by Ukrainian citizens to Poland was 3,886,397 in 1999, rising to 4,428,480 in 2000. In the first six months of 2001 alone there were 2,175,341 such visits.[1] It is a reasonable supposition that most of these visits were shuttling visits. The numbers will certainly fall when the Polish government, in anticipation of EU membership, introduces visas for Ukrainian citizens in 2003. The impact may, however, be less dramatic than might at first sight be expected. Thus shuttle trade across the Polish-Ukrainian border is largely in the hands of foreigners whose visa status may not be directly affected by Polish accession to the EU.

For most of the other CIS countries the LCT issue does not arise in a primary form, because there are no common frontiers with CEE. Russia does, however, have borders with three former Soviet republics — Estonia, Latvia and Lithuania, which are all prospects for EU accession. These are short borders, but LCT across them is important. The fact that Russian citizens already need visas to enter Estonia means, however, that the impact of Estonian accession on that trade will be marginal. A lot of Russian hydrocarbons and minerals are exported via Latvia, but this trade would probably not be significantly affected by accession.

Turkey, another candidate for accession to the EU, has common borders with three CIS countries — Georgia, Armenia and Azerbaijan. Turkey currently enforces a trade blockade with the second of these, in pursuance of a dispute over the recognition of the Armenian massacres of the First World War as genocide. LCT between Turkey and Georgia through the Georgian town of Batumi flourishes, and it would be a big blow to the Georgian economy if this trade were cut off. The Turkish border with Azerbaijan is not very long, and it is with the Nakhichevan region of Azerbaijan. As noted above, this is an enclave between Armenia and Turkey which has no land connection with Azerbaijan proper. Nakhichevan is effectively under blockade from Armenia in pursuance of the

---

[1]D.G. Lukyanenko, *The Impact of European Union Enlargement on Ukraine*, United Nations, Economic and Social Council, Economic Commission for Europe, Coordinating Unit for Operational Activities, 27 February 2002, p. 20.

Nagorno-Karabakh dispute,[2] so that the scope for LCT is severely limited. But if the Nagorno-Karabakh conflict and the Armenian genocide dispute are resolved before Turkey joins the EU, we could see the phenomenon of a rapid growth in Turkey-Azerbaijan and Turkey-Armenia LCT being cut off dramatically when Turkey does finally join the EU and the EU visa regime is introduced on the related borders.

These specific regional issues apart, there are two general trading issues in relation to which enlargement could have a significant effect. One is transit. Russian officials are very concerned about the impact that eastwards enlargement of the EU, and the eastwards extension of EU regulations on pipeline safety, dangerous loads, etc. might have on transit arrangements. While trade between the CIS and the CEECs may be of minor importance, transit through CEE is vital for the HOT of the CIS countries. The other is contingent protection. The Ministry of Economics of Ukraine estimates that EU enlargement will result in a 50–80 per cent drop in Ukrainian metal exports to CEE, which will mean a loss of $210–340 m in export revenue,[3] or 2–3 per cent of the total value of Ukrainian exports.[4] It is not clear how the Ministry has calculated this figure. CEEC duties on imports of heavy industrial products are generally higher than EU, so that enlargement is likely to mean a liberalisation of the CEE steel trade in terms of formal tariff barriers. The key issue here is anti-dumping, specifically the fear that the European Commission will be persuaded by CEEC steel lobbies to impose anti-dumping restrictions on Ukrainian steel-makers even more frequently than happens at present. The Ukrainian Ministry of Economics seems to have made the strongest assumptions about the likely pattern of anti-dumping in its calculations. Economists at UEPLAC (The Ukrainian-European Policy and Legal Advice Centre) were sceptical about this argument when the author interviewed them in late 2000.

---

[2]See fn. 6, Chapter 2.

[3]G. Alekseev, "Ukraina fakticheski okazalas' v torgovoi izolyatsii", *Kievskie Vedomosti*, 11 November 2000, p. 9.

[4]The ministry estimates the total loss of exports consequent on enlargement in the range of $750–950 m, some 6–7 per cent of the aggregate value of exports.

One very specific enlargement issue affecting Russia is that of nuclear fuel. At present Russia commands a substantial market for its nuclear fuel in the countries of CEE currently negotiating for accession to the EU. When these countries actually join the EU, this trade will be cut off completely because Russian nuclear fuel (and possibly also Russian ways of transporting nuclear fuel — see discussion of transit issues above) does not correspond to EU regulations.

The Changing Profile of the Eurasian Trade Pattern

The Soviet inter-regional division of labour was not completely without foundation. In Heckscher-Ohlin terms it was perfectly reasonable for Central Asia to provide cotton for the old-established textile industries of Russia, for Siberia to supply the rest of the Union with hydrocarbons and non-ferrous metals, for Transcaucasia and Central Asia to supply the whole Union with speciality and sub-tropical foodstuffs, and for Ukraine and South Russia to grow wheat for the whole Union.

On a finer calibration, there was a union-wide machine-building complex involving a great deal of IIT. Because the Soviet planning system was very insensitive to locational considerations, inter-regional trade in engineering components often involved "long cross-hauls". So there was micro-specialisation, though it was often anything but cost-effective. There was also "macro-specialisation", within Soviet machine-building, mainly involving Russia and Ukraine. Local trade across republic boundaries was hampered by bureaucratic restrictions, but it was important, particularly in Central Asia.

The main thing that has changed in the post-Soviet period is that the HOT has been globalised. Russian deliveries of oil and gas have been largely re-oriented to the international, hard-currency market. Something similar has happened with Central Asian cotton. The best Georgian wine, formerly the luxury of the Soviet Communist Party elites and their guests, now goes to European markets. Globalisation of the hydrocarbons trade has been inhibited by continuing Russian and Ukrainian control over key pipelines. It has also been hampered by disagreements about how to divide up the hydrocarbon-rich Caspian Sea between the littoral states. But the HOT of the former

Soviet states does now respond largely to world patterns of supply and demand as reflected in world prices. That Russia continues to supply its former fellow Soviet republics with oil and gas, even when they cannot pay, is a partial exception to that rule, but it does not change the overall picture. As far as HOT is concerned, therefore, the macro-regional orientation is largely driven by short-term global price conditions.

In relation to patterns of specialisation within manufacturing, and especially within engineering, the situation is completely different. Here, output comes in the form of heterogeneous, quality-sensitive artefacts rather than standardised commodities. The capacity to make these artefacts stems from a combination of fixed capital and human capital endowment. In relation to the latter, the possession of critical elements of *tacit knowledge* may be a *sine qua non* of successful commercial exploitation. Technology transfer may involve firm-specific information on production processes or product designs. Even to use and run the equipment satisfactorily may involve passing on knowledge about operating methods and ways of doing things that has been built up over extended periods of time.[5]

This is the area where one would expect a clear-cut reorientation towards global, and particularly Western markets, as a way of maximising the impact of the existing fixed and human capital endowment of the given FSU country, and at the same time filling the gaps in that endowment through foreign investment. In practice this has not happened.[6]

---

[5]M. Sharp and M. Barz, "Multinational companies and the transfer and diffusion of new technological capabilities in Central and Eastern Europe and the former Soviet Union", in ed. D.A. Dyker, *The Technology of Transition: Science and Technology Policies for Transition Countries*, Central European University Press, Budapest, 1997, p. 96.

[6]It is estimated that, if machinery exports associated with technical assistance programmes and cooperation agreements with other CIS countries are factored out, Russia has revealed comparative advantage in relation to just 0.1% of total world machinery exports. See V.A. Oreshkin, *Vneshneekonomicheskoi Komplekse Rossii — Problemy i Perspektivy Razvitiya*, Vserossiiskii Nauchno-Issledovatel'skii Konyunkturnyi Institut, Moscow, 2000, p. 6.

One major reason is that international companies have been as reluctant to invest in engineering-based industries in the FSU as they have been eager to in the CEECs, where FDI has been a key factor in transferring key elements of tacit knowledge and upgrading human capital stock, and also in building state-of-the-art supply networks. In the FSU FDI has simply never achieved critical mass, and the upgrading factors it tends to bring have come through only at the level of isolated, individual enterprises.

None of this reasoning has much relevance to Central Asia. Here, levels of industrialisation are generally low, and levels of productivity in the industrial enterprises that do exist generally well below even Russian/Ukrainian standards. In a word, these countries do not have comparative advantage in most areas of manufacturing, so the issue of the development of IIT simply does not arise in the short term.

The regional orientation of Eurasian HOT is heavily influenced by transport links, particularly pipelines. Oil and gas are the same the world over, and it requires no tacit knowledge or protected intellectual property rights to ship them where you will. Thus the globalisation of the hydrocarbon industries of the former Soviet South is basically held up by physical bottlenecks, bottlenecks which Moscow has been prepared to exploit for political reasons. Oil and gas from the Caspian and Central Asia can go West, South (to the Gulf) or east (to China), and the only thing that stops it is the logistic capacity to move them. That logistic capacity is at present very unevenly developed, but the reasons for this are technical and macro-political rather than economic as such.

The situation is very different in relationship to IIT. Let us take Ukraine as an example. Here is a country with a long-established industrial tradition, a well-educated and skilful labour force, and significant concentrations of technological capability in sectors like aerospace, electro-welding and motor vehicles. The scope for profitable Ukrainian involvement in the supply networks which dominate the contemporary industrial world is obvious. But with FDI at nugatory levels, and other forms of inward technology transfer largely ineffective, Ukraine is locked into a vicious circle of economic stagnation and dependence on Russia, with exports per head of population only one half the Russian level. EU technical assistance programmes have sought to clear the way for new paths of interaction between Ukrainian and foreign organisations within the business sector, but the impact has been minimal.

The evolution of the pattern of Eurasian trade since the break-up of the Soviet Union has, therefore, been a complex one, involving multiple interaction of intra-and extra-regional factors. But the dominant trend has been reorientation to the world market. Before turning to an examination of the international institutional setting within which this reorientation has taken place, we pause to look at the ways in which inherited political patterns continue to affect the prosecution of trade policy in the CIS countries.

Influence of the Soviet Political Legacy on Trade Policy

As noted above, some of the CIS countries are today ruled by the same men who ruled them in Soviet times, and in much the same manner that they ruled them in Soviet times. Even in the more reformed CIS countries, the habits formed in the school of Soviet politics are difficult to shake off. The wide prevalence of corruption is only the most obvious manifestation of that. Less obvious but equally important is the survival of the Soviet notions of "blat" (influence, good connections, old boy's networks) and "the economy of agreements" (*ekonomika soglasovanii*), under which in Soviet times a market effectively existed for bureaucratic signatures on pieces of paper with important resource implications. These political influences from the past continue to shape policy today. In the post-Soviet world blat translates into a range of unsavoury power devices extending to blackmail and conspiracy. Most important, it means that post-Soviet leaders will tend instinctively to seek for solutions to post-Soviet problems, including trade policy problems, through the exercise of blat. That means that networks developed in the context of a centrally planned economy may be called upon to address the problems of the market economy, an obvious nonsense in economic policy terms.

One very specific way in which the old "economy of agreements" has been developed and transformed in the post-Soviet world is in terms of what might be called the "economy of exemptions". Here we see how the survival of Soviet-type political habits can influence the implementation of trade policy profoundly. Tariff revenue is a relatively small proportion of the total value of imports in most CIS countries, often smaller than might appear likely from published tariff rates. What that reflects is the crucial importance in post-Soviet states of the prerogative of giving tariff exemptions to favoured interests. All of this is clearly crucial to the whole issue of trade policy. Specifically, the notion of bound tariffs, a crucial element in the GATT, is totally incompatible with the "economy of exemptions".

JOINING THE CLUB: THE CIS COUNTRIES AND THE MULTILATERAL TRADE INSTITUTIONS

WTO Membership

Accession to the WTO is a complex matter, because it involves consideration of a large number of technical trade issues, and because the WTO itself cannot negotiate on behalf of its members (as does the European Commission). In principle, therefore, accession is conditional on bilateral agreement with each individual existing member. Nevertheless Kyrgyzstan and Georgia both managed to join the WTO in 2000 after only brief negotiations, and Moldova and Armenia have since been admitted. Russia has been negotiating for membership ever since the Soviet Union broke up, but has still not managed to conclude negotiations. If joining the WTO is such a difficult matter technically, how can small and impoverished countries like Georgia go so quickly, when Russia, with a formidable establishment of trade negotiators, seems to make such heavy weather of the whole thing? Is it the size of the Russia trade surplus and the country's ability to affect the markets of importing countries that makes the negotiations more complex and hence slower? Is it because the leading Western nations, notably the United States, want to impose some kind of political conditionality on Russian accession? Or have domestic Russian factors been of primary importance? The Russian government has, certainly, been very concerned to *negotiate*, and to try to get the very best deal for Russia. In practice, that has meant standing firm on a number of issues, notably:

1. *Market access* in the area of services, especially in relation to financial services.
2. *Export taxes*: the main incidence of these is on oil. The oil export tax issue is, however, likely to diminish in importance as the international price of oil comes down.[7] It may be more difficult to negotiate over duties on the export of *scrap metal*, which reflect the strength of domestic scrap-using lobbies.
3. *Subsidisation of agriculture*: this is more a matter of principle than of practice. The Russian budget could never accommodate the levels of agricultural subsidisation which Russia is trying to negotiate with the WTO.
4. *Market-economy status*. This is not strictly a WTO matter, but it impinges strongly on the effective WTO status of any given country. Till recently, Russia had quasi-market-economy status with the EU. This meant that full market status had to be negotiated sector by sector, even company by company, which made Russia more vulnerable to anti-dumping actions. In principle, the problem should have been resolved by the August 2002 recognition by the European Commission of Russia as a fully-fledged market economy. There are reports, however, that the Commission is planning to modify its anti-dumping rules in such a way as to permit continued application of non-market economy rules in the case of particular companies or sectors of the Russian economy.[8]

Technical issues apart, there has been a determination on the part of the Russians to *do it themselves*, without the help of foreign consultants. While the Russian government may be better equipped than any other CIS country to do its own negotiations with the WTO, it does suffer from some significant weaknesses of capability, and this has certainly slowed down the pace of negotiations.

---

[7]See postscript to Chapter 3.
[8]*GazetaSNG*, 12 August 2002.

It is not difficult, therefore, to understand why negotiations for accession to the WTO have been so long-drawn-out for Russia. But why did they go so quickly and easily for Georgia and Kyrgyzstan? Smallness is certainly one factor. The foreign trade activity of these two countries does not impinge on any existing WTO member to any significant extent. Politics is another. In both cases the Western powers, and in particular the United States, were anxious to speed WTO accession as a way of consolidating links with the West. Thirdly, the governments of Georgia and Kyrgyzstan were quite happy to allow most of the technical work in the accession negotiations to be done by foreign consultants. Finally, it should be borne in mind that WTO membership does not entail full compliance with the WTO. As long as existing members do not make difficulties, new members can be admitted on the basis of commitments to action in the post-accession period. But this does mean that significant trade problems may remain outstanding even after WTO accession. Three stand out in particular.

1. As long as smuggling and second-economy tax evasion are as prevalent as they are in many CIS countries (notably Georgia), foreign firms will not enjoy genuine level-playing-field conditions.
2. Recent decisions by WTO disputes panels have established the principle that a member-state may legitimately raise a dispute against another member state in relation to domestic policy measures which are implicitly protectionist, even if there is no protectionist intention.[9] The principle remains a contentious one among the great trading powers because of its implications for sovereignty, and it may not be upheld. Even if it is upheld, it may never be invoked against the smaller CIS countries, because their markets are too small for it to be worth anyone's trouble to raise a dispute. For big countries with potentially large markets like Russia and Ukraine the risks are greater.

---

[9]J. Katchen, *Recapturing a Lost Opportunity: Article III:2 GATT 1994 Japan-Taxes on Alcoholic Beverages 1996*, mimeo, undated.

3. It is clear that at present many civil servants and businesspeople in Georgia and Kyrgyzstan have only an imperfect understanding of the implications of WTO accession. This will become more, rather than less, of a problem as the post-accession stage proceeds.

The Energy Charter

The Energy Charter, to which every CIS country is a signatory, involves extension of WTO principles to trade in energy carriers. The Energy Charter is, indeed, the only global trade agreement involving all the CIS countries as well as their main trading partners in other parts of the world. It covers trade in energy carriers, promotion and protection of investment in energy sectors, sovereignty and environmental issues as they relate to energy, and it includes a disputes mechanism.

Energy is, of course, a sector where the usual kinds of trade disputes — relating to dumping and allegations of dumping, etc. — rarely arise. Where there have been disagreements among Charter signatories, e.g. as to whether the provisions of the Charter cover nuclear energy, they have proved difficult to resolve. And the Energy Charter has not helped Russia to obtain the package agreement it wants with the EU covering oil, electricity, nuclear fuel and transit of energy carriers through Europe. In the *Joint Communiqué* published at the end of the Brussels Russia-EU Summit in October 2001,[10] the co-signatories stressed the importance of technical security of transit of hydrocarbons, and "recognised the role" of stable, long-term contracts for energy deliveries. To what extent this represents a movement on the part of the EU towards the Russian position on long-term contracts is not clear.[11] Nevertheless, the Charter stands as a pioneering development, showing the way forward in terms of integration of the CIS countries into the global trading system.

---

[10]*Ministerstvo Inostrannykh Del Rossiiskoi Federatsii, Departament Informatsii Pechati*, 4 October 2001.

[11]In the joint communiqué it is stated that the *Russian side* stresses the importance of long-term contracts for gas supply on a "take or pay" basis.

EU Co-operation

There are now *Partnership and Co-operation Agreements* (PCAs) between the EU and virtually all of the CIS countries. The general view is that they are not very important, providing some kind of political symbol, but offering little by way of trade liberalisation that is not already available through GSP, etc. But this is a part of the world where political symbols are particularly important. Politics apart, PCAs may be more significant in the purely technical sense than is commonly believed in the CIS countries. The fact is that implementation of the PCAs has in most cases only just begun. As with WTO membership in the case of Kyrgyzstan and Georgia, there is a strong impression that governments and business communities may at present have an incomplete understanding of the implications of PCAs. Particularly in areas like investment and IPRs, PCAs may be viewed as a kind of "WTO accession plus". Their potential importance is taken up again in that context in the next section.

CONCLUSIONS

The policy implications of the above are, in a sense, simple and obvious enough. Governments inside and outside the CIS and international organizations should do everything possible to:

- accelerate the accession of *all* CIS countries to the WTO;
- facilitate the process of implementation of CIS PCA agreements with the EU; and
- ensure consistency and sequentiality in the implementation of post-WTO-accession policies.

The reality, however, is less neat. As has emerged repeatedly from the foregoing analysis, the trading problems of the CIS countries will not all be solved simply by joining international clubs. On key issues, further measures need to be taken on a multilateral basis. The issues involved include contingent protection, investment, intellectual property rights, liberalization of the trade in services, trade facilitation and a number of other more technical matters. Here we focus in detail on

the most important of these issues from an economic point of view —
contingent protection and investment.

Guarantees Against Contingent Protection

The global record on guarantees against contingent protection is
very patchy. The WTO disputes mechanism may tend to discourage
"trigger-happy" application of contingent protection, but it does not
narrow the range of application of these instruments as such. Nor
do the PCAs. There is no empirical instance of a free-trade agreement "enhanced" through some limitation on the prerogative to
invoke contingent protection within the Eurasian region. Outside
the region, there are examples of enhanced free trade areas. One is
the European Economic Area (EEA). Given that the members of the
EEA are all advanced industrial countries, with similar economic
structures and engaging primarily in IIT, the lessons to be drawn for
the CIS countries are limited. Still, there are features of the EEA
regime which may be "exportable".

The EEA system is based on three key principles:

1. Waiver of anti-dumping rights is conditional on the introduction
   of an EEA-wide package of competition measures.
2. These packages of competition measures are agreed on a sector-
   by-sector basis.
3. Safeguard measures are not affected by the EEA Agreement.

The linkage of anti-dumping issues to competition issues is an obvious enough one. The sectoral principle in relation of competition regulations makes for fussy negotiations and an uneven pattern of
implementation (there is, for example, no EEA agreement on anti-
dumping/competition in relation to salmon). But in CIS conditions,
this may not be a bad thing. Governments in the region are weak and
corrupt. Industry structures are also corrupt, but many industry lobbies in Russia and Ukraine in particular are extremely well organised.
They also tend to cartelisation, and might, certainly, look askance at
any international agreement that sought to enforce stricter rules of
competition on them. But if the *quid pro quo* were a blanket exemption

from anti-dumping actions, then some sectors, e.g. steel, would surely be interested.

The fact that safeguards are not covered by the self-denying ordinance on contingent protection in the EEA Agreement seems at first sight to be a regrettable omission. In political terms, however, it may be no bad thing. The rules on safeguards are very broad. But the process of taking an action based on safeguards provisions is very complicated, and in practice few such cases come to court. There has never been a safeguards case in the EEA. Maintaining safeguard provisions as an ultimate deterrent, one which will, we hope, never be used, could be an important element in a strategy aimed at persuading CIS industrial lobbies to break up their cartels, and industrial lobbies inside and outside the CIS to stop pestering their governments to apply anti-dumping measures on a broad basis against CIS producers.

Both the EU and the US have been guilty of using contingent protection as a means of backdoor protection against the former communist countries, and it cannot be assumed that they would give up this prerogative lightly, even if there were substantial gains to be made in other areas if they did. In addition, the US in particular continues to oppose the free export of Russian and Ukrainian space, defence and nuclear technology. Any long-term plan for the integration of the CIS economies into the global economy would certainly have to include concerted action to remove this kind of barrier to trade.

While the stress in the area of contingent protection must be laid primarily on the need to reduce the burden of contingent protection on CIS exporters, CIS governments will have to continue to maintain at least minimal arrays of "trade remedies" themselves. After all, genuine dumping does sometimes happen. Present deficiencies of expertise in all the CIS national bureaucracies in this area mean that in practice only powerful and wealthy interests, like steel-making in Russia and Ukraine, are effectively defended, while weaker and more vulnerable interests like Russian textiles receive little meaningful support against dumping. These deficiencies are particularly glaring in the smaller CIS countries, not excluding those that have already joined the WTO. But deputy minister for economic development and trade of the Russian Federation, Maksim Medvedkov, has also recently stressed the need to improve Russian anti-dumping regulations and to teach Russian producers how to proceed with dumping complaints.[12]

International Agreement on Investment

A standard agreement on guarantees and a regulatory framework for foreign investment for all the CIS countries would have the great merit of providing assurances to investors while at the same time ensuring that governments did not engage in a self-defeating competition with each other to attract investment to their particular countries. The PCAs contain a number of level-playing-field provisions in relation to investment, and the European Commission has been prepared to enforce these. WTO membership for all the countries of the region would take them further down the same road. The problems here are primarily political rather than technical, viz.:

1. There is no immediate prospect of Russia making it possible for foreign companies to buy land or natural resource deposits in Russia. The existing production-sharing legislation is unsatisfactory and the prospects of substantial improvement uncertain.
2. As in relation to free trade itself, gate-keeping and corruption at local level can make a mockery of the best imaginable level-playing field agreement on investment.
3. Foreign businessmen who have learned to cope with gate-keeping and corruption in other parts of the world may yet continue to be cautious in their approach to investment in the CIS on account of general considerations of political (in)stability, considerations which may not be significantly affected by the introduction of investment guarantees.

On point 1, negotiations could produce a resolution over the medium term. However obstinate the Russian government may be on some aspects of investment regulation, there is a clear understanding in

---

[12]Interview with Medvedkov published in *Vedomosti*, 9 November 2000.

Russia of the critical importance of foreign investment. A senior official of the Russian Ministry of Economic Development and Trade stated in 2000 that an agreement on investment is more important for Russia than free trade itself.[13] That means that Russia will likely ultimately agree on outstanding investment issues. It also implies that she will be ready to accept free trade if that is a condition of agreement on investment.

Points 2 and 3 present much more difficult problems — deep-seated elements of systemic instability and the perception thereof, which can only be solved in the context of a general resolution of the outstanding transition issues which face *all* the CIS countries to a greater or lesser extent. It is unrealistic to think that international agreements on investment can turn the CIS into a foreign investors' paradise. On this dimension, therefore, policy initiatives can offer incremental improvement, but no final resolution. That in turn means that the impact of free trade in terms of the development of IIT will be less than maximal. This is a somewhat sombre note on which to end, but it is surely an accurate reflection of current reality.

---

[13]Interview by author of Evgeni Manakin, deputy director of the Department for Trade Policy and Multilateral Negotiations of the Ministry of Economic Development and Trade of the Russian Federation, 28 November 2000.

Part IV

The East European Countries and the European Union

Chapter 6

The Dynamic Impact on the Central-East European Economies of Accession to the European Union: Social Capability and Technology Absorption

INTRODUCTION: THE RETURNS TO ECONOMIC INTEGRATION

Whenever economists have sought to gauge the gains from economic integration they have come up with very modest figures. Estimates of the *total* impact, in terms of static trade effects, of the creation of original Common Market are all in the region of 1 per cent. Taking economies of scale and competition effects into account raises the estimate, but only to a still modest 3 per cent. *Ex ante* assessments of the impact of the implementation of the 1992 Single Market programme, making allowance for scale and competition effects, produced estimates of total impact in the range of 4–6 per cent (Holmes, 1999, pp. 49–55; Smith & Gasiorek, 1999, pp. 86–91). *Ex post* evaluations of the Single Market working on the same methodological basis suggest that the actual impact of 1992 may have been somewhat smaller (Smith & Gasiorek, 1999, pp. 91–3).

So what is all the fuss about? If a once-and-for-all increase in GDP of 1 per cent is all that economic integration offers, then it is simply not worth the trouble. Even a once-and-for-all increase of 6 per cent represents no more than two years of normal, healthy economic growth. Surely there must be something more to economic integration than trade creation, economies of scale and more competition? Smith and Gasiorek do, indeed, qualify their conclusions as quoted above thus, citing the work of Baldwin (1989):

> All of the above highlights the possible effects of the "1992" programme on economic performance, but with no reference to the third dimension of our understanding of the effects of integration on national economies, namely the effect on growth. Increased output [could] generate additional savings and investment which would contribute to further output growth. Increasing returns to scale or effects feeding through R&D could produce a permanent increase, not just in income, but in the *growth rate* of income. It is too early to be able to identify such effects, and indeed the methodological problems involved in such an exercise would be colossal... (Smith & Gasiorek, 1999, p. 93).

However difficult it may be just to prove a connection between European integration and European growth trends, never mind quantifying the relationship, it seems only plausible to suppose that there has been some link between the development of European integration since the signing of the Treaty of Paris[1] in 1951 and the impressive and sustained growth performance of most of the European economies over the past half-century, and that it was indeed the prospect of these truly dynamic effects, coupled with an essentially political vision of European unity, that spurred European leaders on to go through an immensely complex and long-drawn-out political process for the sake of integration.

ECONOMIC INTEGRATION AND EASTWARDS ENLARGEMENT: AN OVERVIEW

Eastwards enlargement poses two sets of questions in terms of the economic impact of integration. Firstly, how will it affect economic performance in the European Union as a whole? Secondly, how will it

---

[1]Setting up the European Coal and Steel Community, the first of the European communities.

affect economic performance specifically in the accession countries themselves? The first set of questions is relatively easy to answer. With the combined GDP of the formerly communist accession countries (Estonia, Latvia, Lithuania, Poland, the Czech Republic, Slovakia, Hungary, Slovenia, Romania and Bulgaria) coming to less than 10 per cent of the GDP of the EU as presently constituted, it is inconceivable that eastwards enlargement could have a substantial effect on aggregate economic performance in the bloc, whether in terms of trade creation, scale and competition effects or growth effects.

The second set of questions is much more interesting and much more difficult to answer, and it is this set of questions that will concern us mainly in what follows. Let us take each dimension of the impact of integration in turn.

Trade Effects

Analogy with the analyses of the original common market cited above suggests that these effects may be relatively minor. The argument is that much stronger if we consider that the *Europe Agreements*, originally signed in 1991 between the EU on the one side and Poland, Czechoslovakia and Hungary on the other, and since extended to Slovenia, Romania, Bulgaria and the Baltic countries, set the majority of the accession countries on a path towards free trade with the EU, a path which has now been largely traversed. We should not exaggerate the importance of the Europe Agreements in trade liberalisation terms. After all, 80 per cent of EU imports enter the Union tariff-free in any case (Baldwin *et al.*, 1997, p. 132). The key point here is that the process of liberalisation of trade between the CEECs and the EU, and indeed of the domestic economies of the countries concerned, starts in 1991, not in the (putative) year of accession to the Union. By the time accession to the EU becomes a real possibility, the most glaring structural distortions inherited from communism have already been corrected; these are more or less normal market economies, facing few barriers in their trade with the EU.

Of course, the liberalisation is not complete. The *Common Agricultural Policy* continues to deny the accession countries free trade in agricultural goods with existing EU members. And contingent protection, mainly in the form of anti-dumping actions, still affects some items in the trade of those countries. Thus over the last two quarters of 1998 and the first quarter of 1999 the European Commission took anti-dumping measures against East European producers in relation to iron and steel, fertilisers, hardboard and a number of other products. Governments of the accession states themselves have also been active in the area of contingent protection within the area of the Central European Free Trade Area (CEFTA),[2] with Hungary imposing a steel quota on the Czech Republic in December 1998, allegedly in retaliation against restrictions imposed earlier by the Czech government on imports of Hungarian wheat. There has been a general tendency since 1998 for the Central and East European and Baltic countries to increase support prices and export subsidies for agricultural products, and these have, of course, affected trade between accession countries and between accession countries and third countries, as well as trade between individual accession countries and the EU (ECE, 1999, pp. 150–151).

The various forms of contingent protection have, certainly, had some effect on the performance of the accession countries, and the final removal of anti-dumping and safeguard actions and the like from the array of policy instruments of acceding governments, and of the EU *vis-à-vis* those countries, will have a perceptible trade impact. That impact is, nevertheless, unlikely to change radically the basic arithmetic of the static effects of enlargement on the new member countries. Although some of the accession countries have large agricultural populations, none of them have across-the-board competitive advantage in agriculture, except possibly Hungary, though all have in a few speciality products. Thus with reference to this eternally "sensitive" sector, the situation of the accession countries is, on the whole, rather similar to that of the EU in terms of competitive advantage, though not, of course, in terms of efficiency. It is, perhaps, not surprising, therefore, that the European Commission and the governments of the candidate countries should vie with each other to see how many restraints on agricultural trade they can impose. But if all those restraints were

---

[2]Poland, the Czech Republic, Slovakia, Hungary and Slovenia.

removed between the EU and the accession countries, while remaining in place between the enlarged EU and the rest of the world, the result would be trade re-diversion rather than trade creation, and the impact on the GDP of the acceding countries quite marginal. The impact of contingent protection on *industrial goods* can certainly not be ignored, but many of the emergency quotas and duties imposed under this rubric are short-lived, so that their direct impact on trade is marginal. Finally, we should bear in mind that agricultural protection and contingent protection were two of the things which the Treaty of Rome removed from trade between the original Six. So the fact that these forms of protection still apply to the CEECs does nothing to weaken the analogy with the initial creation of the EEC.[3]

Casual empiricism would suggest, therefore, that the trade effects of enlargement on the acceding countries would not greatly exceed the 1 per cent of GDP estimated for the impact of the original Common Market. Baldwin *et al.* (1997, p. 138) estimate, using a calibrated general equilibrium model, that the total impact on acceding countries of allocation effects (including scale effects but not competition effects, plus a limited range of investment/growth effects: see below) consequent on enlargement would amount to just 1.5 per cent of GDP. Broadly comparable estimates for Slovenia taken by itself, using the same methodology, yield even more modest figures (Stanovnik *et al.*, 1999, pp. 6–8).

Scale and Competition Effects

These are in practice potentially very substantial. Many sectors in the former communist countries still operate largely with the network of

---

[3]Outside the range of the Europe Agreements and CEFTA, CEECs levy a higher average tariff (6.5 per cent) than the EU (3 per cent) (Baldwin *et al.*, 1997, p. 133). It is protection of heavy industry that drives the average CEEC tariff up, and effective levels of agricultural protection *vis-à-vis* the outside world are actually lower than for the EU. Thus accession will reduce levels of protection for some CEEC sectors and increase them for others. These effects may be important, but probably more for partner countries than for the CEECs themselves, which do the bulk of their trading with the EU and each other.

medium-large firms inherited from the communist period. There are no really big firms, no multinationals based in the accession countries, and the typical accession country still has a much smaller proportion of its GDP originating from SMEs than the typical EU member state. (Poland is an exception here.) So there is enormous scope for rationalisation in both directions — for the exploitation of economies of scale *and* exploitation of the economies of small-scale production, and Baldwin *et al.* do not appear to take full account of these regional peculiarities in their estimates of scale effects. Competition policy tends to be one of the weaker areas of policy-making, and "cosy" relationships between producers in given sectors in particular candidate countries tend to be reinforced by the presence or threat of contingent protection measures by the EU or neighbouring countries. Again, the breaking-up of these cosy relationships could have a very significant effect.

The problem here is that while the scale and competition effects of enlargement on the (enlarged) EU would by definition be positive, however small, as would the scale effects taken by themselves in relation to the acceding countries, the combination of scale and competition effects for the latter could be positive or negative. Accession could well liberate the entrepreneurial energies of the management of some of these medium-large firms, and the first Polish, Czech, Hungarian, etc. multinationals could be forged in the conquest of EU markets. New multinationals would provide new markets for the outputs of SMEs, who might themselves expand by competing head-on with SMEs in the existing member-countries of the EU. But accession will also complete the opening-up of the economies of the candidate economies to competition from the existing EU. To the extent that most West European firms, large and small, have already been honed to their optimal size by competition within the existing EU, they may find it relatively easy to conquer the local markets of firms from acceding countries. If they do that through arm's-length trade, the result, *ceteris paribus*, will be a fall in local GDP.[4] No doubt both types of effect would occur in practice, but there is little *a priori* basis for gauging which would be stronger. Thus while combined

---

[4]Though the welfare level of local consumers may rise.

scale and competition effects on the acceding countries could be substantial, they could be positive or negative.

Growth Effects

Important, if difficult to tie down, for the original EU, these are potentially colossal for the accession countries in the context of enlargement. When Baldwin *et al.* allow for the impact of enlargement on levels of investment, but hold all the conditions affecting investment activity constant, they come up with very modest figures. When they introduce into their model the assumption that enlargement will reduce investment risk premia for the acceding countries by 15 per cent, their estimate of the increase in GDP flowing from enlargement rises to 18.8 per cent. Even this estimate, however, is arguably on the modest side, since it does not allow for the possibility of a succession of upward shifts in the production functions of the acceding countries through learning effects. As Table 1 shows, the gap in terms of GDP per head between the candidate countries and

Table 1. GDP per head in the accession countries and the EU, US$, 2001.

	At Official Exchange Rates	At Purchasing Power Parities[†]
Estonia	3,810	10,020
Latvia	3,260	7,870
Lithuania	3,270	7,610
Poland	4,240	9,280
Czech Republic	5,270	14,550
Slovakia	3,700	11,610
Hungary	4,800	12,570
Slovenia	9,780	18,160
Romania	1,710	6,980
Bulgaria	1,560	5,950
EU	18,273[*]	23,892[‡]

[*]Calculated as the Eurostat figure for GDP per head in ECU, multiplied by the average ECU: $ exchange rate for 2001.
[†]Based on the standard of what $1 buys in the US.
[‡]Author's estimate.
Source: World Bank, 2003; Eurostat.

the EU varies considerably, but is generally of the order of 1:4 or higher at prevailing exchange rates. In terms of purchasing power parities the gap is smaller, as we would expect, but still averages nearly 1:2.5. That puts these countries firmly into the category of *catch-up countries*. The scope for catch-up growth is defined by Verspagen (1999)[5] in terms of technological diffusion and spillovers from the leading industrial countries, as constrained by *technological congruence* and *social capability*. He defines the first in terms of:

> ...the match between the technologies in use in the advanced country and those most fit for introduction in the backward country. If there is a mismatch between the two, the opportunities for catch-up-driven growth are reduced. The sectoral distribution of economic activity is one important factor in congruence. For example, one may well imagine that most technologies developed in the industrialized market economies are not very relevant for the most backward economies, which are often still largely agricultural societies. But there are also other factors in congruence, as in the case where the technologically leading country applies very scale-intensive technologies, for which investment opportunities and/or domestic markets in the backward country are too small. In such a situation, technological incongruence would prevent successful catch-up (Verspagen, 1999, p. 31).

The second he defines in terms of:

> ...institutional factors such as educational systems (which supply the human capital necessary for assimilating spillovers), the banking system (which supplies financial capital for catch-up related investment), the political system, etc. (Verspagen, 1999, pp. 31–2).

The concept of social capability is in essence a fairly specific one — it covers the elements in the social and political infrastructure which have a significant affect on flows of human and financial capital, and

---

[5]Following Abramowitz, 1979 and 1994. See also Stehrer & Landesmann, 1999.

on the conditions for application of this capital, in a given society. In practice, it is difficult to make a sharp distinction between social capability and broader concepts like culture and civil society. Thus Landes, in an authoritative work on the origins of differences in levels of economic development between different countries which analyses the factor of social capability systematically, concludes that:

If we learn anything from the history of economic development, it is that culture makes all the difference (Landes, 1998, p. 516).

Contemporary political science, in seeking for a more sharply focused terminology to define the cultural sphere, has picked out the term "civil society" from the seminal stage of modern social science and posited a close relationship between civil society, democracy, economic pluralism and production efficiency (Ferguson, 1996; Putnam *et al.*, 1994; Gellner, 1995). At the level of grand generalisation, "trust" has emerged as the element of culture which makes the crucial difference between advanced and less advanced economies/polities (Fukuyama, 1995; Warren, 1999), and Raiser (1999) has applied this approach explicitly to the problems of the transition countries. But let us for the time being stick to the narrower definition of social capability, blurred at the edges though it may be, and let us see what *a priori* analysis makes of the status and prospects of the accession countries in relation to technological congruence and social capability.

Since most of the leading industrial countries are members of the single market which the acceding countries would be joining, the post-enlargement scope for technological diffusion and spillovers should *in principle* be immense, and the threats posed by technological incongruence limited, given that the acceding countries are already industrialised, and have relatively sophisticated existing human capital stocks. To the extent that there were initial deficits on the social capability side, these should in principle have been substantially made up by the time of accession through the institution-building implicit in the pre-accession process of assimilation of the *acquis communautaire*. In very rough *a priori* terms, therefore, and if we accept that there are no sharp constraints on economic development other than technological congruence and social capability, accession

Table 2.   Growth rates of GDP in accession countries, 1994–2001.

	1994	1995	1996	1997	1998	1999	2000	2001	1994–2001 Ave.
Estonia	−2.0	4.3	3.9	9.8	4.6	−0.6	7.1	5.0	4.01
Latvia	2.2	−0.9	3.7	8.4	4.8	2.8	6.8	7.7	4.44
Lithuania	−9.8	3.3	4.7	7.3	5.1	−3.9	3.8	5.9	2.05*
Poland	5.2	7.0	6.0	6.8	4.8	4.1	4.0	1.0	4.86
Czech Rep.	2.2	5.9	4.3	−0.8	−1.0	0.5	3.3	3.3	2.21
Slovakia	4.9	6.7	6.2	6.2	4.1	1.9	2.2	3.3	4.44
Hungary	2.9	1.5	1.3	4.6	4.9	4.2	5.2	3.8	3.55
Slovenia	5.3	4.1	3.5	4.6	3.8	5.2	4.6	3.0	4.26
Romania	3.9	7.1	3.9	−6.1	−5.4	−3.2	1.8	5.3	0.91
Bulgaria	1.8	2.9	−9.4	−5.6	4.0	2.3	5.4	4.0	0.68

*Note that if 1994 is ignored, the Lithuanian average rises to 3.7.
Source: EBRD, 2002; author's calculations.

to the EU should make it possible for the countries involved to attain something like the EU level of GDP per head over the medium-to-long run, i.e., within 10–20 years.[6] Given that the ten accession countries, Romania and Bulgaria apart, have generally recorded fairly impressive growth rates since coming out of the slump which was a universal feature of early transition (see Table 2; note that the relatively low average GDP growth figure for the Czech Republic reflects the renewed recession into which that country fell following on the financial crisis of May 1997), we can only suppose that a good deal of catching-up would occur over the next couple of decades even if the candidate countries stayed outside the EU. Even if we attributed only half the full potential catch-up effect to accession, we would however be talking about a cumulative growth effect in the region of 50–100 per cent of current GDP levels. This dwarfs other potential (net) gains, and raises the question: why should we bother about trade and competition effects in our analysis of the likely economic impact

---

[6]Note that we neither make nor require any specific assumptions about the relative growth paths of existing EU countries and accession countries here. We simply assume that if there are no significant barriers to catch-up, less developed countries will inevitably catch up, with a time lag of roughly one "learning" generation.

of accession when we can sit back and wait for growth effects on this scale?

The answer to the question lies in the differences in the status of *a priori* analysis in each case. Trade effects in the context of integration accrue more or less automatically. There is a degree of market-driven automaticity in the case of scale and competition effects, though entrepreneurial behaviour is also an important element. Baldwin *et al.* (1997) hold that the reduction in investment risk premia they hypothesise would flow more or less automatically from enlargement as such. They argue this on the basis that:

> On the micro side, EU membership greatly constrains arbitrary trade and indirect tax policy changes. It also locks in well-defined property rights and codifies competition policy and state-aids policy. By securing convertibility, open capital markets and rights of establishment, membership assures investors that they can put in and take out money. Finally, EU membership guarantees that CEEC-produced products have unparalleled access to the EU15 markets. On the macro side, membership puts the CEECs on a path to eventual monetary union, and thus provides a solid hedge against inflation spurts. These two aspects of membership are likely to have a related impact on investor confidence and are likely to be mutually reinforcing (p. 140).

In practice, entrepreneurial and political decision-making would surely be additional variables here — after all risk premia do not move up and down through some anonymous and automatic market mechanism, but because firms, banks and rating agencies make conscious decisions to change them. On the macroeconomic side too (strictly outside the remit of this article), Baldwin *et al.* are surely wrong to simply assume that accession will improve performance. All the CEECs have been plagued by problems of inflation and/or balance of payments deficits. Accession to the EU, more specifically to the Monetary Union, would certainly offer an opportunity to iron out these problems. But in the absence of well-considered national fiscal policies, EMU membership could actually push the CEECs into recession. Once we enter the area of learning effects, therefore, the quality of entrepreneurial and political decision-taking clearly becomes an absolutely crucial factor. A review of the experience of Mediterranean enlargement tends to support the argument that effective exploitation of the growth potential of accession does, indeed, depend on opportunities being taken through good decision-taking by key actors, both inside and outside the acceding country. Thus our *a priori* analysis in this case merely defines the potential for growth effects. It tells us nothing about the extent to which this potential is likely to be exploited. In order to assess that, we need to look more closely at the factors which may constrain the exploitation of the scope for technological diffusion and spillovers.

It is clear that in practice the relationship between the development of social capability and the assimilation of the *acquis communautaire* is fraught with difficulty. The *acquis* strictly deals only with political and infrastructural institutions and systems. There are key elements of social capability like educational systems which it does not address at all. And within the political and infrastructural sphere there are serious problems as to whether all the elements of the *acquis* can be effectively assimilated, whether indeed all its elements are appropriate to the accession countries, and whether the institutions set up under its aegis can be efficiently and honestly administered by local elites.

A comprehensive assessment of the constraints on the building of social capability in the accession countries is beyond the scope of this article. In particular, an adequate treatment of educational policy as an element in the building of social capability would require an article in itself. What we do in the sections that follow is to look in detail at aspects of social capability which impinge most directly on the capacity to absorb technology from abroad, namely R&D systems and banking systems. We then go on to look at the institutional context within which technology diffusion actually takes place and the theme of technological congruence is played out — business alliances, foreign investment, supply networking — before trying to draw some general conclusions. At this stage we are still basically sticking to our narrower conception of social capability, while introducing broader concepts like that of trust as appropriate.

R&D SYSTEMS

In principle the substantial R&D systems inherited by the accession countries from the communist period should represent significant elements of social capability. The reality is more complex. First of all, the quality of the legacy has to be questioned. Understandable weakness of market orientation apart, the old communist *S&T* systems suffered from a number of critical *scientific* weaknesses. While they were strong in basic science, at least in the more traditional hard sciences like physics and chemistry, they were weak in applied sciences, or rather they were weak in science as applied to *innovation*, and weak in emerging disciplines like biotechnology and artificial intelligence. The administrative structures of communist science, dominated by the Academies of Sciences, were conservative and hierarchical, and the process of innovation was understood, to the extent that it was understood at all, in terms of a crude, linear, science-push conception.

While the process of transition has revolutionised the understanding of the process of innovation, it has failed to revolutionise the configuration of *S&T* among the accession countries. The administration of science is still dominated by the old Academies of Science in most of them. A corollary of this has been a tendency to maintain the traditional split between research (Academy of Sciences) and training of postgraduate students (universities), in the face of all the evidence from the West to the effect that the biggest contribution basic research makes to economic development is precisely in terms of training postgraduate students (Senker & Faulkner, 1995; Pavitt, 1996). While *S&T* expenditure as a whole has contracted sharply, expenditure on applied research has contracted more sharply than expenditure on basic science (Gokhberg, 1999), as the Academies have defended their vested interests rather more effectively than the industrial R&D institutes. While the former have suffered significant cuts in funding, the latter have in many cases simply been closed down altogether. And analysis of the pattern of "disciplinary comparative advantage", based on shares in world citations, indicates that the strengths of basic science in the post-communist countries are still very heavily concentrated in Physics, Mathematics and Chemistry, especially Nuclear Chemistry, and in some branches of engineering, notably Instrumentation and Measurement, Spectroscopy and Nuclear Engineering (Kozlowski & Ircha, 1999). The fact that numbers of *S&T* personnel have fallen more gently than expenditure reflects less devotion to science than resistance to redeployment. Policies to encourage the development of "Academy-industry links" adopted in the mid-1990s produced some isolated successes but had no great impact at the aggregate level (Balázs, 1996; Jasinski, 1997). The tendency through the mid-1990s was for the proportion of total GERD (gross expenditure on research and development) financed by the business sector to fall, with Poland as a significant exception.[7] Government continues to finance more than half total GERD in Hungary and Poland. In short, there is a good deal of evidence to suggest that much of the inherited *S&T* complex is still waiting to be restructured, and in extreme cases should be considered a "liability" rather than an asset to the accession countries (Meske, 1999).

Against this background, it is hardly surprising that no clear relationships emerge between statistical series relating to *S&T* and GDP performance over the transition period to date. The downward trend in *S&T* expenditure as a proportion of national income has been fairly uniform across the spectrum of accession countries. There have been significant differences between different accession countries in terms of policy, but these have been differences of emphasis rather than of direction. The sharpness of the cuts in R&D personnel in the Czech Republic, the only country where total personnel has fallen more sharply than expenditure, bears witness to the special muscularity of restructuring policies in the *S&T* sector in that country. But there is no evidence of any impact therefrom on the general level of economic performance in the Czech Republic. Poland, the pacesetter in the early phase of transition, continues to maintain an *S&T* system dominated by the Academy of Sciences and there has been little radical restructuring of R&D in that country, despite the upward trend in

---

[7]Note that, of the accession countries, only the Czech Republic reports proportions of total GERD financed by the business sector comparable to the OECD average.

the proportion of total GERD financed by the business sector.[8] Thus the science and technology sectors of the accession countries continue essentially to live in a world apart, and their role within the aggregate production functions of those economies has still to be clearly redefined. They are therefore ill-equipped for the task of reinforcing social capability for catch-up, and cannot be counted on, at the present time, to play any serious role in the solution of problems of technological congruence.

BANKING SYSTEMS

Banking systems are among the weakest elements in the accession economies. Banks are generally undercapitalised, with balance sheets skewed towards short-term assets and burdened by non-performing loans. Many of the bad loans are inherited from the communist period, but the stock of bad loans has continued to grow in the transition period, even in countries with relatively sophisticated banking traditions like Czechoslovakia/The Czech Republic (Gower, 1997; Zahradnik, 1999). This in turn reflects purely technical deficiencies in credit assessment procedures, and also the strength of specific "borrowing lobbies" and the extent of cross-ownership of banks and companies in the real sector of the economy, against the background of a pervasive notion, largely borne out in practice, that transition states will not allow big banks to go bankrupt. Banks in accession countries also have a poor record as mobilisers of savings. The recalcitrance of all these problems reflects a general lack of competition in the sector.

There is clearly a serious deficit of social capability in the banking sectors of the accession countries at the present time. The extent of the deficit varies substantially between countries, with the Czech Republic perhaps the most problematic in this respect and Hungary in the strongest position. But the Hungarian banking sector is exempt from none of the typical weaknesses of transition country banking sectors. Banks have generally preferred to invest in government paper or lend to

---

[8]That means that in Poland, the (highly dynamic) business sector appears to have been affording substantial financial support to traditional R&D structures.

established, large companies (mostly inherited from the communist period), often with scant regard to the likelihood of the loans being repaid. In the key area of channelling finance to new companies they have played virtually no role. It is again particularly significant that in the Czech Republic, one of the most advanced transition countries, weaknesses in the commercial banking sector were a significant factor in the financial crisis of 1997 (ECE, 1998, pp. 79–81). Here, then, is an area where accession to the European Union, and its implications in terms of opening-up of CEEC banking, could in principle have a huge effect.

> Foreign banks provide not only capital to weak banks, but also expertise in bank management and the technical know-how for creating a competitive environment. Perhaps their greatest advantage is that they can expose the unsound credit business of their domestic counterparts, notably connected lending and lending to loss-making enterprises (Koch, 1998, pp. 76–7).

Since liberalisation of the banking sector is an element of the *acquis communautaire* which has to be in place *before* candidate countries can actually join the EU, this element of competition should be present from the very beginning of enlargement. But will it be sufficient to raise the standard of banking services in the acceding countries to West European standards?

Let us look first at the aggregate data on bank performance in the transition area as a whole. Of the ten candidate countries, Hungary has by far the highest rate of foreign ownership in the banking sector (approaching 50 per cent, with elements of foreign ownership in 30 out of a total of 41 banks). Yet Hungarian banking does not show up as being significantly stronger on any key indicator of banking activity. When we look at banks individually, however, the picture is rather different. On the basis of analysis of reports on 452 banks from the transition area culled from the Bureau van Dijk's Bankscope database,[9] the EBRD found that:

> Foreign participation in banks has been associated with their stronger revenue performance; however, this effect diminishes

_____

[9]Published in *Bankscope*, May 1998.

as the size of a bank increases. In larger banks foreign participation typically involves investments in privatised banks. This result suggests that it may be more difficult for foreign participation to bring about a strong commercial orientation in a privatised bank than in a new private bank established with foreign involvement (EBRD, 1998, p. 129).

This helps to explain the Hungarian puzzle. The rate of foreign ownership in banking is higher in Hungary because the pace of privatisation of existing banks has been high, and because foreign banks have taken up a large proportion of the assets offered for sale. The new owners of these privatised banks have not, however, been able to bring about a transformation in the levels of operational activity of these banks. It is clear, therefore, that privatisation as such is not the key issue in transition banking. What matters, at least in the short-to-medium run, is the willingness of foreign banks to set up *new* banks in transition countries.

A priori reasoning suggests that foreign banks may generally be more prepared to take advantage of accession-related liberalisation in the candidate countries to compete through acquisitions than through wholly new ventures. Central-East Europe is still unfamiliar territory for most of the big Western banks in the sense that they lack personal knowledge of the client base; in that context the importance for risk management of having an experienced (if inefficient) local partner and an existing network of offices and expertise cannot be overstated. In Poland and Slovenia substantial sections of the banking industry remain in public ownership, and the scope for increasing foreign involvement through privatisation in those countries is huge.[10] In the other countries the key issue would rather be foreign participation in already privatised banks, in relation to which restrictions are generally currently in force. Either way, the immediate impact on social

---

[10]In early 2003 just 30–35 per cent of Slovenian banking assets were foreign-owned. The effective degree of foreign control of the industry was, however, substantially higher, with the bulk of bank credit now originating from banks with a dominant foreign interest.

capability in the banking sector would likely be less than dramatic. But over the long run the difference in levels of performance between privatised and new banks would surely disappear. As long as foreign banks are willing to go in and compete in the acceding countries, on whatever basis, therefore, the ultimate impact on social capability in the sector should certainly be a substantial one. We must, however, issue one more caveat. Bank liberalisation in the CEECs will not force Western banks to compete, nor will it force them to overcome their own existing weaknesses. As noted earlier, development of SMEs is a crucial issue for all the transition countries, and the lack of provision of venture capital has been a key bottleneck in this connection. In Hungary, for instance, only 4 per cent of total bank credit went to small enterprises in 1998 (EBRD, 1999, p. 227). But West European credit organisations, which may be supposed to be the ones most likely to take advantage of candidate country liberalisation, are also notably weak in the area of venture capital provision (Cowie, 1999). There are, in any case, serious obstacles to the development of large-scale venture capital activities in transition countries on account of the difficulty of selling on, which venture capital funds normally do after a few years (Sagari, 1992). In Western countries this is normally done through a specialised stock market of the type of NASDAQ. Given the rudimentary level of development of stock markets in the accession countries, development of this kind of financial flexibility is surely at best a long-term prospect.

Our essential conclusions on the likely impact of enlargement on local banking sectors are, accordingly, two-fold:

- The impact is likely to be long-term rather than short-term.
- Key areas of banking activity may remain largely untouched even into the long term.

THE INSTITUTIONAL FRAMEWORK FOR TECHNOLOGY DIFFUSION

Business Alliances

Perhaps the most important form of business alliance over the past decade has been the *outward processing agreement*. This is essentially a form of "putting-out", whereby EU firms supply firms in CEECs with inputs for the latter to make up into finished or semi-finished products and ship back to the EU firm. The trade is explicitly exempt from tariffs. Outward processing agreements are most common in traditional, low-tech sectors like textiles and footwear. The benefit of such arrangements for the putting-out firm resides in the scope created for the accessing of cheap labour. The advantage for the CEEC firms lies in the tariff-free access it provides to the EU market in "sensitive" sectors where non-tariff barriers have only recently been removed, and where there is still no general guarantee against contingent protection. While outward processing generally involves no transfer of "hard" (product/process) technology, it does inevitably result in some transfer of "soft" (management) technology, the area where, indeed, the technology gap between the EU and the CEECs is widest.

The outward processing trade (OPT) was in its heyday in the early 1990s. Since then OPT has declined in importance for the CEEC region as a whole, accounting for just 13 per cent of total CEEC exports to the EU in 1996 compared to 17 per cent in 1993 (Pellegrin, 1999, p. 4), as real wages have risen and trade liberalisation has progressed. It does, certainly, remain very important in particular sectors, notably clothing and textiles, and for particular countries, e.g. Romania. But it is likely to continue to contract once the CEECs are inside the EU. Avoidance of trade restrictions will no longer be an issue. If enlargement produces any trend whatsoever towards convergence of CEEC wage levels to existing EU levels, the acceding countries are likely to become less and less competitive in the outward processing trade *vis-à-vis* alternative hosts, e.g. in the former Soviet Union. The only advantage of enlargement for the outward processing trade will come through reduction in the amount of trade documentation required. But this factor will surely be overwhelmed by the other factors. Thus classic outward processing, a vehicle for technology diffusion of limited if non-negligible importance in the past, is likely to be less important in this regard after enlargement.

Under *Bangalore-type agreements*, Western companies have hired scientists, computer and software engineers, etc. from transition countries to do contract work on major projects while continuing to live and work in their native countries. As with outward processing, the lure for the Western partners here is cheap labour. For the transition country partners, Bangalore-type agreements offer steady work in over-populated sectors at wages which may be low by international standards but are usually above the average for the host country. In many cases Western partners provide equipment, even whole laboratories, to their collaborators under these deals, so that there can be significant element of hard technology transfer here. And, as with outward processing, there is always some soft technology transfer. But East-West Bangalore-type agreements have largely involved people and organisations from the former Soviet Union rather than Eastern Europe simply because the over-supply of scientists and engineers is greater in that region and average wages lower than in the countries of Eastern Europe. Since enlargement is likely to widen the wages gap between the two transition regions, Bangalore-type agreements are likely to be even more heavily concentrated in the FSU in the future than they have been in the past. As with classic outward processing agreements, then, enlargement is likely to reduce rather than increase the technology diffusion role of Bangalore-type agreements in the countries concerned.

Franchise and licensing agreements have been of considerable importance for the CEECs, notably in the software industry and in other specialist supplier sectors. Licensing agreements involve hard technology transfer by definition; in practice franchising is not very different, though there may be more stress on transfer of soft technology in this case. Franchise and licensing agreements have had a notable impact in terms of integrating small CEE firms into global networks in technologically highly dynamic sectors, and allowing them to develop their technological capabilities through the scope for two-way technology transfer which these networks offer. Wage rates as such are not normally a crucial issue in relation to these agreements, but level playing fields are. The supposition must be, therefore, that enlargement will increase the importance of franchise and licensing agreements as vehicles for the diffusion of state-of-the-art technology in the acceding countries. To the extent that specialist suppliers make crucial technological inputs into most of the other sectors of their home economies, the scope for accession-related spillover effects is also broad here.

Foreign Direct Investment

FDI has been a key vehicle of technology diffusion world-wide, and the transition region has been no exception in this regard. Once again, the transfer of soft technology has been of particular importance, against the background of the marked weakness of the communist system in the area of management and organisational science and technology. Major investments by Western multinationals have made crucial contributions to the creation of a modern business technology in the former communist countries, and this is as true of investments by MacDonald's and Coca-Cola as of investments by Ford, Volkswagen and Suzuki. But investments in key industrial sectors like the motor-car industry have been equally important in terms of the transfer of hard technology (state-of-the-art production lines and new models) and the building of supply networks (further discussed in the next section) (Dyker, 1999), and have done much to reinforce the underlying technological congruence of the former communist economies.

That said, it must be admitted that FDI has not maximised its potential for technology diffusion in the transition region. Explicit restrictiveness in related technology transfer has been the exception to the rule, and there have been cases where foreign investors have gone out of their way to help associated companies in transition countries to access more advanced technologies (Havas, 1996). But foreign direct investors in Eastern Europe have generally invested little in R&D facilities as such (Inzelt, 1999; Urem, 1999). Thus they have failed to make up for the deficit in social capability found in domestic R&D systems, and have accordingly left the transition countries still suffering from a key constraint on the scope for effective technology diffusion. At a more general level, case study material confirms that FDI has generated significant streams of asset creation,[11] but that FDI is neither a necessary nor a sufficient condition

---

[11]For a discussion of this concept see Chapter 4.

of asset creation, and that where FDI does create assets it tends to do so only weakly (Dyker & Kubielas, 2000, p. 21).

How are these patterns likely to change with enlargement? If the assumptions of Baldwin *et al.* about falls in risk premia are borne out in practice, even if only partially, we should see significant increases in aggregate volumes of FDI, as well as other forms of foreign investment, into the new member states. Yet we should exercise some caution here, especially in relation to the original five candidate countries — Estonia, Poland, the Czech Republic, Hungary and Slovenia. As Table 3 shows, Poland, the Czech Republic and Hungary between them account for the great bulk of FDI into

Table 3.   Foreign direct investment in Eastern Europe and the former Soviet Union, 2001.

	Cumulative* FDI ($m)	Cumulative FDI Per Capita ($)
Eastern Europe	115,615	1,083
Albania	774	252
Bulgaria	3,924	474
Croatia	6,141	1,370
Czech Republic	26,448	2,578
Hungary	23,914	2,372
Poland	35,690	922
Romania	7,635	341
Slovakia	5,468	1,014
Slovenia	1,994	1,002
Macedonia	836	416
Baltic states	8,261	1,104
Estonia	2,948	2,091
Latvia	2,562	1,072
Lithuania	2,750	747
European CIS[†]	31,304	149
Belarus	952	92
Moldova	671	153
Russian Federation	25,083	170
Ukraine	4,598	90

*From 1988.
[†]Not including Armenia, Azerbaijan and Georgia, in which levels of FDI have been nugatory.
Source: ECE (2000, p. 143; ECE, 2003, p. 239); author's calculations.

Eastern Europe, and for nearly 60 per cent of aggregate cumulative FDI in the transition region as a whole. While absolute levels of FDI into Estonia have been modest, per capita rates of FDI into this small country have been among the highest in the transition region, and cumulative FDI per capita is above $1,000 in Slovenia. In Hungary, FDI as a percentage of annual gross fixed capital formation has been consistently above 20 per cent throughout the transition period, placing that country firmly within the high-FDI group in global terms, and the corresponding ratios for Poland and the Czech Republic have exceeded 20 per cent in recent years. Thus the original five candidate countries are already absorbing levels of FDI that are high by regional, and even by global standards. This pattern no doubt reflects in part a widely held view that Estonia, Poland, the Czech Republic, Hungary and Slovenia are politically stable countries. It may also reflect widespread anticipation of EU membership for these countries. Thus Havas points out, in relation to the car industry, that:

> ... the first major investment decisions had been made before the Central European countries became associate members of the European Union, i.e., economic integration preceded the start of the fairly lengthy and cumbersome process of political integration. Most likely, though, both parties — managers of the Western European automotive firms and Central European government officials — anticipated potential EU membership in their medium term scenarios (Havas, 1999, p. 10).

There is some indication, therefore, that in this (key) industry at least, risk premia were already being cut in the early 1990s. We should, therefore, perhaps expect accession to maintain, even reinforce, the existing trend in aggregate levels of FDI in the original five accession countries, rather than to produce a dramatic jump. Accession could produce more radical changes in the structure of FDI in the new member states if, for instance, the extension of the EU intellectual property regime increased the readiness of foreign companies to invest in R&D facilities in those countries. But there is still a suspicion that failures on the part of the acceding states to build up social capability through the public education and R&D systems in the run-up to accession may make it *increasingly* difficult for companies to implement such investments satisfactorily. This point is brought into very sharp relief if we assume that real wages will rise significantly in the candidate countries after accession. In the past, and in sharp distinction to the outward processing and Bangalore cases, real wages by themselves have not been a key factor in decision-taking on FDI. Rather it has been the relationship between productivity trends and real wage trends that has been critical (Havas, 1999, p. 39). Since real wages are beyond the control of individual firms, control over productivity trends is clearly vital, where long-term direct investment commitments are in question. If there is a danger that that control might be lost because of deficiencies in social capability which the firm feels it can do little about, the consequences could be serious indeed. It must be added in this context that in the past foreign investors in the transition countries have probably erred on the side of caution in relation to their own capacity to change social capability parameters. But this reflects weaknesses of entrepreneurial vision which are unlikely to be corrected by changes in the external regulatory environment.

On balance, therefore, there appear to be no strong reasons for expecting big qualitative changes in the pattern of FDI in Estonia, Poland, the Czech Republic, Hungary and Slovenia after accession.[12] FDI as such will continue to be an important vehicle of technology diffusion, but its general contribution to the process of catch-up will probably increase steadily rather than dramatically.

The prospects for FDI are more mixed for the other five accession countries, which were given the go-ahead to begin negotiations for accession by the Helsinki European Council of 1999. The early 2000s saw big increases in FDI inflow into Slovakia, Latvia and Lithuania, indicating a strong anticipation effect, of the kind visible for the first five applicants from the early 1990s. But cumulative FDI

---

[12]This is not necessarily to dispute the validity of the assumptions of Baldwin *et al.* in relation to investment *as a whole* in these countries. Indeed those assumptions are arguably much more plausible in relation to financial and portfolio investment than in relation to direct investment.

per capita is still below $500 in Bulgaria and Romania, the two countries not scheduled to accede in 2004.[13] There is a hint, here, that investors may have suspected, right from the start, that Romania and Bulgaria would not be allowed in at the same time as all the others. Those suspicions may have combined, and indeed been partly based on, lingering doubts about political stability in these countries, especially in Romania. The perception, indeed the reality, of special problems of social capability may have been a further inhibiting factor in the case of Romania and Bulgaria. As argued above, membership of the European Union will not solve all problems of social capability overnight. But it will provide a substantial guarantee of political stability, and it should mean, following the Baldwin argument, that risk premia on investments will be cut significantly for Romania and Bulgaria, and sooner rather than later, now that the two Balkan countries have a definite date for accession, if not an absolute guarantee of accession. For Latvia, Lithuania and Slovakia, then, FDI trends are already converging to those of the original five applicants, suggesting that, for these countries too, accession will reinforce an existing trend rather than induce a break in trend. For Romania and Bulgaria accession-related increases in FDI are likely to be more dramatic than for the other eight countries, though they will probably be spread out over the years leading up to accession.

Supply Networks

Supply networks are of central importance in the present context for two reasons. Firstly, they represent an important element of social capability. Second, they are key conduits of technology spillover. We take these two aspects in turn.

In a mature market economy supply networks represent an important form of business organisation intermediate between fully internalised structures and fully externalised, market-based relationships.

---

[13]The Copenhagen European Council of December 2002 opened the door for accession for Slovakia, Latvia and Lithuania (along with all of the first five) in May 2004, while postponing Romanian and Bulgarian accession until 2007.

Price parameters play a key role in the mediation of supply network relationships, but the role is not an exclusive one as it is in the case of commodity trade. Quality is perceived as a key variable which has to be individually monitored, and there may be a significant degree of integration of functions like R&D and design which are normally organised on a hierarchical rather than a (quasi-)market basis within the integrated firm. Supply networks may also play a key role as vehicles for the transfer of *tacit knowledge*, which cannot be effected through arm's-length market transactions because it requires ongoing human contact. In the context of all this, trust, and detailed knowledge of partners' capabilities, play an essential role. Elements within supply networks are generally identified as:

- First-tier suppliers, who collaborate actively with the main firm on the design and production of complex components (e.g. gearboxes and engines in the case of the automotive industry).
- Second-tier suppliers, who supply advanced single components to first-tier suppliers.
- Third-tier suppliers, who supply simple components to second-tier suppliers.

The assessment of the role of supply networks in the former communist countries is greatly complicated by the legacy from the past. In the centrally planned economies like the Soviet Union, Poland[14] and Czechoslovakia, informal supply networking based on position within the *nomenklatura* pecking-order and good connections was an essential way of compensating for the rigidities and deficiencies of the official supply system. In the market socialist systems of Yugoslavia and Hungary supply networking was better integrated into the official system, but still tended to be dominated by the dimension of political influence and connections. In both cases supply networking was part of a strategy of survival, rather than a vehicle of best practice. In both cases the *linkages* within the networks tended to be stronger than the *nodes*.

---

[14]There was a brief period of limited market socialism in Poland during the 1980s, probably too brief significantly to affect the pattern of networking.

In the context of transition, this legacy is clearly at best ambivalent. Most notably in the Russian case, the persistence of traditionally Soviet patterns of networking has tended to hold back rather than facilitate the emergence of supply networks in the Western/Far Eastern sense (Harter, 1998). In Poland and Czechoslovakia/the Czech Republic, by contrast, the "clean-break" nature of the political transformation largely destroyed the old *nomenklatura* networks in terms of industrial networks (though not within the financial sphere), so that there was a much stronger sense of a "fresh start" in the building of supply networks in these countries. In Hungary and Yugoslavia/Slovenia, there have been elements of positive continuity in networking. This is also the case for Estonia, where firms, especially those operating in high-tech areas, enjoyed a good deal of quasi-market autonomy even in the Soviet period. But these elements of positive continuity tend to go hand in hand with a certain persistence of the old survival approach to networking.

All of this helps us to understand the key importance of foreign firms in relation to the building or refashioning of supply networks as networks of social capability in the accession countries. Whether because a clean break with the communist past has left a vacuum, or because greater continuity with the past has bequeathed an ambivalent legacy, local supply networks cannot simply be left to upgrade their social capability by themselves. They need exogenous impetus in the form of lead firms that are strong in both financial and organisational terms, and which have a secure position within their sector, globally as well as nationally. In principle, that could be a local firm. In practice, it is nearly always a foreign firm. When we add in the dimension of technology spillover through networks, the role of foreign firms becomes essential.

To say that the role of foreign firms in technology spillover through networks is a crucial one is not, however, to say that it is always fulfilled. Foreign investors in the accession countries rarely use local firms as first-tier suppliers. On the other hand, many first-tier suppliers are, in fact, joint ventures between established Western suppliers and local firms, located in the host country. This may not be ideal from the technology transfer point of view, and may indeed tend to reinforce the tendency for FDI not to develop local R&D and design capabilities. Havas is clear, however, that, in the case of the automotive industry at least, "it is not feasible to 'raise' — or keep alive — 'national' first-tier suppliers" (1999, p. 37). The implication is that the role of second-tier/third-tier supplier is the best the transition countries — even those leading transition countries now preparing for entry into the EU in May 2004 — can hope for right now, and that wholly-owned first-tier suppliers will come later, once local firms have moved up the learning curve a bit and basic technological congruence has been established. This is a plausible enough argument, but we must enter one caveat. Second- and third-tier suppliers are generally in a weak market position, because what they do can generally be done equally well by a large number of other firms. This leaves them open to abuse of market position by lead firms or first-tier suppliers, and there have been some striking cases of such abuse in the accession countries (Havas, 1999, p. 34). Abuse of monopoly power kills trust, and therefore destroys the capacity of supply networks to generate increases in social capability. It excludes by definition any significant transfer of technology, since it involves treating suppliers as commodity producers.

It is not clear that accession will significantly affect any of these points. Shared membership of the EU will do little to reinforce the cultural foundations of trust in the broadest sense. But it will make it easier to build the more specific kind of trust on which supplier networks rely, in part because it will facilitate and simplify the formal, contractual side of networking and the paperwork of international deliveries. In the end, however, choices by lead firms of first-tier suppliers are taken essentially on technological grounds, and the *acquis communautaire* has little to say about technology as such. Introduction of EU competition law into the acceding countries could in principle help to defend second- and third-tier suppliers against crude exploitation, but the principle is unlikely to be implemented unless major strides are made towards strengthening local capabilities in the areas of commercial and competition law. *International production networks* (IPNs), built around key elements of intellectual property and designed to access heterogeneous capabilities across frontiers

(Borrus & Zysman, 1997), are bound to expand their activities in East European countries as the latter accede to the EU, possibly creating a new, technologically sophisticated, form of outward processing. But IPNs were initially developed — with great success — by American companies in East Asia, where there are no common markets and where intellectual property regimes are weak and non-standardised. So there are no strong grounds for arguing that in the East European case accession will be a *critical* factor in the development of IPNs. As in relation to FDI *per se*, therefore, we have to conclude our discussion of supply networks on a cautious note. Development of supply networks could be a major factor of catch-up in the accession countries. But that development is likely to take place over a very long period, with no dramatic acceleration following enlargement, and significant shortfalls in social capability on this dimension will persist for the foreseeable future.

CONCLUSIONS

Analysis of the potential growth effects of EU eastwards enlargement on the acceding countries suggests figures which dwarf even the most optimistic estimates of the impact of short-run trade, scale economies and competition factors. But realisation of that potential depends on the capacity of the acceding countries to absorb new technologies, and on the active presence of organisations capable of diffusing technology and generating technological spillovers, and of financing all these activities. While there are no insuperable difficulties in relation to any of this, all of the accession countries *in practice* suffer from significant deficiencies of social capability and significant levels of technological incongruence, factors likely to impede the process of institutionalisation of technology diffusion. This conclusion emerges strongly from a line of analysis based mainly on a fairly narrow understanding of the concept of social capability. Broadening out the picture to take full account of the dimensions of culture, civil society and trust can only strengthen it further. Membership of the EU will be an important enabling factor in the resolution of the difficulties identified. But it will not provide an immediate solution to any of them.

Governments and firms must take positive steps to take advantage of the new possibilities, if the prospect of catch-up for Central-East Europe is not to be banished to the very long term, and if eastwards enlargement is not to impose intolerable distributional strains on the European Union.

REFERENCES

Abramovitz, MA (1979). Rapid growth potential and its realization: The experience of the capitalist countries in the postwar period. In *Economic Growth and Resources*, Vol. I, E Malinvaud (ed.). London and New York: Macmillan Press.

——— (1994). The origins of the postwar catch-up and convergence boom. In *The Dynamics of Technology, Trade and Growth*, J Fagerberg *et al.* (eds.). Aldershot: Edward Elgar.

Balázs, K (1996). *Academic Entrepreneurs and their Role in Knowledge Transfer*. STEEP Discussion Paper No. 37, SPRU, University of Sussex.

Baldwin, R (1989). The growth effects of 1992. *Economic Policy*, 9, 247–81.

Baldwin, R, J Francois and R Portes (1997). The costs and benefits of eastern enlargement: The impact on the EU and central Europe. *Economic Policy*, 24, 125–76.

Borrus, M and J Zysman (1997). Globalisation with borders: The rise of Wintelism as the future of industrial competition. In *Enlarging Europe: The Industrial Foundations of a New Political Reality*, J Zysman and A Schwartz (eds.). University of California at Berkeley.

Cowie, H (1999). *Venture Capital in Europe*. London: Federal Trust.

Dyker, DA (1999). Foreign direct investment in transition countries: A global perspective. In *Foreign Direct Investment and Technology Transfer in the Former Soviet Union*, DA Dyker (ed.). Cheltenham: Edward Elgar.

Dyker, DA and S Kubielas (2000). Technology and structure in the Polish economy under transition and globalisation. *Economic Systems*, 24(1), 1–24.

Economic Commission for Europe (ECE) (1998). *Economic Survey of Europe, 1998, No. 1*. New York and Geneva: United Nations.

——— (1999). *Economic Survey of Europe, 1999, No. 1*. New York and Geneva: United Nations.

——— (2000). *Economic Survey of Europe, 2000, No. 1*. New York and Geneva: United Nations.

——— (2003). *Economic Survey of Europe, 2003, No. 1*. New York and Geneva: United Nations.

European Bank for Reconstruction and Development (EBRD) (1998). *Transition Report 1998*, London.

———— (1999). *Transition Report 1999*. London.

———— (2002). *Transition Report 2002*. London.

Ferguson, A (1996). *An Essay on the History of Civil Society*, edited by Fania Oz-Salzberger. CUP.

Fukuyama, F (1995). *Trust: The Social Virtues and the Creation of Prosperity*. Harmondsworth, Middlesex: Penguin.

Gellner, E (1995). *Bedingungen der Freiheit: Die Zivilgesellschaft und ihre Rivalen*. Stuttgart: Klett-Cotta.

Gower, P (1997). *Banking Development in the Czech Republic: An Analysis of Credit Allocation*. D.Phil. thesis, University of Sussex.

Gokhberg, L (1999). The transformation of R&D in the post-socialist countries. In *Innovation and Structural Change in Post-Socialist Countries: A Quantitative Approach*, DA Dyker and S Radošević (eds.). Dordrecht: Kluwer.

Harter, S (1998). *The Civilianisation of the Russian Economy: A Network Approach*. D.Phil. thesis, University of Birmingham, U.K.

Havas, A (1996). Foreign direct investment and intra-industry trade: The case of the automotive industry in Central Europe. In *The Technology of Transition: Science and Technology Policies for Transition Countries*, DA Dyker (ed.). Budapest: Central European University Press.

Havas, A (1999). *Changing Patterns of Inter- and Intra-regional Division of Labour: Central Europe's Long and Winding Road*. Budapest: mimeo.

Holmes, P (1999). The political economy of the European integration process. In *The European Economy*, 2nd Ed., DA Dyker (ed.). Harlow: Longman.

Inzelt, A-M (1999). The transformation role of FDI in R&D: Analysis based on material from a data bank. In *Innovation and Structural Change in Post-Socialist Countries: A Quantitative Approach*, DA Dyker and S Radošević (eds.). Dordrecht: Kluwer.

Jasinski, A (1997). *Academy-Industry Relations for Innovation in Poland*. STEEP Discussion Paper No. 41, SPRU, University of Sussex, August.

Koch, EB (1998). Banking sector reform in the transition economies — a central banking perspective. In *Economic Survey of Europe 1998 No. 2*, pp. 67–81. New York and Geneva: Economic Commission for Europe, United Nations.

Kozlowski, J and D Ircha (1999). The structure of disciplinary comparative advantage in post-communist countries. In *Innovation and Structural Change in Post-Socialist Countries: A Quantitative Approach*, DA Dyker and S Radošević (eds.). Dordrecht: Kluwer.

Landes, D (1998). *The Wealth and Poverty of Nations: Why Some are so Rich and Some are so Poor*. New York and London: W.W.Norton.

Meske, W (1999). Transformation of R&D in central and eastern Europe: Asset or liability? In *Innovation and Structural Change in Post-Socialist Countries: A Quantitative Approach*, DA Dyker and S Radošević (eds.). Dordrecht: Kluwer.

Pavitt, K (1996). National policies for technological change: Where are the increasing returns to economic research? *Proc. of the National Academy of Sciences USA*, 93(12), 693–12, 700, November.

Pellegrin, J (1999). *German Production Networks in Central/Eastern Europe*. WSB-Berlin Discussion Paper FS 1 99-304, January.

Putnam, R *et al. Making Democracy Work: Civic Traditions in Modern Italy.* Princeton, NJ: Princeton University Press.

Raiser, M (1999). *Trust in Transition*. EBRD Working Paper No. 39. London.

Sagari, S and G Guidotti (1992). *Venture Capital: Lessons from the Developed World for the Developing Markets*. Washington: International Finance Corporation, The World Bank.

Senker, J and W Faulkner (1995). *Knowledge Frontiers: Public Sector Research and Industrial Innovation in Biotechnology, Engineering Ceramics, and Parallel Computing*. Oxford: Clarendon Press.

Smith, A and M Gasiorek (1999). Measuring the effects of "1992". In *The European Economy*, 2nd Ed., DA Dyker (ed.). Harlow: Longman.

Stanovnik, P, B Majcen and V Lavrac (1999). *Country Report: Slovenia*. Paper presented to workshop *Winners and Losers of EU Integration in Central and Eastern Europe*, Budapest.

Stehrer, R and M Landesmann (1999). *Convergence Patterns at the Industrial Level: The Dynamics of Comparative Advantage*. WIIW Working Paper No. 11, October.

Urem, B (1999). R&D behaviour of firms in transition economies: An analysis of the key determinants. In *Innovation and Structural Change in Post-Socialist Countries: A Quantitative Approach*, DA Dyker and S Radošević (eds.). Dordrecht: Kluwer.

Verspagen, B (1999). A global perspective on technology and economic performance. In *Innovation and Structural Change in Post-Socialist Countries: A Quantitative Approach*, DA Dyker and S Radošević (eds.). Dordrecht: Kluwer.

Warren, M (ed.) (1999). *Democracy and Trust*. Cambridge: CUP.

World Bank (2000). *World Development Report 2003*. Washington DC.

Zahradnik, P (1999). Banks in the Czech republic: Current state and prospects. In *Capital Markets in Central and Eastern Europe*, C Helmenstein (ed.). Cheltenham: Edward Elgar.

Chapter 7

"East"-"West" Networks and their Alignment: Industrial Networks in Hungary and Slovenia

INTRODUCTION

Industrial Networks in the Context of Economic Transition

Traditional microeconomics has been dominated by the concept of the *firm*. Firms have been viewed as discrete organisations, relating to each other through the medium of arm's-length trade, and maintaining an absolute distinction between internal and external domains. Recognition in the post-war period of the growing importance of international firms has seen the development of theories of foreign direct investment (FDI) to supplement the traditional theory of the firm, but transnational corporation (TNC) theory has largely held fast to the traditional view of the firm in that it has interpreted foreign investment primarily as a means of extending the domain of internalisation across international borders (Dunning, 1988).

Over the past decade or so there has been a growing recognition that in the real world of contemporary business the patterns of linkage between companies may be at least as important as the companies themselves, and that those patterns may involve forms of transaction and business relationship which defy neat pigeon-holing as either internal or external. Buyer-supplier relations are fundamental to the working of a market economy. Economic activity, however, is not a simple matter of supply and demand in perfect markets without interaction/transaction costs. In a real economy buyers and suppliers have to communicate to each other their delivery requirements, what they can provide, what help they can offer in producing something new, what time scales are involved, what terms of payment are acceptable, and so on, all in a volatile environment where they do not know exactly how much they will need, what future prices will be like, and how reliable their partner really is. Relationships that help to overcome market uncertainties and aid in communicating needs and capabilities can, indeed must, develop between buyers and suppliers. The basis, depth, breadth and development of these links may vary depending on the environment in which companies are embedded.

In developing the theory of international production networks (IPNs), scholars like Zysman (Zysman & Schwartz, 1997) have argued that global business is increasingly dominated by networks, based not on equity ownership as such, but rather on ownership of intellectual property rights and control over key technologies. Research on patterns of regional development has highlighted the importance of localised networks as vehicles for the exploitation of external economies of scale. And networks have also been pinpointed as key instruments of technology transfer, and hence of innovation, involving public- or semi-public-sector actors like government agencies and universities as well as firms as such (Freeman & Soete, 1997). Finally, supply networks have been identified as key elements in the success of the newly industrialising countries (NICs) of East Asia (Hobday, 1995). The ambivalent nature of networks in terms of the internalisation/externalisation dichotomy is highlighted by the range of socio-legal bases used as a framework for their operation. Contracts can be important, but networks are often based as much on trust (such as one would normally find *within* a company) as on formal legal commitments.

All of these dimensions of industrial networking are of particular importance in the context of transition from communism. The ex-communist countries are, in a sense, NICs *manqué*. Communist development strategy was essentially based on industrial development, with clearly defined sectoral priorities (primarily on heavy industry) and strong (if in practice not very clear) ideas about how different enterprises should relate to each other in hierarchical terms. The Soviet Union and the GDR were notable for their development of the *ob"edinenie* (association)/*kombinat* principle, under which groups of cognate enterprises were brought together in pyramidal structures with highly centralised formal structures, in keeping with the principles of centralised, command planning which generally informed the planning systems of those countries. In practice these industrialised pyramids were rather less centralised than they were supposed to be, because the centralised system could not cope with the realities of industrial supply without some help from "grey" market elements (Dyker, 1992). Under Yugoslav market socialism, which prevailed in Slovenia until 1991, similar pyramids were established within the framework of "complex organisations of associated labour" (*sestavljene organizacije združenega dela — SOZD*) and "basic organisations of associated labour" (*temeljne organizacije združenego dela — TOZD*) (Dyker, 1990). In Hungary the 1970s witnessed a process of concentration of industrial production capacity in bigger enterprises, a process that was then, to a degree, reversed in the 1980s, though big enterprises remained dominant. These policy themes were played out against the background of a varied organisational structure, with trusts, associations and big enterprises heading a variety of hierarchies involving different patterns of mutual dependence and inter-firm linkage. Details apart, Yugoslav/Slovenian and Hungarian hierarchies were generally flatter than in the Soviet/East German case, because they formed part of national economic systems based, to a degree, on market principles, and the primary units within industrial pyramids retained a substantial degree of operational independence in Yugoslavia and Hungary. Mainly for that reason, supply networks in Hungary and Yugoslavia developed in a qualitatively different way from the more conventional, centrally-planned, socialist systems. But there were other differences as well. In Hungary, many of the most successful conglomerates were in the agricultural and food sectors, in despite of traditional communist priorities. And in

Slovenia, one of the most prominent SOZDs was the electronics giant Iskra, which managed to maintain competitiveness in a sector in which most of the communist economies were notoriously weak. Iskra's annual exports in the 1980s averaged around $400 m. Some of this went to Western markets, and although the question of price competitiveness is clouded by the complex system of tariffs and export incentives in force in the old Yugoslavia, there can be no doubt that Iskra products were competitive, in terms of quality, on those markets.

Formal industrial hierarchies were reinforced, sometimes to a degree modified, by Communist Party links and "old boys" networks' going back, in many cases, to the period of the Second World War. The result was structures with very powerful linkages — at their most powerful in the military-industrial complex (Harter, 1998). But while the *linkages* were strong, the *nodes* were weak. Communist industrial networks transferred little technology or know-how, because the nodes involved had little knowledge, tacit[1] or otherwise, that was worth transferring, and because they were not plugged into the international networks which tend to provide the most powerful conduits of technology transfer. There were exceptions, particularly in the market-socialist countries. The Iskra network in Yugoslavia/Slovenia did provide significant channels of technology interchange, and there were a few islands of such interchange in the Hungarian pharmaceuticals industry. But the typical industrial network in Hungary or Yugoslavia was no more dynamic than the typical network in the Soviet Union. And the static nature of most networks was reflected in the universal crisis of productivity which overtook the entire communist bloc[2] in the 1970s and 1980s, and which was one of the main underlying reasons for the collapse of the communist economic systems.

---

[1]Tacit knowledge is knowledge that cannot be transferred through conventional means such as license documentation and training manuals. It is embedded in a particular organisation or a particular group of people, and can only be transferred through continual, hands-on contact between transferer and transferee. See Rosenberg and Frischtag, 1985, Preface.

[2]China is an exception for reasons that do not require detailed discussion in the present context.

Transition, Transformation and Network Realignment

In studying the development/redevelopment of industrial networks in the transition period, we are seeking to identify the extent to which industrial networks do, or may, contribute to the redynamisation of the economies concerned — the reestablishment of efficient channels of technology transfer, the reinforcement of upward trends in productivity, the reintegration of regional industrial complexes, including those that cut across international borders, and effective reintegration into global economic processes. We are also looking to situate this process of redevelopment within the framework of the broader emerging pattern of "East"-"West" network alignment. In that context we are aiming to situate the Hungarian and Slovenian firm in relation to markets, in relation to an overlapping complex of local, national and global networks, and in relation to the EU and the Hungarian and Slovenian states (see Fig. 1 below). The research is based on broad engagement by the authors in the process of industrial transformation in the target countries and a wide reading of the industrial organisation literature from those countries, reinforced by c.50 in-depth company interviews from each of them.

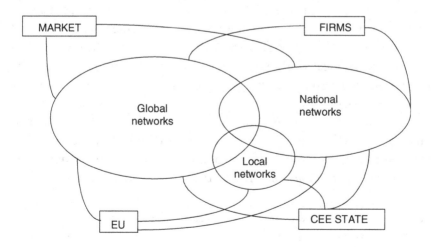

Fig. 1. "East"-"West" networks and their alignment.

MARKETS AND NETWORKS: CONTRACTS, TRUST AND THE MEANING OF CLOSE COOPERATION

Trust and Contracts

To what extent are supply networking relationships in Hungary and Slovenia driven by trust and embodied in informal commitments, rather than in the formal commitments of contracts and legal recourse? The theoretical literature on trust suggests that the formal and informal aspects of business negotiation are essentially complementary.

> The more *formal* processes of negotiation, transaction, and administration associated with most business transactions are also accompanied by *informal* processes of sense-making, understanding, and committing. The informal processes that take place in each of these formal stages of putting together a business deal provide opportunities for economic actors to directly experience the observance of norms such as equity or reciprocity (Ring, 1997, pp. 129–30).

Still, consideration of the general weakness of legal and institutional structures in the former communist countries might lead us to expect a less balanced view of formal and informal aspects of business negotiation in our two target countries. In fact, our interviews provided a very strong affirmation of Ring's view of the complementarity of formal and informal aspects. Trust and contracts emerged as in no sense alternatives.[3] In an ideal world you would have both. Trust is certainly the most important thing, particularly for smaller firms, but however much trust there is, there is no harm in having a contract as well, even if it is an essentially open-ended contract which can be modified to take account of changing circumstances as cooperation between the firms concerned develops. The key point is that contracts are uniformly seen as *codifications of trust*, rather than as threats. As such, they do

---

[3]There is a degree of "spread" around this modal view of the matter in the interviews. But where interviewees expressed strong views to the effect that either contracts or trust were more important in one response, they often contradicted this position in other responses.

not offer the networking firm options, but simply allow him to reinforce and "cap" an essentially informal relationship with a formal layer.

In one sub-group of the interview sets the picture is somewhat different. Relations between foreign owners (a very important group in Hungary) and their subsidiaries are articulated largely on the basis of standard and special contracts, in accordance with circumstances, and there is little evidence of any kind of special relationship going beyond contracts. Even here, however, there is no impression of contracts being seen as a *substitute* for trust. Rather the general principle is that firms trust other firms because they have trusted them in the past and have had no reason to regret that trust. The interview material in relation to foreign firms and their subsidiaries suggests that this is a process that takes time, even when you actually *own* the firm whose trust is in question. It also implies that the dialectic of trust and formal commitment may be significantly different in the case of international networks from that of national and local ones.

The Relationship Between Closeness of Cooperation and Depth of Cooperation

A priori reasoning would suggest that *close* cooperation, defined in terms of cooperation in R&D, would normally imply *deep* cooperation, defined in terms of a sharing of strategic management functions.[4]

---

[4]The distinction between close and deep cooperation appears frequently in the literature, but the terminology used varies from author to author. Lundvall (1992), Dosi (1988), Avadikyan *et al.* (1993), Storper (1994) and Sabel (1994) stress the importance of "learning networks", i.e., networks which involve not just R&D, but *innovation*. Inzelt (1999), in her study of R&D cooperation in Hungary, distinguishes between "skin-deep" and "root-and-branch" cooperation. In discussing learning networks, Sabel also uses the term *thickness* to describe the capacity of a network to raise the performance levels of participants through critical transfers of knowledge; see also Bianchi and Miller (1994) and Dei Ottati (1994). Tanaka (1998) describes "accumulated technology zones" in Japan within which 'information and experiences, new technical knowledge and orders from outside are circulated to each other ... even by walking or bicycling ... Waves of product innovations have been supported by process innovation based on this networking" (p. 122).

In conditions of transition, however, the picture may not be so simple. Firms may engage in R&D cooperation as part of a short-term survival strategy oriented exclusively to the domestic market, while the R&D activity of foreign-owned firms may be largely geared to the adaptation of existing designs and products for specific markets or clients (Inzelt, 1999). A classic example of close cooperation that does, indeed, mean deep cooperation is provided by one of our Slovenian interviewees, which we will refer to as SL-41. SL-41 cooperates closely with its suppliers on the design of components, and with its clients in the design of final products. Cooperation is continual, with frequent face-to-face meetings, maximising the scope for the transfer of tacit knowledge, and technological cooperation with buyers is intimately connected with the transfer of knowledge about market conditions from buyers to the firm. One of the Hungarian firms interviewed (let us give it the code name HU-15) shows a rather different pattern. Here is a classic first-tier supplier, 100 per cent foreign-owned, which has, up to now, practised very close, and deep, R&D cooperation with the lead firm. But the tendency is for the depth of R&D cooperation to *diminish*, with plans to set up a separate R&D centre at HU-15 in 2001. And this is happening because the lead firm and owner of HU-15 see it as a way of increasing the overall R&D *effectiveness* of the whole group.

SUPPLY HIERARCHIES AND NETWORK ALIGNMENTS

The Relationship Between Closeness of Cooperation and Position in the Hierarchy of Supply

Just as the relationship between closeness of cooperation and depth of cooperation is a complex one, so the relationship between closeness of cooperation and the hierarchy of supply relationships is not straightforward. If we think in terms of classic three-level hierarchies,[5] we would expect that second- and third-tier suppliers could be involved in anything from close to minimal cooperation. Our interviews did, indeed, confirm that hypothesis. *A priori* reasoning suggests that

---

[5]See Chapter 4, fn. 6; see also Chapter 6.

first-tier suppliers would, *ipso facto*, be involved in close cooperation. In this case, however, the interviews present a more complex picture than indicated by the *a priori* reasoning. There is certainly a clear relationship between product complexity and intensity of cooperation, stronger on the buyer than on the supplier side, and that makes sense in *a priori* terms if we think of first-tier suppliers as companies that design and make complex, customised products. But there are individual case studies that diverge sharply from this picture. Thus a Slovenian interviewee (SL-15), which makes alternators, starter motors and DC motors for the car industry, is a first-tier supplier which collaborates on R&D with its suppliers, but not with its customers. The reason for this, however, is not the weakness of its R&D profile, but rather its *strength*. SL-15 is powerful enough in R&D to be able to exercise the design and R&D function independently of its main buyers, though always with the specific requirements of those buyers in mind. And there is an added twist to this story, which brings into sharp relief the technological dynamism which so often underlies the evolution of supply networks. SL-15 is technologically independent now, but it began its technological odyssey by taking out licenses from an international firm which is, today, one of its main buyers, a firm which has indeed, been reluctant to transfer more than the minimum amount of technology to its suppliers. SL-15's success in building a position of technological independence on the basis of this modest beginning echoes the experience of Japanese and Korean firms in the 1960s and 1970s (Bell, 1997, p. 68). Moving back to the case of HU-15, it is clear that if the policy of developing separate R&D at HU-15 is taken to its logical conclusion, HU-15 could cease to have even close, never mind deep, R&D cooperation with its lead company and owner. Matters are in practice unlikely to go that far. However strong HU-15 becomes in relation to R&D, it will always need to be able to exchange tacit knowledge with the lead company, and that is impossible without close cooperation. Furthermore, while development of the separate identity of HU-15's R&D activity may mean less intensive cooperation as such, it is likely to deepen the R&D *division of labour* between HU-15 and the other companies in its group.

Patterns of Supply Hierarchy, Levels of Economic Development and Ownership Patterns

Detailed perusal of the interviews brought out one very striking and interesting difference between our two target countries. While there are one or two domestically-owned first-tier suppliers in Hungary, they are a rare breed, and only one of them was included in the interview set. In Slovenia, by contrast, we found a number of domestically-owned companies operating as first-tier suppliers to foreign companies within the interview set. This is no doubt in part a reflection of the fact that general levels of social productivity, as reflected in GDP per capita, is substantially higher in Slovenia than it is in Hungary.[6] But it is particularly interesting that all of the Slovenian-owned first-tier suppliers are daughter-companies of the old, communist-era electronics giant Iskra. It seems, then, that specific elements of know-how and human capital inherited from *particular companies* developed during the previous period may have been a crucial factor in establishing first-tier-supplier status here. These inferences find support in independent, sector-specific case studies. Thus Havas (1999) concludes, on the basis of a case study of the automotive industry in Hungary, Poland, and the Czech Republic, that "indigenous suppliers cannot survive without a foreign partner — with which they have long-term contracts — or being taken over...At least some of them, however, can perform much higher value-added tasks, by exploring and continually developing their skill base, as partners of, or acquired by, foreign-owned first- or second-tier suppliers...One thing is sure...It is not feasible to 'raise' — or keep alive — 'national' first-tier suppliers." (pp. 36–7). Bleak as this assessment may sound, it does hold out hope that the economies concerned may, as dynamic economies, hope to pass the crucial threshold within the next few years.[7]

Can foreign-owned first-tier suppliers help domestically-owned firms to achieve that status? Hungary is a particularly useful reference

---

[6]Slovenia's GDP per capita was $9,780 in 2001, compared to a corresponding figure for Hungary of $4,800 (World Bank data).
[7]For a discussion of the growth prospects of these economies, see Chapter 6.

country in relation to this question because it has so many foreign-owned firms. Where foreign owners compel their subsidiaries to give preference to suppliers within the group (which usually means a foreign supplier), the answer is clearly no. But where foreign-owned first-tier suppliers have their origin in privatisation of existing firms rather than greenfield developments, the general pattern is for them to retain their supply network links with domestic companies. An example is a foreign-owned Hungarian firm which we interviewed, and which we will refer to as HU-2. That company clearly perceives its own business interest in raising its suppliers from the status of *lohnarbeiter* to that of independent, second-tier suppliers. But it does not help them to address the task of progressing from the status of independent second-tier supplier to that of first-tier supplier. HU-15 has used its market power to force second-tier suppliers to raise their game, and conducts joint R&D operations with its most important supplier — but that supplier is, in fact, owned by the same international company that owns HU-15! Another Hungarian interviewee (alias HU-38) is an outstanding, foreign-owned, first-tier supplier, but all of its own main suppliers are also foreign-owned. While foreign-owned first-tier suppliers differ widely, therefore, in their strategies *vis-à-vis* other suppliers, there is no evidence from our interviews to suggest that they do much to help domestic firms win promotion to a higher level within the supply hierarchy.

Can a foreign-owned second-tier supplier use its links with an international group to help it to develop into a first-tier supplier? One Hungarian firm we interviewed (alias HU-18) started off as an outward processor before establishing itself as in internationally competitive producer of advanced auto components like automotive cables and car radios. It is now aiming to progress from technical cooperation with its main customer — its owner — to the establishment of an independent R&D system, which should provide a foundation for the achievement of first-tier-supplier status while at the same time reducing the degree of technical cooperation with the owner company. Another Hungarian interviewee (we called it HU-27) has, under foreign ownership, moved up from the status of second-tier to that of first-tier supplier in the sector of electronic valves. It has, at the same time, tended to move away from its parent company, while simultaneously conducting an explicit policy of developing domestic Hungarian third-tier suppliers. So our answer to this second question is more positive than our answer to the first.

How Important is it to be a First-tier Supplier?

As the cases of HU-15 and SL-15 illustrate graphically, to be a first-tier supplier is to be, in a sense, a "champion" of the supply networks — to participate actively in the generation and exchange of new scientific and technical knowledge, to develop new product lines, to engage in the matrix of supply relations at the points where the scope for the exploitation of quasi-rents is at its highest. You can be a market leader at home and abroad as a second-tier supplier, but you are condemned to remain a kind of commodity supplier. It must be remembered, however, that there are no first-tier suppliers without supply hierarchies, and the notion of supply hierarchy has been developed very much on the basis of the patterns prevalent in the key automotive and electronics industries. Some of the companies we interviewed live in a much simpler world. A prime example is alias HU-21, a firm producing medical equipment for prosthesis and implantation. HU-21 is the leading company of its kind in Hungary, and operates a system of continuous innovation. It is a paragon of "nimbleness", being able to deliver complex products within a few hours of order — clearly a crucial business advantage in an area of medical technology where an hour may represent the difference between life and death. It encourages its main clients — doctors — to become actively involved in its R&D programmes. HU-21 is one of Hungary's top companies, and it is 100 per cent domestically owned. It is a key technology networker, admittedly within a small and highly specialised area. But it will never show up as a first-tier supplier because it is, in fact, a first-, second- and third-tier supplier rolled into one.

Networking and Outward Processing

Outward-processing agreements have played a key role in the globalisation of the CEECs during the 1990s, and have been of particular importance in relation to German business involvement in Poland, for example, where equity ownership raises political problems. Thus German OPT with Poland accounted for over 30 per cent of total EU15 OPT with the CEE-4 (Poland, Hungary, the Czech Republic and Slovakia) in 1996 (Pellegrin, 1999, p. 4). OPT agreements were in the first instance designed to exploit the scope for gaining exemption from tariffs on goods imported into the EU in cases where the materials used in the manufacture of the goods concerned had been exported from the EU in the first place. But while there has been some levelling-off in volumes of OPT in recent years, as trade liberalisation has reduced the value of such exemptions, the OPT trade category remains an important one for the CEECs.

The sectors involved are usually low-technology sectors, where R&D hardly comes into the question. Thus in 1996 textiles and clothing, footwear and furniture, together accounted for nearly 75 per cent of total OPT re-imports into the EU (Pellegrin, 1999, p. 6). That is not to say that outward processing relationships involve no transfer of "soft" management and organisational technology from lead firm to collaborating firm. But it does mean that lead firms do not consider it necessary, in the context of relatively simple production technologies, to internalise the determinants of labour productivity through acquisition of the supplying firm. Here lead firms are basically looking for cheap labour, confident that collaborating firms can keep control of labour productivity — and knowing that if they fail to do so, the financial loss will be theirs, not the lead firm's. None of this is to suggest that there is nothing in outward-processing deals in traditional sectors for the collaborating firm. It does gain access, even if only indirect, to international markets, and it can, with shrewd management, gain much more in the way of technology transfer than the lead firm might consider minimally necessary.

Where cross-border business relationships in other sectors take an OPT form, the content of the relationship may be much more dynamic and far-reaching. The one "middle-tech" sector which figures significantly in the aggregate statistics for OPT is electrical machinery, which accounted for 13.6 per cent of total OPT re-imports into the EU in 1996 (Pellegrin, 1999, p. 6). And here case material demonstrates the possibility of OPT-based trajectories which may take firms a long-way beyond the basic OPT model.

The case of Vilati (Budapest) is illuminating in this respect. Vilati is a small company producing control systems, printed circuit boards and other electrical and electronic components. Although it has several OPT partners, Vilati has a privileged relation with Brunswick Bowling (US). It is integrated into the production chain of its main OPT partner in a rather flexible way, but it does not purport to recover independence, nor does it count on integrating its partner's production chain and upgrad[ing] its position within it. In fact, if Vilati is more loosely associated to its foreign partners than if it were full integrated, this is not to say that its relations are more fragile, or unstable. Its strategy is indeed to establish its reputation as reliable and technologically updated supplier of component system[s] to Original Equipment Manufacturers [OEM]. In this case OPT is used as a vehicle for implementing methods of production in line with the new requirements of international competition in terms of flexibility and quality. OPT goes together with the automisation and the decomposition of the production process into stages which are more independent and "de-integrated" from one another (Pellegrin, 1999, p. 16).

Material from the interviews provides striking confirmation of Pellegrin's interpretation of middle-tech OPT, and suggest that it may extend beyond the area of electrical machinery. Thus a Slovenian interviewee which we will refer to as SL-35 is a classic instance of outward processing in the sense that its main supplier is also its main buyer. But SL-35 makes highly sophisticated plastic products for biomedicine, mostly for dialysis. And while the initial competitive advantage of SL-35 in OPT was very much based on cheap labour, the company has learned, as real wages have risen in Slovenia, to shift the emphasis to quality and flexibility. A similar story is unfolding with another Slovenian company (alias SL-43), a second-tier supplier of auto parts, specialising in driver seats, which has, over less than a decade, worked up from a straight OPT position to one whereby the buyer is looking to pursue joint development with the firm. HU-2, which produces coupler heads and trailer parts, is the only firm in Hungary that produces such parts to the given level of technology and precision, and it exports under its own name. But in addition it has an OPT relationship with a foreign firm which is also its part- (50 per cent) owner, with the foreign firm selling some of HU-2's output under *its* trademark. Interestingly, HU-2 also has OPT-type relations with its own domestic suppliers, in the sense that it procures materials for them as well as buying their output. But it sees this arrangement as purely temporary. Again, the impression is that OPT is an essentially functional arrangement, which may correspond to a particular stage in the development of a firm, but which can be quickly jettisoned by mutual consent as conditions change. Changes in corporate policy *vis-à-vis* OPT can be quite dramatic, and far-reaching in their implications. Thus in 1999, a Hungarian manufacturer of complex pieces of machinery (alias HU-19), decided to hive off OPT operations into a separate company, cutting the total workforce by 50 per cent in the process (though there had been no significant increase in real wages over the previous few years). Even where the OPT stance of a particular company is in evolution, it rarely involves much that could be described as R&D. But the infrequency of OPT-based R&D cooperation does not mean that OPT generally excludes innovation. Thus one modest Hungarian engineering firm we interviewed (alias HU-25), with half its turnover accounted for by OPT, has still managed to introduce a significant number of new products in recent years. In one key respect, the pattern of OPT among the firms interviewed is quite different from the standard pattern of OPT in low-tech sectors. In those latter sectors, the whole point, for the lead firm, is *not* to get involved in ownership of the suppliers. Among engineering firms, at least in Hungary, firms doing OPT are often wholly or partly owned by the lead firm. This makes sense, because the more technologically complex the activity, the more operations there are that may have to be to some degree internalised to the lead firm if they are to be carried out efficiently. In all this lead firms, and indeed to a degree subsidiary firms, retain much of the flexibility of the basic OPT model, because the subsidiary firms involved are usually small, with modest asset endowments, so that divestment is generally as easy as investment.

These particular case-studies of OPT in engineering sectors cannot be taken to be typical of OPT in general, just as engineering cannot be taken to be typical sectors of the Slovenian and Hungarian economies. But they do demonstrate that there is *scope* within the framework of OPT to develop flexible business relationships which can help collaborating firms to absorb both hard and soft technology from lead firms, to react quickly and sensibly to changes in real wage costs, and to develop product range and quality to the extent that they can come on to international markets as OEM manufacturers. Thus the material from the interview sets confirms that OPT is much more than just a ruse to exploit loopholes in foreign trade regulations, and may survive and indeed develop in an age when those loopholes have ceased to be relevant, as a major vehicle of international supply networking.

Cooperation with Buyers as a Springboard for Upgrading and Innovation

One of the strongest themes to emerge from the research, strongly reinforced by the interview responses, is that of the buyer company as teacher. Buyers are consistently the most important sources of technology transfer, consistently the strongest pressure for increases in operational efficiency. In many cases they provide training courses for suppliers' workforces. The buyer does not, of course, become a teacher through pure altruism. He helps suppliers to become more innovative and more efficient because he demands of them continual reductions in the prices of their supplies. So the systematic transfer of knowledge to suppliers is simply the other side of merciless pressure for cost reduction. From the interviews, we take one medium-sized precision engineering company (alias SL-24) as illustrative of how this process may transform the position of a given firm within the supply hierarchy. Traditionally a producer of meters, chronometers and timers, and one of the top companies in Europe in this market,

SL-24 has found that, with the development of computers, the market for their established specialities is in decline. They have moved over into auto component supply, and aspire to first-tier supplier status, but do not as yet possess the technologies to support that status. Their strategy for acquiring the necessary technologies is essentially based on development of their relationship with their main buyer. Through cooperation with that company they have obtained an enormous amount of knowledge in the area of quality and work organisation, and have been able to introduce the system of continuous improvement. The buyer has also advised them in relation to development of their factory workspace and the introduction of new technology. In a word, SL-24's main buyer has given the Slovenian company an opportunity to overcome a technological and organisational barrier which might otherwise have proved insurmountable.

Cooperation with Buyers as a Vehicle of Market Research/ Information Networking

The teaching role is certainly the loftiest role that buyers play. But it is not the only one. The buyer-teacher is also often the market researcher. Researching Western markets is always a problem for firms from the transition countries with few inherited networks with the West and limited funds. For small firms, researching markets is a problem worldwide. It is hardly surprising, then, that a large number of firms among our interview sets stressed their main buyers as key sources of information on market possibilities. This has important implications for the nature of networks. While at the level of technology and production cooperation they may tend to lock in, at the level of general market information they actually open up new possibilities for supplier firms — at one level internalising or partially internalising "hard" processes, while at an other actually increasing the scope for externalised, market-driven transactions. Owners may play the same role as suppliers of market information — especially when they are foreign owners. Once again a relationship which is in the first instance constraining may at some levels actually increase the firm's effective scope for independent action.

INDUSTRIAL NETWORKS AND THE TRANSITION STATE

Most of the state aid policies currently carried on in Hungary and Slovenia will have to be abandoned on, or even prior to, accession. But there seems to be no reason why Slovenia's *clustering programme* and Hungary's *sub-contracting programme* should not continue. Neither of these programmes has been in operation long enough for assessment of results to be feasible. A few *a priori* points can, however be made, viz.:

- *Clusters in Slovenia*: the proven capacity of the Slovenian economy to support first-tier suppliers means that there is genuine potential to build and reinforce vertically integrated industrial clusters within Slovenia. But the research project underpinning the clustering programme found that not a single one of the identified "production-service systems" actually met the set criteria for a cluster (in terms of the given firm having at least three partners having cooperation with at least another three partners). This reflects the dearth of vertically-integrated big (i.e., effectively transnational) companies in Slovenia which could act as hubs within industrial districts. Given how small Slovenia is, and given that in the developed industrial regions of the world clusters run along main lines of communication rather than being concentrated in "points" (see Veltz, 1991), it hardly needs stressing that effective clustering policy will have to involve effective cooperation between national and EU levels. This seems to be a significant weak point in the Slovenian programme.
- *The Subcontracting Programme in Hungary*: this is primarily an information service aimed at briefing national and international business communities on the capabilities of SMEs in relation to industrial supply. Given the extreme weakness of the old communist system in the field of information, this is, indeed, an important service. But information alone will not help Hungarian firms to graduate to the status of first-tier supplier. The Hungarian subcontracting programme also offers educational and training services. These could be crucial in terms of correcting the imbalances in established education and R&D systems, and therefore helping companies to

make real progress in terms of upgrading their capabilities. In all of this, however, it should be borne in mind that it is generally bigger firms that have the closest cooperation links (this generalization receives strong support from our interview responses). SME development is rightly a policy priority in Hungary, as it is in many other transition countries. But it is clear that SME development is likely to *broaden out* the supply networking base rather than upgrade it.

One very important rider must be added to this *a priori* analysis on the clustering and sub-contracting programmes. Our interviewees were largely negative, often quite scathing, about state programmes for industrial development. The few exceptions were companies which had benefited from specific incentives (usually in the context of foreign investment) or grants for specific purposes like the introduction of a quality control system. Private entrepreneurs are *generally* sceptical about state intervention in the economy, whichever country they come from, and it would be wrong to accept the evaluations of the interviewees on this matter uncritically. But the clustering and sub-contracting programmes will not work without a measure of cooperation from the business community. It is not clear that that cooperation will be forthcoming. What is clear, looking ahead to the next section, is that accession to the EU is unlikely to affect business attitudes to such programmes in any way.

IMPLICATIONS FOR EU ACCESSION

An Overview

A priori reasoning suggests that accession to the European Union by Hungary and Slovenia would automatically strengthen the key networking factors highlighted in this chapter (pages 176–189), viz.:

- Foreign investment makes for close cooperation; EU accession will surely make for more foreign investment.
- Inclusion in the internal market will facilitate exports from Hungary and Slovenia, thus strengthening the "learning through networking" tendency.

- Inclusion in the internal market will, *ipso facto*, make it easier for Slovenian and Hungarian firms to achieve optimum scale of operations, which should be conducive to closer cooperation.
- Membership of the EU for the target countries will make it easier for foreign companies to trust local companies, notably through the extension of the EU intellectual property rights regime to them. This should, again, be conducive to closer cooperation.
- The combined operation of all these factors should make it easier for Hungarian and Slovenian firms to: (a) upgrade their technological level and (b) attain the status of first-tier suppliers.

Each of these points finds support in more general arguments and empirical investigations in relation to the two target countries and to the transition region as a whole, and in the responses to our interviews. In some cases, however, important caveats and riders need to be entered, viz. the following.

Foreign Investment

As Table 3, Chapter 6, shows, Hungary is one of the leaders in the transition region in terms of stock of FDI and cumulative FDI per capita. FDI as a percentage of annual gross fixed capital formation has been consistently above 20 per cent in Hungary throughout the transition period, placing that country firmly within the high-FDI group in world terms. Hungary's outstanding performance on FDI inflow has been a function of a number of factors, notably a favourable legislative regime for FDI and an approach to privatisation which has facilitated sell-offs to large, wealthy (i.e., in most cases foreign) companies. The foreign investment regime has until recently been less favourable in Slovenia than in Hungary, and even now, after the passage of EU-harmonised FDI legislation, enforcement of these new laws on local players remains problematic. The process of privatisation has also been much slower in Slovenia. We should, therefore, not be surprised to find that Slovenia accounts for a relatively modest proportion of total FDI in the region. Yet Slovenia's FDI per capita is still higher than that of Poland, the country with the biggest stock of FDI in the region. There is a strong suggestion here that investors have to a great extent *anticipated* accession of these five countries to the EU, just as governments have to a considerable extent anticipated accession in terms of regulatory and institutional reforms. In the case of Hungary in particular, we should therefore be cautious about predicting a new leap in levels of FDI with accession. Membership of the EU will surely help to ensure that FDI in that country continues to grow, but the impact on the trend line may be minimal. The Slovenian cases is somewhat different. Here, accession will complete the process of change in the laws on foreign investment, and will also involve the dismantling of the system of state aids which has been an important indirect barrier to foreign acquisition of Slovenian companies. Taking the two countries together, however, accession is unlikely to make a dramatic difference to trends in FDI.

Trust

As argued earlier, trust and contracts should not be seen as alternatives. Rather, good contracts, or at least good contract law, makes for trust, while trust, in particular trust in courts, is in turn a key condition for the implementation of the rule of law in the commercial sphere, as in other spheres. How will accession to the European Union strengthen this virtuous circle for Hungarian and Slovenian firms? To the extent that it improves the enforceability of contracts in Hungarian and Slovenian courts, to the extent that in improving and strengthening competition law within those countries it reins in abuse of monopoly power against third-tier suppliers, and to the extent that it fills *lacunae* and removes weaknesses and inconsistencies in domestic regulatory regimes, it should make lead partners, mainly foreign partners, more willing to build close cooperative links with firms from those countries, while at the same time making it more difficult for them to exploit those cooperative links for purely short-term corporate advantage. But we should be cautious about pressing this conclusion too hard. One of the most striking qualitative features to emerge from our interviews is the universal aversion to domestic courts of law as a recourse when firms are let down by partners. Virtually every firm we interviewed declared that such action would only ever be taken as a very last resort. In a word, firms trust their partners, even their bad partners, more than they trust the courts. This distrust of the courts no doubt reflects weaknesses in the regulatory regime as well as in the legal system *per se*. It does, nevertheless, suggest that there is some fundamental deficiency of *social capability* in the Slovenian and Hungarian legal systems. The literature on economic "catch-up" argues that making up for such deficiencies is a long-term process (see Verspagen, 1999). Accession to the EU could reasonably be expected to facilitate and hasten that process, but not to solve the problem in a day. And as long as Slovenian and Hungarian firms remain reluctant to use their own courts of law, foreign firms are likely to remain at least as cautious. To that extent, the nexus of trust and contract enforceability is likely to strengthen gradually rather than dramatically after accession.

The extension of EU intellectual property protection to the target countries should remove a very specific factor which has hindered the development of trust on the part of Western companies *vis-à-vis* Eastern partners up to now. IPNs (see discussion at the beginning of this chapter), built around key elements of intellectual property and designed to access heterogeneous capabilities across frontiers (Borrus & Zysman, 1997), are bound to expand their activities in East European countries as the latter accede to the EU. But IPNs were initially developed — with great success — by American companies in East Asia, where there are no common markets and where intellectual property regimes are weak and non-standardised. So there are no strong grounds for arguing that in the East European case accession will be a *critical* factor in the development of IPNs.

Closeness of Cooperation

Granted that a whole range of accession-related factors will have a positive, indirect impact on closeness of cooperation, we can pose two basic questions:

- Will accession *in itself* make it easier to develop close cooperation?
- Will it become easier to use close cooperation as a springboard for deep cooperation?

It is, in fact, difficult to see how accession *per se* could have a major direct impact on the scope for developing close cooperation. The ability and the readiness to engage in the exchange of tacit knowledge is in the first instance a function of the corporate strategies of the companies involved and the professional ethos and attitudes of their employees, variables hardly likely to be significantly affected by the signature of international treaties. It does also seem to be dependent to an important degree on the degree of *technological congruence* (see Chapters 4 and 6) between the firms involved. A sophisticated German machine-tool company will not, for instance, be interested in setting up close cooperation with a village blacksmith's shop in rural Hungary or Slovenia. And research done on the Polish economy shows that foreign investors in that country have evinced a strong preference for investment in activities based on the same generic technologies as are used in their plants located in more advanced countries (see Chapter 4). Technological congruence is clearly primarily a function of inherited capital, human capital and technology endowments. None of those factors will be significantly affected by the act of accession in itself. But to the extent that accession increases investment by reducing risk premia, as strongly argued by e.g. Baldwin, Francois, and Portes (1997), the rate of replacement of capital stock will accelerate after accession, and this could make technological closeness significantly easier to attain. Our interviews show clearly that close cooperation generally goes together with generosity on the part of lead firms in relation to IPRs, and it will certainly be easier for lead firms to be generous with their intellectual property in CEE once it is protected by EU law in that region. Beyond that, accession may produce a degree of *rapprochement* between the business cultures of Western and Central-East Europe which could facilitate the transfer of tacit knowledge. But this would be a slow process, unlikely to produce any significant impact in the short run.

The same basic arguments apply to the close cooperation/deep cooperation issue. There is clearly no deep cooperation without technological congruence, and if accession makes lead firms feel more secure, in IPR terms, about close cooperation, then surely it will make them feel more secure about deep cooperation. The convergence of business culture factor could be rather more important in relation to deep than to "merely" close cooperation. In addition to encouraging deep cooperation, accession may positively discourage cooperation that is close, but shallow. As our interviews show, that kind of close cooperation is usually part of the survival strategy of a firm intent on subsisting from day to day. By increasing the strength of competition, accession will tend to force firms like that to sink or swim, and this may have a significant impact on the balance of deep and shallow cooperation.

Attaining the Status of First-tier Supplier

Every specific accession-related factor, whether it be improved frameworks for FDI and intellectual property protection, improved access to market or easier optimisation of production capacity, will help firms from Hungary and Slovenia to become first-tier suppliers, because it will increase the willingness of international firms to develop long-term relations with firms from those two countries, because it will remove constraints on the efficient utilisation by the Hungarian and Slovenian firms of their countries' factor endowments, and because it will facilitate integration into the currents of micro-specialisation which have dominated the evolution of the pattern of intra-industry trade within the existing EU over the past four decades. But the evidence from Slovenia and Hungary suggests (though it certainly does not prove) that the capacity to operate as a first-tier supplier is in the first instance a function of levels of aggregate social productivity and firm-specific capabilities. So it is not enough to be able to use your factor endowments efficiently — you may have to *improve* that endowment in order to achieve first-tier-supplier status.

How will accession improve aggregate social productivity? Not through specific impacts, but rather through the positive influence of accession on aggregate growth rates of GDP in the accession countries. There are strong *a priori* arguments for expecting just such an acceleration of economic growth after enlargement. But if the acceleration does not materialise, the macroeconomic conditions for the development of first-tier supplier status will remain problematic. On the microeconomic side, how can accession enhance the capabilities of specific firms? The opening-up of markets, the exploitation of economies of scale will certainly help firms to improve their capabilities as well as to marshall them more efficiently. To the extent that accession produces increased flows of FDI, that will also help. Stricter policing of intellectual property rights probably will, but might not. Where Slovenian and Hungarian firms have had difficulty in defending their own IPRs against predation from outside the EU (mostly from the Far East), membership of the EU should make it easier for them to protect and develop their in-house intellectual property base. Where, however, lead firms are inclined to be restrictive in their IPR policy *vis-à-vis* suppliers in the target countries, EU membership will make it easier for them to be so. As noted in the last sub-section, however, far more of the firms interviewed reported generous IPR policies *vis-à-vis* close collaborators than did the opposite behaviour.

Deficiencies of social capability as discussed above may have a direct effect on levels of social productivity and particular capabilities at firm level. More specifically, weaknesses in the public-sector R&D and education sectors may impose severe constraints on the learning processes which serve as the primary vehicle for the enhancement of, in particular, human capital endowment, at the level of both firm and society. Education systems in the ex-communist countries have struggled to keep up with the demands imposed on them by the process of transformation. But it is R&D systems in particular that have remained stubbornly unreformed through ten years of transition and EU technical assistance (see Chapter 6).

While the process of transition has revolutionised the understanding of the process of innovation, it has failed to revolutionise the configuration of *S&T* among the accession countries. The administration of science is still controlled by the old Academy of Sciences in Hungary, as it is in Poland. In Slovenia the Academy is less important, but structures are still dominated by a conservative scientific lobby. In both countries science managers pursue conservative scientific policies, oriented largely to personal and institutional survival. In Slovenia the business sector is currently the main funder of R&D in the country, but the government continues to finance more than half total GERD in Hungary. In short, much of the inherited *S&T* complex in the Hungary and Slovenia is still waiting to be restructured.

There is no basis for believing that accession to the EU will have any impact on this stubborn problem. So one major obstacle to the enhancement of social productivity and firm-level capabilities, and indirectly to the attainment by companies of first-tier-supplier status, is likely to survive into the long term.

Accession and Outward Processing

As noted earlier, OPT developed initially as a way of exploiting the scope for duty-free export of raw materials from EU countries to CEECs followed by duty-free re-import of the same materials, made up, into the EU. As it blossomed in the early mid-1990s, it was largely restricted to traditional low-tech sectors like textiles, and the prize, for the EU entrepreneurs involved, was access to cheap labour.

Accession to the EU for Hungary and Slovenia will mean the end, not only to tariffs on the interface with the existing Union, but also to the possibility of contingent protection — anti-dumping measures and the like. In that sense, the whole original motive for engaging in OPT will fall away. And with wage levels in the accession countries converging to Western (or at least Southern) European levels after enlargement, the underlying *economic* rationale for OPT will weaken. A strictly "neo-classical" model of OPT might, therefore, predict the total disappearance of this category of trade with, or soon after, accession. The responses to our interviews suggest a rather different path. The essential definition of OPT is the identity of main supplier and main buyer. The interviews show that such an arrangement does not exclude technology transfer and innovation in product lines, and may, indeed, provide a basis for dramatic increases in the levels of capability of the firm concerned in the middle-tech sectors that we are primarily concerned with in this study. Given that, and given that accession to the EU will at least get rid of the complex paperwork associated with OPT at the present time, accession may actually lead to an increase in some types of OPT. But the increase may be short-lived, because, as the interviews strikingly show, the more dynamic the OPT relationship, the more likely it is to evolve into something qualitatively different. We return to this theme in our concluding paragraphs.

Climbing the Technological Ladder

Whatever the difficulties associated with specific networking "milestones" like the attainment of first-tier-supplier status, one of the strongest impressions to come out of our interviews is of a dominant upward mobility in terms of technology, product range, etc. The first decade of transition witnessed a substantial increase in real wages in Slovenia but not in Hungary.[8] Competition at the lower end of the technological ladder from low-wage countries like China has, nevertheless, increased for both of them. So our target countries have discovered a truth which has, indeed, been evident to the developed industrialised countries for many years — that you cannot stand still on the technological ladder; you have to keep moving up, otherwise you go out of business. Supply networking has not shielded Hungarian and Slovenian companies from the competitive pressures which force this upward movement. But it has made the upward movement less painful, because it has facilitated the acquisition of the new technologies which that upward movement requires. Accession to the EU will affect the networking elements conducive to this upgrading process only to a marginal extent. But in unifying markets, including labour markets, it will increase the pressure on companies in Hungary and Slovenia to upgrade further. On the most optimistic scenario, higher wages will simply induce a higher valuation of the existing human capital endowments of the transition countries and greater efforts to ensure, through networking, that those endowments are efficiently marshalled. The downside risk is that the competitive pressures are too powerful, that companies are not strong enough, in themselves and in their networking capacity, to respond positively. In practice, some companies will past the test, others will not. The results of the interviews suggest that the pass rate will be fairly high.

---

[8]Real gross wages in constant US dollars actually fell by 2.5 per cent in Hungary 1992–98, while in Slovenia they rose over the same period by 30.3 per cent — *source*: national statistics.

CONCLUSIONS

How far has our research succeeded in filling the "empty boxes" of Fig. 1? We have evoked a picture of the Hungarian and Slovenian firm as a striving, learning organisation, strongly dependent on an interactive complex of local, national and global networks as a source of information, learning and innovation. The degree and pattern of dependence varies, and Hungarian firms are generally more dependent on global networks than Slovenian. Close cooperation does not always mean deep cooperation, and deep cooperation can sometimes involve a reduction in the level of *dependence* on (N.B. not in that of integration into) global networks. A much more homogeneous picture emerges in relation to the extent of skepticism about the role of the state in relation to network-building. The picture may not be wholly typical — a good deal of our material is anecdotal, and our interview sets not wholly representative. But it is surely accurate for a large number of companies from the target countries.

The policy-related implications of these conclusions are essentially straightforward. Companies will continue to upgrade their firm-specific capabilities in function of their involvement in networks, and of trends in the general level of social productivity and social capability in their respective countries. The impact of national support programmes will be marginal. Accession to the EU will facilitate the strengthening of networks in the target countries through its impact on FDI, IPR regimes and systems of legal recourse. But it will do so by reinforcing existing trends rather than producing breaks in trend. Accession will make it easier for firms from Hungary and Slovenia to develop closeness and depth in their networking relationships, and to achieve first-tier supplier status. But the impact will be gradual rather than dramatic. Accession could well result in a short-term increase in the volume of some types of OPT. In the long-run, however, the impact is likely to be in the opposite direction. In assimilating the Hungarian and Slovenian labour markets to the West European, accession should tend to increase real wages in those countries, which is likely to force their companies to increase the rate at which they climb the technological ladder — as the only alternative to bankruptcy. In a word, the pattern of network alignment and realignment will reflect the interaction of the logic of markets and the imperatives of developing intra-firm capabilities, with the public sector playing a strictly subsidiary role.

REFERENCES

Avadikyan, A *et al.* (1993). *Coherence, Diversity of Assets and Network Learning.* Mimeo, BETA, Strasbourg: Université Louis Pasteur.

Balázs, K (1996). *Academic Entrepreneurs and their Role in Knowledge Transfer.* STEEP Discussion Paper No. 37. SPRU, University of Sussex.

Baldwin, R, J Francois and R Portes (1997). The costs and benefits of eastern enlargement: The impact on the EU and central Europe. *Economic Policy*, 24, 125–76.

Bell, M (1997). Technology transfer to transition countries: Are there lessons from the experience of the post-war industrializing countries? In *The Technology of Transition: Science and Technology Policies for Transition Countries*, DA Dyker (ed.). Budapest: Central European University Press.

Bianchi, P and L Miller (1994). *Innovation, Collective Action and Endogenous Growth: An Essay on Institutions and Structural Change.* Mimeo, Department of Economics, University of Bologna.

Borrus, M and J Zysman (1997). Globalisation with borders: The rise of Wintelism as the future of industrial competition. In *Enlarging Europe: The Industrial Foundations of a New Political Reality*, J Zysman and A Schwartz (eds.). University of California at Berkeley.

Dei Ottati, G (1994). Trust, interlinking transactions and credit in the industrial district. *Cambridge Journal of Economics*, 18(6), 529–46.

Dosi, G (1988). Institutions and markets in a dynamic world. *The Manchester School*, 56, 119–46.

Dunning, JH (1988). *Multinationals, Technology and Competitiveness.* London: Unwin Hyman.

Dyker, DA (1990). *Yugoslavia: Socialism, Development and Debt.* London: Routledge.

―――― (1992). *Restructuring the Soviet Economy.* London: Routledge.

Dyker, DA and S Kubielas (2000). Technology and structure in the Polish economy under transition. *Economic Systems*, 24(1).

Economic Commission for Europe (ECE) (2000). *Economic Survey of Europe 2000 No. 1.* New York and Geneva: United Nations.

Freeman, C and L Soete (1997). *The Economics of Industrial Innovation*, 3rd Ed. London: Pinter.

Gokhberg, L (1999). The transformation of R&D in the post-socialist countries. In *Innovation and Structural Change in Post-Socialist Countries: A Quantitative Approach*, DA Dyker and S Radošević (eds.). Dordrecht: Kluwer.

Harter, S (1998). *The Civilianisation of the Russian Economy: A Network Approach.* D.Phil. thesis, University of Birmingham, U.K.

Havas, A (1999). *Changing Patterns of Inter- and Intra-regional Division of Labour: Central Europe's Long and Winding Road.* Budapest: mimeo.

Hobday, M (1995). *Innovation in East Asia: The Challenge to Japan.* Aldershot: Edward Elgar.

Inzelt, A-M (1999). The transformation role of FDI in R&D: Analysis based on material from a data bank. In *Innovation and Structural Change in Post-Socialist Countries: A Quantitative Approach*, DA Dyker and S Radošević (eds.). Dordrecht: Kluwer.

Jasinski, A (1997). *Academy-Industry Relations for Innovation in Poland.* STEEP Discussion Paper No. 41, SPRU, University of Sussex, August.

Kozlowski, J and D Ircha (1999). The structure of disciplinary comparative advantage in post-communist countries. In *Innovation and Structural Change in Post-Socialist Countries: A Quantitative Approach*, DA Dyker and S Radošević (eds.). Dordrecht: Kluwer.

Lundvall, B-A (ed.) (1992). *National Systems of Innovation.* London: Frances Pinter.

Pavitt, K (1996). National policies for technological change: Where are the increasing returns to economic research?. *Proc. of the National Academy of Sciences USA*, 93(12), 693–12,700, November.

Pellegrin, J (1999). *German Production Networks in Central/Eastern Europe.* WSB-Berlin Discussion Paper FS 1 99–304, January.

Ring, P (1997). Processes facilitating trust in inter-organizational networks. In *The Formation of Inter-Organizational Networks*, M Ebers (ed.). New York: OUP.

Rosenberg, N and C Frischtag (eds.) (1985). *International Technology Transfer: Concepts, Measures and Comparisons.* New York: Praeger.

Sabel, C (1994). Learning by monitoring: the institutions of economic development. In *Handbook of Economic Sociology*, N Smelser and R Swedberg (eds.). Princeton University Press.

Senker, J and W Faulkner (1995). *Knowledge Frontiers: Public Sector Research and Industrial Innovation in Biotechnology, Engineering Ceramics, and Parallel Computing.* Oxford: Clarendon Press.

Storper, M (1994). Territorial economies in a global economy: The challenge to developing countries. *Review of International Political Economy*, 2(3), 394–424.

Tanaka, H (1998). Integration, transformation and modernization in Hungary — an analysis of Hungarian machinery industry. *Kochi University Review of Social Science*, 62, June 1998, 119–45.

Veltz, P (1991). New models of production organisation and trends in spatial development. In *Industrial Change and Regional Development*, G Benko and M Dunford (eds.). London: Belhaven.

Verspagen, B (1999). A global perspective on technology and economic performance. In *Innovation and Structural Change in Post-Socialist Countries: A Quantitative Approach*, DA Dyker and S Radošević (eds.). Dordrecht: Kluwer.

Zysman, J and A Schwartz (1997). *Enlarging Europe: The Industrial Foundations of a New Political Reality.* University of California at Berkeley.

Part V

Technology and Transition

Chapter 8

Key Actors in the Process of Innovation and Technology Transfer in the Context of Economic Transition

INTRODUCTION

Why are innovation and technology transfer such critical factors in the process of economic transition? Quite simply because they were among the weakest elements in the old, communist economic systems from which transition is being made. Communist ideology placed great stress on science and technology — but in a scientistic way that reflected little understanding of the reality of technological processes. Post-war Western capitalism, too, was often guilty of placing too much faith on a linear, "science-push" conception of the technological process which was no more sensitive to the realities of innovation and technology transfer than was Stalinist socialism (Bush, 1946). But the forces of competition — more specifically the impact of a new culture of innovation springing from the ancient cultures of East Asia — ensured that by the 1970s government and business in the West was beginning to understand that "big science" is not the first and last word in the study of patterns of technological dynamism. In Great Britain, where high levels of expenditure on basic science seemed to be systematically correlated with poor economic performance, the point was brought home with particular sharpness. At the same time, science and technology policy analysts began to lay more and more stress on the concept of "tacit" knowledge, which can only be transferred to individuals through extended "insider" activity within key innovation teams.

In the countries of socialism, the forces of political inertia, unchallenged by any form of competition, political or economic, ensured that there would be no such evolution of attitudes to technical change. The parallel failure to institute meaningful economic reform meant that at the level of the firm all the incentives were to fulfil formal "plans" for innovation, rather than do anything to change fundamentally the kinds of products they made, and the ways they made them. The communist system of social control, far from encouraging the formation of small informal groups within which tacit knowledge could be passed on and assimilated, tended to induce passivity, fragmentation and "internal emigration". While every socialist country continued to spend a substantial proportion of its GDP on *S&T*, productivity ceased to grow from the 1970s onwards right across the region. In extreme cases like that of Poland in the 1980s, where special political factors greatly exacerbated the underlying systemic problems, productivity started to fall sharply. Of course many factors contributed to the deterioration in productivity performance, but there can be no doubt that among them technological weaknesses played a central role.

> Results on the highest international standard were achieved only in a few cases. R&D was rarely integrated with production. Scientists and engineers were appreciated mainly for their intellectual capacities. Their contribution to economic development was rather limited (Mosoni-Fried, 1997, p. 14).

THE LEGACY

So much for the past. How much difference does it make today, more than a decade after the start of transition? I would argue that it does, indeed, make a substantial difference. The *institutional structure* of all the post-socialist countries remains distorted in a way that is inimical to effective technology transfer. Most obviously, the structure of the network of specialist research institutes is still in flux, and indeed the very issue of what role such institutes should play in the mature market economy of the future continues to be controversial. But the structure of industry, too, presents fundamental problems. While R&D in the West is dominated by small firms and giant firms, the industrial sectors of the transition economies are still largely populated by the medium-large firms (enterprises) inherited from communism. At governmental level, in many transitional countries, notions of "big science" and "science-push" have still not been laid to rest.

Equally important is the legacy of trying to cope with the distortions of the past — if you like, the legacy of transition itself. As research institutes, and their individual staff members, have sought to survive in a financially hostile environment, often on the basis of informal or even semi-legal "moon-lighting" with very little R&D content as such, the problem of fragmentation, and the allied problem of weak tacit knowledge transfer, has in many cases actually got worse. Under pressure from tight macroeconomic policies and increasingly severe competition, including from abroad, industrial firms have faced chronic liquidity problems, and R&D expenditure has been the first item to be squeezed. Thus the pressure of competition has actually had the opposite effect to what we would expect in the West (where established firms are, of course, generally in a position to take a long-term view of the impact of R&D expenditures on competitiveness). The networks of industrial R&D institutes, which might have provided an alternative focus for applied R&D, have largely disappeared with the demise of the systems of industrial ministries of which they formed a part. Nor are these problems a monopoly of the less advanced countries in transition.

Research cooperation inside Hungary is even weaker than it used to be. Most R&D units in the business sector are known only by those who are working in the same field. Only organisations belonging to the state-budget sector are clearly identified by the Central Statistical Office; others are voluntarily present or non-present in the official statistics. According to our experiences, the new technology-intensive firms are only exceptionally listed in the R&D sector (Mosoni-Fried, 1997, pp. 13–14).

THE NEW INSTITUTIONAL AGENDA

In this context, the cause of strengthening the capacity of the transition economies to innovate and transfer technology has had to be taken up largely by new institutional actors, and institutional actors brought in from outside. New firms in the region nearly always start off as *small and medium-sized enterprises* (SMEs), and while the pattern varies widely from country to country, there is evidence that R&D SMEs are one of the strongest sub-groups within the overall category. Thus in Russia, for instance, SMEs specialising in the implementation of new technologies report an average rate of profit 60 per cent higher than the average for all SMEs in Russia (Pripisnov, 1996). A specific form of technology-oriented SME is the *academic spin-off*, which differs from the kind of moonlighting operation discussed earlier in that it *is* genuinely technology-oriented, it *does* provide scope for the transfer of tacit knowledge, and it tends to integrate (through the market) rather than further fragment the R&D system. Most important, it is in the *business* of technology transfer. The more spin-offs there are, the more competitive that business is, and, consequently, the more powerful the underlying innovatory impetus in the economy. The development of academic spin-offs has been best documented in the case of Hungary (Balázs, 1996), but has also been noteworthy in Poland (Jasinski, 1997). An outstanding Polish example is that of ATM, a small firm founded in the late 1980s by a couple of professors from Warsaw Technical University, which now manufactures and exports flight recorders, against stiff (and not always wholly ethical) competition from the major American producers (Dyker, 1996). Overall, however, SMEs remain at best precocious infants within the transition economies, often weak and hesitant in marketing themselves, and having nothing like the impact they typically have in Western economies.

Rather more important, and increasingly important with every year that passes, has been *foreign direct investment* (FDI). FDI has been particularly valuable as a vehicle for the transfer of management, or *soft* technology,[1] and it is probably fair to say that no major piece of FDI in Eastern Europe and the former Soviet Union has failed to transfer, at minimum, the capacity to organise an office on the Western model, and up to Western standards (Dyker, 1999). On the transfer of *hard* (product and process) technology[2] the record is more mixed. Some sectors in some countries of the region have simply not needed hard technology, e.g. the Russian space-launch industry (see Bzhilianskaya, 1999). In sectors where hard technology transfer has been needed, the policy of Western firms has varied widely. In some cases, it has been extremely restrictive, seeking to maximise any East-West technology transfer while keeping West-East technology transfer at the minimum necessary to allow the subsidiary to do its job (Sharp & Barz, 1997, pp. 107–8). In others, Western investors seem to have gone out their way to maximise the ramified scope for technology transfer from West to East (Havas, 1997, p. 227). Direct investment in supply chains has been uncommon, though not unheard of, and international investors have a very mixed record on the encourage-ment of the development of local supply chains.

Against such a background, it is hardly surprising to find that the overall impact of FDI, in terms of improving the technological capa-bilities of host economies, has been less than it might have been. Macroeconomic analysis suggests a predominance of *asset absorption*, as opposed to *asset creation*, in FDI. In other words, investment has tended simply to access existing resources, rather than transforming those resources (in particular human capital resources) (Dyker & Kubielas, 2000).

---

[1]The notion of soft technology covers the "invisible" technology of organisation, e.g. management hierarchies, incentive systems, etc. It also includes office technol-ogy as such, e.g. communications systems, computer networks, etc.
[2]As production processes are increasingly computerised, the distinction between hard and soft technology may obviously become blurred at the edges.

FDI is not the only vehicle for international business integration and international technology transfer. Various kinds of *alliances, outward processing agreements, franchises, etc.* have developed in numbers since the start of transition. Thus in the information technology field, over the period 1989–94, more strategic technology alliances were formed with the involvement of firms from Russia than for any other country in the world (Radošević, 1999). The problem here, however, is that we have very little idea how much real technology transfer is going on under the rubric of these alliances. We are on much more solid ground with outward processing, which typically involves substantial transfer of soft technology but little of hard technology. Aimed as it is at the accessing of cheap labour for labour-intensive processes, it represents asset absorption, pure and simple. Case-study evidence suggests that franchising may be a very important way of transferring both soft and hard technology in high-tech sectors, and of building a platform from which local franchisers can start to develop their own technological dynamism, eventually integrating back into the global technology network of the firm that gave them the franchise in the first place (Dyker, 1996) — clearly asset creation *par excellence*. But franchising is not developing on an aggregate scale which would permit best practice under this heading to revolutionise whole economies. In what follows, we subsume non-equity based international cooperation under FDI.

Finally, there is *government*. While industrial ministries have largely disappeared in the transition region, ministries of science and technology, or their equivalent, have in the main survived, to promulgate programmes in which raising the efficiency of technology transfer invariably features as a goal. Policy implementation here, as in other regards, has, however, been generally ineffectual — partly because science and technology ministries have tended to concentrate their attention on the science sector, rather than on the key private sector actors in the technology transfer process, as discussed above, partly through lack of funds, and partly through sheer conservatism of outlook. As we have seen, none of the organisations with potential for technology transfer have really "pulled their weight". Government has, perhaps, been the most disappointing of all in this regard. The obvious question that arises at this point is: given that SMEs, academic spin-offs, foreign-owned subsidiaries, franchisers, government departments, etc. seem uniformly unequal to the scale of the challenge of upgrading the process of innovation and technology transfer in the transition countries, might some recombination of those elements provide the critical mass that does not at present exist?

ELEMENTS OF AN INTEGRATED TECHNOLOGY TRANSFER SYSTEM

The new vision that emerged as theorists and practitioners sloughed off the science-push idea in the West was of the process of innovation as an *interactive* process, within which "science and technology development in practice is characterised by the constant occurrence of interactions; *vertically*, between mono- and multidisciplinary research and technology development as well as between technology development and production innovation, and *horizontally*, between technologies as well as between science disciplines" (Schaffers & Smits, 1997, p. 2). On the organisational dimension, big firms, small firms, government departments, higher educational institutions, research organisations, etc. all participate in the innovation process. In that context it would be misleading to think that just because a particular firm or department was "big" that it was therefore at the "top" in hierarchical terms.

> Innovation and technology development are the result of a complex set of relationships among actors in the system, which includes enterprises, universities and government research institutes... For policy-makers, an understanding of the national innovation system can help identify leverage points for enhancing innovative performance and overall competitiveness... Policies which seek to improve networking among the actors and institutions in the system and which aim at enhancing the innovative capacity of firms, particularly their ability to identify and absorb technologies, are most valuable in this context (OECD, 1997, p. 3).

In such a system it is the matrix, the network, that is crucial. Individual elements within the matrix do not need to have critical mass in themselves — as long as they are adequately linked in with adjacent elements. In this understanding of the process of innovation and technology transfer, therefore, the stress is on technological networks, rather than on the elements that make up the networks. In that context the very distinction between innovation and technology transfer begins to lose its significance. In an interactive system there is no innovation without technology transfer, and effective technology transfer is itself, in most cases, only possible if the organisation providing the vehicle for transfer has a degree of innovatory capability.

This is at once bad news and good news for the transition countries. It is bad news in the sense that networking has always been the biggest weakness of the *S&T* systems of those countries. It is good news in the sense that the interactive vision of the technology transfer process shows how elements which in themselves have only a minor impact may, in concert, be able to produce a real transformation of the whole process of innovation in the context of transition. If we believe, as I think we must, that the negative legacies of the past are not immutable, then we must believe that, in this case, the good news is bigger news than the bad news.

The conclusion to which this argument tends is obvious enough. If the dynamic elements in the transition economies — the foreign-owned firms, the franchises, the high-tech SMEs and the spin-offs — could only get together, in the way they do in the West, the vicious circle of weak innovation/technology transfer would be broken. But that is, of course, to state the problem rather than solve it. Let us try to list the main obstacles, inherited inertia apart, to the reintegration of the fragmented innovation/technology transfer systems of the transition countries.

1. Irrespective of their attitude to the transfer of hard technology, transnational corporations (TNCs) generally keep their central R&D activities located in the home country (General Electric/ Tungsram and Sun Microsystems are notable exceptions in relation to Eastern Europe and the former Soviet Union). If we

accept the argument that you cannot effectively absorb the innovations of others unless you know how to innovate yourself, then this is indeed a major obstacle in the way of "deep integration".

2. The origin of transition region spin-offs is completely different from that of their Western counterparts. In the West, spin-offs are spun-off from other companies. In the East, they are spun off from research institutes. Even where Eastern spin-offs can make a real contribution to technology transfer, therefore, they are up against the problem that come from a "different world" from that of their prospective clients.

3. The weakness of TNC networking within the transition region is largely a function of the perception that potential local suppliers (some of them academic spin-offs, as discussed above) are not competitive, in terms of price, quality or both. In other words, there seems to be a *prima facie* case that transition countries do not generally enjoy comparative advantage in supplier sectors, despite their abundant endowment in labour in general, and in the relevant specific types of human capital. Of course the perceptions of the TNCs may be wrong. But it is clear that if an investor does not even think he can make a profit out of asset absorption, he is unlikely to get involved in asset creation.

4. To the extent that effective networking is dependent on government, weakness in government may clearly be a critical obstacle to the creation of an effective interactive system.

Of course, none of these obstacles are insuperable. Rather we consider them simply to sharpen our understanding of the underlying issues. TNCs, for instance, may still concentrate their big labs in their home country, but the current trend is actually to deconcentration.

> R&D increasingly is being moved closer to major customers, and/or areas with more favourable R&D conditions... The foreign proportion of R&D in promising fields developed in an even more dynamic manner than the foreign share of sales. Apart from the legal framework, contact with leading academic research facilities in the respective fields is an important factor in the choice of R&D location (Albach *et al.*, 1996).

A particularly striking example of this is the way that European chemicals firms have tended to shift their biotechnology laboratory activity to the United States (Thomas, 1998).

Up to now, this new trend has been in evidence largely within the developed industrial world. But it has surfaced in the transition region, e.g. in terms of the setting-up by major Western companies of software and computer labs in Russia, to take advantage of the unique human capital resources released after the break-up of the Soviet military-industrial complex. It will develop further in that region to the extent that core research capacities are effectively restructured in such a way that they can respond efficiently and flexibly to the needs of the TNCs and in such a way as to ensure that both sides can make money out of the deal, or alternatively present themselves as worthy objects of acquisition policy. Either way, core research capacities need a good dose of the soft technology transfer which usually only comes after a deal with a foreign company has been clinched. Public sector technical assistance programmes have done something to fill the gap — but not enough. They could do much better, and, in combination with more muscular management in-house, possibly achieve a major breakthrough in terms of making core research capacities in the transition countries look like an attractive investment.

Again, the problem of the non-commercial origin of the typical East European spin-off is only an insuperable one if we believe that nothing can ever be changed. Certainly, the managements of the medium-large firms inherited from the old system may, under difficult transition conditions, be reluctant to be persuaded that "academics" can help them. Even here, however, it is important to bear in mind that in many cases, under the old system, enterprises did have long-term links with particular research institutes. There is no reason of principle why those links should not be inherited by transition-period spin-offs from those same institutes, and redeveloped as the most vigorous of the medium-large firms rediscover the capacity to invest in future competitiveness. Finally, the TNCs have few prejudices. If they perceive the prospect of profitable sub-contracting to an academic spin-off from the transition region they will do it. What is clear is that the spin-off must be in a position to organise its work coherently, market its services properly, and take a reasonably long view on financial matters. Given that many spin-offs were originally created as financial improvisations with cash flow primarily in mind, that is a tall order. Here, then, is where the spin-offs need help from the public sector:

- to provide facilities in the form of innovation centres or science parks that can provide a congenial environment, strengthen linkages *between* spin-offs and exploit economies of scale in things like marketing; and
- to open up special channels for the financing of more long-term projects, including innovative projects for which a client has not yet been found.

That brings us round to point 4 above. Can the typical East European/post-Soviet government really be trusted to set up innovation centres and science parks which are not just real estate speculations, to coordinate spin-off activity and provide some kind of venture capital facility? Up to now, the governments of the region have signally failed on all of these, and similar, policy issues. Again, we must not assume that nothing can ever be changed. But changing the typical East European state is likely to be a special challenge.

On TNC supply networking within the region, there is no need to be excessively despondent. However unsatisfactory the present situation is, the trend is in the right direction, as evidenced by a survey conducted in Hungary.

> According to our … survey, multies play a significant *economic role as contractors*: many new technology-oriented or R&D-intensive forms are connected to them as suppliers. In these cases mostly [the] financial situation of the firms is strengthened. Besides, they are forced to meet the contractor's claim on a very high level, in due time and on low prices. All the resources and knowledge have to be mobilized. It is a difficult but good training for companies and individuals, who were accustomed to [a] less productive economic system (Mosoni-Fried, 1997, p. 22).

Matters are much less advanced in Russia, as one might expect. Still, Pripisnov (1999) finds that supply links between foreign investors and SMEs are developing (in both directions), especially where SMEs specialising in scientific services are involved, and that in general SMEs with better developed supply links with foreign-owned firms tend to be more innovative — all of this despite the fact that there is very little FDI as such in Russian SMEs.

As in relation to academic spin-offs, government can help reinforce positive trends through marketing in the broadest sense — the dissemination of information on the entire supplier landscape in the given country. But beyond that the private sector can be trusted here to take the matter largely into its own hands. The common interest between foreign investors and local suppliers is such a palpable one, that they should probably be largely left to do their own deals. Tax breaks or the like for foreign investors using local suppliers would run the risk of insulating the suppliers from the need to raise their game, and of thus largely losing the benefit to the economy as a whole. Local content minima still come within the range of what is permissible in terms of the international commercial code, but can backfire in the case of countries with small domestic markets. In a number of countries, notably in the former Soviet Union, steps need to be taken to ensure that SMEs in general play on a "level playing field", untroubled by local government chiefs who can be arbitrary and sometimes rapacious, or protection racketeers who are invariably rapacious.

CONCLUSIONS

What lessons for the future can we draw on all this? It seems almost banal to repeat that critical mass is critical. Yet the reality of the transition countries is that:

- The innovation process remains fragmented.
- The transition countries dispose of many positive elements of innovatory dynamism.
- Positive action is needed to bring these together so as to create the interactive matrix whose existence is taken for granted in a mature market economy.

Much of that positive action will be generated by the market itself, and it should be the first duty of government to ensure that the market is allowed to get on with the job. To that extent, policy on innovation can simply be seen as an extension of policy on privatisation, competition, etc. But government does have other, more positive duties to perform in the business of integrating the innovation process, and it is not clear that it is, at present, capable of performing these duties. Even the maintenance of basic law and order, so crucial for small companies, seems to be beyond the capabilities of many transition governments, especially in the former Soviet Union. More specifically, existing ministries of science and technology often seem to hinder rather than facilitate the emergence of a more realistic understanding of the nature of innovation and the elaboration of corresponding programmes of technical assistance to help research institutes restructure, to develop networks of innovation centres, to strengthen venture capital facilities, etc. In the vision of a virtuous circle of interaction between foreign companies, indigenous small enterprises and government, it is always government which seems most likely to break the circle. While helping government to raise its game can be a thankless task, it is surely the action most likely to have a substantial exogenous impact on the process of innovation and technology transfer in the transition region over the medium term. Radical reorganisation, even abolition, of existing science and technology ministries may be a necessary first step in all this.

REFERENCES

Albach, H *et al.* (1996). *Innovation in the European Chemical Industry.* WZB, Berlin, Discussion Paper No. 52.

Balázs, K (1996). *Academic Entrepreneurs and their Role in Knowledge Transfer.* STEEP Discussion Paper No. 37, SPRU, University of Sussex.

Bush, V (1946). *Endless Horizons.* Washington DC: Public Affairs Press.

Bzhilianskaya, L (1999). Foreign investment in the science-based industries of Russia. In *Foreign Direct Investment and Technology Transfer in the Former Soviet Union*, DA Dyker (ed.), pp. 64–83. Cheltenham: Edward Elgar.

Dyker, DA (1996). The computer and software industries in the East European economies — a bridgehead to the global economy? *Europe-Asia Studies*, 48(6), 915–30.

Dyker, DA (1999). Foreign direct investment in transition countries — a global perspective. In *Foreign Direct Investment and Technology Transfer in the Former Soviet Union*, DA Dyker (ed.), pp. 8–26. Cheltenham: Edward Elgar.

Dyker, DA and S Kubielas (2000). Technology and structure in the Polish economy under transition and globalisation. *Economic Systems*, 24(1), 1–24.

Havas, A (1997). Foreign direct investment and intra-industry trade: The case of the automotive industry in Central Europe. In *The Technology of Transition. Science and Technology Policies for Transition Countries*, DA Dyker (ed.). Budapest: Central European University Press.

Jasinski, A (1997). *Academy-Industry Relations for Innovation in Poland*. STEEP Discussion Paper No. 41, SPRU, University of Sussex, August.

Mosoni-Fried, J (1997). *Structural Changes in Industrial R&D in Hungary: Losers and Winners*. Paper presented to NATO ARW No. 970451, *Institutional Transformations of S&T Systems and S&T Policy in Economies in Transition*, 28–30 August, Budapest.

OECD (1997). Working group on innovation and technology policy. *National Innovation Systems: Background Report*, OLIS, 27 February.

Pripisnov, V (1996). *The Development of Small and Medium-Sized Enterprises (SMEs) in Russia 1993–95*. STEEP Discussion Paper No. 35, SPRU, University of Sussex.

———— (1999). Foreign investment in small and medium-sized enterprises in Russia. In *Foreign Direct Investment and Technology Transfer in the Former Soviet Union*, DA Dyker (ed.), pp. 84–101. Cheltenham: Edward Elgar.

Radošević, S (1997). Alliances and emerging patterns of technological integration and marginalisation of Central and Eastern Europe within the global economy. In *Foreign Direct Investment and Technology Transfer in the Former Soviet Union*, DA Dyker (ed.), pp. 27–51. Cheltenham: Edward Elgar.

Schaffers, H and R Smits (1997). *The Strategic Position of Research Organisations in Tomorrow's Markets for Technological Knowledge*. Paper presented to NATO ARW No. 970451. *Institutional Transformations of S&T Systems and S&T Policy in Economies in Transition*, 28–30 August, Budapest.

Sharp, M and M Barz (1997). Multinational companies and the transfer and diffusion of new technological capabilities in Central and Eastern Europe and the former Soviet Union. In *The Technology of Transition: Science and Technology Policies for Transition Countries*, DA Dyker (ed.). Budapest: Central European University Press.

Thomas, S (1998). Biotechnology in Europe. In *The European Economy*, 2nd Ed., DA Dyker (ed.). Harlow: Addison Wesley Longman.

Chapter 9

Technology Exchange and the Foreign Business Sector in Russia[*]

INTRODUCTION

The aim of this paper is to study the process of development and dissemination of technology in Russia through the medium of cooperation between Russian organisations and foreign firms, and/or the employment and training by foreign firms of Russian nationals.[1] In principle, the study does not limit itself to any particular institutional form. In practice, it has to start by looking at foreign direct investment, as the dominant, and best documented, form of technology-oriented international business collaboration. According to commonly

---

[*]This article is based on a report commissioned by the OECD and presented at the conference "The Future of Russian Science and Technology", Moscow, 15–16 December, 1998. It draws primarily on sources published in English and Russian. These published sources have been supplemented by interviews with executives of foreign companies investing in Russia and Russian civil servants with responsibilities in the area. For reasons of confidentiality, those latter sources cannot be named. Where such a source has been used, it is marked (C) in the text.
[1]Thus we do not discuss systematically the role of public-sector technical assistance programmes and the like in technological processes. On these see Mirskaya, 1997.

accepted definitions, any investment worth more than 10 per cent of the total equity of the host organisation counts as direct investment. That means that a wide range of joint ventures between Russian companies and institutes, on the one hand, and foreign firms on the other, count as direct investment. It is this very broad grouping that we investigate first, before going on to look at other forms of technological alliance or contractual relationship.

FOREIGN DIRECT INVESTMENT IN GLOBAL CONTEXT

Foreign direct investment (FDI) is widely perceived as one of the key resource flows in the contemporary international economy. It is strongly identified with multinational corporations (MNCs), and has not escaped the political controversy that has sometimes surrounded the latter. But the balance of opinion has changed over the past couple of decades, and while specific elements of FDI may still come in for criticism on health, environmental or distributional grounds, FDI in the aggregate is generally viewed as a positive factor of economic development. It is, certainly, easy to exaggerate the purely quantitative impact of FDI. In 1999 total world FDI outflow was $845 b — 14 per cent of total world gross fixed capital formation (UNCTAD, 2000, p. xvi). Thus the great bulk of fixed investment is still carried on within the boundaries of individual states. Of course there are wide variations between countries, and a number of countries, especially in East Asia, owe much larger proportions of their total investment to FDI. Still, FDI remains a minor source of investment finance at the global level. Its key importance, therefore, has to be sought in other areas. Those areas have generally been identified in terms of *technology transfer*. Any suggestion that there is a *unique* relationship between FDI and international technology transfer should be treated with scepticism, and we shall return at a later point to the issue of alternative forms of international technology transfer. But it is commonly believed that FDI tends to disseminate technological best practice, and the empirical record at the global level vindicates that belief.

What kinds of technology transfer are we talking about? Most obviously about the transfer of:

Process and Product Technology — *"Hard" Technology*

To the extent that hard technology transfer in the contemporary world is crucially dependent on the transfer of *tacit knowledge*, which can only be transferred within the framework of tightly knit teams of executives and scientists, it can only be done efficiently within the boundaries of one firm. To use Dunning's terminology, particular firms may enjoy firm-specific technological advantages which can be transferred efficiently only through a mechanism internal to the firms itself (Dunning, 1988). Of course, such processes of hard technology transfer can occur within the frontiers of one state, and indeed often do in the advanced capitalist countries. Given Russia's special technological strengths in specific areas, purely domestic hard technology transfer on a significant scale is therefore not ruled out. Nor is "reverse" technology transfer, where the hard technology is transferred from the host company to the foreign investor. But in the "catch-up" countries in general (i.e., NICs and transition countries (TCs)), key elements of hard technology will usually come from abroad.

Management, Organisational and Office Technology — *"Soft" Technology*

In seeking to internalise firm-specific or other advantages, investing companies have to impose their own corporate organisational structures on subsidiaries or partners. Those organisational structures are, in the modern world, crucially dependent, not only on patterns of human organisation within the firm, but also on specific forms of electronic networking, etc. It will therefore be impossible for the firm to impose its organisational structure without transferring "soft" technology, in terms of the disposition of hierarchies, lines of responsibility, the use of intra-firm E-mail systems, etc. While FDI normally carries hard technology transfer, while indeed hard technology is often part of the *raison d'être* of FDI, it is possible to envisage FDI without hard technology transfer, and indeed not difficult to find examples of it. Soft technology transfer, by contrast, *is a sine qua non of foreign direct investment.* To put the point even more strongly, even if an investing company did not want its management technology to be transferred, it would not be able to stop it.

The implication is that, even where there is no soft technology gap as such, soft technology will be transferred in the course of FDI, simply in order to create an integrated system. In practice, where the catch-up countries are concerned, there *is* generally a technology gap, so that there will be a genuine learning process here. And that process will have to be addressed explicitly, hence the enormous stress placed on training of local personnel by MNCs in the context of FDI.

Networking, building of supply chains, etc.

The ramifications of a particular element of FDI often go far beyond the original investment. Particularly in sectors with highly complex input-output linkages like the automotive industry, the normal pattern is for networking out from the core investment, to *first-tier suppliers,* who will usually actively cooperate with the core enterprise in areas like design as well as in the manufacture of components, and then on to *second- and third-tier suppliers,* whose role is generally limited to the latter dimension. First-tier suppliers may be industrial firms or research institutes. Second- and third-tier suppliers will normally be industrial firms. In principle, networking amplifies the process of technology transfer through a process of ramified dissemination. No two networks are identical, however, and the impact of a particular supply chain on the overall technological level of the host economy will depend on a wide range of factors:

- the policies of the investing company towards technology transfer outside the company (i.e., externalisation of firm-specific advantages);
- the extent to which sub-contractors are actually able to "raise their game";
- whether first-tier suppliers are domestic firms, as opposed to foreign firms or subsidiaries; and
- the precise manner in which the relationships between the different tiers of suppliers are set up.

Thus while FDI-induced networking will always have some knock-on effect, it may be difficult to maximise that effect.

Locational Factors in FDI Decisions

Specific FDI decisions are based on the perception and scope for internalisation, not only of firm-specific advantages, but also of *location-specific advantages.* So it is not enough for the investing firm to have something special to offer. The prospective host country has to have something special as well. Economists have traditionally viewed locational factors in international economic relations in terms of broadly defined factors of production. And since in the context of FDI the investing firm by definition provides the capital, attention focuses on the other two main factors of production, labour and land (including natural resources). Thus FDI in the Third World is predominantly cheap-labour-seeking and/or land/natural-resource-seeking. But just as the bulk of trade in the modern world is between developed countries (mostly in the form of intra-industry trade), so the bulk of FDI also flows between the developed countries, in which labour is generally equally dear, and land and natural resource endowment (North America and Australia apart) equally meagre. Thus there are clear parallels between intra-industry trade and intra-industry FDI. In the context of a complex and dynamic world, specific firms/institutes or clusters of firms/institutes in specific countries or regions develop specific capabilities. Other firms seeking to stay on the technological leading edge will have to do business with these firms. And where there are, e.g. crucial issues of intellectual property, the business will ultimately have to be internalised within some of these firms.

FDI IN THE TRANSITION REGION

Over the past decade or so FDI has run at fairly high levels in the TCs, particularly in Central-East Europe (CEE) (see Chapter 6). We can summarise the experience of CEE in relation to FDI under the following headings:

1. FDI in CEE has hardly ever been driven by a quest for cheap labour (OECD, 1994; Mutinelli & Piscitello, 1996; Estrin *et al.*, 1997). That does not mean that wage costs, and indeed price factors in general, have not been an important element in

decision-taking. It does mean that they have rarely represented a *decisive* factor, because it is not wage costs as such, but rather the relationship between wages and productivity that will determine how profitable a project in manufacturing is. And it is the key importance of controlling that relationship that pushes the prime mover in the direction of internalisation through FDI, and makes the transfer of managerial and organisational technology, as an instrument of that control, absolutely essential.

2. There is a general correlation between levels of FDI and rates of growth of labour productivity, levels of exports, and improvement in the structure of exports as measured by the share of the machinery and engineering sectors in total exports. In Hungary, foreign investment enterprises (FIEs) accounted for 77.5 per cent of total exports in 1996, while the share of machinery and engineering in total exports increased from 20 per cent in 1990 to 52 per cent in 1996 (Hunya, 1998, pp. 12 and 18). This clearly underlines the tremendous importance of soft technology transfer through FDI as a factor enabling FIEs to raise their business game, but it also suggests substantial elements of transfer of hard technology.

3. The experience of Eastern Europe in relation to supply networks has been mixed. There has been substantial foreign investment in the car industries of Poland, the Czech Republic and Hungary, and this yields a rich seam of case material (Havas, 1997; 1999; Ellingstad, 1997; Martin, 1998; Dyker, 1999). Generally, the Hungarian experience has been the most positive in terms of the extent of supply networking out from the FIE, though development has been constrained by difficulties experienced by suppliers in meeting quality requirements. The extent of supply networking out of the Volkswagen/Škoda plant in the Czech Republic has been impressive, but local (as opposed to foreign or foreign-owned) suppliers have tended to be relegated to the position of second- and third-tier suppliers, so that they have not been involved in design activities, and have tended to be treated as "commodity" producers, with all that implies in terms of pressure to cut prices. In Poland, most of the foreign-owned car plants have brought their own suppliers with them.

4. The experience in relation to the impact of FDI on R&D as such is mixed. A statistical study of the activity of more than 100 FIEs spending money on R&D in Hungary 1992–95 (Inzelt, 1999) found that:

   a. FIEs with above 75 per cent foreign ownership tend to spend substantially more on R&D in relation to total sales than domestically-owned firms.
   b. The higher the foreign ownership stake, the higher do relative R&D expenditures tend to be.
   c. As time went on, R&D expenditures per FIE tended to rise.
   d. FIEs tended progressively to cut expenditure on contract R&D.
   e. R&D within the framework of FDI tends to be "skin-deep", in the sense that it is focused on product development and adaptation rather than basic or applied research.

5. The record of government influence on these patterns is uneven. Governments of host countries have found it difficult to hold foreign companies to their commitments in relation to levels of investment (e.g. Volkswagen/Škoda) and to prevent abuse of monopoly power. But they have been able to impose effective local-content requirements, and this has been a major factor in the development of supply networks in the automotive industry. A scheme under which the Hungarian government offers grants to foreign firms setting up R&D laboratories in Hungary has generated positive results (Inzelt, 1999).

Overall, the experience of CEE demonstrates that FDI can be a major factor of productivity enhancement. It is less evident from the CEE material that it will necessarily strengthen the indigenous science and technology base of the host country. In other words, it is simply not clear whether FDI in TCs produces "shallow" or "deep" integration (Radošević & Dyker, 1997). TC governments are not powerless in these matters, but it would be unrealistic to imagine that the government of any transition government could ever have the "clout" of the US government or the European Commission. Thus CEE experience provides no blueprints — for Russia or for any other country. But it does provide a useful checklist of key issues, which will help us to structure our discussion of the Russian case.

STRATEGIC AND TECHNOLOGICAL ALLIANCES IN THE TRANSITION REGION

As noted earlier, the distinction between an alliance and FDI based on a minority equity holding is an artificial one. Nevertheless there are forms of alliance which have no equity content as such, but which may be particularly important for catch-up countries, including TCs. *Outward-processing agreements* have played a key role in the globalisation of the CEECs during the 1990s, and have been of particular importance in relation to German business involvement in Poland, for example, where equity ownership raises political problems. Thus German OPT with Poland accounted for over 30 per cent of total EU15 OPT with the CEE-4 (Poland, Hungary, the Czech Republic and Slovakia) in 1996 (Pellegrin, 1999, p. 4).

The sectors involved are usually low-technology sectors, where R&D hardly comes into the question. Thus in 1996 textiles and clothing, footwear and furniture together accounted for nearly 75 per cent of total OPT re-imports into the EU (Pellegrin, 1999, p. 6). And here lead firms clearly believe that collaborating firms can be trusted to organise their own production lines, so that full internalisation of the operation is not required. That is not to say that outward processing relationships involve no transfer of soft technology from lead firm to collaborating firm. But it does mean that lead firms do not consider it necessary, in the context of relatively simple production technologies, to take control of the determinants of labour productivity. Here, in contrast to the pattern with FDI, lead firms are indeed looking for cheap labour, confident that collaborating firms can keep control of labour productivity — and knowing that if they fail to do so, the financial loss will be theirs, not the lead firm's.

But not all alliances involving TCs are low-tech. Over the period 1984–94 Hungary, Poland, Czechoslovakia and the FSU (mainly Russia) reported a very high incidence of strategic alliances in information technology (Vonortas & Safioles, 1996). We have no systematic information on the content of these alliances, and some of them may have been purely opportunistic, as insiders sought to circumvent restrictions on privatisation in the early years of transition. But there is surely some indication of a breadth of opportunity for science and technology cooperation in an area where human capital resources in the region are substantial. Case material from the software sector would tend to corroborate this latter thesis, with licensing and franchising agreements with international companies furnishing software firms in TCs with a springboard for technological dynamism. The latter are then able to exploit this springboard as a basis for integrating back into the global system which provided the licenses and franchises in the first place, ultimately generating a process of *two-way technology transfer* (Dyker, 1996). Even where the cross-border business relationship takes an OPT form, the content of the relationship may carry a significant technology element where the sector involved is a "middle-tech" one like electrical machinery (see Chapter 7).

Taking alliances into consideration certainly broadens out the picture of international business collaboration as it affects TCs. Here we find relationships more reminiscent of those between metropolitan countries and NICs than of those between different parts of Europe. But here also we find relationships nested within highly dynamic, high-tech sectors, where alliances seem to provide a necessary element of flexibility which equity-based relationships cannot match. What alliances have not up to now been able to provide is a basis for complex supply networking. It is surely inconceivable that the vehicle-manufacturing multinationals could have gone into CEE on the basis of outward processing. Yet the case of Vilati (see Chapter 7) suggests that what has been inconceivable in the past may not be inconceivable in the future. Indeed when we look at the whole gamut of possible equity- and non-equity-based relationships, we have to conclude that almost anything is possible, that almost anything can be to a degree mutually beneficial, while always bearing in mind that in practice few international business collaborations have been as beneficial for the TCs as they might have been.

THE PATTERN OF FOREIGN INVESTMENT AND ALLIANCES IN RUSSIA

It hardly needs saying that Russia is a unique country, even among TCs. It is one of the few TCs to dispose of a raw material endowment rich enough significantly to affect patterns of foreign trade and foreign investment. It is the only TC where geographical and climatic factors have a major bearing on investment decisions. Russia shares with the other TCs a substantial endowment in human capital. Even here, however, there are special factors contingent on the concentration of the old Warsaw Pact's military-industrial complex in the Soviet Union, primarily in Russia. Russia is also unique among TCs in terms of the potential size of its domestic market, and we must expect this also to affect the pattern of inward investment.[2]

The basic contours of the overall pattern of foreign investment in Russia are laid out in Table 7, Chapter 3. The main characteristics of the FDI situation are clear enough — absolute levels have been low, and the modest upward trend of the mid-1990s was cut off by the financial crisis of August 1998. In 2000 and 2001 net inflow of FDI was actually negative, according to EBRD estimates (EBRD, 2002, p. 193). While this reflects primarily increases in FDI *outflow*, gross inflow of FDI has never recovered the level of 1997, averaging something under $3 b per annum 1999–2002 (ECE, 2003, p. 239). Thus FDI has been an essentially minor, but not insignificant, resource flow in the Russian case.

This basic pattern of foreign direct investment in Russia comes out clearly from the figures on inflow and stock by branch, presented in Table 1. Fuel is an important target for FDI, as might be expected, given Russia's natural endowments, and it can dominate investment inflow in particular periods, e.g. the first half of 1999. But in cumulative terms it is no more important a target than the food industry. Over 30 per cent of cumulative FDI has gone to assuage traditional Soviet/Russian weaknesses in the production and distribution of food and in the distribution network at large, i.e., in sectors where the main technologies being transferred are soft rather than hard. The c.20 per cent of total cumulative FDI that has gone to telecommunications (note that the inflow figure for the first half of 1999 was much lower) has likewise aimed to fill a gap left by communism, though here the transfer of hard technology has been much more

---

[2]But note that access to the domestic market has tended to be a central motivation for FDI in CEE too — partly because firms have tended to view market access in that part of the world in *regional* rather than purely national terms.

Table 1.   FDI inflow into Russia, first half of 1999 and cumulative, by sector.

	First half of 1999		Cumulative	
	$ m	% of total	$ m	% of total
Total	2,428.8	100.0	11,692.5	100.0
Fuel	995.1	41.0	2138.7	18.3
General commercial activity	46.9	1.9	375.3	3.2
Finance and credit	66.2	2.0	—	—
Trade and public catering	318.3	13.1	1153.0	9.9
Food industry	483.2	19.9	2317.7	19.8
Non-ferrous metallurgy	3.6	0.1	292.4	2.5
Transport	129.3	5.3	341.5	2.9
Forestry, pulp and paper	—	—	465.4	4.0
Communications	68.7	2.8	2208.5	18.9
Mechanical engineering and metal working	51.6	2.1	470.4	4.0
Ferrous metallurgy	61.8	2.5	—	—

Source: FIPC.

important. When non-ferrous metallurgy and timber and paper are added into fuel, the total share of cumulative FDI going to raw-material-based sectors rises to nearly 25 per cent. The only branch of manufacturing that figures significantly within total cumulative FDI is mechanical engineering and metal-working, which holds the main scope for networking and spillover effects, and inflow into this sector fell to almost negligible proportions in the first half of 1999.

In the sections that follow, reference is made to the specific FDI experience of a number of these sectors. In addition, detailed *case studies* of the hydrocarbon industries, and of one key sector of the engineering industry, are laid out in a separate section.

What about the pattern of FDI by size of enterprise? Investor companies have on the whole been big companies, though with a significant volume of investment coming from small and (in particular) medium-sized enterprises from Central Europe. As far as host enterprises are concerned, we have no official data, but we do have sample-survey data. In interpreting this data, we have to bear in mind the peculiar size distribution of firms in Russia. Gazprom apart, there are no really big firms. And while there are a large number of small firms (employing under 100 people), they account for only around 10 per cent of official employment (rather more when allowance is made for the second economy). It is only to be expected, therefore, that the great bulk of FDI should be in either existing medium-large firms or greenfield developments. It is, nevertheless, surprising that a survey of 841 small enterprises carried out at the beginning of 1997 discovered only five SEs actually hosting FDI. What the survey also discovered, however, was that the intensity of business relations between SEs and foreign firms and foreign-owned firms is greater in the high-tech sectors, that such relationships afford significant advantages to the SEs involved in terms of soft technology transfer and training for their staff, and that SEs working closely with foreign firms and foreign-owned firms tend to be more innovative than other SEs, at least on the product-design and marketing sides, if less clearly so on the production technology side (Pripisnov, 1999). All this suggests that small Russian enterprises have a big potential role to play in the development of FDI in Russia, but as elements in supply networks rather than as hosts of FDI as such.

In the absence of any comparable data on alliances, we can only guess at the pattern of non-equity relationships that has evolved over recent years. Alliances are probably mainly concentrated in the high-tech and information technology sectors. Hagedoorn and Sedaitis (1997) found a high correlation between non-equity relationships and the intensity of the R&D component in the strategic technology alliances and joint ventures they studied. For both these reasons, partners must surely come predominantly from the OECD countries. Hagedoorn and Sedaitis found that, within their sample, the pure alliance form (i.e., with no equity element at all) tended to exhibit a relatively even balance of West-to-East and East-to-West technology transfer. More than that it is not possible to say at the general level with any confidence.

Table 2 shows the extent to which Russian R&D organisations and innovation-oriented enterprises[3] have become involved in alliances with foreign partners. The figures are not insignificant, and they grew steadily up to 1996, but they are still not high, and they

---

[3]It is not clear exactly how this category is defined.

Table 2.   The internationalisation of Russian R&D.

	1993	1994	1995	1996	1997	1998
Number of wholly or partly foreign-owned R&D-performing organizations	2	—	25	43	43	61
As percentage of all R&D organizations	0.4	—	0.6	1.0	1.0	1.3
Number of joint ventures in R&D and related activities	305	510	800	813	608	306
Number of employees	9,100	8,900	9,600	9,000	5,300	4,900
Number of innovating enterprises involving foreign ownership						
Active in R&D	—	—	13	11	11	—
Active in patenting and licensing	—	—	2	3	4	—
Active in production design	—	—	2	7	10	—

Source: Nauka Rossii v Tsifrakh, 1997, pp. 12, 14 & 85; *Nauka Rossii v Tsifrakh, 1998*, pp. 12, 14 & 85; *Nauka Rossii v Tsifrakh, 1999*, pp. 12, 14 & 85.

experienced something of a collapse in 1997–98 (though note that where foreign ownership is involved they held up better). They show that the reported degree of internationalisation of R&D as such is, in fact, a good deal lower than the reported degree of internationalisation of, for example, the oil industry (see case study 1). Outstanding cases like the American branch of the Institute of Theoretical Physics of the Russian Academy of Sciences apart, the incidence of formal international R&D collaboration has been noticeably lower for Russia (and indeed for the former Soviet Union in general) than for the Central-East European countries (Mirskaya, 1997). There is, surely, a substantial degree of underreporting here in the Russian case (the incidence of underreporting may have increased since 1997), as R&D organisations conceal their foreign partnerships to avoid cuts in core funding, and groups within institutes do their own international deals with institute management turning a blind eye as the price of keeping the institute together. It is, of course, difficult to obtain more than scattered, anecdotal evidence on this section of the "grey" economy. In studying the impact of R&D collaboration with foreign organisations within the framework of FDI and alliances, therefore, we have to focus on production enterprises rather than R&D organisations.

Beyond FDI and formal alliances lies a largely uncharted area of informal contacts, alliances and exchanges. (Note that here "informal" does not necessarily mean "grey" in the sense that that word was used in the past paragraph.) To the extent that informality is conducive to the transfer of tacit knowledge, these relationships must play a significant role in processes of technology transfer in both directions. Thus a Russian scientist who works in the West for five years will return to Russia with upgraded scientific capabilities and a grasp of how state-of-the-art laboratories are organised, and will probably have left a significant legacy of (Russian) scientific and technical knowledge with his hosts. He will, furthermore, take the network he has built up over the five years home with him. In some cases, Russian scientists have been able to build up powerful international networks without ever spending long periods abroad. The bulk of this kind of cooperation goes on within the public sector rather than the business sector (Mirskaya, 1997). But there are exceptions, notably in the case of the British healthcare consortium (Glaxo, Wellcome and Zeneca) operating in the Urals, which brings Russian doctors over to the UK for training within the framework of a commercial agreement that also involves sale of pharmaceuticals and medical equipment, and some elements of countertrade (Barz, 1999). Specific examples of this nature apart, academic networks do increasingly overlap with business networks, so that even purely academic cooperation must have a significant impact on foreign business sector activity in Russia. It is impossible to comment further on the basis of existing information.

THE PATTERN OF TECHNOLOGY TRANSFER THROUGH FDI AND ALLIANCES IN RUSSIA

How does the particular pattern of FDI in Russia affect the pattern of technology transfer? In relation to *soft technology*, not at all. As noted earlier, transfer of managerial and organisational technology is a *sine qua non* of effective FDI. In Russia, where the essentially non-commercial management culture of the old system of central planning is peculiarly deep-seated, this is *a fortiori* the case. If the foreign investor is not able to impose the essential elements of his management system and culture the project is doomed to failure.

The situation with respect to *hard technology* is much more complex. In many areas, for example that of fast food, there is virtually no hard technology to transfer — the organisational side is everything. There are broad areas of middle-tech engineering where the levels of technology inherited from the Soviet Union are competitive, if not absolutely leading-edge (Dyker & Radošević, 1994), so that "brownfield" investments in these sectors are again largely exercises in organisational rationalisation. There are areas of hard technology, e.g. in the oil industry, where transfer has been crucial in the past, but where the Russian side to a great extent caught up in the course of the 1990s (C; see case study 1). But we should not downplay the role of hard technology transfer too much. There are very specific areas of hard technology, e.g. nuclear safety, aero engines and telecommunications, environmental protection (see case study 1) where transfer of process technology has been, and remains crucial. And when we switch our attention from process to product technology, we see a different picture altogether. Thus in food processing, for instance, the design of products specifically for the Russian market, based on thoroughgoing market research and taking into account all the special characteristics of the Russian market, including the limited spending power of most families, has been key (C). Thus inward transfer of hard technology is of central importance, but the degree of importance varies greatly from sector to sector, and even from operation to operation.

FDI in Russia has also served as a vehicle for *East-to-West technology transfer*. The market for East-to-West technology transfer is conditioned by three key features of the Soviet legacy.

1. The "over-development" of specific elements within the Russian human capital stock on account of key weaknesses in the technology

array of the Soviet Union. Examples include software design, where the inadequacy of Soviet computers, in particular their limited memory capacity, spawned a level of "ingeniousness" on the part of Soviet software specialists which would have been unnecessary in a Western context, but which could be turned to other, profitable, uses once the system was opened up to global influences (Katkalo, 1993). Sometimes this kind of thing resulted in the development of a specific technology which subsequently proved to be commercially viable in the transition context. An example is horizontal drilling for oil, which was developed in the USSR because Soviet steel was not good enough to make the bits necessary for conventional, vertical drilling (C). Beyond that, it tended to result in the development of specific capabilities. There is wide agreement, for example, that in the mid-1990s the best Russian computer programmers were better than the best in the OECD area (Dyker, 1996; Barz, 1999).

These elements of human capital have been successfully used as a basis for FDI in related sectors. In software and integrated computer system development, biotechnology, medical technology, opto-electronics, polymer-optical fibres and energy technology, Western multinationals have been able to harness the related capabilities in the service of global technological development programmes (Dyker, 1996; Barz, 1999; C). Such programmes have involved a significant amount of West-to-East technology transfer as well as East-to-West. But, unique among major forms of FDI in Russia, they do seem to be critically dependent for their commercial success on the low wages which the Russian specialists involved are prepared to accept. This, then, is a "Bangalore"-type system of FDI, whereby Western multinationals contract out specific elements of development work to specialists from countries where, for one reason or another, wages are at a comparatively low level.

2. The priorities and capabilities of the military-industrial complex resulted in the development of a range of technological capabilities and specific, high-tech products, e.g. military aircraft, rocket launchers (see case study 2), extra-hard metals, special alloys, etc. In some cases it has been possible to transform these directly into

hard-currency export industries. In others, that goal has been achieved indirectly, through the process of conversion, e.g. with the use of Soviet/Russian rocket-launching technology to launch Western telecommunications satellites (see case study 2). This is an area where the hard technology transfer may be two-way, as, for example, where Western engines have been installed in Russian aircraft, or only East-to-West, as with some areas of space launching (see case study 2). By the early-mid-1990s quite complex business structures had already been set up in some sectors to exploit the scope for East-to-West technology transfer from the Russian military-industrial complex. Thus in 1993 the German metals company Metallgesellschaft set up a 50:50 joint venture with fourteen leading Russian research institutes from the military sector, with the aim of marketing Russian metals technologies in the West (Barz, 1999).

3. The isolation of the Soviet Union sometimes resulted in the development of "marsupial" technologies — technologies which might never have been developed under the competitive pressures of a market system (just as the kangaroo would never have survived if Australia had not been cut off from the rest of the world), but which may now contribute crucial elements of technological diversity to a globalised technological system. An example is the development of technologies for the launching of rockets from ships and sea-platforms, submarines and heavy aircraft (see case study 2). Originally developed out of considerations of military security, these "alternative" technologies offer multinational companies technological options which help them to respond flexibly to changing patterns of relative cost in their areas of investment.

The best illustrations of how these three elements may come together in particular cases come from the computer and software industries. Thus the Moscow Centre for SPARC Technology (MCST), the creation of Boris Babayan, the father of the Elbrus-2 supercomputer (widely used in the Soviet space and nuclear programmes), has made significant contributions to the development of workstation technology. MCST is financed by Sun Microsystems. ParaGraph, a leading

Russian software company, also with its roots in the military-industrial complex, was a pioneer of the technology of computer handwriting recognition. Again, ParaGraph had to do a deal with Apple Computers to develop that technology commercially. Cooperation with Apple has now extended into the fields of compression, 3D graphics and virtual reality. ParaGraph has also worked together with Elsag-Bailey of Genoa on off-line recognition, and with the Sanctuary Woods company on a multimedia project (Dyker, 1996).

We saw in the last section that the pattern of development of small enterprises in Russia holds out some promise of the development of *production and technology networks* built around foreign-owned firms. In practice, the promise has yet to be fulfilled. Paradoxically, this state of affairs may be related to the very *strength* of existing networks — of the traditional, Soviet type, especially in military-oriented sectors which are usually the main repositories of scientific and technological capabilities. Case material shows that the style of networking inherited from the past tends to be too hierarchical, too rigid on lines of authority, not rigid enough on observance of contracts, unable to integrate where the Soviet system divided (e.g. design and production) and unable to devolve effectively what was often centralised under the Soviet system (e.g. component supply) (Harter, pp. 144–8; Richet & Bourassa, 1998). All of this represents a challenge rather than an insurmountable obstacle for the foreign investor. But it is a challenge that has still not been effectively taken up, notably by that most important industrial networker, the motor-car industry. Current plans for foreign investment in the Russian automotive industry focus mainly on the setting-up of *screwdriver assembly* inside Russia. There is, however, some prospect that this will develop into genuine supply-network-building. Thus the agreement between Opel and Avtovaz on joint product of the Opel Astra T-3000 platform for the Russian market envisaged initial assembly largely on the basis of imported parts, but with local content rising to 35–40 per cent by 2002 and 70 per cent by 2004 (Dagayev, 1999, p. 8). Ford's St. Petersburg plant currently imports 95 per cent of its components. In response to the problem, however, the International Finance Corporation set up a project in 2002 to help Ford develop a supply chain in Russia (involving Russian and foreign companies).

PROBLEMS OF TECHNOLOGY TRANSFER THROUGH FDI AND ALLIANCES

The aggregate level of FDI in Russia is low in relation to the size of the country and the resources it has to offer. Why so? Every organisation and company involved in FDI and alliances has a particular experience and particular insights into these matters. At the risk of oversimplifying, we have structured this section in terms of the typical preoccupations of the "Russian side" and the "investor side".

From the Russian Point of View

• Fear of the "Maquiladora" phenomenon: "Maquiladora" factories, set up in northern Mexico on the basis of US FDI, are characterised by low wages, low levels of investment in training, and weak networking within the host region. It must be emphasised that the Maquiladora phenomenon is not a wholly negative one. Its operation in Mexico has improved levels of technology and capability, increased productivity and created new jobs (Ellingstad, 1997). But it is not calculated to maximise the impact of FDI on the Mexican economy as a whole, it fails to transfer benefits on a large scale to workers, and it tends to reinforce Mexico's colonial status *vis-à-vis* the US.

   In practice, Russia does not need to worry too much about the Maquiladora phenomenon. As noted earlier, cheap labour is rarely a key factor in FDI in Russia, or indeed in the transition area as a whole. And it must be stressed that Maquiladora is a phenomenon of the Mexican *border* region with the US (similar patterns can be found in China's border region with Hong Kong — see Chan Oi, 1999), and it is difficult to imagine it developing outside that specific geographical context. Russia simply does not have any border regions with advanced capitalist economies, Finland and Japan excepted. If the political obstacles to major investment inflows from Japan are ever removed, Maquiladora-type investment (and outward processing as a form of alliance) could certainly develop in the Russian Far East.

- Non-tariff barriers against Russian exports: Russia has suffered a good deal from anti-dumping duties and quotas and other forms of contingent protection over the past decade or so, and this has hampered her in seeking to follow her comparative advantage, e.g. in relation to the export of non-ferrous metals, notably aluminium, and base chemicals. But anti-dumping measures have generally had little connection either with FDI or with technology transfer. The aluminium case is a partial exception, in that the complex of restrictions hammered out in 1993 by the European Commission and the various producer interests themselves did involve promises of Western investment in Russian aluminium and provision of Western technology to clean up Russian production facilities (Dyker, 1994, pp. 49–52). Much more important in the present context has been the case of space-launching (see case study 2), where development of substantial programmes of joint investment and joint marketing between Western and Russian providers has gone on against the background of restrictions imposed by the US government through successive Russian-US Trade Agreements on the sale of Russian space-launching services on the world market. FDI and alliances effectively ease the trade restrictions imposed on Russian producers, because the output of joint ventures in this field do not count as "Russian". But even joint ventures can fall foul of US security restrictions. Thus, for instance, Boeing was fined $10 m by the US government for breaching non-proliferation of rocket technologies regulations in connection with its involvement in the SL project, and Pratt and Whitney was investigated with respect to their cooperation with Energomash (see case study 2) (Ivanova, 2000, pp. 5–7).[4]

---

[4]The Pratt and Whitney-Energomash partnership was finally cleared by Congress in April 2000.

• Fear of the destruction of the Russian *S&T* base: there are widespread fears among the Russian science and technology establishment that the impact of globalisation on Russian *S&T* will be, at best, large-scale "asset-stripping", at worst liquidation of Russia's independent *S&T* base. These fears are by no means groundless. Brain drain is a real problem, though probably not as critical as sometimes suggested.[5] The Bangalore phenomenon often extends a life line to individuals or small research groups, but generally has little to offer the big research institutes, and may even harm their interests to the extent that it encourages "moonlighting", with staff using institute equipment to fulfil what are in effect private contracts. There have also been cases where purportedly scientific agreements have been used as a cover for the pirating of Russian technologies (C; Ivanova, 1998, p. 10). And as the Hungarian material cited earlier shows, even where there is genuine investment in the local *S&T* base, the cooperation may be only skin-deep and the implications for basic and even applied research negative. Still, it has to be borne in mind that skin-deep cooperation is better than no cooperation at all. Most important of all, we should not blame globalisation for all the ills of the Russian *S&T* system. Those ills flow mainly from the Soviet inheritance, from the fact that the Russian *S&T* system is oversized and distorted in its pattern of specialisation, and is structurally extremely ill-suited to the needs of a market economy. These problems have been addressed but slowly, and it is this that poses the real threat to the Russian *S&T* base. Foreign business involvement can do something to pump new funds into the sector and move it in the right structural direction. In practice, as Table 2 indicates (and taking into account the likely degree of underestimation in the figures contained in that table), the involvement of the foreign business sector in cooperation with R&D organisations as such has been on a minor scale. It would be quite unrealistic to imagine that the fate of Russian *S&T* lies in the hands of FDI and alliances.

---

[5]The number of R&D workers emigrating annually from Russia fell from 2,300 in 1993 to 1,900 in 1996 and 1,200 in 1997. See *Nauka Rossii v Tsifrakh* 1998, p. 40.

- Fears of restrictions on West-to-East technology transfer in the context of FDI and alliances: these fears are widespread (Ivanova, 2000), and receive a good deal of confirmation from Western sources. Within the framework of Bangalore-type agreements, Western investors generally aim to give their Russian partners only the minimum amount of firm-specific technology they need to do the job (C; Sharp & Barz, 1997, pp. 107–8). More broadly, however, as East European experience shows, a lot depends on the individual investing firm, and the conduct of Suzuki in Hungary in this regard, for example, has been exemplary (Havas, 1997, pp. 224–9). Global experience indicates that, where there is genuine collaboration in the setting-up and management of production lines, it will be difficult for investing companies to prevent the transfer of hard technology. As noted earlier, it is simply impossible for Western partners to stop the transfer of soft technology in cases where they need to impose control over the whole operation. Restrictiveness in relation to technology transfer is, therefore, probably not a critical problem on big projects, though with some variation between firms. There is more of a problem with smaller deals, within the framework of which investors transfer limited amounts of equipment and know-how, but leave the organisation of the operation to local partners.

From the Western Point of View

- Unsatisfactory legal framework: this is one of the principal obstacles to the maximisation of the volume of FDI in Russia. Tax is a central element, with Western investors unhappy about levels of tax and also the speed with which the effective tax burden can change. Individual Western firms have produced charts based on time series of effective tax burdens which look like switchbacks (C).[6] An additional complication affecting Western companies operating in the regions of Russia is the penchant for local political bosses to impose their own, arbitrary charges on foreign companies. Such

---

[6]NB a good deal has been during the Putin era to simplify and stabilise the tax system.

volatility in the tax regime makes investment planning impossible, especially for firms with long time horizons. The simple solution to that problem is, of course, not to invest. Company law, intellectual property rights, property law, bankruptcy law and legal recourse also present a whole range of difficulties. There have been many cases in Russia of foreign shareholders being prevented from exercising their shareholding rights in particular Russian companies through manipulation of shareholders meetings, or the issue by management of new blocks of shares without the knowledge of existing shareholders. The intellectual property rights situation is unsatisfactory, and this has been a significant obstacle to investment in sectors like pharmaceuticals, where the cost of investing in the development of new drugs makes companies particularly sensitive to IPR risks; foreign companies also cite IPR problems as a reason why they are restrictive about the extent of West-to-East technology transfer within the framework of deals involving mainly technology transfer in the opposite direction. For the oil industry, the lack of a proper legal framework for production-sharing, the most common basis for FDI from the oil multinationals elsewhere in the world, continues to symbolise the generally unsatisfactory state of the business environment. Where disputes do arise, Western companies find that taking action through Russian courts is very difficult, and that even when they secure a favourable judgement, the judgement may not be implemented. Opaque bankruptcy laws mean that it may in practice be impossible for Western firms to seize assets as a way of recovering debts.

- Fears of political instability: this point is graphically illustrated by the reactions of foreign companies already investing in Russia to the rouble crisis of August-September 1998. While the breakdown in the banking system attendant on the crisis caused cash-flow problems for all of them, possible changes in the real exchange rate and therefore the real dollar wage were in many cases viewed as being of minor importance, either because the local wage bill was not an important element of costs, or because staff were effectively paid in dollars. Firms primarily oriented to the domestic Russian market saw the crisis as an opportunity to reinforce the competitive advantage they already had. So on strictly economic grounds the crisis was seen by many investing firms as being on a minor scale. But *all* investing firms were concerned about the generalised uncertainty the crisis had brought with it, with political uncertainty viewed as being more serious than economic uncertainty as such (C).

- Western investors perceive major problems in imposing their *firm-specific* "technology culture" on Russian firms. Even where local managers are eager to collaborate, they may have serious problems in comprehending the key importance of "value engineering". Foreign companies still find it difficult to talk about the cost side of deals to potential suppliers, often receiving the response "just tell us what you want and we'll make it" (C). But some suppliers *are* managing to make the transition to a set of attitudes appropriate to a market economy, and the supposition must be that as the younger generation moves up into the top positions in industry, the problem will be largely solved. At the broader level of 'business culture' as a whole, significant local peculiarities are likely to remain. But that is true of many countries in the world, and there is no reason why it should present insuperable problems to investment in Russia.

- Trying to sell technologies "off the shelf" or "out of the store cupboard": this problem stems from a misinterpretation of technology as an *artefact* (a "thing made by human workmanship"). The confusion may arise because of the traditional dominance of military and space R&D in Russia — where technologies and artefacts do, to a great extent, coincide (see case study 2). More generally, while a given technology may produce artefacts, and may indeed use artefacts to produce other artefacts, the technology itself must be understood as a *process*, a *body of knowledge*. In Western technology management thinking, development of a new technology always starts with the problem to be solved — and the potential market for the solution. Only once those have been defined does "hard" technology development work actually begin. So there are no technologies "off the shelf" in the West, except to the extent that Western companies may use or sell obsolescent technologies in less developed parts of the world. Western companies *are* prepared to buy Russian technologies off the shelf because they are generally interested in technological alternatives, as discussed under the heading of marsupial technology, above, and indeed some foreign engineering companies do good business translating and reformatting Soviet/Russian patent and design documentation (C). But few of these technological alternatives are actually developed *directly* for commercial application (sea-based space launching is an exception: see case study 2). The bulk of them are simply used to broaden and enrich the core technology files of the given Western firm. The implication of this is that active and equal technological cooperation between Russian and foreign companies means working together on a project *from the conceptual phase onwards*, and applying all the technological capabilities of both sides to the solution of the problems addressed. Of course many Western companies do not want active and equal technological cooperation, preferring more limited, perhaps less equal relationships. If Russian scientists and technologists want to encourage potential Western partners to change their ways of thinking, they must be prepared to change theirs, and that means getting rid of their "off-the-shelf" mentality.

CASE STUDIES

The Oil and Gas Industries

At the end of 1994 there were around 140 oil and gas joint ventures involving foreign participation in Russia. The cumulative volume of actual investment up to that point was in the region of US$3 b, more or less equally divided between oil and gas. By the beginning of 1998 the number of projects had increased substantially, now ranging from exploration and development/production and refurbishment/ enhanced recovery through to refining and processing and the development of terminals, while the cumulative investment to that point had reached around US$5.5 b.[7] Hydrocarbons are seen by many

---

[7]It does not appear to have increased much, in net terms, since then. Major investment announcements in 2003 indicate, however, that it is likely to increase significantly in the period 2003–2010.

executives as a flagship of FDI, showing other sectors the way, and also helping to build supplier networks within Russia (C). For our purposes the sector serves to bring out a number of special features of the FDI process, the importance of raw material endowment apart, viz.:

- However important firm-specific and location-specific advantages may be (and in the case of Russian hydrocarbons both are clearly very important), firms will only proceed with a specific investment if it fits in with their corporate strategy.
- In globalised industries, of which oil and gas are the prime examples, that corporate strategy will, by definition, be a global strategy. That means that investments in Russia, or in any other potential host country, will be implemented to the extent that they fit in with a set of priorities which will doubtless include profitability, but which will also include security of supply, market penetration and a host of other factors.
- Most of those other factors will be very long-term factors. Thus a globalised industry is obliged to work in terms of a long-term horizon of, say, ten to fifteen years, in making specific investment decisions. Since it is impossible to predict the movement of key parameters like real wages and the price of oil over such a long time-span, the strategic planner in the globalised company is forced to depend on alternative-scenario-building, risk analysis, etc. rather than on straightforward estimates of Present Value.
- By the same token short-term factors which may be of key importance for other sectors and other firms will not figure prominently in the global strategic planner's deliberations, except to the extent that those short-term factors actually change best guesses in relation to longer-term factors.
- While upstream oil and gas activity is not generally considered to have wide-ranging networking potential, Western oil companies are sub-contracting within Russia, exploiting the improvements in performance which some supplier companies have achieved, while putting pressure on those performing less well to do better (C). This trend is reinforced by the tendency for the big Russian oil companies to hive off specialist service operations to separate companies.

- The technology gap between the Western multinationals and the domestic Russian oil and gas industries is closing. Just as Russian engineering companies are figuring more and more as suppliers to the multinationals, so Russian oil and gas companies are increasingly sub-contracting their technology work to international and domestic technology service companies, thus lessening their technological dependence on the MNCs. Gazprom, the giant Russian gas producer, which is more than 90 per cent Russian-owned, is the centre of a key technology network developing aeroengine technology for use in the pumping of gas. This network includes Western MNCs like Pratt and Whitney and Rolls Royce, and also a number of domestic Russian aerospace firms (Ivanova, 1999). Lukoil, Russia's biggest oil-producer and also predominantly Russian-owned, implemented an ambitious programme of investment during 1998 which allowed the company to cut average extraction costs by 10 per cent between 1997 and 1998. The investment programme was partly financed from foreign sources, and involved a wide range of cooperation agreements with both foreign and Russian companies, but did not involve any MNC taking a significant new equity share in Lukoil ("Lukoil riding high", 1999; Radošević, 1999).[8] There are, therefore, real prospects that hard technology transfer and FDI may be decoupled in the hydrocarbon sectors. Russian dependence on Western hard technology will continue in specific areas like gas compression and transmission into the medium term. Environmental-impact minimisation is another area where foreign involvement is likely to remain crucial for some time, with, for example, the US-Russian joint venture Polar Lights leading the field with the development of ice pad drilling technology ("Polar lights", 1999; see also "Small might be beautiful", 1999). Where Western companies are likely to retain a firm-specific advantage into the long term is in relation to project

---

[8]Atlantic Richfield (Arco) took an 8 per cent holding in Lukoil in 1995–6. In 1996 Arco and Lukoil set up a joint venture, LukArco, which may have played a key role in the management of the 1998 investment programme.

management and the application of communications and information technology, i.e., essentially the soft technology of oil and gas exploration and development (C; Ivanova, 1999; "New petrol storage facility", 1999; Khartukov, 1999).

The Space and Aerospace Industries

These are sectors where Russia has large accumulations of human capital, substantial potential competitive advantage, and a range of marsupial technologies which have met with a good deal of interest among potential Western collaborators. Major types of collaboration in this field have included:

- Joint ventures aimed at remedying a specific weakness in the capabilities of the Russian industry, e.g. the agreement between GE Aviation and Rybinsk Motors to produce the CE Aviation CT7 aero engine at the Rybinsk plant, for use in the new Sukhoi-80 executive jet, and also for export (Ivanova, 1998, p. 15). A similar agreement has been concluded between Pratt & Whitney and Perm Motors in relation to the PS-90A engine (Ivanova, 2000, pp. 15–16).
- Alliances designed to transfer specific pieces of Russian hard technology to the Western partner, such as the agreement between Pratt and Whitney and Energomash whereby the latter will initially make the "low-cost and robust" RD-180M engine for the Lockheed Martin Atlas IIAE space-launch vehicle, with production (under license) gradually moving to the US over an eight-year period (Ivanova, 2000, pp. 6–7).[9]
- Joint ventures designed to market a particular piece of Russian technology worldwide, e.g. the LKEI (Lockheed-Khrunichev-Energiya International) joint venture, which has sole rights in relation to the use of the Proton booster rocket, designed by Khrunichev (Bzhilianskaya, 1999).

---

[9]The first commercial launch of an Atlas III launch vehicle powered by an RD-180M engine was successfully completed in May 2000. An improved Atlas IIIb vehicle was successfully launched for the first time in February 2002.

- Joint ventures designed to develop a particular piece of marsupial technology for the Western market, like the SL (Sea Launch) joint venture, involving Energiya, Yuzhnoe from Ukraine, Kvaerner (building the rig) and Boeing (doing the finance and marketing), dedicated to the launching of satellites from platforms floating in the Pacific Ocean;[10] and Sea Launch Services (SLS), a joint venture between the Russian association RAMCON and the US Sea Launch Investors, with a booster rocket specially adapted for sea launches, the *Priboi*, being expressly designed by the Russian side (Bzhilianskaya, 1999).
- Technological alliances like those between Boeing, DASA and Airbus and the Zhukovskii Central Aerohydrodynamics Institute relating to specific research projects being carried out by Zhukovskii for its Western partners (Ivanova, 2000).

A central theme in this varied picture is the recognised value of Russian hard technology. A less obvious but no less central theme is the essential role of Western soft technology, and also of Western finance, in bringing Russian technology to the global market (Ivanova, 2000). That transfer of soft technology is essentially a learning process is highlighted by reports that Khrunichev may now be considering ending its partnership with Lockheed, on the grounds that it has now learned enough to "go it alone" (Ivanova, 2000, p. 5). This assessment is at odds with the evidence from the oil and gas industries to the effect that Russian dependence on Western soft technology will persist into the long term. There may be an important inter-sectoral difference here, but only time will tell. The evidence from the space sector on the westwards transfer of marsupial technology confirms the operational importance of this kind of technology transfer, but also confirms that, even here, technologies cannot simply be taken off the shelf — they have to be redeployed, and in some cases specific elements may have to be newly developed from

---

[10]SL ran into serious problems in March 2000 with a failed launch. The problem was almost certainly a software one. Since then, five successful launches have been carried out.

scratch. There are elements of the Bangalore system in some of the case studies from the space and aerospace sectors, notably in relation to Zhukovskii's various partnerships, but these elements do not seem to be dominant.

SUMMARY CONCLUSIONS

- Collaboration with the foreign business sector, through FDI and the creation of formal and informal production and technological alliances, has brought significant benefits to Russia, in terms of inward and outward transfer of technology, but has not had a critical impact on the level of performance of the Russian economy, at general or sectoral level. The specialised R&D sector is no exception in this regard.
- While outward technology transfer has been restricted to the field of hard technology, inward technology transfer has encompassed soft technology and (more selectively) hard technology.
- As the hard technology gap has narrowed, so inward transfer of soft technology has tended to come even more to the fore.
- Business enterprises rather than R&D institutes have been the main vehicle for inwards and outwards technology transfer, though the role of R&D institutes is almost certainly understated by the official statistics.
- FDI remains the main specific channel of technology transfer, but sectoral case studies suggest that its importance relative to other channels may now be diminishing.
- While the scope for involving small Russian enterprises in international R&D-oriented collaboration is substantial, it remains unexploited. One of the main reasons for this is the continued failure of Russian industry to develop contemporary patterns of supply networking. More widespread foreign ownership across the range of industrial sectors might do something to rectify this situation, but the key initiatives will have to come from within the Russian business and government community.

- While Russian scientific and industrial leaders still tend to view foreign business with some suspicion, foreign businessmen continue to view Russia as a difficult environment and a poor risk in investment terms. The differences in view are to some extent attitudinally-based, but there are genuine problems on both sides, the solution of which would greatly increase the scope for mutually beneficial cooperation. These problems will not be solved unless some kind of overarching process of bilateral dialogue is set up.

- It is unrealistic to expect much from government policy in this field. State programmes to reorganise the R&D sector may, if properly conceived, have some impact, but given the limited role of specialist R&D organisations in international technology transfer, that impact will inevitably be limited. A much more promising field for government action is in relation to problems of corporate governance and property rights. These are among the main problems lying behind the disappointing aggregate figures for FDI inflow, and the failure of key industrial sectors to develop the modern supply networks necessary if the technology transfer content of foreign investment and international alliances is to be maximised. It is, therefore, in the solution of these problems that international cooperation could have the biggest impact. How such international cooperation could be set up in the Russian case is, however, problematic. In the case of the CEECs, the aspiration to membership of the EU offers, indeed imposes, a largely ready-made system of regulation and governance on states in the form of the *acquis communautaire*. The Russian state has no such aspirations, and the Russian government and business community are unlikely to want to import, lock stock and barrel, a foreign system of regulation and governance, whatever its pedigree. But the creation of some kind of permanent EU-Russia commission to consider these matters could be immensely useful, not just in relation to technical matters but also as a trust-building exercise. It would ideally draw its membership from officials on both sides, but also business and scientific leaders, and it could serve as a key conduit for the channelling of best practice in regulation and governance to Russia.

In a word, it could provide the most important kind of technology transfer of all.[11]

REFERENCES

Barz, M (1999). British and German MNCs in Russia and the FSU — evidence from the Western side. In *Foreign Direct Investment and Technology Transfer in the Former Soviet Union*, DA Dyker (ed.), pp. 102–54. Cheltenham: Edward Elgar.

Bzhilianskaya, L (1999). Foreign direct investment in the science-based industries of Russia. In *Foreign Direct Investment and Technology Transfer in the Former Soviet Union*, DA Dyker (ed.), pp. 64–83. Cheltenham: Edward Elgar.

Chan Oi, W (1998). *Hongkong's Foreign Direct Investment in Guangdong Province and its Impact on Industrial Restructuring and the Transformation of Overseas Trade.* D.Phil. dissertation, University of Sussex.

Dagayev, A (1999). *Trading Technology for Market Access: Strategic Technology Alliances in Russia and the Ukraine in the 1990s. International Co-operative Agreements in Russian Automobiles and Telecom Services Sectors.* IMEMO, Moscow, mimeo, August, Tacis-Ace Project No P95-4003-R.

Dunning, JH (1988). *Multinationals, Technology and Competitiveness.* London: Unwin Hyman.

Dyker, DA (1994). Russian perceptions of economic security. *Tokyo Club Papers*, No. 7, pp. 33–56.

——— (1996). The computer and software industries in the East European economies: A bridgehead to the global economy? *Europe-Asia Studies*, 48(6), 915–30.

——— (1999). Foreign direct investment in transition countries: A global perspective. In *Foreign Direct Investment and Technology Transfer in the Former Soviet Union*, DA Dyker (ed.), pp. 8–26. Cheltenham: Edward Elgar.

Dyker, DA and S Radošević (1994). *Industrial Restructuring in the Baltic Countries.* PSBF Briefing, Royal Institute of International Affairs, London.

---

[11]Under the Rubric of the *Common European Economic Space* (*Obshchee evropeiskoe ekonomicheskoe prostranstvo*) — CEES, the October 2001 Brussels Russia-EU Summit set up a "High-Level Group" to press forward with the elaboration of the CEES idea within the framework of the Partnership and Cooperation Agreement. In a progress report to the EU-Russia Summit of 29 May 2002 the High-Level Group stressed the importance of regulatory convergence, picking out the areas of standards, technical regulations and conformity assessment, customs, financial services, accounting/auditing, transport, *space launching*, public procurement, telecoms and competition as key areas of common work.

EBRD (1998). *Transition Report 1998.* London.
——— (1999). *Transition Report 1999.* London.
——— (2002). *Transition Report 2002.* London.
Economic Commission for Europe (ECE) (1998). *Economic Survey of Europe in 1998 No. 1.* New York and Geneva: United Nations.
——— (1999). *Economic Survey of Europe in 1999 No. 1.* New York and Geneva: United Nations.
——— (2003). *Economic Survey of Europe in 2003 No. 1.* New York and Geneva: United Nations.
Ellingstad, M (1997). The Maquiladora syndrome: Central European prospects. *Europe-Asia Studies,* 49(1), 7–21.
Estrin, S, K Hughes and S Todd (1997). *Foreign Direct Investment in Central and Eastern Europe.* London: Pinter and RIIA.
Hagedoorn, J and JB Sedaitis (1997). *Partnerships in Transition Economies: International Strategic Technology Alliances in Russia.* MERIT, Maastricht and Stanford University, Stanford, November.
Harter, S (1998). *The Civilianisation of the Russian Economy: A Network Approach.* D.Phil. thesis, University of Birmingham, U.K.
Havas, A (1997). Foreign direct investment and intra-industry trade: The case of the automotive industry in Central Europe. In *The Technology of Transition: Science and Technology Policy for Transition Countries,* DA Dyker (ed.), pp. 211–40. Budapest: Central European University Press.
——— (1999). *Changing Patterns of Inter- and Intra-regional Division of Labour: Central Europe's Long and Winding Road.* Budapest, mimeo.
Hunya, G (1998). *Integration of CEEC Manufacturing into European Corporate Structures by Direct Investments.* The Vienna Institute for International Economic Studies, mimeo.
Inzelt, A-M (1999). The transformation role of FDI in R&D: Analysis based on material from a databank. In *Innovation and Structural Change in Post-Socialist Countries: A Quantitative Approach,* DA Dyker and S Radošević (eds.), pp. 185–201. Dordrecht: Kluwer.
Ivanova, N (1998). *Strategic Technology Alliances (STA) in the Russian Innovation System.* IMEMO, Moscow, mimeo, Tacis-Ace Project No P95-4003-R.
——— (1999). *Trading Technology for Market Access. International Co-operative Agreements in Russia and the Ukraine. Gas Industry.* IMEMO, Moscow, mimeo, August, Tacis-Ace Project No P95-4003-R.
——— (2000). *Strategic Alliances in Russian Aerospace Industry: Cooperate to Survive.* IMEMO, Moscow, mimeo.
Katkalo, VS (1993). *Institutional Structure and Innovation in Emerging Russian Software Industry.* St. Petersburg, mimeo.
Khartukov, E (1999). Reshaping the landscape. *Petroleum Economist,* 66(11), November, 22–6.

"Lukoil riding high and forecasting even higher" (1999). *Financial Times. East European Energy Report*, No. 93, June, pp. 8–10.

Martin, R (1998). Central and Eastern Europe and the international economy: The limits to globalisation. *Europe-Asia Studies*, 50(1), 7–26.

Mirskaya, EZ (1997). International scientific collaboration in the post-communist countries: Modern trends and priorities. *Science and Public Policy*, 24(5), 301–8.

Mutinelli, M and L Piscitello (1996). Strategic motivations leading firms to invest in Central and Eastern Europe: Evidence from the Italian case. In *Foreign Direct Investment and Transition: The Case of the Visegrad Countries*, G Csáki, G Fóti and D Mayes (eds.). Budapest: Institute of World Economics.

Nauka Rossii v Tsifrakh 1997. Kratkii Statisticheskii Obzor (1997). Ministry of Science and Technology, Moscow.

Nauka Rossii v Tsifrakh 1998. Kratkii Statisticheskii Obzor (1998). Ministry of Science and Technology, Moscow.

Nauka Rossii v Tsifrakh 1999. Kratkii Statisticheskii Obzor (1999). Ministry of Science and Technology, Moscow.

"New petrol storage facility" (1999). *Financial Times. East European Energy Report*, No. 91, April, pp. 32–33.

OECD (1994). *Assessing Investment Opportunities in Economies in Transition*, Paris.

Pellegrin, J (1999). *German Production Networks in Central/Eastern Europe*. WSB-Berlin Discussion Paper FS 1 99-304, January.

"Polar Lights wins Russian environment award" (1999). *Financial Times. East European Energy Report*, No. 92, May, p. 27.

Pripisnov, V (1999). Foreign direct investment in relation to small enterprises in Russia. In *Foreign Direct Investment and Technology Transfer in the Former Soviet Union*, DA Dyker, pp. 84–101. Cheltenham: Edward Elgar.

Radošević, S (1999). *Restructuring and Growth of Post-Socialist Enterprises through Alliances: The Cases of "Gazprom" and "Lukoil"*. IMEMO, Moscow, mimeo, Tacis-Ace Project No P95-4003-R.

Radošević, S and DA Dyker (1997). Technological integration and global marginalization of Central and East European economies: The role of FDI and alliances. In *Restructuring Eastern Europe: The Microeconomics of the Transition Process*, S Sharma (ed.), pp. 111–27. Cheltenham: Edward Elgar.

Richet, X and F Bourassa (1998). *Restructuring of the East European Car Industry*. *Final Report*, TSER workshop on Restructuring and Reintegration of Science and Technology Systems in Economies in Transition, Berlin, June.

Sharp, M and M Barz (1997). Multinational companies and the transfer and diffusion of new technological capabilities in Central and Eastern Europe and the former Soviet Union. In *The Technology of Transition and Technology Transfer in the Former Soviet Union*, DA Dyker (ed.), pp. 95–125. Cheltenham: Edward Elgar.

"Small might be beautiful" (1999). *Petroleum Economist*, 66(1), January, p. 36.

UNCTAD (2000). *World Investment Report 2000.* New York and Geneva: United Nations.

Vonortas, NS and SP Safioles (1996). *Strategic Alliances in Information Technology and Developing Country Firms: Recent Evidence.* World Bank, Private Sector Development Department, 26 March, Washington D.C., mimeo.

Chapter 10

Building the Knowledge-Based
Economy in Countries in Transition:
From Concepts to Policies[*]

INTRODUCTION

There is increasing evidence of shifts in the industrial and occupational structure of the OECD economies towards a *knowledge-based* profile (OECD, 1996).[1] In this respect the transition countries are lagging behind the leading OECD economies. But if trends and performance in the lead countries are critical to an understanding of the changing pattern and pace of technological progress in the follower nations (Chandler & Hikino, 1997), we can expect that the shift towards a knowledge-based profile will eventually occur in the transition countries as well.

*The work that forms the basis for this paper was funded by the World Bank and the EU DGXII TSER programme.
[1]Like the OECD (1996), we define knowledge-based economies as those which are directly based on the production, distribution and use of knowledge and information.

Knowledge and Learning and the Transition Context

Activities which underpin the knowledge-based economy may be divided into *knowledge creation*, or knowledge investments, and *knowledge diffusion*, or distribution. This distinction is essential to an understanding of the problems surrounding the knowledge-based economy, as innovation is driven not only by intra-firm activities, but equally by interaction between firms. Effective knowledge distribution through formal and informal networks is essential for good economic performance (Nelson, 1993; Lundval *et al.*, 1992; David & Foray, 1995; Edquist, 1997; Antonelli, 1998).

Knowledge-creating activities are undertaken both through formal R&D activities (mainly in firms and their R&D labs; universities, and other public or private R&D organisations) and through non-R&D activities (in the engineering and production departments of firms; in trading organisations; in technology-transfer organisations; and on the part of users). Knowledge diffuses through diverse forms of inter-firm interaction, and by interaction between firms and organisations at other levels, including public-sector organisations. This multi-layered pattern of knowledge generation and distribution is well captured in Matthew's notion of *economic learning*.

The concept of economic learning captures the notion that some economies seem to be able to accommodate changes (e.g. products, technologies, markets) better than others. They do so partly through the flexibility of their firms themselves, but also through their capacities to promote inter-organisational linkages and collaboration and, above all, through the capacity of public institutions to imbibe and develop innovations, and then disseminate those innovations in various forms to firms, thus accelerating the process of adaptation (Matthew, 1996, p. 161).

Matthew makes a useful distinction between first-, second- and third-order economic learning. First-order economic learning takes place *within* firms (organisations). Second-order learning takes place *between* firms through arrangements like sub-contracting, licensing, consortia, equity partnerships or joint ventures. Third-order economic learning "takes place both outside and within firms but in such a way that their operating conditions are changed. It is 'meta-learning', or learning how to learn; it takes place at the level of the economic system as a whole. Its efficacy depends critically on the design and functioning of the economy's institutional framework" (Matthew, 1996, p. 161). In the outcome, "some economies learn faster than others because of differences in their national structure of innovation, or, more generally, within the institutional frameworks that support third-order economic learning" (ibid, p. 170).

What is specific when we apply Matthew's taxonomy to the situation in the transition countries is that radical change is taking place at all three levels of learning. Transformation of socialist production units into firms as business units involves a great deal of intra-organisational learning. The breakdown of the old branch structure of the economy necessitates the development of new inter-firm linkages, and especially of direct links with foreign firms. Finally, the changing boundaries between private and public sectors should lead to new, nationally specific structures of innovation.

The inherited uniformity of enterprise form is another specificity of the transition situation that is historically conditioned. The Soviet-type economies "consisted of firms of a single type, namely large volume-producers, or of enterprises which had other objects or proportions, but which in practice, had to abide by the same rules of behaviour as the large enterprises" (Yudanov, 1997, p. 414). In addition, the failure to institute meaningful economic reform meant that at the level of the firm all the incentives were to fulfil formal "plans" for innovation, rather than do anything to change fundamentally the kinds of products made, and the ways they were made. The communist system of social control, far from encouraging the formation of small informal groups within which tacit knowledge could be passed on and assimilated, tended to induce passivity, fragmentation and "internal emigration". Misconceived forms of integration and anti-innovative bias had a severely depressing effect on productivity. All of this inhibited interaction and division of labour between different types of firm, and stunted the development of product differentiation. The "biological" notion of the importance of diversity of organisational forms for dynamic efficiency has been at the core of much of the analysis of changing production networks in economies in transition (see Grabher & Stark, 1996).

The proposition that flows from these insights, and which is developed in this paper, is that the strength of the structural shift towards the knowledge-based economy in the transition countries depends on:

1. the diversity of enterprise types;
2. the intensity of knowledge exchange and diffusion among enterprises; and
3. the role of public institutions in fostering intra- and inter-organisational learning.

The General Policy Framework in the Transition Countries

It is hardly surprising that the dominant policies in the transition countries are transition policies. Transition policies are, however, geared to macroeconomic stabilisation and institutional convergence towards the market economy, rather than towards growth and structural change. In the present context we must, then, start from a position of scepticism as to how conducive transition policies have been to structural change towards a knowledge-based economy. Specifically, the rationale which forms the basis of transition policies and the rationale for policies to support learning are not the same. While the former are based on the market failure rationale, policies for learning have to be more broadly based because of the specific features of knowledge as a "commodity" with strong public good and network elements, in the context of pervasive strategic uncertainties in the transition countries. (See Teubal, 1997; Radošević, 1994, 1997).

While transition policies and policies for structural change may in principle be complementary, the relationship is in practice complex. Privatisation is an indispensable condition for restructuring, but it does not by itself restructure. If pursued as the main objective through rapid, mass sell-offs, it may even inhibit restructuring (cf. the experience of the Czech Republic and Russia). In particular, privatisation of banks is not sufficient to ensure that capital will be directed towards exports and industry, rather than towards real estate, securities and imports (Gower, 1997). Improved corporate governance at the firm level and the breaking-up of large enterprises are seen as the ultimate objectives of enterprise restructuring (see EBRD, 1998). However, the breaking-up of large enterprises does not necessarily lead to positive outcomes at branch level. Price and foreign trade liberalisation, too, are necessary rather than sufficient conditions for restructuring. In some instances the radical opening-up of an economy may actually freeze structural change.

In the light of these problems there is a clear need for better integration of structural and transition policies, to induce economic growth and initiate structural change. In this context we try here to answer two questions. First, what is the impact of existing transition and other policies on the promotion of structural change towards a knowledge-based economy? (Section 2). Second, how can *new* policies for enhancing the knowledge-based economy be developed and integrated into mainstream policies? (Section 3).

THE IMPACT OF EXISTING POLICIES ON THE KNOWLEDGE-BASED ECONOMY IN THE TRANSITION COUNTRIES

We distinguish here between different policies affecting knowledge generation and distribution on the basis of whether the impact is explicit or implicit. Of course the explicitness or implicitness of any given policy tells us nothing about the intensity of the impact on the process of formation of the knowledge-based economy.

Under the heading of explicit policies we analyse R&D policies. The key implicit policy is privatisation, but we also highlight the possible impact of investment policy, monopoly and competition policy, labour market policy, foreign direct investment policy and regional policy. Tax policy has both explicit and implicit aspects.

R&D Policy

R&D policy explicitly aims at improving knowledge generation in the economy and society. The large "stock" of R&D employment inherited from the socialist period should have come through as an advantage in the transition period. For the time being, however, R&D "assets" are still largely seen as liabilities. This is partly a matter of quality and relevance in the new market context; partly of structural and organisational mismatches (e.g. the high share of extra-mural R&D) and of still weak demand for R&D.

We pointed out earlier that patterns of knowledge generation and distribution are partly determined by the role of public institutions through, in Matthew's terms, third-order economic learning. Public R&D policy is an important ingredient in this process, and it may play an important role in turning R&D into an asset for the transition countries. The four key dimensions here are *autonomy, openness, competition* and *relevance* (see Table 1 below).

R&D systems in the transition countries were in the past part of the government, or under direct state control. In almost all transition countries, R&D institutions are now self-governing and autonomous in terms of establishing criteria of quality and promotion. They are open to international cooperation, and in several countries foreign funding has started to play a significant role in aggregate R&D budgets. However, progress in terms of competition is uneven (Frankl & Cave, 1997). In part, this lack of progress can be ascribed to objective factors like the small size of R&D communities and consequent peer-review problems. It also reflects the slow pace of change in systems and criteria of funding, and especially of the balance between institutional and project/grant-based funding. The rate of advance in this respect is rather uneven across countries, but in no transition country has the problem been solved. Lying behind all this is the problem of 'path-dependency'. The R&D sectors that cope best with competition and peer review are the ones that were already strong under the

Table 1. Assessment of progress in reforms of public R&D in transition countries.

Autonomy	+++++
Openness	++++
Competition	++--
Industrial relevance	----

Scale: +++++ significant change; ---- no change.

old system and should in many cases ideally be the first targets for restructuring and downsizing (Kozlowski & Ircha, 1999).

The dimension of industrial relevance is the one on which least progress has been made. Since 1989 there have been various initiatives to strengthen *academy-industry links*, often supported by foreign funding.[2] In the period immediately after 1989 this was seen as a magic formula for commercialising accumulated R&D capabilities and the whole oversized R&D sector. It represented a continuation of the initiatives undertaken in a number of socialist countries during the 1980s, when R&D systems were under pressure to become more viable commercially. (For Bulgaria see Simeonova, 1994; for Hungary see Balázs, 1994; for Russia see Orel *et al.*, 1995, pp. 310–311.) In the event, the fundamental changes in the economic environment after 1989 left the academy-industry links initiative looking rather inadequate, due to very weak demand for R&D from industry.

R&D institutes in the transition region operate under two different regimes: the market regime of direct contracts for R&D, and the non-market regime of public funding for R&D. While their responses are also shaped by their internally developed strategies, it is these two exogenous factors that primarily influence the way they adjust. The restructuring responses of R&D institutes are influenced by the tightness and stringency of the two regimes, and by exogenous restructuring policy as such. To sharpen the picture we have developed a matrix (Chart 1) involving two basic criteria: first, the specific features of the dual regime of operation under which R&D institutes operate in a particular case; second, the (non)existence of active restructuring policy directed at the micro level by higher-level bodies, and the corresponding extent of passive restructuring at the level of the institute itself. This enables us — at the cost of a degree of simplification — to distinguish clearly between different national patterns within the transition region.

---

[2]Here we use the term "academy-industry links" not to refer specifically to Academies of Sciences, but rather to denote all links involving non- "in-house" R&D organisations.

Contrasting National Patterns of Restructuring[3]

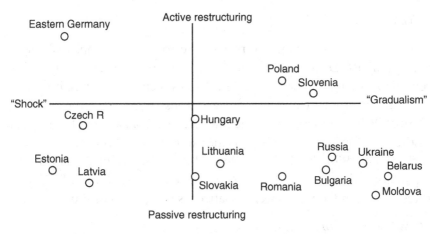

Chart 1. National patterns of R&D reconstructing in post-socialist economics.

"Shock without Therapy"

The Czech government rejected any structural policy *vis-à-vis* the microeconomic level within the R&D system (Schneider, 1998). It abruptly withdrew financial support from the majority of industrial R&D institutes at an early stage in the transition process. Since 1991, manufacturing companies in the Czech Republic have had to finance their R&D activities themselves. Under the privatisation programme, R&D institutes were treated as 'normal' production enterprises. This shock without therapy led to the wholesale conversion of the activity profile of R&D institutes to services and production. In Estonia and Latvia the industrial branch institutes, which had served the interests of the Soviet military and industrial complex, were largely closed down, primarily because they had no purpose in young, small economies. In Estonia the sector was virtually eliminated, and this probably represents the most radical change in the system of R&D institutes in the transition region. In Latvia the policy line was to combine closures and cuts in subsidies, which led to a radical

---

[3]This section draws on Radošević (1996, 1999).

reduction in the number of organisations (Martinson, Dagyte & Kristapson, 1998).

"Shock with Therapy"

Germany may seem from one perspective to be an exemplar of shock therapy in R&D, in view of the speed and scale of cut-backs, after reunification, in the eastern German R&D system. The fact is, however, that the government initially gave generous subsidies to the old East German R&D institutes, subsequently making evaluations of individual institutions, on the basis of which they were then actively restructured. (Schneider, 1995 & Meske, 1996). The availability of administrative capability and finance made it possible to restructure all the R&D institutes in eastern Germany over a relatively short period of time.

"Gradualism with Some Therapy"

The Polish government also pursued (or at least attempted to pursue) a policy of active restructuring, but in a gradualist manner. It changed the principles of public funding of R&D by ranking R&D institutes on the basis of direct (perhaps imperfect) individual appraisals. However, a number of R&D institutions, including a large number of industrial R&D institutes, still receive (modest) statutory subsidies (see Jablecka, 1995; Jasinski, 1997).

As a result of its self-management legacy from the old Yugoslavia, Slovenia has inherited fewer structural problems than other post-socialist countries. The absence of industrial branch institutes means that the problem in this case basically reduces to the development of policy for enhancing enterprise R&D. As in other transition countries, we have seen a downsizing of industrial R&D as a result of the break-up of large firms in Slovenia. However, the government has tried to counter the process by developing co-funding of experimental development, setting up a venture capital fund, and developing innovation policy (Stanovnik, 1998).

"Gradualism without Therapy"

The path that most of the post-socialist countries have followed in relation to industrial R&D is one of passive adjustment and gradualism. In

Russia, Romania and Bulgaria institutional financing is still dominant, and there are no systematic attempts actively to restructure the R&D system (Peck *et al.*, 1997; Simeonova, 1997; Sandu, 1998). In these countries the slogan of "salvation of national science" has served as a cover for saving jobs in the R&D sector. Although in Russia the Ministry of Science and Technology has officially abandoned the policy of salvation of science, and initiated prioritisation in funding and differentiation among institutes by granting to 60 of them the status of "State Scientific Centre", the result has been to allow institutes to survive (barely), rather than redevelop (Gaponenko, 1995). The reasons for this pattern include inherited R&D systems heavily concentrated in institutes, and inconsistent policies on transition in general.

In Lithuania, in contrast to the other two Baltic countries, the block funding of industrial R&D institutes has been maintained, with some of them being transformed into state institutes and others surviving on state contracts (Martinson, Dagyte & Kristapson, 1998). Ukraine, Belarus and Moldova are all cases where the status quo in industrial R&D is being maintained in conditions of continuous cutbacks in public funds and decreases in demand from industry (Malitsky *et al.*, 1998; Nesvetailov, 1997; Kramarenko, 1998). The state remains the only customer of R&D institutes, which are surviving through a variety of strategies, including long, unpaid vacations for their staff. In Belarus the dominant aim is the conservation of the R&D system in its old form (Nesvetailov, 1997). The lack of any systematic policy for active restructuring leaves a big gap in the array of survival strategies developed by R&D institutes.

"Shock and Gradualism without Therapy"

The cases of Hungary and Slovakia do not fall clearly within our matrix. Here, inconsistent government policies have actually resulted in a combination of shock therapy and gradualism. Hungary embarked on a programme of evaluation of industrial R&D institutes as early as 1992, but this was not followed up with any systematic policy of restructuring (see Mosoni-Fried, 1995; Balázs, 1994). The outcome has been deterioration and ultimately collapse of the network of industrial institutes in the course of prolonged and unsystematic attempts to restructure them. In Slovakia, industrial institutes were privatised in the first round of voucher privatisation (while Slovakia was still a part of Czechoslovakia). Here too, however, there has been a failure to come up with any systematic policy. The current situation is characterised by policy stalemate, a combination of "muddling through" and passive adjustment (see Zajac, 1997).

The Impact of Privatisation Policies

As noted earlier, lack of organisational diversity was one of the main factors behind the low innovation capacity of the socialist economies. The dearth of small firms and specialised suppliers, and the absence of close co-operation among different types of firm, made it virtually impossible to develop innovatory potential. Privatisation was supposed to correct this weakness. In practice, things have not worked out so neatly. Privatisation policy usually has multiple objectives, generally not fully compatible. Privatising quickly to achieve a fairer distribution of wealth (as in the Czech Republic) or to make it impossible for resistance to build up (e.g. Russia) is plainly not conducive to maximising budget revenues or to achieving good corporate governance with core owners and strong external supervision (a nominal objective in all post-socialist countries). And rapid privatisation often means slow restructuring, or, in the extreme case of Russia, no restructuring at all. What have been the implications of these tensions and incompatibilities for the creation of the knowledge-based economy?

In the early years of transition, privatisation policies aimed, as a general rule, to break up large enterprises. These, however, play a key role in innovation and R&D in the developed market economies (see Chandler & Hikino, 1997), in terms of both in-house R&D and sub-contracted R&D. Table 2 shows that the incidence of innovative activity is higher among big firms than among small firms in the post-socialist countries also. Russia is a partial exception here, with one key innovation survey showing an inverted-U shape distribution of innovative firms, suggesting that neither very large nor small enterprises are innovative (Table 3). Note, however, that in terms of innovation *expenditures* the very large enterprises still dominate. There is

Table 2. Innovating enterprises[a] by size of work-force (percentage of total number of firms in each size category).

Size of work-force	1990–92 EU*	Size of work-force	1995 Russia**	Size of work-force	1992 Poland***	1994–96 Poland****	Size of work-force	1993–95 Romania******
20–30	45%	below 50	21%	6–60	48%	16%	20–49	2.70%
30–50	47%	51–200	42%	51–500	59.30%	33%	50–199	9.60%
50–100	61%	201–1,000	52%	501–2,000	87.90%	72.50%	200–499	26.30%
100–300	70%	1,000–5,000	74%	2,001 and above	92.30%	87.50%	500–999	36.30%
300–1,000	83%	5,001–10,000	83%				1,000 and above	52.90%
1,001 and above	90%							

* Evangelista *et al*., 1997.
**Gaponenko, 1996.
*** GUS, 1998.
****Niedbalska, 1997.
***** CSO, 1996.
[a]i.e., enterprises carrying out development and introduction of new and improved products or processes.

Table 3. Percentage distribution of number of innovating enterprises[a] and volume of innovation expenditures by size of work-force, Russia, 1995.

Employment size	Innovating enterprises (%)	Innovation expenditures (%)
Below 49	1.70	0.30
50–99	4.20	0.30
100–199	11.80	4.90
200–499	19.60	3.60
500–999	16.30	6.20
1,000–4,999	35.10	25.20
5,000–9,999	7.30	27.90
10,000 and above	4.0	31.60
Total	100	100

Sources: Gokhberg and Kuznetsova, 1999.
[a]See note to Table 2.

no reason to doubt, then, that in the transition region, as elsewhere, big firms are key generators and absorbers of R&D, investing in R&D themselves and helping to maintain the level of market demand for R&D.

The impact of deconcentration policies on R&D is most clearly delineated in the case of the former GDR. In the old East Germany, "companies with more than 10,000 employees no longer exist, while almost 80 per cent of all R&D personnel in the private sector are employed in companies with less than 500 employees, with the bulk of that 80 per cent employed in companies with less than 100 employees" (Meske, 1997, p. 7). About 20 per cent of total R&D employment is in privatised spin-offs from sectoral research institutes operating as private research companies. The rest of industrial R&D is in small, technology-oriented companies with between 1 and 19 employees, and in the R&D subsidiaries of West German and foreign companies. Against this background it is hardly surprising that industrial R&D employment in the former GDR fell by 74 per cent between 1989 and 1993 (Meske, 1997). The importance of the point is brought out strongly when we look at the experience of the Czech Republic, where the policy was to leave industrial R&D to sink or swim, but where there was no policy of deconcentration of industry.

(The number of Czech firms employing between 1,000 and 2,500 decreased from 259 in 1990 to 174 in 1993, while the number with more than 2,500 employees actually increased from 103 to 133 — Müller, 1997, p. 25) Here the fall in the total number of industrial R&D personnel was just 48 per cent between 1989 and 1994, and there has been a trend for large enterprises to reintegrate industrial R&D institutes back into their own structures (Müller, 1997).

East German experience shows that a policy of breaking up large enterprises can have a serious negative effect on demand for R&D. However, the core of the argument here is not about large enterprises as such, but rather about the lack of diversity of enterprise forms which privatisation may generate. Shortage of dynamic small firms is just as serious an obstacle to innovation dynamics and knowledge diffusion as shortage of big firms, as is palpably obvious from the case of Russia. Furthermore the number of small firms in a given economy is in itself no guarantee that a diversity of role and strategy among small firms will develop. As argued by Gabor (1997) in the case of Hungary, too many small firms with low levels of technological competency, operating within the framework of a semi-formal economy, indicates a *dual* economy rather than a *diverse* one. The same point can be made in relation to corporate governance. Where rapid privatisation has resulted largely in *nomenklatura* privatisation, as most notably in the case of Russia, the "new" owners tend to be generally uninterested in innovation; more insidiously, they tend as a group to operate in terms of the rules of thumb and mores of the old Soviet-type economy. Thus their socio-political homogeneity greatly reinforces the impact of their lack of technological imagination (see Chapters 2 and 3). There can be little doubt that this was one of the main elements in the structural crisis which hit the Russian economy in mid-1998 (Hosking, 1998).

Labour-related Measures, Education and Training Policies

The knowledge-based economy is marked by increasing labour market demand for more highly skilled workers, who in turn enjoy wage premiums (OECD, 1996). In the transition countries investment in knowledge-intensive technologies is still at a modest level, so that there is as yet little pressure from the demand side for upgrading of skills. More specific evidence from Russia indicates that demand for skilled labour is still low (see Kovaleva, 1999). On the supply side, the scale of active labour measures remains modest in the post-socialist countries as compared to developed economies, and is clearly unequal to the task of developing the knowledge-based economy. The share of such measures in GDP in 1994 ranged from 0.25 per cent in Slovakia to 0.48 per cent in Hungary (OECD, 1997). There is a real training component here, but the training system is still burdened with social functions, and re-training activity remains undeveloped. Failures of coordination between public agencies and firms are a big problem in this latter respect. In a word, the traditional system of enterprise-based training has collapsing, and no new system has been put in place.

Relatively high levels of human capital are often cited as a comparative advantage of post-socialist countries. While this may be true in relation to the structure of the existing labour force (stock),[4] the situation is not so favourable when it comes to trends in enrolment rates (flow). During the 1980s these fell. During the 1990s the transition countries managed to maintain, at least on average, the enrolment rates of the 1980s (Hutschenreiter *et al.*, 1999). In some post-socialist countries, increased enrolment rates have actually produced some reexpansion of higher education (see Auriol, 1997). However, the number of teachers remains stagnant, indicating that the quality of education provided may be falling.

The education system does not seem to be a major factor constraining evolution towards a knowledge-based economy, but it is certainly not a catalyst in that direction. Thus one looks in vain for strong pressures for upgrading of the human capital stock from either demand or supply sides. Even if supply-side policies in education were much more muscular, and much better coordinated with the demand side and with other elements of policy, that by itself would not revolutionise the economy. This is an area that is unlikely, therefore, to provide key policy levers.

---

[4]Kozlowski and Ircha (1999) argue that even under the old system the human capital base was never developed to match the S&T system.

Investment Policy

The main problem with investment in the transition countries is not its (admittedly low) aggregate level, but rather its structure (EBRD, 1995). The capital stock inherited from communism is grossly distorted, featuring a wealth of (often obsolescent) physical production capacities, and a gross deficiency in relation to organisation, finance and marketing functions, and specifically in relation to IT. Investment patterns over the past decade or so have done something to correct these distortions in the leading transition economies (essentially the Visegrad group), but in the others, and especially in the former Soviet Union, sharp falls in levels of investment in production capacity have been compensated, if at all, by new investment in housing (usually luxury housing for the *nouveaux riches*), rather than by large-scale investment in business systems and/or new technologies. The cost of this tendency for investment to reinforce rather than correct the inherited distortions in the capital stock is high indeed. For, as argued in the EBRD *Transition Report 1995* (EBRD, 1995, p. 126, Box 7.1), it is new investment that primarily promotes the kinds of market-based interaction between industrial, financial and infrastructural sectors which can generate increasing returns through the accessing of a specific form of external economy of scale intimately tied up with the process of 'learning through investment'. It is clear that, in a transition context, it would be unrealistic to expect private firms to internalise, even partially, these externalities, in the way that is common among the TNCs of the West, except to a limited extent through the investments of those same TNCs in the transition region. There is a role for the public sector here, and a rich prize to be won, though the conditions under which the role could be effectively played remain problematic.

Monopoly and Competition Policy

Contrary to popular perceptions, the industrial structures of the post-socialist countries are not exceptional. It is striking that the US and Russia, for example, have quite similar industrial structures (see Dyker & Barrow, 1995). As argued by Amsden *et al.* (1994) "transition economists were correct in stressing that too small a proportion of out-put was produced by small firms, and that white elephants in certain industries required downsizing and vertical disintegration. Yet, they failed to recognise that in other industries fragmented and sub-optimal plants and enterprise size were the bottleneck" (pp. 90–96).

The problem is that policy-makers have tended to confuse eco-nomic concentration with inappropriate firm size, and this has resulted in a policy emphasis on anti-monopoly rather than pro-competition measures. If there is one lesson that can be drawn from studies on comparative industrial structures in post-socialist countries, it is that, in transition conditions, pro-competition policy aimed at reducing barriers to entry is much more likely to have a significant impact than any anti-monopoly policy. Indeed, in the context of weak capacity to implement policy, anti-monopoly policy is often simply hi-jacked by the monopolists for their own ends (Dyker & Barrow, 1995). Pro-competitive policies have the double advantage of being focused on the right variables, and being relatively immune to "capture" by sec-toral interests, because they aim to destroy old structures, rather than to replace them with new. Those transition countries negotiating for accession to the EU are under pressure to develop pro-competition policies as an element in their assimilation of the *acquis communau-taire*. But the process is a slow one, and the countries of the former Soviet Union remain unaffected by that process.

Policy on Foreign Direct Investment

Policy-makers in post-socialist countries naturally want to increase the inflow of foreign direct investment (FDI). FDI offers the prospect of significant supplements to weak aggregate domestic investment. It is also seen, as indeed it is throughout the world, as a key vehicle for the transfer of technology. But the policies of individual transition gov-ernments on FDI have often been inconsistent and unstable. In the first years of transition the tendency was for local production and employment to be traded for market access and privileged tax and tar-iff status. TNCs in key sectors came together to organise themselves in pursuit of special deals, and by the mid-1990s Western MNCs had become the transition countries' most effective lobby for protection (EBRD, 1994). Since then, the trend has been towards more level playing fields, but there is still plenty of scope for individual firms to make special deals which may be more conducive to short-term profit maximisation for the company and solution of short-term social and political problems for host governments than to any acceleration of the pace of structural change.

In practice, FDI always has some restructuring impact. Even where there is minimal transfer of "hard" (product, process) technology, even where there is abuse of dominant position, FDI will always lead to transfer of "soft" (management, office) technology, whether the investing company intends it or not (Dyker, 1999). But transfer of soft technology alone will not lead to "catching-up". Rather it will produce a pattern of "shallow" integration which provides substantial technological benefits to the host economies, but leaves them in a position of permanent retardation *vis-à-vis* the advanced industrial economies. New empirical research indicates that even where are significant elements of transfer of hard technology, the dominant form of integration through FDI as such is of the shallow variety (Urem, 1999; Inzelt, 1999).

Though there has been some development of supply networking between investing TNCs and local firms, particularly in the Visegrad countries, the local firms involved have usually been relegated to the position of second- or third-tier supplier,[5] which excludes them from most of the technologically more dynamic elements of networking (Ellingstad, 1997; Martin, 1998). It may be surmised that as time passes and globalised learning processes are reinforced, the obstacles to "deep" integration, which would set the transition countries on a path to catch-up, would diminish. But there is always the danger that foreign companies which have established dominant positions in particular transition economies will actually slow the rate of technology transfer to the minimum 'entry-preventing' level as time goes on. Clearly, then, pro-competition policies need to be implemented at least as energetically in relation to foreign as to domestic firms.

---

[5]See Chapter 4, fn. 6; see also Chapter 6.

Regional Policy

As a result of systematic neglect under the old regimes, regions are usually only weakly developed in the transition region in the administrative sense, and as innovative milieux. Because they were entrusted with few real responsibilities under the old system, local and regional authorities find that they simply lack the capabilities to implement today's transition agenda. The notion of decentralised innovation policy, which has enjoyed such a vogue in the West over the past couple of decades, is particularly difficult for them to grasp. In addition, local and regional government has still not been put on a sound fiscal basis in a number of important transition countries. Western technical assistance programmes, e.g. to help develop regional innovation centres, have had some impact, but it can be concluded from OECD studies on industrial policies in post-socialist countries that it is still too soon to speak of regional policy as such in the transition region. On the other hand, economic differences across regions are already increasing, and are likely to increase more, which further reinforces the case for proactive regional policy.

The current situation is characterised by increasing tension between regional and central levels which in some countries has turned into a major political issue (e.g. Russia). Given the lack of labour mobility in transition countries, regional differentiation in unemployment rates, already marked, is very likely to persist and intensify over the foreseeable future. It is worth noting that the areas with the highest unemployment rates are also those with the highest rates of long-term unemployment, indicating the strength of the structural factor in unemployment in the region, especially in the so-called "rust-belt" areas. That in turn means that a high level of unemployment may exert little dampening effect on tendencies towards wage inflation. This is an added reinforcement to the case for regional policy, in particular in terms of help with retraining and assistance in finding new jobs. To be fully effective, of course, such limited human capital policies have to be backed up by regional policy on innovation as such.

Thus "the development of the local economy, as a basic task of local governments, requires the development of a more comprehensive local policy than the simple entrepreneurial mentality" (Peteri, 1993, p. 40). Local government in the modern world has to be businesslike, but that is not to say that it can be run like a business. To be effective, it has to be prepared to act in the areas of human capital formation, environment and regulation, and to take on a coordinating role, both within its region and in terms of relations between its region and other regions. In a word, it has to be prepared to act like a *government*. Up to now hesitant moves in the direction of more businesslike local government in the transition region have not generally been matched by any movement towards more *strategic* local government, such as might use the authority and competencies of the state at that level to develop the given region as a cluster of economic activities in interaction with other clusters of economic activities.

Tax Policy

Tax policy can offer specific incentives for R&D activity by allowing firms to write off all or part of their R&D expenditures against tax, or by giving research institutes non-profit-making status. Other elements in tax policy, such as accelerated depreciation for capital equipment or import duty exemptions for imported equipment, can in principle have a significant impact on R&D. But if we are to gauge the total impact of tax policy on R&D activity, we have to look at the whole gamut of tax measures in a given country. Tax policies in post-socialist countries have not been notable for their consistency, and they have changed frequently over time and varied widely between countries. To the extent that they have focused on a common theme, that theme has been short-term revenue maximisation in support of macroeconomic policies aiming at minimisation of aggregate budget deficits. In this context collection of taxes among private individuals and small companies has been particularly problematic, and that has had a doubly negative effect. It has resulted in the imposition of an excessively heavy burden of taxation on big companies, and it has left much of the SME sector outwith the range of impact of tax policies altogether. Against that background it is unrealistic to expect the tax system of a transition country to play even the limited role in R&D

policy it plays in the advanced industrial countries, and this situation is unlikely to change over the medium term.

PROSPECTS FOR DEVELOPING POLICIES TO ENHANCE THE KNOWLEDGE-BASED ECONOMY IN THE POST-SOCIALIST COUNTRIES

In this section, we seek to develop a conceptual framework which takes into account the need for policies for learning and for enhancing knowledge generation and diffusion in the transition region, and thus allows us to reformulate some of key issues that emerged in Section 2. We base the analysis on Matthew's taxonomy of different orders of economic learning.

The Conceptual Framework — Key Elements

Analysis of the heritage of the transition countries clearly indicates the absence of system integration capabilities, i.e., elements of first- and second-order economic learning. The pervasiveness of co-ordination failures in post-socialist countries points to the importance of support, not only of knowledge generation through R&D policy, but also of knowledge distribution or diffusion, and indeed of higher orders of economic learning.

Swaan's (1995, 1997) analysis represents a rare attempt at quantitative assessment of transition country capabilities, albeit based on qualitative judgements. Using *World Competitiveness Report* data, Swaan makes a comparison of transition countries with East Asian and other economies. His conclusion is that:

> Post-socialist economies are strong in capabilities that either involve a high level of codified, transferable knowledge, or types of tacit knowledge that are not related to commercial application and marketisation. On the other hand, capabilities that are valued very low, both in absolute and relative terms, invariably involve a high degree of tacit knowledge and require complex co-operation to be effective (such as the implementation of organisational and technological strategies, or time required for

product development and marketisation respectively). Between these two extremes are capabilities that do involve tacit aspects, but merely on an individual level, such as managerial skills and various social attitudes (for example entrepreneurship or risk taking) (Swaan, 1997, pp. 7 and 8).

In a similar analysis based on Hungary alone, Swaan concludes that deficiencies are almost all related to complex organisational capabilities involving a high degree of market-related tacit knowledge and complex (inter)organisational co-operation: the effectiveness of strategies, the time required for product development and marketisation, the implementation of total quality management and the level of technology and R&D (Swaan, 1995).

Swaan's picture is confirmed by research on emerging systems of innovation in transition countries (see Radošević, 1999). This work also indicates two crucial weakness of post-socialist countries, both essentially originating from the communist heritage, viz.:

- system integration capabilities at product level; and
- process integration capabilities at firm level.

By system integration at product level we mean integration of different functions (finance, R&D, engineering, procurement, production, sales) as a necessary condition of innovation dynamics. The capability to implement such integration is relatively undeveloped in transition countries because under communism enterprises were only production units, with many of these integrative functions being delegated to administrative organs. By process integration at the firm level we mean the organisation of production and innovation across several tiers of suppliers who are all involved, to different degrees, not only in production, but also in innovation. In the socialist period, process integration was the responsibility of either branch ministries or inter-ministerial bodies.

In market economies these integrative functions are carried out by producers or users (not always perfectly, of course, cf. earlier comments about the marginalisation of second- and third-tier suppliers). Under the socialist system, by contrast, it was largely government bodies or design organisations that performed such network organiser functions as were performed. There was a degree of system integration capability in research institutes, but only for products, not for processes. Customers and users were not strong initiators of change. Even when they had the money to place their own contracts for R&D (in the 1980s) they showed little concern for the final results. The system integrators at the process level were ministries. But the organisation of processes that involved multi-technology products was almost impossible where it involved more than one ministry. Sometimes this would lead to parallel development, a kind of simultaneous "reinvention of the bicycle".

In terms of Matthew's economic learning categories, system integration deficiencies at product level fall within the first-order economic learning (organisational learning) category, while process integration at the firm level represents a dimension of second-order economic learning. The policy implication is that transition governments cannot avoid issues of collective learning and inter-firm co-operation, and are driven to establish mechanisms of third-order learning. As we saw in the last section, spontaneous development of new networks in the transition countries has come, to a considerable extent, through a revival of old linkages to form conglomerates that are new in form but hardly novel in content. If these new business forms are to be given a genuinely novel content, and if the impact of foreign investment is to attain critical mass, key measures in the area of *regulation* and *technological infrastructure* will have to be implemented as conditions for effective technological learning. The good news is that, if these key measure can be implemented, the specific government failures detailed in Section 2 will be at best dealt with, at worst largely neutralised.

In Chart 2 we develop a policy framework based on these two dimensions of technological learning in transition conditions. The *x* axis shows whether learning is individual or collective (i.e., supported by the technology infrastructure). The *y* axis differentiates between two types of market environment: a non-regulated market where monopolies, unfair competition, and short-term rent-seeking dominate over long-term growth considerations and incentives for innovation; and a regulated or "ordered" market environment where

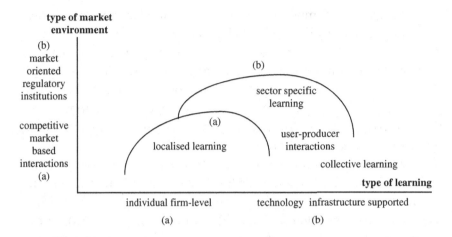

Chart 2. Technological Learning Under Two Policy Regimes.

interactions are mediated through market-oriented regulatory institutions like competition policy and supervision of utilities and banks, etc.

Our argument, as summarised in Chart 2, is that the rate of technological learning is higher in a context where learning is not only intra-firm, but also involves interactions between firms and other organisations, and where market interactions are structured in a way that is supportive to investment and the control of monopolies. That in turn means that the rate of learning in the economy as a whole is higher if inter-firm learning is fostered through technology infrastructure and market-oriented regulatory institutions (path (b) in the chart).

Market Regulation

Markets are not institution-free. Developed market economies are dominated by institutions that directly or indirectly regulate markets. Here we will briefly discuss two such elements of regulation — banking regulation and corporate governance regulation — which are particularly important for the rate of technological learning, referring back, as appropriate, to the relevant elements of existing indirect policy as laid out in Section 2.

Self-organised, competitive, market-based interactions are not *necessarily* conducive to innovative behaviour. Even where they are conducive to individual firm learning, they may generate markets susceptible to monopoly and rent-seeking. As we saw in Section 2, if competition is to be maintained, explicit policies have to be put in place to curb monopoly, or, better, to encourage competition, in particular through the lowering of entry barriers. In the banking sector, there are some additional problems.

Privatisation and competition in *capital markets* do not by themselves create sufficient conditions for banks to be efficient in restructuring (Gower, 1997). Poor information flows lay transition financial systems open to problems of moral hazard, looting and insider dealing on a huge scale. Low levels of professional capability in transition banking systems mean that credit allocation mechanisms are weak and prone to error, leaving wide scope for established lobbies to manipulate the banking system to their own, narrow (and usually non-innovative) ends. Market failures are much more pervasive in capital than in commodity markets. This means that the state's role in regulating the banking system is absolutely crucial. This is one sector which definitely cannot simply be left to self-organise.

The dominant source of investment in transition countries is retained earnings. This can be positive, to the extent that it allows firms to grow and develop in an "organic" way. It may, however, tend to perpetuate the existing industrial structure, creating a real danger of "lock in" to inferior technologies. A mature system of investment finance is one that balances external and internal sources of finance. A key condition of such balance is a system of regulation for the banking system which pushes it towards long-term, innovation-oriented investments while maintaining its competitive character. Creating such a system is, it must be stressed, something of a tight-rope act. Excessively rigid regulation, too much emphasis on prudence, can reduce the level of competition between banks and increase the average spread between borrowing and lending rates, which reduces the efficiency of resource mobilisation by reducing the volume of investment that can be supported by a given level of savings. Where too little regulation hands market power to banks, the result may be exactly the same. Against this background it is not difficult to understand why most transition governments are reluctant to rely entirely on private markets to allocate capital.

In seeking to formulate policy with respect to the banking and financial sectors, these governments are faced with a difficult dilemma. The easiest way for the state to exert influence over the pattern of bank lending is through retention of substantial elements of state ownership of banks (cf. the French experience with the indicative planning system in the decades after the Second World War). In practice, continued direct state involvement in banking, in the context of the peculiar historical legacy that burdens the transition countries, is likely to produce perverse results. Soft budget constraints will not be hardened up, good money will continue to be thrown after bad, and the cycle of non-performing loans will continue to operate. The difficulty here is that, as Gower (1997) has shown, even after privatisation, post-communist banks may continue to exhibit many of the bad old habits. It remains unclear how transition governments can mould a framework for private financial activity which will ensure effective mobilisation of savings, efficient allocation of loanable funds, and a positive orientation towards investment in new production lines and technologies, which yet avoids the pitfall of politicisation of decision-taking in the name of trying to "pick winners" or foster "national champions". Foreign technical assistance schemes to set up venture capital institutions have shown positive results, but the quantitative impact of such schemes has been largely negligible. Foreign take-overs of domestic banks has strengthened balance sheets but has had little immediate effect on banks as lenders to growing enterprises (EBRD, 1998, Part 2). It is, indeed, clear that institution-building in the financial sector will, like other key elements of institution-building, have to be a mainly domestic affair. And it will have to go forward hand-in-hand with other key elements of institution-building — at the level of government, in the civil service, in industry itself, and in the new and rapidly developing sector of industrial services.

A second area of regulation crucially important for (third-order) technological learning is *corporate governance*. The predominance of *nomenklatura* privatisation throughout the transition region means that the governance of companies is everywhere dominated by insiders from the old regime. The practical implications of that vary greatly from country to country. Thus in Poland, *nomenklatura* capitalists in the business sector, like former communists in politics, often seem to differ from their "cleaner" compatriots in terms of a *greater* degree of commitment to market disciplines. In the former Soviet Union, by contrast, *nomenklatura* capitalists have generally set their faces firmly against the generalised introduction of such disciplines, and have frequently behaved in an arbitrary, even illegal, manner *vis-à-vis* foreign investors (Hanson, 1997). Most important in the present context, they tend to be steadfastly conservative in the technological area, holding to the belief that the hard technology inherited from the Soviet Union is perfectly adequate for most purposes, and refusing to recognise the importance of soft technology.

Outside the former Soviet Union it is quite difficult to generalise about the technological attitudes of *nomenklatura* capitalists. But it must be recognised that insider control is always a problem, especially where strategic investors, whether domestic or foreign, are seeking to take control over large blocks of assets and fundamentally redirect the pattern of their application. Here the weaknesses of corporate governance structures conspire with the weaknesses of the banking systems of the region. It is against that background that the holding companies and other forms of conglomerates which have sprung up throughout the region over the past few years must be assessed. Themselves dominated by *nomenklatura* capitalist interests, they nevertheless represent the more dynamic elements within that socio-economic formation. What is clear is that if the new conglomerates are to be accepted as a "fact of life", it is that much more important to impose on them a structure of governance which ensures that strategic investment will not simply be used as a cover for asset stripping and the extension of political power. The challenge here to young and inexperienced transition states is huge, but it is a challenge that must be met.

Technological Infrastructure

In this sub-section we use Matthew's analytical approach to reassess and reformulate a number of the elements from Section 2, especially the sub-sections on R&D itself, privatisation, investment, including foreign, and regional policy.

Infrastructure is an element of the economic system used by enterprises in common, and technology infrastructure is an element of a given industry's technology that is jointly used by firms in competition with each other (Tassey, 1996). In more concrete terms, it is "the set of specific industry-relevant capabilities which have been supplied collectively and which are intended for several applications in two or more firms or user organisations" (Justman & Teubal, 1996, p. 23). Technology elements held in common are important for supporting and complementing individual firms' technological activities (for example, in relation to testing facilities), and lack of them may seriously constrain firms' growth. Technology infrastructure thus offers an important external economy of scale, on the basis of which firms can pursue interactive technology development and compensate for the lack of some elements of technology in-house.

The special importance of building up technology infrastructure in the transition context hardly needs emphasising. Thus, for example, the market value of the current excess supply of engineers and R&D specialists could be greatly enhanced by technology infrastructure which provides general technical support for entrepreneurs, in tandem, perhaps, with a venture capital facility to provide the financial support. But while infrastructure is crucial for private enterprise and investment, it does not follow from this that the building-up of the infrastructure should be entirely the responsibility of government. Particularly in a transition context, fiscal exigencies may make it impossible for the state to finance every aspect of technological infrastructure; the government may in any case lack the capabilities to do a good job in some areas of that infrastructure. Finally, in areas like telecoms, where technology is transforming an old natural monopoly into an (almost) normal competitive sector, there is simply no need for government to become deeply involved on the financial side, whether the country in question is in transition or not.

In the post-socialist countries the danger of market failure, in this as in other areas, is an especially acute one. Widespread but mostly unsuccessful attempts across Eastern Europe to set up technology parks and business incubators are a case in point (see Webster, 1996). In the Baltic states we find some particularly telling examples. The government-backed technology park in Tallinn is supposed to be an exercise in planned spillovers, but it actually operates as an *ensemble* of unrelated companies. Only a few hundred metres away, however, is EKTA, an association of electronics and software companies which receives no support from the state, but within which there is intensive interaction and complementarity between companies. Puzzles like this are by no means unknown outside the transition region, but the scale of potential government failure in that region, against a background of financial stringencies, means that the whole approach to the building of technology infrastructure has to be emphatically decentralised. Paradoxically in countries with a socialist background, technology infrastructure policy for transition needs to be much closer to the customer, designed and financed in co-operation with the customer. In addition to direct government-led public initiatives, infrastructural functions can be created through the support of *private* provision of *public* services (through information services, consultancy organisations, university-industry consortia, semi-public networks of innovation centres, etc.). A "bottom-up" approach should ensure that there is demand for the services provided. Voluntary industry associations, too, can function as builders of the technology infrastructure, targeting quite specific branch needs and financing their operations through members' fees and customer contributions.

Market Regulation and Technology Infrastructure — A Synthesis

It is clear that intra-firm learning is insufficient to ensure industrial and technological change for long-term growth in the transition region. Only when intra-firm (first-order) learning expands into collective or network-based (second-order) learning can deeper structural change be guaranteed. Only with the development of market-oriented regulatory institutions and technology infrastructure can the process of collective (third-order) learning be effectively sustained. The novelty of our perspective lies in its stress on the mutual dependence of the two elements and the way that that mutual dependence should shape policy actions. Neither wholly free-market-led nor wholly government-led development of market institutions and technology infrastructure will deliver transformation towards a knowledge-based economy. Development of network-based learning is the key condition, and it is strongly dependent on the development of meso-institutions, "non-market mechanisms of articulation of markets" (Robertson, 1992) like private/public councils, business associations, industrial groups, etc., which can play a key role in the development of "voluntary" regulation while at the same time helping to fill the "empty boxes" of technology infrastructure.

CONCLUSIONS

In this paper we have tried to analyse the policy issues involved in the transformation of transition countries into knowledge-based economies. The general conclusion is that there is no strong synergy between transition policies in the narrow, macro-economic sense and the required shift towards the knowledge-based economy. It is undoubtedly the case that general liberalisation policies are essential to the transformation process. They ensure freedom of action for enterprises, freedom to pursue profitable opportunities, and thus may be considered necessary conditions for the building of a knowledge-based economy. But they are clearly not sufficient conditions.

Of all the basic transition policies, it is privatisation which has the biggest direct implications for the knowledge base of the countries concerned. But the preoccupations of privatisation programmes are manifold, and restructuring and growth of enterprises are not always at the top of the list. The basic criterion for assessing privatisation policies from a knowledge-based economy perspective is the extent to which they allow for the diversity of enterprise forms, sizes and strategies which is essential for knowledge diffusion and generation. Privatisation also strongly influences the pattern of development of inter-firm networks (second-order economic learning) and the way that public policy mediates the process of economic development (third-order economic learning). But is no exaggeration to say that without satisfactory levels of corporate governance, privatisation will deliver none of these levels of economic learning.

What about R&D as such? Whether policy on R&D should be in the direction of active or passive restructuring, gradual or radical reduction in public funding, should clearly be decided on the basis of *policy implementation capability*. The lower that capability, the higher the costs of gradualism could be in terms of erosion of the real R&D base and weakening of any impetus towards restructuring, and the more attractive the option of rapid privatisation of industrial R&D activities. Either way, effective policy is policy which aims at supporting activities (projects) and not institutions *per se*, and which supports a limited number of consistent and administratively feasible goals.

We should expect that the whole R&D system itself will change structurally. In that context, intra-organisational restructuring will probably dominate over the development of bridging institutions as such.[6] The bridging function will most likely be absorbed into newly restructured enterprises, universities, R&D service companies, industrial associations or R&D centres, rather than being provided by institutions specialising solely in transfer services. In other words, the bridging function will develop as a complementary rather than as a stand-alone function. Bridging functions will be supported by these various actors because in that way they can better understand customer needs. Where independent bridging organisations survive, they will do so largely by evolving into full-scale SMEs, with their own specific in-house capabilities, including knowledge-transfer capabilities.

Rather than lingering over systemic details, R&D policy priorities in the post-socialist countries should focus on the "big picture" — on enhancing demand for technology within enterprises, and on restructuring R&D supply from top to bottom. It must be recognised that stabilisation of the R&D sector is impossible at radically reduced levels of expenditures unless the organisations, functions and structure of R&D are totally transformed. Policy needs to tackle supply, demand and bridging functions in an *integrative* way.

---

[6]For discussion of this issue in the context of developing countries, and of the implications of that experience for transition economies, see Bell, 1996.

More generally, policy for enhancing the knowledge-based economy requires a broad range of intermediate institutions, because knowledge is an odd kind of "commodity" which transcends private-public boundaries. At the regional level, the key task is to build up new agencies, some public-sector, some mixed public/private, the job of which is to strengthen horizontal information flows, and build new, operational business links on that basis.

Institutions located in the "grey zone" between government and business can represent a variety of public-private interfaces, and can thus act as key "traders" in knowledge. They are not strongly present in transition countries because they represent a dimension of civil society, a category that was largely suppressed in socialist times. Financial institutions which would normally exercise some of these civil society functions are also undeveloped. But against the background of pervasive government failure in relation to top-down policies in the transition economies, there is simply no alternative to developing the civil society of knowledge and business intermediation, including financial institutions, as a foundation for effective systems of regulation and technological infrastructure.

REFERENCES

Antonelli, C (1998). Localised technological change, new information technology and the knowledge-based economy: The European evidence. *Journal of Evolutionary Economics*, 8(2), 177–198.

Amsden, AA, J Kochanowicz and L Taylor (1994). *The Market Meets its Match: Restructuring the Economies of Eastern Europe*. Cambridge University Press.

Auriol, L (1997). Developments in university research of Central and Eastern European countries since 1990: Statistical analysis. In *Research at Central and East European Universities: Conference Proceedings*, pp. 25–36. Krakow: Jagiellonian University Press.

Balázs, K (1994). *Small Firms in and around Academia* (A-IR, Hungarian Case Study). Institute of Economics, Budapest, August 1994.

Bell, M (1997). Technology transfer to transition countries: Are there lessons from the experience of the post-war industrializing countries? In Dyker (ed.), pp. 63–94.

Central Statistical Office (1995). *Activitatea de Inovare Tehnologica in Interprenderile Industriei Prelucratoare*. Central Statistical Office of Romania, Bucharest.

Chandler, DA and T Hikino (1997). The large industrial enterprise and the dynamics of modern economic growth. In A Chandler *et al.* (eds.).

Chandler, DA, F Amatori and T Hikino (1997). *Big Business and the Wealth of Nations*. Cambridge University Press.

David, PA and D Foray (1995). Accessing and expanding the science and technology knowledge base. *STI Review*, OECD, Paris.

Dyker, DA (ed.) (1997). *The Technology of Transition. Science and Technology Policies for Transition Countries*. Budapest: Central European University Press.

——— (1999). Foreign direct investment in transition countries — a global perspective. In Dyker (ed.), pp. 8–26.

——— (ed.) (1999). *Foreign Direct Investment and Technology Transfer in the Former Soviet Union*. Cheltenham: Edward Elgar.

Dyker, DA and M Barrow (1995). *Monopoly and Competition Policy in Russia*. The Royal Institute of International Affairs, London.

Dyker, DA and S Radošević, (eds.) (1999). *Innovation and Structural Change in Post-Socialist Countries: A Quantitative Approach*. Dordrecht: Kluwer.

Edquist, C (ed.) (1997). *Systems of Innovation: Technologies, Institutions and Organisations*, London: Pinter.

Ellingstad, M (1997). The Maquiladora syndrome: Central European prospects. *Europe-Asia Studies*, 49(1), 7–21.

European Bank for Reconstruction and Development (EBRD) (1994). *Transition Report 1994*. London.

——— (1995). *Transition Report 1995*. London.

——— (1998). *Transition Report 1998*. London.

Evangelista, R, T Sandven, G Sirilli and K Smith (1997). *Measuring the Cost of Innovation in European industry*. Paper presented at the International Conference "Innovation Measurement and Policies", EC, Eurostat; DGXIII, pp. 20–21 May 1996, Luxembourg.

Frankl, SM and J Cave (1997). *Evaluating Science and Scientists. An East-West Dialogue on Research Evaluation in Post-Communist Europe*. Budapest: Central European University Press.

Gabor, I (1997). Too many, too small: Small entrepreneurship in Hungary — ailing or prospering? In Grabher and Stark (eds.).

Gaponenko, N (1995). Transformation of the research system in a transitional society: The case of Russia. *Social Studies of Science*, 25, EASST Special Issue.

Gaponenko, N (1996). *Transformation of the System of Innovation in a Society in Transition: The Case of the Russian Federation*. Paper presented at the UN/ECE Seminar on State Policy in Economies in Transition, Analytical Centre on Science and Industrial Policy, Moscow.

Glowny Urzad Statystczny (1998). *Dzialalnosc Innowacyna Przedsiebrostw w latach 1994–1996*, Warsaw.

Grabher, G and D Stark (eds.) (1997). *Restructuring Networks in Post-Socialism: Legacies, Linkages, and Localities.* Oxford University Press.

Gokhberg, L and I Kuznetsova (1999). Measuring innovation activities of industrial enterprises in Russia. In Knell, Hutschenreiter and Radošević (eds.).

Gower, P (1997). *Banking Development in the Czech Republic: An Analysis of Credit Allocation.* Thesis for the degree of D.Phil., University of Sussex.

Hanson, P (1997). What sort of capitalism is developing in Russia? *Communist Economies and Economic Transformation,* 9(1), 27–42.

Hosking, G (1998). Russia has to re-establish trust, even if it means price controls. *The Independent,* 29 August 1998, Weekend Review, p. 3.

Hutschenreiter, G, M Knell and S Radošević (1999). Restructuring innovation systems in central and eastern Europe. In Hutschenreiter, Knell, and Radošević (eds.).

Inzelt, A-M (1999). The transformation role of FDI in R&D: Analysis based on material from a databank. In Dyker and Radošević (eds.), pp. 185–201.

Jasinski, A (1997). *Academy-Industry Relations for Innovation in Poland.* STEEP Working Paper, No. 41, SPRU, University of Sussex.

Jablecka, J (1995). Changes in the management and finance of the research system in Poland: A survey of the opinions of grant applicants. *Social Studies of Science,* 25, EASST Special Issue.

Justman, M and M Teubal (1996). Technological infrastructure policy (TIP): Creating capabilities and building markets. In Teubal *et al.* (eds.).

Kekic, L (1996). Assessing and measuring progress in the transition. *Economies in Transition: Regional Overview,* 2nd quarter 1996. Economist Intelligence Unit, London.

Knell, M, G Hutschenreiter and S Radošević (eds.). *Restructuring of Innovation Systems in Central Europe and Russia.* Cheltenham: Edward Elgar.

Kovaleva, N (1999). Higher education and the labour market in Russia: Trends in the transition period. In Dyker and Radošević (eds.), pp. 429–45.

Kozlowski, J and D Ircha (1999). The structure of disciplinary comparative advantage in post-communist countries. In Dyker and Radošević (eds.), pp. 107–22.

Kramarenko, VG (1998). What is the fate of S&T in the Republic of Moldova? In Meske *et al.* (eds.), pp. 150–152.

Lundvall, B-A (ed.) (1992). *National Systems of Innovation — Towards a Theory of Innovation and Interactive Learning.* London: Pinter.

Malitsky, B, V Onoprienko and L Kavunenko (1998). Toward a national STS in Ukraine. In Meske *et al.* (eds.), pp. 129–140.

Martin, R (1998). Central and Eastern Europe and the international economy: The limits to globalisation. *Europe-Asia Studies,* 50(1), pp. 7–26.

Martinson, H, I Dagyté and J Kristapsons (1998). Transformation of R&D systems in the Baltic states. In Meske *et al.* (eds.), pp. 108–117.

Matthew, J (1996). Organisational foundations of the knowledge-based economy. In OECD.

Meske, W (1996). Academic-industry relations in East German innovation. In A Webster (ed.).

Meske, W (1997). *Institutional Transformation of STS in Economies in Transition: The Unique Problem of the Complexity of Changes on Different Levels*. Paper presented to TSER project "Restructuring and Reintegration of S&T Systems in Economies in Transition" workshop, Berlin, DIW, January 23–24, 1997, WZB, Berlin.

Meske, W *et al.* (eds.) (1998). *Transforming Science and Technology Systems — The Endless Transition?* Amsterdam: IOS Press.

Mosoni-Fried, J (1995). Industrial research in Hungary: A victim of structural change. *Social Studies of Science*, 25, EASST Special Issue.

Müller, K (1997). The Institutional Transformation of the S&T-System in the Czech Republic (Country Report). Unpublished paper, WZB, Berlin.

Nelson, R (ed.) (1993). *National Systems of Innovation: A Comparative Study*. Oxford: University Press.

Nesvetailov, GA (1997). Transformation of Science and Technology System in Belarus (Country Report). Unpublished paper, WZB, Berlin.

Niedbalska, G (1999). Polish innovation surveys: The state-of-the-art, analysis of results and plans for the future. In Knell, Hutschenreiter and Radošević (eds.).

OECD (1996). *Employment and Growth in the Knowledge-based Economy*. OECD Documents, Paris.

——— (1997). *Science, Technology and Industry Outlook 1996*. Paris.

Orel, VM (1995). Sotsial no-ekonomicheskie aspekty razvitiya nauki v Rossii. In *Sotsialnaya Dinamika Sovremennoi Nauki*, VZ Kelle, EZ Mirskaya and SA Kugel *et al.*(eds.). Moscow: Nauka.

Peck, M, J Gacs and L Gokhberg (1997). *Russian Applied R&D: Its Problems and Promise*. IIASA Research Report, Laxenbourg.

Peteri, G (1993). From the "enterprising" local government towards local economic development. In *Private Sector Development and Local Government in Hungary*, Papers and Proceedings of a conference organized by the Centre for International Private Enterprise and the Public Policy Institute Foundation, Eger (Hungary), pp. 10–11 September 1993, Budapest: Public Policy Institute Foundation.

Radošević, S (1994). Strategic technology policy for Eastern Europe. *Economic Systems*, 18(2), 87–116.

——— (1996). Restructuring of R&D institutes in post-socialist economies: Emerging patterns and issues. In A Webster (ed.).

——— (1997). Strategic policies for growth in post-socialism: Theory and evidence based on the case of Baltic states. *Economic Systems*, 21(2), 165–196.

Radošević, S (1998). Transformation of S&T systems into systems of innovation in central and eastern Europe: The emerging patterns of recombination, path-dependency and change. *SPRU Electronic Working Papers Series* No. 9, University of Sussex, Brighton.

—— (1999). Restructuring of research, technology and development in countries of central and eastern Europe. In Hutschenreiter, Knell, and Radošević (eds.).

Robertson, N (1992). Economic articulation: A neglected dimension of economic performance? *ISS Working Paper Series*, 122, April. The Hague: Institute of Social Studies.

Sandu, S (1998). Industrial R&D reforms in Romania. In W Meske *et al.* (eds.)., pp. 244–52.

Schneider, C (1995). *Systemic Transformation and its Impact on Industrial Innovation Networks: The Case of the "Research-Plc" in Eastern Germany.* Paper presented at the workshop "Discontinuous Institutional Change and the Economic System: Theory and Evidence", July 8–13, Castel Ivano, Italy, ROSES-CNRS, Paris, mimeo.

—— (1998). Institutional Transformation in the Industrial R&D Sector — Changes in Organisational Structures, Functions, and Interrelations: Analysis by Country: Czech Republic (Country Report). Unpublished paper, WZB, Berlin.

Simeonova, K (1994). *Innovation Capacities Embodied in Academy – Industry Relations: Bulgarian Case.* Bulgarian Academy of Sciences, mimeo.

—— (1997). The Institutional Transformation of the S&T System in Bulgaria Directed to a New (National) Innovation System (Country Report). Unpublished Paper, WZB, Berlin.

Stanovnik, P (1998). The Slovenian S&T transition. In Meske *et al.* (eds.), pp. 98–107.

Swaan, W (1995). *Capabilities and Competitiveness of the Hungarian Economy.* Paper presented at the conference "Hungary: Towards a Market Economy", Budapest, Hungarian Academy of Sciences, 20–21, October.

Swaan, W (1997). *Capabilities and Institutional Change: Post-Socialist Economies and Later Industrialising Economies Compared.* Paper presented to the First Paris Workshop, European Association for Comparative Economic Studies, 29–30 September.

Teubal, M (1997). A catalytic and evolutionary approach to horizontal technology policies (HTPs). *Research Policy*, 25, 1161–88.

Teubal, M *et al.* (eds.). *Technological Infrastructure Policy: An International Perspective.* Dordrecht: Kluwer.

Urem, B (1999). R&D behaviour of firms in transition economies: An analysis of the key determinants. In Dyker and Radošević (eds.), pp. 173–84.

Yudanov, A (1997). USSR: Large enterprises in the USSR — the functional disorder. In A Chandler *et al.* (eds.).

Webster, A (ed.) (1996). *Building New Bases for Innovation: The Transformation of the R&D System in Post-Socialist States.* Anglia Polytechnic University, Cambridge.

Zajac, S (1997). Institutional transformation of the S&T System in Slovakia (Country Report). Unpublished paper, WZB, Berlin.

Part VI

Patterns and Prospects

Chapter 11

Economic Performance in the Transition Economies: A Comparative Perspective

INTRODUCTION: CONTRASTS AND COMMON FEATURES IN GENERAL PATTERNS OF ECONOMIC PERFORMANCE

Some dozen or so years after the beginning of the process of restoration of market/capitalist economic systems in Eastern Europe and the former Soviet Union, and with the new millennium just begun, we find ourselves in an ideal position to review the results of the early phase of the transition process. Given that the main features of the old system were invariable, and given the goal of restoring capitalism is shared by every country in the region, it is perhaps surprising that the impact of transition on basic output trends has been so variable between countries (See Table 1). But this is an advantage from the analytical point of view, because it allows us to use inter-country comparisons to gauge the relative importance of different factors of transition. Before attempting to do that, however, let us take a look at the features that are common throughout Eastern Europe and the former Soviet Union. *All* the economies of the region suffered a dramatic collapse of output in the early 1990s, no doubt inevitably given the depth of the

Table 1. Eastern Europe and the former Soviet Union: Basic economic indicators 1990–2001 (annual percentage change).

	1990	1991	1992	1993	1994	1995	1996	1997	1998	1999	2000	2001
GDP												
Eastern Europe	**-7.9**	**-11.5**	**-6.0**	**-1.7**	**3.9**	**5.9**	**4.1**	**2.8**	**1.8**	**1.7**	**3.7**	**3.0**
Albania	-13.1	-27.7	-9.7	11.0	9.4	8.0	9.1	-7.0	8	7.3	7.8	7.0
Bosnia & Hercegovina	1.6	—	—	—	—	—	—	—	—	—	9.1	8.0
Bulgaria	-9.1	-11.7	-5.7	-1.5	1.8	2.1	-10.9	-6.9	3.5	2.4	5.8	4.9
Croatia	-8.5	-20.9	-9.7	-3.7	0.6	7.1	6.0	6.5	2.5	-0.4	3.7	4.3
Czech Rep.	-1.2	-14.2	-6.4	-0.9	2.6	5.9	4.1	1.0	-2.2	-0.4	2.9	3.6
Hungary	-3.3	-11.9	-4.3	-2.3	2.9	1.5	1.3	4.6	4.9	4.2	5.2	3.8
Poland	-11.6	-7.0	2.6	3.8	5.2	7.0	6.1	6.9	4.8	4.1	4.0	1.1
Romania	-8.2	-12.9	-8.2	1.3	3.9	7.1	4.1	-6.9	-5.4	-1.2	1.8	5.3
Slovakia	-2.5	-11.2	-7.0	-3.2	4.9	7.3	6.9	6.5	4.4	1.9	2.2	3.3
Slovenia	-4.7	-8.1	-5.4	1.3	5.3	4.1	3.1	4.6	3.9	5.2	4.6	3.0
FYR Macedonia	-10.2	-12.1	-13.4	-14.1	-7.2	-1.2	0.7	1.5	2.9	4.3	4.6	-4.6
FR Yugoslavia	-8.4	-11.2	-26.2	-27.7	2.5	6.1	5.9	7.4	2.5	-17.7	6.4	6.2
Baltic states	**-3.9**	**-11.5**	**-32.5**	**-17.5**	**-0.2**	**2.1**	**3.7**	**7.6**	**4.5**	**-1.7**	**5.4**	**6.2**
Estonia	-8.1	-10.0	-14.2	-8.6	-2.7	4.3	4.0	11.4	4.0	-0.7	6.9	5.3
Latvia	2.7	-10.4	-34.9	-14.9	0.6	-0.8	2.8	6.5	3.9	1.1	6.8	7.6
Lithuania	-6.9	-13.1	-39.3	-27.1	1.0	3.0	4.2	6.1	5.1	-3.9	3.9	5.7
CIS[1]	**-3.4**	**-11.5**	**-17.8**	**-11.5**	**-14.5**	**-5.5**	**-4.4**	**1.1**	**-3.0**	**4.5**	**8.3**	**6.2**
Armenia	-8.2	-8.8	-52.3	-14.8	5.4	6.9	5.8	3.1	7.2	3.3	6.0	9.6
Azerbaijan	-11.3	-0.7	-22.6	-23.1	-19.7	-11.8	1.3	5.8	10.0	7.4	11.1	9.9
Belarus	-3.2	-1.2	-9.6	-9.5	-12.6	-10.4	2.8	11.4	8.4	3.4	5.8	4.1
Georgia	-4.3	-20.1	-40.3	-39.4	-30.0	2.6	8.6	11.3	2.9	3.0	2.0	4.5
Moldova	-1.5	-18.7	-28.3	-4.8	-31.2	-1.9	-7.8	1.6	-8.6	-3.4	2.1	6.1
Russia	-2.0	-12.8	-19.2	-12	-12.7	-4.1	-4.9	0.8	-4.9	5.4	9.0	5.0
Ukraine	-3.6	-11.6	-13.7	-14.2	-22.9	-12.2	-10.0	-3.2	-1.7	-0.2	5.9	9.1
Former GDR	**-15.5**	**-19.2**	**7.8**	**5.8**	**9.9**	**5.2**	**1.9**	**1.7**	**2.0**	**1.4**	**2.1**	**-0.7**

	1990	1991	1992	1993	1994	1995	1996	1997	1998	1999	2000	2001
Industrial output												
Eastern Europe	**-15.1**	**-18.5**	**-10.0**	**-3.0**	**6.7**	**8.0**	**5.8**	**5.6**	**0.8**	**0.3**	**8.4**	**3.2**
Albania	-7.5	-41.9	-30.1	2.5	-18.6	-7.2	13.6	-5.6	21.8	16.0	12.0	-20.0
Bosnia & Hercegovina	0.9	-16.2	—	—	—	60.8	87.3	35.7	23.8	10.6	8.8	12.2
Bulgaria	-17.2	-22.2	-15.9	-10.0	8.5	9.1	-8.3	-10.2	-12.7	-9.3	5.8	0.7
Croatia	-11	-28.5	-14.6	-5.9	-2.7	0.3	3.1	6.8	3.7	-1.4	1.7	6.0
Czech Rep.	-3.3	-24.4	-7.9	-5.3	2.1	8.7	1.8	4.5	1.6	-3.1	5.4	6.8
Hungary	-4.5	-19.1	-9.8	3.9	9.5	4.5	3.4	11.1	12.5	10.4	18.7	4.1
Poland	-24.2	-11.9	3.9	7.3	11.9	9.7	8.3	11.5	3.5	3.6	6.7	0.0
Romania	-19.0	-22.8	-21.9	1.3	3.3	9.4	9.9	-7.2	-16.8	-2.2	8.2	8.2
Slovakia	-4.0	-17.6	-14.1	-10.6	4.6	8.3	2.4	1.7	3.8	-3.0	9.3	5.6
Slovenia	-10.5	-12.4	-13.2	-2.8	6.4	2.0	1.0	1.0	3.7	-0.5	6.2	2.9
FYR Macedonia	-11.0	-17.2	-15.8	-14.6	-10.6	-10.8	3.1	1.6	4.5	-2.6	3.5	-10.1
FR Yugoslavia	-11.7	-17.6	-22.4	-37.4	1.2	3.8	7.5	9.5	3.6	-23.1	11.2	0.0
Baltic states	**-2.5**	**-3.4**	**-33.5**	**-33.9**	**-15.7**	**1.3**	**4.6**	**9.4**	**5.6**	**-8.0**	**7.1**	**12.5**
Estonia	-5.6	-7.2	-38.9	-26.6	-2.0	1.9	2.9	13.4	2.3	-3.4	13.1	7.5
Latvia	-0.2	-0.7	-34.8	-38.1	-6.8	-3.7	5.5	13.8	3.1	-5.4	4.7	8.4
Lithuania	-2.8	-3.5	-30.0	-34.2	-28.0	5.3	5.0	3.3	8.2	-11.2	5.3	16.9
CIS[1]	**-1.1**	**-7.8**	**-18**	**-12.5**	**-21.5**	**-5.9**	**-2.8**	**2.6**	**-3.0**	**9.2**	**11.6**	**6.7**
Armenia	-7.5	-7.7	-48.2	-10.3	5.3	1.5	1.2	0.9	-2.7	5.3	6.4	3.8
Azerbaijan	-6.3	4.8	-23.7	-7.0	-22.7	-17.2	-6.7	0.3	2.2	3.6	6.9	5.1
Belarus	2.1	-1.0	-9.4	-7.4	-17.1	-11.7	3.5	18.8	12.4	10.3	7.8	5.4
Georgia	-5.7	-22.6	-45.8	-26.6	-39.7	-9.8	7.7	8.2	-2.7	7.4	6.1	-1.1
Moldova	3.2	-11.1	-27.1	-10	-27.7	-3.9	-6.5	0.0	-15.0	-11.6	7.7	14.2
Russia	..	-8.0	-18.0	-14.1	-20.9	-3.3	-4.0	2.0	-5.2	11.0	11.9	4.9
Ukraine	-0.1	-4.8	-6.4	-22.4	-27.3	-12.0	-5.1	-0.3	-1.0	4.0	12.4	14.2
Former GDR	**-27.3**	**-49.1**	**-6.4**	**5.8**	**13.9**	**5.8**	**4.6**	**5.8**	**7.6**	**7.4**	**10.5**	**3.7**

[1] Including the Asian members of the CIS, not separately listed.

Source: Various editions of the *Economic Survey of Europe*, Economic Commission for Europe, United Nations, Geneva.

systemic changes taking place, and no doubt exacerbated by the collapse of the CMEA trading system. *None* has made a really impressive recovery from that collapse, at least in purely quantitative terms, with the best of them having only recently recovered the output levels of the 1980s. *Some* have actually fallen into renewed recession, after the initial recovery (Bulgaria 1996–97, the Czech Republic and Romania 1997–99, Poland 2001–present). In almost every country the close relationship between GDP growth and growth in industrial production characteristic of the old communist days has been maintained, despite the rapid development of the services industry in the region as a whole.

There are, at the same time, very striking contrasts between the growth performance of individual countries and groups of countries. Until recently, Poland stood out as a star performer, outstripping all the other countries of the region. At the level of sub-regions, we can see that the Central-East European group (Poland, the Czech Republic, Slovakia, Hungary and Slovenia) have performed significantly better than any of the other major groups of transition economies in purely quantitative terms. The gap between them and the others is, of course, even bigger when we take into account qualitative variables like law and order, civic renewal, etc. The fact that these five (among others) are now about to accede to the European Union can be interpreted as in part a reward for relatively good performance on the major aggregate indicators of transition. It does, of course, at the same time increase the gap between them and the others. Overall, the former Soviet Union compares poorly with Central-East Europe on quantitative performance, against the background of widespread disintegration of the social fabric, though both CIS and Baltic countries have been narrowing the gap since 1999. The former Soviet Union remains a large and disparate area, and there has been wide variation in performance between different sub-groups of successor states. All of the Transcaucasian CIS countries reported positive growth throughout the period 1996–2001, but only after particularly steep falls in GDP levels in the preceding years. The two main CIS economies, the Russian and Ukrainian, were still showing declines in GDP in 1996, and hopes raised by the achievement of a modest 0.8 per cent increase in GDP in Russia in 1997 were cruelly dashed in 1998 in the aftermath of the financial crisis which overtook the country in the middle of that year. But recovery from the crisis was swift, and the Russian economy has performed well in aggregate terms since then. In Ukraine, recovery in GDP growth rates had to wait for the new millennium, but the recovery has been sustained. In Moldova, recovery has been extremely weak.

Economic performance in the countries of South-East Europe through the last decade of the 20th century was dominated by the impact and aftermath of the Yugoslav war. Not surprisingly, most of these countries reported weak growth over that period, after a dramatic collapse in output levels in the early 1990s. The main exceptions are Croatia, where GDP growth trends 1995–97 shadowed Polish, and Bulgaria, where apparently favourable initial conditions for economic transformation were belied by a pattern of relentless contraction of GDP through the late 1990s. Romania flattered to deceive in the mid-1990s, before descending into a renewed output collapse in 1997–1998. There have been modest recoveries in both Bulgaria and Romania in the early 2000s, while GDP growth in Croatia has fallen away. The NATO bombardment of Yugoslavia (Serbia & Montenegro) in 1999 precipitated a renewed collapse of production in that country, from which recovery has been weak.

In a region of generally poor-to-mediocre overall economic performance, then, only a small group of countries can be said to have "made it", in terms of reestablishing some kind of sustained pattern of economic growth. Others have managed two-three years of continuous growth at different points in time, but have not been able, at least up to the present time, to maintain the impetus. Yet others continue to flounder in something between recession and stagnation. How are we to explain these differences? In terms of initial conditions? In terms of the quality of economic policy-making? Before trying to answer those questions, let us broaden out the picture of economic performance by looking at figures on inflation, unemployment and productivity.

UNDERLYING PATTERNS OF TRANSFORMATION — MACRO STABILITY AND INCREASES IN EFFICIENCY

Table 2 suggests an intriguing, but complex relationship between macroeconomic stabilisation and recovery in terms of growth. There

Table 2.   Eastern Europe and the former Soviet Union: Inflation (percentage change) and unemployment (percentage of total work force), 1990–2001.

	1990	1991	1992	1993	1994	1995	1996	1997	1998	1999	2000	2001
Inflation (December/December)												
Eastern Europe												
Albania	—	104	266	85	15.0	6.0	17.4	42.0	7.8	−1.0	4.2	3.5
Bosnia & Hercegovina	—	—	—	—	94.7	−34.2	3.2	12.2	2.2	−0.4	3.4	1.5
Bulgaria	19.3	254	79	73	122.0	33.0	311.1	578.7	0.9	6.2	11.2	4.8
Croatia	—	223	766	1,538	−3.0	3.7	3.5	4.0	5.6	4.6	7.5	2.5
Czech Rep.	—	57	11	21	10.3	7.9	8.7	9.9	6.7	2.5	4.1	4.2
Hungary	28.9	35	23	23	21.3	28.5	20.0	18.4	10.4	11.3	10.1	6.9
Poland	558.4	70	43	37	29.4	22.0	18.7	13.2	8.5	9.9	8.6	3.6
Romania	5.7	166	211	257	61.9	27.7	56.8	151.7	40.7	54.9	40.7	30.2
Slovakia	—	61	10	23	11.8	7.4	5.5	6.5	5.5	14.4	8.3	6.5
Slovenia	—	118	201	33	18.3	8.6	8.8	8.8	6.6	8.1	9.0	7.1
FYR Macedonia	—	—	—	350	55.1	11.2	0.3	4.5	−1.0	2.4	6.1	3.7
FR Yugoslavia	—	120	8,991	2.2E +14	8E +09	110.7	59.9	10.3	45.7	54.0	115.1	40.5
Baltic states												
Estonia	—	283	969	88	41.8	28.8	14.9	12.3	6.8	3.9	5.0	4.3
Latvia	—	172	950	109	26.1	23.3	13.2	7.0	2.8	3.3	1.9	3.0
Lithuania	—	216	1,020	410	45.0	35.5	13.1	8.5	2.4	0.3	1.5	2.1
CIS[1]												
Armenia	—	174	729	2,260	1,763	32.0	5.6	21.8	−1.2	2.1	0.4	2.8
Azerbaijan	—	102	1,063	981	1,787	84.5	6.8	0.3	−7.6	−0.5	2.1	1.5
Belarus	—	94	1,016	1,682	1,957	244.2	39.1	63.4	181.6	251.3	108.0	46.3
Georgia	—	—	767	11,647	9,198	57.4	12.6	7.3	10.8	11.1	4.6	3.4
Moldova	—	98	941	1,576	104.6	23.8	15.1	11.1	18.2	43.8	18.5	6.4
Russia	—	100	1,468	911	214.8	131.4	21.8	11.0	84.5	36.7	20.1	18.8
Ukraine	—	84	1,240	4,474	401.1	181.7	39.7	10.1	20.0	19.2	25.8	6.1
Former GDR	—	—	**11**	**9**	**3.5**	**2.6**	**1.6**	**2.3**	**1.1**	**0.2**	—	—

	1990	1991	1992	1993	1994	1995	1996	1997	1998	1999	2000	2001
Unemployment												
Eastern Europe	—	9.4	**12.4**	**14.0**	**13.6**	**12.5**	**11.8**	**11.9**	**12.6**	**14.6**	**15.2**	**15.6**
Albania	9.5	9.4	27.0	22.0	18.0	13.1	12.1	14.9	17.6	18.2	16.9	15.0
Bosnia & Hercegovina	—	—	—	—	—	—	—	39.0	38.3	39.0	39.4	40.0
Bulgaria	1.8	11.5	15.6	16.4	12.8	11.1	12.5	13.7	12.2	16.0	17.9	17.3
Croatia	—	14.1	17.8	16.6	17.3	17.6	15.9	17.6	18.6	20.8	22.6	23.1
Czech Rep.	0.7	4.1	2.6	3.5	3.2	2.9	3.5	5.2	7.5	9.4	8.8	8.9
Hungary	1.7	7.4	12.3	12.1	10.4	10.4	10.5	10.4	9.1	9.6	8.9	8.0
Poland	6.5	11.8	14.3	16.4	16.0	14.9	13.6	10.3	10.4	13.1	15.1	17.4
Romania	1.3	3.1	8.2	10.4	10.9	9.5	6.3	8.8	10.3	11.5	10.5	8.6
Slovakia	1.6	11.8	10.4	14.4	14.8	13.1	12.8	12.5	15.6	19.2	17.9	18.6
Slovenia	—	10.1	13.3	15.5	14.2	14.5	14.4	14.8	14.6	13.0	12.0	11.8
FYR Macedonia	—	24.5	26.8	30.3	33.2	37.2	39.8	42.5	—	43.8	44.9	41.7
FR Yugoslavia	—	15.7	24.6	24.0	23.9	24.7	26.1	25.6	27.2	27.4	26.6	27.9
Baltic states	—	—	**2.1**	**4.5**	**5.3**	**6.5**	**6.4**	**6.3**	**7.3**	**9.1**	**10.0**	**10.1**
Estonia	—	0.1	1.6	5.0	5.1	5.0	5.6	4.6	5.1	6.7	7.3	7.2
Latvia	—	—	2.3	5.8	6.5	6.6	7.2	6.7	9.2	9.1	7.8	7.7
Lithuania	—	0.3	3.6	3.4	4.5	7.3	6.2	6.7	6.9	10.0	12.6	12.9
CIS[1]	—	—	**2.7**	**3.6**	**4.4**	**5.8**	**6.2**	**7.6**	**8.5**	**8.3**	**7.1**	**6.2**
Armenia	—	—	3.5	6.3	6.0	8.1	9.7	11.0	8.9	11.5	10.9	9.8
Azerbaijan	—	0.1	0.2	0.7	0.9	1.1	1.1	1.3	1.4	1.2	1.2	1.3
Belarus	—	—	0.5	1.3	2.1	2.7	4.0	2.8	2.3	2.0	2.1	2.3
Georgia	—	—	0.3	2.0	3.8	3.4	3.2	8.0	4.2	5.6	—	—
Moldova	—	—	0.7	0.7	1.0	1.4	1.5	1.7	1.9	2.1	1.8	1.7
Russia	—	0.1	4.7	5.5	7.1	8.9	9.3	11.2	12.4	12.2	9.8	9.0
Ukraine	—	—	0.3	0.4	0.3	0.6	1.5	2.8	4.3	4.3	4.2	3.7
Former GDR	—	—	—	—	**13.5**	**14.9**	**15.9**	**19.4**	**17.4**	**17.7**	**17.2**	**17.6**

[1] Including the Asian members of the CIS, not separately listed.

Source: Various editions of the *Economic Survey of Europe*, Economic Commission for Europe, United Nations, Geneva.

certainly seems to be no special virtue in getting inflation right down to zero. The only transition economies claiming rates of inflation below 2 per cent in 1998 were Azerbaijan and Bosnia, hardly front-runners in terms of renewed economic development. Indeed if we look at the inflation data for all the countries of the region for 1999–2001, we see a remarkably flat picture. The great majority of them report annual rates of inflation of between 2 and 20 per cent, and there is no pattern of correlation between the pecking order for inflation and that for economic growth. In Poland, the inflation rate has come down as growth has stalled over recent years. In Hungary, growth rates of GDP have accelerated over recent years, as inflation rates have remained relatively high. And in Slovenia, GDP growth and inflation have accelerated together since 1998. Surveying the whole transition period, we can see that consistent reductions in infla-tion, year-by-year, have been more important than good performance on inflation in any one year, and that makes sense in terms of what we understand of the impact of inflationary trends on business and con-sumer expectations. Even here, however, the correspondence is far from complete. Russia to mid-1998 is as good an example as Poland of a steady reduction in inflation from initially high levels — yet in terms of output recovery, the two countries stand at opposite ends of the spectrum. Certainly, the dimension of *initial impact* seems to be important — thus in Poland the inflation rate had been reduced to some 40 per cent by as early as 1992, whereas in Russia it was still over 100 per cent in 1995. To that extent, the *shock therapy* argument is surely proven. Sustainability is also important. Again, it is worth noting that inflation has gone down in Poland in every single year since 1990 except 1999. In Russia, by contrast, the financial crisis of mid-1998 and the subsequent reversion to high rates of inflation exposed in dramatic fashion the dangers of basing macroeconomic stabilisation policies on foreign borrowing and non-payment of wages and salaries in the public sector. But the overall pattern of the figures for growth and inflation over the whole region and the whole period leaves us in no doubt that macroeconomic stabilisation is a necessary, but not sufficient condition of effective economic transformation. If we want to penetrate deeper into the underlying factors of economic transformation we must clearly go beyond aggregate macroeconomic data to the level of structural indicators as such.

What do the unemployment figures tell us? To the extent that effective economic transformation means shaking labour out of sunset industries and redeploying it in sunrise industries (and services), we might expect to see sharp initial increases in unemployment, followed by gradual, sustained reductions, in the "first division" countries. In fact, the only countries that follow this pattern are Hungary (fairly weakly) and Slovenia (very weakly). In Poland, unemployment starts rise sharply again from 1999, well before the output recession sets in in that country. In Slovakia unemployment goes high and stays high. In the Czech Republic it starts off low and stays low until the fallout of the 1997 financial crisis and the consequent recession begins to show. It does not start to fall again as output recovers in the early 2000s. The pattern is similar in Romania. But here average rates of unemployment are much higher, and there is a weak downward trend in the early 2000s. In the countries of the former Soviet Union, unemployment has stayed remarkably low — under 5 per cent in most cases. Does this tell us that that less muscular transformation policies (taking macroeconomic policy orientation as a crude proxy for transformation policy as a whole) do, at least, make for less unemployment? Certainly Russia, which has followed a more consistent reform line than any other CIS country, reports, along with Armenia, the highest unemployment figures in that region. But the low reported unemployment figures of countries like Ukraine do, in fact, reflect concealed unemployment on a massive scale. If account is taken of the number of workers in that country who are on indefinite unpaid leave (but still with social security benefits), the rate of employment rises to around 30 per cent, comparable to that of beleaguered Macedonia, which suffered from the "double blockade" (the UN against Serbia and Greece against Macedonia) during the years of the first Yugoslav war, which has only just begun to repair the damage inflicted in that period, but which is at least more honest in its reporting of unemployment.

Like the inflation figures, then, the unemployment data tell us a good deal, but not enough. They tell us that if you do something

Table 3.   Eastern Europe and the former Soviet Union: Measured labour productivity, 1991–2001 (annual percentage change).

	1991	1992	1993	1994	1995	1996	1997	1998	1999	2000	2001
Total labour productivity[a]											
Albania	-26.7	19.0	14.6	-1.4	11.4	11.3	-6.3				
Bulgaria	1.4	1.0	0.1	1.2	0.5	-11.0	-4.3				
Croatia	-12.7	0.1	2.6	3.0	3.0	6.0	7.3				
Czech Rep.	-9.3	-3.9	0.7	1.8	2.1	3.4	2.0				
Hungary	-2.3	6.8	4.7	5.3	3.4	1.8	4.5				
Poland	-1.2	7.2	6.4	4.2	5.1	4.1	4.0				
Romania	-12.5	-5.9	5.5	4.5	12.9	5.4	-7.8				
Slovakia	-2.4	-7.5	-1.3	6.0	5.3	6.1	7.1				
Slovenia	-0.3	1.3	5.1	7.2	4.2	3.6	4.8				
FYR Macedonia	-9.5	-9.1	-9.2	-2.0	7.3	5.3	6.2				
FR Yugoslavia	-8.9	-25.4	-28.8	4.6	7.5	6.4	9.0				
Estonia	-11.9	-8.2	3.8	-1.5	4.5	4.7	11.6				
Latvia	-9.6	-32.3	-8.0	4.0	-0.3	5.7	4.5				
Lithuania	-15.2	-32.5	-27.3	-7.2	5.0	5.1	5.5				
Armenia	-11.1	-38.4	-6.7	8.4	7.8	8.8	7.8				
Azerbaijan	-5.2	-19.3	-22.9	-17.9	-11.6	-0.7	5.6				
Belarus	1.3	-7.2	-9.4	-10.2	-4.1	3.8	11.3				
Georgia	-12.4	-24.2	-33.0	-28.2	3.5	8.4	6.5				
Moldova	-17.5	-28.4	-0.2	-30.9	-2.5	-7.1	2.4				
Russia	-3.1	-12.4	-7.1	-9.7	-1.2	-4.2	2.9				
Ukraine	-7.2	-8.1	-12.2	-19.9	-14.4	-7.3	-0.5				

Industrial labour productivity[b]

	1991	1992	1993	1994	1995	1996	1997	1998	1999	2000	2001
Albania	—	—	—	—	—	—	-8.8	27.9	—	57.0	—
Bulgaria	-5.2	-3.1	-2.8	12.6	6.6	-7.2	-6.4	-9.0	-3.7	18.4	6.4[c]
Croatia	-13.4	-0.8	-6.4	1.8	13.5	4.0	11.2	-2.1	1.4	4.4	8.4[c]
Czech Rep.	-21.4	-0.2	-0.5	7.9	8.6	2.6	5.6	2.2	0.1	8.2	6.9[c]
Hungary	-7.2	-0.2	16.3	14.7	10.5	4.3	9.3	7.5	9.4	20.2	2.3
Poland	-4.2	16.6	9.7	12.8	6.0	9.1	11.2	4.6	9.6	13.5	6.4[c]
Romania	-18.7	-10.0	10.4	8.6	16.2	8.8	-4.9	-12.0	-1.7	15.5	10.9[c]
Slovakia	-10.7	-3.6	-5.0	8.0	8.3	2.4	3.7	8.2	-0.7	12.8	4.1[c]
Slovenia	-2.3	-3.2	6.8	11.2	5.8	2.0	5.5	4.8	1.2	6.9	2.1[c]
FYR Macedonia	-9.9	-9.7	-9.4	-5.0	—	10.3	10.0	8.4	-1.7	8.4	-4.8[c]
FR Yugoslavia	-11.4	-17.1	-35.7	4.0	6.5	10.0	13.0	6.5	—	15.1	0.2[d]
Estonia	—	-28.1	-12.0	—	—	7.6	20.3	4.4	4.3	9.2	6.1[c]
Latvia	4.8	-28.6	-19.8	5.7	4.0	11.8	10.0	2.2	-5.1	2.5	9.2[c]
Lithuania	-5.5	-25.9	-23.2	-12.7	14.9	9.6	3.3	9.3	-10.0	7.5	18.2[c]
Armenia	-0.3	-41.4	0.3	7.5	20.0	20.2	12.4	6.4	13.0	15.6	3.4
Azerbaijan	7.3	-18.6	3.1	-20.0	-12.0	6.0	17.3	-1.5	0.4	11.0	4.4
Belarus	0.7	-3.5	-7.5	-13.1	-0.9	4.7	18.6	10.9	9.4	8.2	5.7
Georgia	—	—	—	—	—	49.9	40.8	-3.7	—	—	—
Moldova	-4.3	-25.5	69.9	-23.6	12.0	-4.9	2.4	-10.8	3.2	7.0	11.4
Russia	-6.3	-13.8	-12.0	-11.4	4.5	1.2	12.1	-0.1	8.9	9.5	3.4
Ukraine	-4.0	-1.8	-3.0	-19.0	-10.6	2.4	8.9	2.1	13.9	19.1	14.9

[a]GDP per employed person.

[b]Gross industrial output per person employed in industry.

[c]First nine months.

[d]First six months.

Source: Various editions of the *Economic Survey of Europe*, Economic Commission for Europe, United Nations, Geneva.

about transformation you get high unemployment; if you do nothing, you get even higher. To dig deeper into the structural dimension, we need to turn to data that tells us something directly about trends in the efficiency with which the employed labour force is being used. The figures on labour productivity presented in Table 3 give us a broad picture of those trends.

The productivity figures do, in fact, produce a much more starkly delineated picture of the pecking order of transition economies. This time Poland, Hungary and Estonia stand out high above all the others, with figures for industrial productivity growth averaging nearly 10 per cent. The Czech and Romanian recoveries of recent years have also been strongly based on industrial productivity growth. Most of the CIS countries have reported high rates of growth of industrial productivity since 1999, though industrial productivity levels in these countries remains generally below what they were in the early 1990s.

Generalisations about overall productivity trends are difficult in the absence of figures for total labour productivity for recent years. But it is clearly industry that is taking the lead in pushing up levels of efficiency in the transition economies. How does this square with the fact that it is the service sectors rather than industry that have been the main growth areas in many of the countries of the region since 1990? Quite simply because industrial labour productivity has risen largely through the slimming-down of labour forces, which has released labour for employment in the "new" service sectors — and into unemployment. Movement of labour from relatively low productivity industrial sectors into relatively high has, by contrast, been of minor importance as a factor of increased aggregate productivity, even among the first division countries. Indeed industrial recovery in the region has largely taken the form of recovery in traditional, low-to-medium-skill sectors like metallurgy, engineering and chemicals, and this is as true for, e.g. Poland, as it is for any other country.

Just as structural trends have been fairly uniform across the region, so also we find that, while productivity *performance* has varied strikingly, the *pattern* of productivity trends has shown key common features, at least in Eastern Europe. A fair generalisation for the whole sub-region would be that the tendency since around 1992 has been for overall productivity to grow, under the impetus of rapid growth in industrial productivity. In the countries where general economic performance has been less impressive, the gap between overall productivity and industrial productivity performance has been wider, suggesting a failure, in these cases, on the part of industry to "drag along" the other sectors of the economy (including the services sector) with it. The only exception to the pattern is Slovakia, where productivity performance has been as good for the economy as a whole as it has been for industry.

The picture in the former Soviet Union is somewhat different. Here, there are simply no trends, no patterns, up to 1996. Since then the statistics indicate a tendency for most of the countries in the sub-region to fall into the East European pattern of positive growth in total labour productivity driven by high growth in industrial labour productivity. Certainly the collapse in productivity in all these countries the early 1990s was quite dramatic, and it is in any case too early to say whether the figures reported for the last few years represent any kind of stable, sustained upward trend. But to the extent that there is a trend at the sub-regional level, it is a trend of convergence between Eastern Europe and the former Soviet Union.

To sum up this section, then, countries that have managed to grow in terms of GDP have generally done so on the basis of upward trends in productivity, with industrial productivity taking the lead. To put the point somewhat differently, countries that have managed to do something about industrial productivity have generally managed to do something about overall productivity, though there has been wide variation in the relationship between the two productivity series. The general tendency has been for "the recent recovery in many East European countries ... sharply [to] increase the labour productivity of those already employed rather than creating a net rise in new jobs" (ECE, 1997, p. 112), and Hungary stands out as the only country that has managed to increase productivity and reduce unemployment at the same time. In the former Soviet Union the failure to produce sustained GDP growth in the 1990s was matched by at best hesitant upward trends in labour productivity. In the 2000s, by contrast, both GDP and industrial productivity trends have been sharply upwards.

Productivity, then, must be a central element in any full explanation of the differences in economic performance between different transition countries. But while it is a central element, it cannot be an ultimate explanation, because levels of productivity are essentially an effect, rather than a cause. Relative success in macroeconomic stabilisation no doubt plays some role in determining productivity trends, in that labour incentives are stronger and business decision-taking easier, the more stable are prices. But there is clearly a lot more to productivity trends than shock therapy. We investigate further in the next section.

SOURCES OF PRODUCTIVITY ENHANCEMENT IN CONDITIONS OF TRANSITION

Given the generally positive assessment of privatisation programmes in the West, it might be expected that the *radical privatisation programmes* implemented in most of the transition countries since the early 1980s might have something to do with productivity trends. In fact, as Table 4 shows, there is no clear pattern of relationship between pace and extent of privatisation and productivity performance across the region. Russia, one of the most thoroughgoing privatisers, is one of weaker performers on productivity. Poland, a leader in the field in terms of productivity performance, has been a laggard in relation to privatisation. Slovenia, too, is near the bottom of the privatisation league, with only Yugoslavia (Serbia/Montenegro), among European transition countries, below it.

We must not take this argument too far. All transition economies have privatised, and if they had not, the general economic state of the region would surely be much worse than it is today. Countries with relatively very low rates of privatisation like Moldova (not in the table) also show poor performance on productivity. Most significant of all, the range of variation in privatisation indicators over the majority of transition countries is by 2002 really quite narrow. It is, nevertheless, quite clear that privatisation has not, in itself, been a key factor in the dynamics of transition. And this is hardly a surprising result. Privatisation has produced results in the West because it has

Table 4. The contribution of the private sector to GDP in selected transition countries, 1991–2002.

	1991	1992	1993	1994	1995	1996	1997	1998	2000	2002
Bulgaria	27	38	41	42	48	45	50	50	70	70
Czech Rep.	17	28	45	56	66	75	75	75	80	80
Hungary	30	47	55	60	65	70	75	80	80	80
Poland	42	47	52	53	58	60	65	65	70	75
Romania	24	26	32	39	45	60	60	60	60	65
Slovakia[a]	—	22	26	58	65	70	75	75	75	80
Slovenia	—	—	—	—	—	45	50	55	55	65
Yugoslavia	—	—	—	33	—	—	—	—	—	—
Latvia	—	—	—	55	—	60	60	60	65	70
Lithuania	16	37	57	62	65	65	70	70	70	75
Kyrgyzstan	26	28	39	43	—	50	60	60	60	60
Russian Federation	—	14	21	62	70	60	70	70	70	70

[a]Including the cooperative sector.
Source: ECE, 1997, p. 92; 1998, p. 122; various editions of EBRD *Transition Report*.

brought about changes in management, which have in turn brought about changes in key operational variables like productivity. The generally negative correlation between privatisation and productivity in Russia is actually quite easy to explain in terms of the failure of the former to produce any significant changes in patterns of *corporate governance*. It has proved particularly difficult in Russian conditions for new owners to oust incumbent managers and play any kind of strategic investor role.

The development of transparent and liquid capital markets in Russia has been hampered by policy choices *made during the rapid large-scale privatisation process* and by an environment in which property rights are not well defined or protected. In general, insider owners (managers and workers) have acquired particular advantages in monopolising information about their firms and holding on to assets in the face of attacks by outside investors, and in ousting partners from the control of profitable assets where the partners lack relevant contacts. In this way the

development of a functioning market...for corporate control
has been delayed (Hanson, 1997, p. 34, emphasis added).

Corporate governance does, indeed, always seem to be a problem
with fast-track, voucher-based privatisations, even when the special
political problems of the communist legacy that affect Russia are not
present. Thus in the Czech Republic, where the "velvet revolution"
largely cleared out the old *nomenklatura*, problems of corporate governance similar to those experienced in Russia emerged against the
background of a similar approach to privatisation (Gower, 1997).
While the reasons for the slow rate of privatisation in Poland and
Slovenia are multiple, "carefulness" about corporate governance is
certainly one of them (Belka & Krajewska, 1997, pp. 25–27; Mrcela,
1996, p. 17).

If the dynamic efficiency of management is the key variable in productivity performance, and if privatisation is at best a necessary condition for the fostering of such dynamic efficiency, what other factors
can provide sufficient conditions, whether singly or in combination?
The ones that spring immediately to mind are *foreign direct investment (FDI)*, the incidence and pattern of activity of *small and
medium-sized enterprises (SMEs)*, and the *intensity of domestic and
international competition*. Also worthy of consideration in terms of
its potential direct effect on productivity trends is *the status of the
national S&T system*. Let us take these in turn.

Why should we expect FDI to improve business efficiency? Most
obviously because it may result in the transfer of "hard" production
technologies, whether of process or product. This kind of technology
transfer has been particularly prominent in the transition region in
relation to FDI in the automotive and automotive components industries, in the computer systems and software sectors, in some branches
of chemicals like glass production, and in the oil industry (Dyker,
1996; Estrin, 1996a, 1996b; Havas, 1997; Watson, 1996). There
have been cases of Western multinationals adopting restrictive policies
in relation to outward technology transfer in the context of FDI
(Sharp & Barz, 1997), but this has not been the dominant pattern.
And where there has been significant transfer of hard technology, it

has often been backed up and "multiplied" through impacts on supplier industries. Thus Volkswagen/Škoda, for example, obtain 80 per
cent of their inputs (in an industry with a very high rate of input/
output ramification) from local suppliers. Ford and Audi, in their
operations in Hungary, have gone one step further, actually setting up
component-manufacturing subsidiaries in that country, but again in
the expectation that these plants would obtain sub-components from
locally-owned firms (Havas, 1997).

The process of transfer of "soft" management technology has
been more universal. In some cases Western firms, in taking control
of given firms in the transition region, have followed a policy of leaving the production floor more or less as it was, and simply superim-
posing their own management system and management technology,
in terms of software systems, on the firm (Dyker & Radošević, 1994).
In others, for example, in the Russian space-launching industry,
where there is a significant element of technology transfer from East
to West, the soft technology is essentially exchanged for hard technology (Bzhilianskaya, 1999). Where there is transfer of both hard and
soft technology, the two transfer processes tend to interact, and in
some sectors, e.g. in computer systems and software, this process of
interaction tends ultimately to generate significant innovatory impetus within the host firm (Dyker, 1996). It is not an exaggeration to
say that where there is FDI it is simply not possible for the investing
firm to prevent transfer of soft technology. And once given management technologies are transferred to particular firms through contact
with foreign firms, they tend to disseminate through the rest of the
economy fairly quickly.

While the case-study evidence on FDI is generally markedly positive, the macroeconomic evidence is indicative rather than emphatic.
As Table 3, Chapter 6 shows, the cumulative inflow of FDI into the
region has been substantial in absolute terms and per head of population. And the great bulk of it has gone to the three leading transition
countries, Poland, the Czech Republic and Hungary. The clearest
evidence of a causal link running from FDI to productivity, and
indeed to business efficiency in general, comes from Hungary, where
FDI has accounted for more than 20 per cent of gross fixed capital

formation throughout the transition period. Thus enterprises hosting
FDI accounted for 36.1 per cent of total employment in Hungarian
manufacturing in 1996, but 61.4 per cent of manufacturing sales and
77.5 per cent of exports of manufactures (Hunya, 1998, p. 12).
Estonia seems to fit in with the Hungarian pattern, though conclusive
evidence is lacking. The Czech case does *not* fit very well. High levels
of FDI penetration did not prevent the Czech economy going into
recession in 1997, though it should be noted that rates of growth in
industrial productivity kept up rather well in the Czech Republic
1997–1998, and have accelerated sharply since. In the Slovenian case,
good productivity performance has been accompanied by moderate
rates of FDI inflow, with no clear evidence on how the latter has
affected the pattern of productivity growth. Even more problematic is
the case of Poland, where the surge of FDI comes only in the late
1990s, raising suspicions that in this case FDI inflow may have been
as much a *result* as a cause of generally successful transition. Again, it
has to be said that that surge could not prevent the Polish economy
slipping into recession in the early 2000s. The negative evidence, on
the other hand, is generally supportive of the hypothesis of a causal
link between FDI and productivity performance.

Looking at the totality of the evidence, it is clear that FDI has been
an important factor of economic performance in the post-socialist
region. And there is a particularly clear relationship between FDI and
medium-term industrial labour productivity trends. There are hints
that the causal link between FDI and economic performance may be a
two-way one, and this is hardly surprising. Firms' investment decisions
are clearly affected by assessments of the local economic and business
environment in the proposed host country, and these assessments are
based, *inter alia*, on the performance variables that we have been looking at. The experience of Hungary shows how virtuous circles involving FDI and economic performance can be built up. It is nevertheless
clear that foreign direct investment is far from offering a complete
explanation of the pattern of economic performance among the transition countries. In the case of Poland in particular, there is simply no
clear relationship between the two. So there must be more to the story
than just FDI. What about domestic structural and policy factors?

Small and medium-sized enterprises are a key component of advanced industrial systems (Humphrey & Schmitz, 1996), and indeed SMEs (defined as companies employing up to 100 people) account for over 50 per cent of total employment in the European Union and between 60 and 80 per cent of the corresponding totals for the Mediterranean members of the EU. High-technology SMEs play a particularly important role in those economies, but usually in symbiosis with bigger companies. In the transition economies, SMEs have been of special importance for two main reasons. Firstly, they have effectively provided an alternative model of privatization — a model of "bottom-up" privatisation which is by definition untouched by the problems of legacies from the past in general, and of corporate governance in particular, which tend to afflict "top-down" privatisation. Secondly, they provide an outlet for the redeployment of a particular human-capital resource in which the transition countries are unusually rich — science and research and development workers (Balázs, 1996) (see below for further discussion). Still, the overall level of SME activity in the transition region remains low. Small and medium-sized enterprises accounted for just 12 per cent of total employment in Russia in 1997 (Pripisnov, 1999), and the figure is even lower in a number of other transition countries. But there is a wide range of variation between countries, and it is striking that countries like Poland, Hungary and Slovenia, which have good records on productivity growth, also report SME employment as a proportion of total employment at above 20 per cent (OECD, 1997, p. 103; Bobinski, 1998; Gábor, 1997)[1].

The reasons for this pattern are not hard to find. Efficiency in the SME sector is consistently well above average. Thus in Russia in 1994, for example, with just 3 per cent of the fixed capital stock and 10 per cent of the labour force (not counting part-time workers), SMEs produced 12 per cent of the total volume of goods and services in the country and accounted for one-third of total profits generated

---

[1]Note that István Gábor (1997) is sceptical about the relationship between the size of the SME sector and general levels of economic performance.

(Pripisnov, 1996). In countries like Russia, where the SME sector is relatively small, and is not growing as a proportion of the total economy, the direct impact of this on overall productivity trends has been very limited. In countries like Poland and Slovenia, where the SME sector is big, is growing, and maintains an efficiency lead over the rest of economy, the direct impact is substantial indeed (Jakupovic, 1994; Rems *et al.*, 1997; OECD, 1997, p. 103; Bobinski, 1998). To the extent that the SMEs concerned operate as "technology brokers" for the rest of economy (see Dyker, 1996; Balázs, 1996), there may be substantial indirect effects as well. Here, however, there is evidence of negative structural trends in recent years. Thus in both Poland and Russia, for example, the proportion of "high-tech" SMEs among total SMEs fell through the late 1990s (Niedbalska, 1999; "Rossiiskii", 1996, pp. 688–689). So in assessing the impact of SME activity on general productivity trends, we have to stick mainly to the direct impacts — a discouraging result for countries like Russia, where direct impacts are inevitably low, because the sector is so small relative to the rest of the economy. Even so, variations in levels of SME activity do appear to have been a significant, if not necessarily determining factor in relation to variations in overall productivity performance.

The *intensity of domestic and international competition* is the most difficult factor of productivity enhancement to assess. All the transition countries have monopoly and competition legislation, but often, and particularly in the former Soviet Union, the implementation of this legislation is blocked, or distorted out of all recognition, by entrenched groups (Dyker & Barrow, 1994, pp. 14–15; Hockuba, 1996, p. 19). The peculiar pattern of monopoly inherited from communism — whereby just one plant serves an entire region, or even an entire country, with a particular product — could not survive in a developed market economy, because it would be relatively easy in that context for domestic companies in related fields, or foreign companies in the same field, to *contest* those markets. Foreign direct investment has, indeed, sometimes been able to play this role in the transition countries, e.g. in the motor car industry and in petrol distribution. But there has not been enough FDI in the majority of transition countries for it to make a critical difference. Given the extent of domination of insiders and insider alliances of one kind or another in the pattern of industrial ownership and control in all the transition countries, challenging other people's markets, or indeed other people's right to manage, is still the most difficult thing to do. Import liberalisation has made a big impact — though because domestic producers in the food and consumer goods industries have generally been unable to stand the heat of international competition, there has been some tendency here for domestic monopolies or cartels to be replaced by foreign. Finally, monopolistic elements in Western markets have hampered the export efforts of transition countries, mainly through contingent protection in relation to "sensitive" sectors like steel and textiles, but also through the operation of internationally sanctioned cartel agreements, e.g. the one that has prevented the Russian space-launch industry, one of Russia's few areas of high-tech comparative advantage, from gaining its rightful share of the world space-launch market (Bzhilianskaya, 1999).

What can we conclude from all this? All the transition economies continue to suffer severely from monopoly and other restraints on competition, some domestically generated, some originating from the global economic sphere. All have introduced a substantial degree of competition from outside through import liberalisation. All transition countries have had difficulties in finding an appropriate way of regulating competition in the peculiar conditions of post-communism. But the countries of the former Soviet Union and the less developed countries of the Balkans seems to have had more difficulty here than the Central-East European countries. And that seems to make sense in terms of generally higher standards of state administration in that last group of countries — and also in terms of the pressure on states in line to accede to the EU to come into line with the *acquis communautaire* on this, as on other policy dimensions, *prior* to accession. To that extent, consideration of monopoly and competition issues helps us a little in our efforts to understand why the Central-East European countries have performed better in relation to productivity than the rest of the transition region, but only a little.

As Table 5 shows, the transition countries inherited large-scale *science and technology (S&T) complexes* from the old regimes.

Table 5.   Gross domestic expenditure on R&D (GERD) as a percentage of GDP (A) and total number of R&D workers per 1,000 employed (B).

	1990		1991		1992		1993		1994		1995		1996		1997		1998		1999		2000	
	A	B	A	B	A	B	A	B	A	B	A	B	A	B	A	B	A	B	A	B	A	B
Czech Rep.	—	—	—	16.3	1.71	12.0	1.23	8.0	1.14	7.3	1.04	4.4	1.07	4.5	1.16	—	1.24	—	1.25	—	1.35	—
Hungary	—	—	—	—	1.05	5.3	0.98	5.2	0.89	5.2	0.74	4.8	0.66	4.9	0.72	5.7	0.68	5.5	0.69	5.6	0.81	6.1
Poland	1.2[a]	—	0.9[a]	—	0.92[a]	—	—	—	0.82	4.6	0.74	4.9	0.76	4.8	0.71	5.4	0.72	5.3	0.75	5.4	0.70	5.3
Russia	2.0	25.8	1.5	22.7	0.75	21.3	0.78	18.6	0.80	16.2	0.75	16.0	0.80	15.5	0.97	16.2	0.92	15.2	1.01	15.4	1.09	15.6
Ukraine	1.62	—	1.5	—	1.05	—	1.08	—	1.08	—	1.08	—	1.15	—	1.45	—	—	—	—	—	—	—

[a]Estimates subject to a wide margin of error.

Sources: Various editions of OECD, *Main Science and Technology Indicators*; *Nauka Rossii vs Tsifrakh 1998*, CSRS, Ministry of Science and Technology, Moscow; Jasinski, 1994, p. 120.

Expenditure on *S&T* in relation to GDP fell sharply in the early 1990s before generally stabilising, in some cases even recovering a little, from around 1995, but the post-socialist countries continue to spend more on R&D than other countries with comparable levels of GDP per head. And numbers of *S&T* workers have generally held up at least as well as *S&T* expenditure.

In principle it should be possible to take these complexes as representative of the degree of endowment of the transition economies in human capital, a major element in the economic growth processes of all the developed and newly developing countries in the world. In practice, matters are not so easy. While the communist *S&T* systems were strong in basic science, at least in the more traditional hard sciences like physics and chemistry, they were weak in applied sciences, or rather they were weak in science as applied to *innovation*, and weak in emerging disciplines like biotechnology and artificial intelligence. The administrative structures of communist science were, not surprisingly, poorly adapted to the needs of the market economy, and the process of innovation was understood, to the extent that it was understood at all, in terms of a crude, linear, science-push conception.

While the process of transition has revolutionised the understanding of the process of innovation, it has failed to revolutionise the structures of *S&T* in the region. The administration of science is still dominated by the old Academies of Science in most of the countries of the region. While *S&T* expenditure was a whole has contracted sharply, expenditure on applied research has contracted more sharply than expenditure on basic science (Gokhberg, 1999). The fact that numbers of *S&T* personnel have fallen less dramatically reflects less devotion to science than a resistance to redeployment. Policies to encourage the development of "academy-industry links" adopted in the mid-1990s produced some isolated successes (see discussion above) but had no great impact at the aggregate level (Balázs, 1996; Jasinski, 1997).

Against this background, it is hardly surprising that no clear relationships emerge between statistical series relating to *S&T*, on the one hand, and productivity performance and economic performance in general on the other. The downward trend in *S&T* expenditure as a proportion of national income over the early transition period was fairly uniform across the spectrum of transition performers, running from Poland down to Ukraine. The sharpness of the cuts in R&D personnel in the Czech Republic, the only country where total personnel has fallen more sharply than expenditure, bears witness to the muscularity of restructuring policies in the *S&T* sector in that country. But there is no evidence of any impact therefrom on the general level of economic performance. Poland, the pacesetter in transition, continues to maintain an *S&T* system dominated by the Academy of Sciences and there has been little radical restructuring of R&D in that country. Thus the science and technology sectors of the transition economies continue essentially to live in a world apart, and their role within the aggregate production function of those economies has still to be clearly redefined. This is not to say that R&D factors can do nothing to help us explain differentials in economic performance in the region. It is rather to suggest that the relationship between the R&D *system* and those operational R&D factors is still tenuous.

EXPLAINING THE TRANSITION PECKING ORDER: A MORE GENERAL APPROACH

Variations in the degree of effective control over monopoly do, then, provide a few inklings of why some transition economies have done better than others, variations in the degree of development of the SME sector tell us rather more. FDI is full of potential and has had a significant impact, clearly differentiated by country; but is far from the whole story. Trends in the *S&T* system have had no visible impact whatsoever. Putting the four factors together, we are still a long way short of a complete explanation of why the pattern of transition performance has been so uneven. So let us leave the microeconomic approach for the time being and take a look at some of the aggregate and composite indicators that we did not consider in our opening sections. Let us start with aggregate investment. If FDI, as a specific component of investment, offers a less than full explanation of performance trends, can we learn something by looking at the overall investment picture? Table 6 presents data on trends in gross fixed capital investment from 1993, the year in which signs of recovery began to show in the stronger transition countries. The picture for

Table 6.   Gross fixed capital formation in Eastern Europe and the former
Soviet Union, 1993–2001 (annual percentage change).

	1993	1994	1995	1996	1997	1998	1999	2000	2001
Bulgaria	−17.5	1.1	16.1	−21.2	−22.1	16.3	25.3	15.4	19.9
Czech Republic	−7.7	17.3	21.0	8.7	−4.9	−3.9	−4.4	5.3	7.2
Hungary	2.0	2.5	−4.3	6.7	8.8	13. 3	6.6	7.7	3.1
Poland	2.9	9.2	16.5	19.7	21.7	14.2	6.5	2.7	−8.8
Romania	8.3	20.7	6.9	5.7	−3.0	−5.1	−10.8	4.6	6.6
Slovakia	−4.1	−5.1	−0.2	39.8	14.5	11.0	−18.8	1.2	9.6
Slovenia	11.9	12.6	16.8	9.2	11.3	12.9	19.1	0.2	−1.9
Estonia	10.0	10.2	4.0	11.4	12.5	8.1	−15.2	13.3	9.1
Latvia	−15.8	0.8	8.7	22.3	11.1	11.1	−6.3	20.0	17.0
Armenia	−24.0	−35.0	−17.3	10.3	12.4	11.9	0.5	16.2	4.0
Azerbaijan	−39.0	89.0	−18.0	111.4	67.0	45.0	−2.0	2.6	20.6
Belarus	−15.4	−17.2	−29.6	−3.1	23.1	10.1	−4.0	2.3	−2.3
Georgia[a]	−62.0	−0.5	38.0	11.0	36.0	80.0	—	—	—
Moldova	−44.0	−51.0	−3.4	24.9	−4.7	9.2	−23.1	−8.7	17.3
Russian Federation	−25.8	−26.0	−7.5	−16.9	−4.6	−6.6	−1.7	14.6	8.1
Ukraine	−30.5	−41.1	−30.8	−22.7	−6.7	3.0	0.1	12.4	6.2

[a]Total investment outlays.
Source: Various editions of the *Economic Survey of Europe*, Economic Commission for Europe, United Nations, Geneva.

the period 1993–96 is very striking. Most of the East European and Baltic countries report substantial net increases in gross fixed investment over the period 1993–96, with Poland, Slovenia and Romania, the three top performers on productivity in that period, plus the Czech Republic, standing out. The picture for the CIS countries is of disastrous cumulative falls in aggregate investment, paralleling their very poor performance on productivity, with signs of recovery coming only in 1996, and even then not in Russia and Ukraine, the biggest of the CIS economies.[2] In recent years trends have been more

[2]The one exception is Azerbaijan, which reports very big increases in total investment outlays in 1994 and 1996. These presumably reflect big, discrete foreign investments in the Azeri oil industry. So here is a case where FDI appears to have made a big impact on *aggregate* investment, but without making any corresponding impact on productivity.

mixed, with the Romanian and Czech recessions showing up clearly in the investment figures (though with the causation no doubt running from output drop to investment drop), and a no less clear-cut recovery in investment in both these countries in the early 2000s. In Poland, investment trends seem to have *presaged* the downturn in GDP growth of 2001. A number of the CEE and Baltic countries had a bad year for investment in 1999, but since then the upward trend has generally reestablished itself, with only Slovenia following the Polish pattern. In the CIS, too, 1999 was for many countries a poor investment year, but recovery since then has been quite impressive, Moldova and Belarus apart. Reference back to Table 3 confirms a general correspondence between these investment trends and productivity trends, Belarus's improbably high reported rates of growth of industrial productivity apart.

The recovery in investment in the smaller CIS countries has clearly been too short-lived for us to posit any clear-cut line of causation running from investment to productivity and output. In the case of countries like Hungary, Estonia and Slovenia, where investment has been rising strongly and consistently since 1994 (apart from Estonia in 1999 and Slovenia in 2001), the situation is, however, rather different. Of course, investment is effect as well as cause of economic growth, even in the medium-to-long-term, and it is clear that high rates of investment in these countries do reflect relatively high levels of business confidence which are themselves the result of transition successes. But these high rates of investment must clearly now have filtered through in terms of increases in production capacity, and this must form a major element in any explanation of why these countries have performed better in terms of output and productivity than the majority of the transition countries.

Our provisional conclusion, then is that the variations in economic performance between transition countries can to a substantial extent be explained in terms of investment — aggregate investment — and within that foreign direct investment, with differences in rates of development of SMEs and policy stances *vis-à-vis* monopoly and competition coming in as secondary factors, and variables relating to the *S&T* system adding nothing to the overall hypothesis. It is interesting to compare our analysis with that of Laza Kekic (1996). Kekic takes a radical approach, in hypothesising that the main determinants of differences in performance between different transition countries may have been essentially external to the approach to transition itself. He focuses on three main factors, viz.:

1. *Initial conditions*, as measured by a composite index reflecting the pre-transition foreign trade orientation and external debt situation, level of GDP per head, structure of the economy in terms of industry and services, energy intensity of the economy, and government expenditure as a percentage of GDP (as a proxy for extent of economic reform under communism);
2. *Political cohesion*; and
3. *Inflows 1990–94 of official medium-term funds and official grants.*

Kekic found that:

> Ordinary least squares regressions, in a variety of specifications, show that initial conditions, official foreign inflows and a dummy variable for countries engaged in civil strife accounted for two thirds of the cross-country variation in output performance in 1989–95[3] (for the 11 countries of eastern Europe alone almost 90 per cent of the variation) ... Our findings on the influence of institutional reform are at variance with optimistic assessments of the impact of rapid change. No specifications yield a positive impact. The most robust results in fact suggested a negative impact of the extent of institutional change, once other factors were taken into account, although the level of statistical significance was low (1996, p. 9).

Does that mean that analysis of transition policy is a waste of time? Certainly not. For Kekic's analysis supplements rather than negates our own analysis. While it manages to explain the bulk of cross-country variation in performance in terms of the specified variables, it fails to

---

[3]Note that Kekic included the Asian transition countries of Kazakhstan, Kyrgyzstan, Uzbekistan, Turkmenistan and Tajikistan in his calculations.

explain why Poland — or indeed Slovakia, Estonia and Latvia — have done as well as they have. Thus for four countries with outstanding productivity performance the Kekic model clearly suggests the policy/institutional factors — or something else as yet unspecified — *have* been important. And if Kekic had regressed his variables against productivity rather than output, he might have found that Slovenia and Hungary (which underperforms on his specifications) overperform as well. Finally, Kekic's period of analysis is one characterised by unusually high levels of inflow of public funds, and this inflow must have been a major factor in keeping up investment rates (in the countries in which they were kept up) in the early period of transition. Since 1994 the importance of official inflows has fallen sharply. The interesting thing is that this has not prevented investment in the most dynamic transition economies from continuing to grow rapidly.

But Kekic's results also help us to refine our microeconomic analysis. It is surely significant that the countries which are strongest on initial conditions are among those strongest on SME development and monopoly/competition policy, because experience of radical economic reform under communism, one of the things that gives you a high index of initial conditions, implies that much longer a history of SME development, and of the need for regulation of competition and monopoly. What the Kekic approach does warn us against are the dangers of concentrating on very narrowly specified variables. Thus if we want to understand the importance of things like small business development and state regulation, we have to see them in the broader context of initial conditions or, in the case of overperformers like Poland, of a *combination* of initial conditions and good transition policies.

CONCLUSIONS

We have seen that there is a well delineated pattern of comparative performance among the transition economies, a pattern which is clear enough in output terms but even clearer in terms of productivity. In seeking to find an explanation for these variations we have found that broad macroeconomic trends and very specific, microeconomic variables provide insights, but not a full explanation. Recourse to more aggregate, macroeconomic data gives a clearer picture of the overall pattern, and suggests that investment may be the key explanatory variable, always allowing for the causal ambivalence displayed by investment in any model of economic activity. More broadly-based analysis focusing on initial conditions, social cohesion and financial support from abroad gives a very satisfactory explanation of the overall pattern of variation in the early period of transition, while at the same time suggesting that for the top performers other factors, which we may surmise to be predominantly policy/institutional factors, have been important. In the later period initial conditions and social cohesion have surely continued to be important, but privately funded investment activity, and within that foreign direct investment have become increasingly so. And it is within that context that *S&T* factors have played an important role. As the history of socialism in Eastern Europe and the former Soviet Union amply demonstrates, high rates of investment are of little use, unless the investments are being made in the right place. Science and technology, whether domestic or foreign, make unique contributions to the process of investment decision-taking, and in this sense *S&T* activity actually has a much bigger role to play than it did under the old system. But the *S&T* *systems* of the transition countries remain basically out of harmony with the patterns of demand for *S&T* services that transition imposes. Looking to the future, it is clear that the more important investment becomes, the more important must R&D become. The extent to which that challenge will be taken up *within* the transition countries themselves remains to be seen.

REFERENCES

Balázs, K (1996). *Academic Entrepreneurs and their Role in Knowledge Transfer.* STEEP Discussion Paper No. 37, SPRU, University of Sussex.

Belka, M and A Krajewska (1997). *The Polish Bank and Enterprise Restructuring Programme: Debt/Equity Swaps. Survey Results.* CERT Discussion Paper No. 97/14, Department of Economics, Heriot-Watt University, Edinburgh.

Bobinski, C (1998). Polish business. Small enterprises optimistic. *Financial Times*, 8, January.

Bzhilianskaya, L (1999). Foreign direct investment in the science-based industries of Russia. In *Foreign Direct Investment and Technology Transfer in the Former Soviet Union*, DA Dyker (ed.). Cheltenham: Edward Elgar.

Dyker, DA (1996). The computer and software industries in the East European Economies — A bridgehead to the global economy? *Europe-Asia Studies*, 48(6), 915–30.

Dyker, DA and M Barrow (1994). *Monopoly and Competition Policy in Russia*. London: Royal Institute of International Affairs, p. 31; reprinted in *Challenges for Russian Economic Reform*, A Smith (ed.). Washington DC: Chatham House, Brookings Institute, 1995, pp. 79–115.

Dyker, DA and S Radošević (1994). *Industrial Restructuring in the Baltic Countries*. PSBF Briefing, Royal Institute of International Affairs, London.

Economic Commission for Europe (ECE) (1997). *Economic Survey of Europe in 1996–1997*, Geneva: United Nations.

——— (1998). *Economic Survey of Europe 1998 No. 1*, Geneva: United Nations.

——— (1999). *Economic Survey of Europe 1999 No. 1*, Geneva: United Nations.

Estrin, S, S Todd and K Hughes (1996a). *Volkswagen Bordnetze GmbH Case Study*, CIS — Middle Europe Centre. Discussion Paper Series, No. 33, London Business School.

——— (1996b). *Guardian Industries Limited Case Study*, CIS — Middle Europe Centre. Discussion Paper Series, No. 29, London Business School.

Gábor, I (1997). Too many, too small: Small entrepreneurship in Hungary — Ailing or prospering? In *Restructuring Networks in Post-Socialism. Legacies, Linkages and Localities*, OUP, G Grabner and D Stark (eds.), pp. 158–75.

Gokhberg, L (1999). The transformation of R&D in the post-socialist countries. In *Innovation and Structural Change in Post-Socialist Countries: A Quantitative Approach*, DA Dyker and S Radošević (eds.). Dordrecht: Kluwer.

Gower, P (1997). *Banking Development in the Czech Republic: An Analysis of Credit Allocation*, D.Phil Dissertation, University of Sussex.

Havas, A (1996). Foreign direct investment and intra-industry trade: The case of the automotive industry in Central Europe. In *The Technology of Transition. Science and Technology Policies for Transition Countries*, DA Dyker (ed.). Budapest: Central European University Press.

Hanson, P (1997). What sort of capitalism is developing in Russia? *Communist Economies and Economic Transformation*, 9(1), 27–42.

Hockuba, Z (1996). *The Emergence of Market Competition in Transforming Economies*, Economic Discussion Papers No. 20, Faculty of Economic Sciences, University of Warsaw.

Humphrey, J and H Schmitz (1996), The triple C approach to local industrial policy *World Development*, 24(12), 1859–77.

Hunya, G (1998). *Integration of CEEC Manufacturing into European Corporate Structures by Direct Investments*. Vienna Institute for International Economic Studies, mimeo.

Jakupović, E (1994). Procvat male privrede. *Ekonomska Politika* (Belgrade), 2219, 17 October, p. 22.

Jasinski, A (1994). R&D and innovation in Poland in the transition period. *Economic Systems* 18(2), 117–40.

——— (1997). *Academy-Industry Relations for Innovation in Poland*. STEEP Discussion Paper No. 41, SPRU, University of Sussex, August.

Kekic, L (1996). *Assessing and Measuring Progress in the Transition*. Paper presented at Reading University, September 18.

Mrcela, AK (1996). *Privatization in Slovenia: A Review of Six Years of the Process of Ownership Transformation*. CASE Studies and Analyses 71, Warsaw.

Niedbalska, G (1999). Polish innovation surveys: The present situation, analysis of results and plans for the future. In *Innovation and Structural Change in Post-Socialist Countries: A Quantitative Approach*, DA Dyker and S Radošević (eds.). Dordrecht: Kluwer.

OECD (1997). *Economic Surveys — Slovenia 1997: Special Feature, Economic and Financial Restructuring*. Centre for Cooperation with the Economies in Transition.

Pripisnov, V (1996). *The Development of Small and Medium-Sized Enterprises (SMEs) in Russia 1993–95*. STEEP Discussion Paper No. 35, SPRU, University of Sussex.

——— (1999). Foreign direct investment in relation to small enterprises in Russia. In *Foreign Direct Investment and Technology Transfer in the Former Soviet Union*, DA Dyker (ed.). Cheltenham: Edward Elgar.

Rems, M, M Rojec and M Simoneti (1997). *Ownership Structure and Performance of Slovenian Non-Financial Corporate Sector*. Institute of Macroeconomic Analysis and Development, Ljubljana.

Rossiiskii Statisticheskii Ezhegodnik 1996 (1996). Moscow: Goskomstat Rossii.

Sharp, M and M Barz (1996). Multinational companies and the transfer and diffusion of new technological capabilities in Central and Eastern Europe and the former Soviet Union. In *The Technology of Transition. Science and Technology Policies for Transition Countries*, DA Dyker (ed.). Budapest: Central European University Press.

Watson, J (1996). Foreign investment in Russia: The case of the oil industry, *Europe-Asia Studies*, 48(2).

Chapter 12

Building Social Capability for Economic Catch-Up: The Experience and Prospects of the Post-Socialist Countries

ECONOMIC GROWTH IN CONDITIONS OF TRANSFORMATION: THE RECORD TO DATE

As Table 1 shows, the post-socialist countries are in general relatively poor ones. Many have levels of GDP per head of under $1,000 at official exchange rates, and even at purchasing power parities (PPPs), which take into account relative price differences between countries, the majority of the countries of the region have levels of GDP per head under $8,000, i.e., less than one-third the EU average. At the top end of the spectrum the Czech Republic and Slovenia stand out, with levels of GDP per head at PPPs between a half and three-quarters the EU average. At the bottom lie a number of countries of the former Soviet Union, plus (probably) Bosnia, where GDP per head at PPPs is under, or not much more than, $3,000. Against a background of relative poverty, therefore, the range of levels of GDP per head is much wider than is found among the member countries of the EU. This pattern of intra-regional variability becomes even more clearly delineated when we take into account regional variations within countries. While the wealthiest regions of countries like

Table 1.   GDP per head in the post-socialist countries and the EU, $US, 2001.

	At official exchange rates	At purchasing power parities[2]
Eastern Europe		
Albania	1,230	3,880
Bosnia & Hercegovina	1,056	
Bulgaria	1,560	5,950
Croatia	4,550	8,440
Czech Rep.	5,270	14,550
Hungary	4,800	12,570
Poland	4,240	9,280
Romania	1,710	6,980
Slovakia	3,700	11,610
Slovenia	9,780	18,160
Baltic states		
Estonia	3,810	10,020
Latvia	3,260	7,870
Lithuania	3,270	7,610
CIS		
Armenia	560	2,880
Azerbaijan	650	3,020
Belarus	1,190	8,030
Georgia	620	2,860
Moldova	380	2,420
Russia	1,750	8,660
Ukraine	720	4,150
EU	18,273[1]	23,892[3]

[1]Calculated as the Eurostat figure for GDP per head in Euro, multiplied by the average Euro: $ exchange rate for 2001.
[2]Based on the standard of what $1 buys in the US.
[3]Author's estimate.
Source: World Bank, 2003; Eurostat; EBRD, 2002 (for Bosnia & Hercegovina).

Poland and Russia still lag far behind the EU average, their poorest regions have levels of GDP per head of under $1,000.

Although these inequalities are to a great extent inherited, Table 1, Chapter 11, demonstrates that they have intensified through the period of transition. It is the most prosperous of the post-socialist countries/regions that have grown fastest since 1990. Indeed it is *only* the more prosperous of the post-socialist countries that have managed any kind of sustained growth through the 1990s and early 2000s, with the poorest countries in the region at best just beginning to come out of the trough of the transition recession in the early 2000s. When we take into account the importance of the "grey" economy, particularly in the poorer transition economies,[1] the picture flattens out somewhat, with the "real" gap between the transitional economies as a whole and the advanced industrial economies, and the gap between the richer and poorer transition economies, narrowing. But factoring in second economy estimates does not change the basic picture.

What do the bald statistics tell us about the underlying economic situation of the post-socialist countries? They tell us, first of all, that these are all catch-up, or at least potential catch-up countries. Even the most advanced of them still face a huge gap in terms of GDP per head *vis-à-vis* the developed capitalist economies. They tell us, secondly, that, even for the poorest of the post-socialist countries, endowed, as they are, with huge reserves of underemployed labour, and in some cases with substantial mineral and hydrocarbon wealth, *extensive development* on the old communist pattern, based on mass mobilisation of human and natural resources, is no longer an option. However different they may be, however contrasting their experience of transition, the post-socialist countries can only catch up on the basis of *intensive development*, founded on the consolidation and enrichment of human capital and knowledge stocks.

It is clear from all this that *S&T* and trends in *S&T* must, in some sense, be fundamental to the whole business of transformation. For there is no enrichment of human capital, no accretion to knowledge stocks without *S&T*. But in this context *S&T* has to be understood in

---

[1] A survey of the second economy in Serbia conducted in December 2000 found that grey economic activity accounted for 30 per cent of total labour supply in that country at that time. See G. Krstić & B. Stojanović, "Osnove reforme tržišta rada u Srbiji (3)", *Ekonomska Politika* (Belgrade), No. 2573, 13 August 2001, p. 28.

a very broad sense. It has to be understood to include education and training, and all the myriad elements of design and organisation which mesh in with R&D proper at the level of the company, and also in many areas of public administration. It encompasses the "soft" technology of management systems, quality control and logistic precision as well as the "hard" technology of product and process innovation. Within that broad concept, *S&T activity* as defined and reported in statistical yearbooks is an important, but not uniquely important element. For our purposes, *S&T* has to be understood as everything that contributes to intensive development, therefore *everything that raises productivity*, and it is again significant that the pattern of differential performance among the post-socialist countries is that much more sharply delineated when we look at the productivity record (Table 3, Chapter 11), with Hungary, Poland and Estonia standing out particularly impressively in relation to labour productivity in industry, while most of the CIS countries have barely recovered the levels of productivity they reported at the end of the communist period.[2] Before pursuing the implications of these propositions about *S&T*, productivity and general economic performance in greater depth, we must pause to dig deeper into the basic notion of catch-up. Does catch-up simply mean drawing level with the EU, the US and Japan in terms of GDP per head? Are there limits to purely quantitative catch-up in that vein? If so, what factors lie at the root of these limits?

CATCHING UP: A CONCEPTUAL FRAMEWORK

In the simple but incisive theory of catch-up put forward by Verspagen (1999) following Abramovitz (1979; 1994), the scope for catching up is defined in terms of the scope for diffusion of technology (again, in the broadest sense) from the advanced countries to the catch-up countries. Just as the level of GDP per head (i.e., the level of

---

[2]Some allowance should, of course, be made for communist statistical exaggeration and the generally poor quality of industrial goods under communism.

social productivity) in the former countries is determined by their human capital and knowledge stocks, and the efficiency with which they use those stocks, so the ultimate limits to economic growth in the latter countries are determined by their ability to assimilate those knowledge stocks and bring their own human capital stocks up to the same level. If economic development is universally dependent on the same productivity-enhancing factors, what is to stop all countries ending up at the same level of development?

Verspagen picks out two main groups of factors which may inhibit catch-up through technological diffusion — *technological congruence* and *social capability*.[3] He defines the first in terms of:

> the match between the technologies in use in the advanced country and those most fit for introduction in the backward country. If there is a mismatch between the two, the opportunities for catch-up-driven growth are reduced. The sectoral distribution of economic activity is one important factor in congruence. For example, one may well imagine that most technologies developed in the industrialized market economies are not very relevant for the most backward economies, which are often still largely agricultural societies. But there are also other factors in congruence, as in the case where the technologically leading country applies very scale-intensive technologies, for which investment opportunities and/or domestic markets in the backward country are too small. In such a situation, technological incongruence would prevent successful catch-up (Verspagen, 1999, p. 31).

---

[3]Among other factors that can affect the rate of technological diffusion are, for example, cultural and geographical factors, and the dimension of political stability. There is little evidence that geographical factors present any absolute barriers to technological diffusion, while the political stability variable can be subsumed under the category of social capability. Culture is more difficult to tie down. Landes (1998, p. 516) argues that "if we learn anything from the history of economic development, it is that culture makes all the difference". I would argue that cultural factors, important though they are, impact on economic development primarily through the medium of social capability.

The second he defines in terms of:

> institutional factors such as educational systems (which supply the human capital necessary for assimilating spillovers), the banking system (which supplies financial capital for catch-up related investment), the political system, etc. (Verspagen, 1999, pp. 31–2).

The concept of social capability is clearly related to that of *social capital*. Thus Putnam (1993), following Coleman (1988), argues that:

> Stocks of social capital, such as trust, norms, and networks, tend to be self-reinforcing and cumulative. Virtuous circles result in social equilibria with high levels of cooperation, trust, reciprocity, civic engagement, and collective well-being ... Defection, distrust, shirking, exploitation, isolation, disorder, and stagnation intensify one another in a suffocating miasma of vicious circles. This argument suggests that there may be at least *two* broad equilibria toward which all societies that face problems of collective action (that is *all* societies) tend to evolve and which, once attained tend to be self-reinforcing (p. 177).

In the present context, however, the notion of social capital presents two critical difficulties. Firstly, it focuses on *inputs* rather than *outputs*, and offers no explanation of how social capital interacts with other inputs — other forms of capital — and with other factors of production. Partly, for that reason, it says little about *economic development*.

> Whilst (sic) much effort has gone into examining the indices of social capital in both qualitative and quantitative terms, much less attention has been devoted to the mechanisms by which such measures of social capital lead to discernible differences at the economic level. Does more social capital, for example, lead to a higher growth rate or merely to a different growth path or the same growth rate on a higher base? (Fine, 2001, p. 92).

Because the notion of social capability focuses on outcomes, and because it subsumes the dimension of learning, it avoids these difficulties: it provides a supple framework within which issues of development and catch-up can be assessed. Vicious circles of poverty and virtuous circles of prosperity can be accommodated by the framework, but they enter the analysis as secondary rather than primary factors, helping to explain the *patchiness and unevenness* of development as it has unfolded since the end of the Second World War. In social capability analysis no country or society is condemned to eternal backwardness.

It goes without saying that social capability may be expressed through widely differing sets of institutions in different countries, and indeed that technological congruence may be established by organisational structures quite unique to the catch-up country. Thus Germany, the most successful catch-up country of the 19th century, and Japan, the most successful of the 20th century, have both been notable for the extent to which they have maintained nationally distinctive institutions and structures, and indeed used these, not only as vehicles for inward technology transfer, but also as vehicles of leading-edge technological progress, once catch-up had been achieved.

In the real world, shortfalls in social capability may constrain the establishment of technological congruence, and indeed incomplete technological congruence hamper the development of social capability, where governance is heavily technology-dependent (e.g. in relation to computer and software systems). But the distinction is in principle a clear one, and it provides a sound basis for making an initial assessment of the growth and development prospects of the post-socialist countries. Before doing that we must pause to examine the relationship between social capability/technological congruence and *S&T* systems in the broadest sense.

THE KEY ROLE OF *S&T* IN THE CATCH-UP PROCESS

Let us start by stating the obvious. It is primarily through *S&T* (in the broadest sense, and in combination with the strategic activities of companies) that technological congruence is established. It is through innovation, strictly (hard) technological and (soft) organisational, that key deficiencies in social capability are made up. Less obvious, perhaps, is the importance of science *per se vis-à-vis* base social capability in terms of general levels of education and applied knowledge. This is something that comes through only when we start to look at the spin-off effects of basic scientific research. Let us briefly enumerate those effects.

First, there is the transfer of new methodologies and instruments from the field of basic research to that of commercial application. R&D results in themselves are by no means the only thing that R&D gives to industry. Experimental science has its own internal technological dynamic, a dynamic which has already created X-rays, the computer and the laser, all of which originated as research machines. But the innovativeness of experimental science as such has sometimes gone well beyond the invention of specific machines.

> The emergence and diffusion of new technologies of instrumentation ... are central and neglected consequences of university basic research ... [The] eventual economic impact of basic research is commonly expressed through the medium of new instrumentation technologies and the life histories of these new technologies (Rosenberg, 1992, p. 381).

In addition, the instrumentation innovations of experimental science have tended to be interdisciplinary in their impact, so that the overall financial return on them has gone far beyond the boundaries of specific sectors. The PACE survey found that instrumentation was the second (out of four) most important input of publicly financed research organisations into industry (Arundel *et al.*, 1995).

Among the spin-off effects of investment in basic research, the creation of a pool of skilled graduates is generally recognised as one of the most important. It is too easy to dismiss new graduates as "greenhorns" who know nothing about the real world. In fact, new graduates tend to embody crucial elements of tacit knowledge, i.e., knowledge embodied in individuals and small, tightly-knit groups, which cannot be codified, and which can normally only be transferred through very close personal contact and/or within the confines of these small groups. The tacit knowledge attributes of new graduates are especially important when the new graduates are working in highly dynamic sectors like information technology.

> As far as companies are concerned, formal qualifications are ... evidence of researchers' tacit ability to acquire and use

knowledge in a meaningful way. This attitude of mind…is a most important contribution to new product development (Senker, 1995).

Equally important, that basic truth remains valid, irrespective of whether the particular young graduate has actually been trained for the specific purposes of the industry he or she finds himself working in. In other words, experimental science generates not only its own (transferable) physical capital in the form of instrumentation, but also its own (transferable) human capital. Indeed in some cases, e.g. that of radio astronomy, human capital spin-off (to a wide range of sectors, some of them very far removed from radio astronomy) has been far more important than instrumentation spin-off.

> The advanced technologies required for the measurement of faint or fleeting signals, the electronics skills required to build the instruments, and the computing skills required to analyse the complex data are all potentially transferable to other applications. Since its formation in 1994 the PPARC [The UK Particle Physics and Astronomy Research Council] has actively encouraged the transfer of technologies used in its research programmes to other sectors (Department of Trade and Industry…, 1996, p. 140).

While the pattern is particularly noticeable in relation to astronomy and particle physics, the statement can be generalised to Mathematics and Physical Sciences across the board. Comparison of two surveys (complete in 1986 and 1991) of graduate employment in computer services industries in Canada, for example, found that

> despite some decline, among the Batchelor graduates, at least two in five continued to report a specialization in Maths/ Physics, with fewer than one in five from Engineering/Applied Sciences, which was about the same as the share from Commerce/Management. Among the work force with a Master's degree, at least one third reported Maths/Physics, followed now by Commerce/Management who contributed at least one quarter…Among people with a Doctorate, in the second survey, Maths/Physical Sciences took over as lead contributor from Engineering/Applied Sciences (Hansen, 1997).

It is, of course, not only new graduates who carry tacit knowledge. An entire complex of professional networks develops from the basic science sector which provides crucial reservoirs and conduits of tacit, and also informal[4] knowledge for industry. The whole circuit of academic conferences, workshops, etc., provides an invaluable platform for widening the knowledge base of industry. What is particularly interesting in this context is the fact that in the developed industrial countries many company R&D units follow a policy of publishing in academic journals, *inter alia* simply to maintain their own presence on these academic circuits — and to ensure that they have full access to all their highways and byways. More specifically, the fact that researchers working within company R&D departments show, through publications, that they are operating on the same level as their academic colleagues, and therefore have something to offer them, means that they can participate in full in the process of swopping (barter) of scientific information and ideas that goes on within the academic world itself.

We would not expect all the specific spin-offs from basic research to operate as strongly in catch-up as in advanced countries. Thus the development of innovatory instrumentation, for example, is likely to be largely the preserve of the advanced industrial countries. But the training and networking spin-offs are surely universal. In relation to scientific networks it is important to note, furthermore, that even in conditions of globalisation in the business world and complete freedom of academic intercourse, they do tend to be culture-bound. Thus the PACE survey found that:

> Domestic public research is substantially more important to respondents than foreign sources, suggesting that the public research infrastructure is one of the most important national assets for supporting innovation (Arundel *et al.*, 1995, p. ii).

This point is clearly as important for catch-up countries as for advanced industrial countries.

---

[4]That is, knowledge which, unlike tacit knowledge, can be codified, but which can only be passed on through "hands-on contact".

Beyond specific technological breakthroughs or specific networking impacts, basic research can have a huge impact in terms of developing the capacity for technological problem-solving. Outside
specific fields like chemicals and electronics, the direct impact of
academic research on industry is limited. It is particularly limited in
the non-electrical engineering industries. Thus in the Yale Survey
(Klevorick *et al.*, 1995), industries like motor vehicles, guided mis-
siles and aircraft production figure prominently among the industries
that cite knowledge of science as an important input into their activities, but not at all among the sectors that rate university research as
such as important. More specifically, the car industry, for instance,
shows itself to be heavily dependent on mathematics and computer
science. The reason is that:

> Theoretical prediction, modelling and simulation of large sys-
> tems, often accompanied by measurement and empirical testing
> of subsystems and components, has increasingly substituted for
> full scale empirical testing of complex systems, and this requires
> design tools and analytical methods grounded in phenomeno-
> logical understanding (Brooks, 1994, p. 480).

The scarcity value of the capacity to solve complex problems, often
through simulation, clearly stems from the fact that it originates from
the tacit-knowledge-rich networks discussed earlier. It is, therefore,
perhaps the most important single spin-off from publicly financed
basic research. In a transition country where the private sector is still
in the process of learning the problem-solving orientation, the importance of this point is self-evident.

There is, then, a consensus in the developed industrial countries
that a strong foundation in basic research is a key condition of innovatory dynamism and industrial competitiveness. Adding this in to
the more direct impact that *S&T* has with respect to the establishment of technological congruence and the rectification of specific
gaps in social capability, the central importance of *S&T* in the catch-
up process, or indeed in any process of economic development, seems
beyond doubt.

TECHNOLOGICAL CONGRUENCE AND SOCIAL CAPABILITY IN THE CONTEXT OF ECONOMIC TRANSFORMATION

It seems unlikely at first sight that problems of technological congruence would present major obstacles to successful catch-up in the case of the post-socialist countries. While there is a real sense in which they are developing countries, their general levels of education are much closer to those of Western Europe and North America than those of the Third World. Literacy is virtually universal, and basic engineering skills are well developed among a large proportion of their respective populations. These are emphatically *industrialised* countries, even if their patterns of industrialisation have often been ill-conceived. Domestic markets are in many cases small, but regional integration schemes like the Central European Free Trade Area (CEFTA) and the Baltic Free Trade Area, and, more important, the fact that a number of countries are on the point of acceding to the EU, have ensured that this is not a major constraint on the establishment of technological congruence. Wages are low, and the influence of this on the structure of trade is visible in terms of pronounced revealed comparative advantage in traditional, labour-intensive goods in a number of countries (Kubielas, 1999). But when transnational companies go into the post-socialist region with big investments, e.g. in the motor car industry, they are seeking to maximise firm-specific advantages as well as local advantages, and that means working within the framework of established company technological systems (Dyker & Kubielas, 2000). The mere fact that so many TNCs have gone into CEE with large-scale investments in the automotive industry, and turned these investments to profitable account, is proof that, while low wages provide trading opportunities, they do not close off technological options in the post-socialist region.

In practice, the picture with respect to technological congruence is not quite as rosy as this initial sketch suggests. While foreign car firms have met no serious obstacles in setting up state-of-the-art production systems employing mainly local people in their CEE transplants, they have found it impossible to integrate local firms into their supply networks as first-tier suppliers, i.e., suppliers of complex components involving R&D and design work as well as production. In practice, first-tier suppliers in the automotive industry in the region are always either wholly-foreign owned subsidiaries or joint ventures, with local firms relegated to the position of second- or third-tier suppliers, supplying single components with little or no in-house R&D or design content (see Chapter 6 for detailed discussion).

This is not to say that automotive supply networks have not operated at all as diffusers of state-of-the-art technology and best practice in the post-socialist countries. But the diffusion of that technology and those practices out from initial investments has been, and continues to be, incomplete. There comes a point in the development of complex business networks, it seems, where generalised engineering skills are no longer enough, where full participation and the establishment of full technological congruence demands a combination of very specific "hard" technological capabilities with high-level "soft" management capabilities. If that combination is absent from key areas of business networking, the process of catch-up will come to a halt well short of the "goal" of equality with the advanced industrial countries.

Similar arguments can be marshalled in relation to the dimension of social capability. In principle, accession to the EU, and by implication assimilation of the *acquis communautaire*, should provide a ready-made framework within which public administration in the post-socialist countries can rapidly converge to EU standards. In practice, matters are not so easy. Only a minority of the countries of the region have immediate prospects of membership of the EU, and while the *acquis* does have some impact on the other countries, the impact diminishes the more distant the prospect of EU membership becomes. Even for the accession countries, there must be serious doubts as to whether all the elements of the *acquis* can be effectively assimilated, whether indeed all its elements are appropriate to the accession countries, and whether the institutions set up under its aegis can be efficiently and honestly administered by local elites. There are, furthermore, key areas of the public sector which are not covered in the *acquis* at all. Education is one of them. And while it may be the inherited "stock" of education that mainly determines the technological congruity of a given society with the advanced industrial societies, it is the current flow of educational services that determines the level of social capability in terms of assimilation of new skills. Lastly, there are areas of business infrastructure which may be partly public sector, partly private, which are just as crucial in relation to the development of social capability, and which again are at best partially addressed by the *acquis communautaire*. Among these we can pick out *R&D systems* and *banking systems* (see detailed discussion in Chapter 6).

THE IMPLICATIONS FOR CATCH-UP IN PRACTICE

Granted that the post-socialist countries cannot deliver first-tier suppliers to the car industry right now, is it not reasonable to suppose that the will "learn" to do so over the long term, i.e., over the next ten-fifteen years? Reasonable, perhaps, but it is difficult to argue that the process will be an automatic one. Corporate strategy may drive particular firms to seek to "teach" their partners in CEE how to be good first-tier suppliers. There seem to be elements of this in the policies of Magyar Suzuki, one of the smaller automotive transplants in the post-socialist region, for example (Havas, 1999). But there is nothing in the competitive (or rather, in this case, oligopolistic) mechanism to *force* them to do so. And even where the lead firm is keen to develop local supply capabilities, it cannot *force* local firms to come up to standard, as again exemplified in the Magyar Suzuki case. Exactly the same point can be made in relation to banking. Over the long run the difference in levels of performance between privatised and new banks will surely disappear. So as long as foreign banks are willing to go in and compete in the acceding countries, on whatever basis, therefore, the ultimate impact on social capability in the sector should surely be a substantial one. But bank liberalisation in the post-socialist countries will not *force* Western banks to compete in those markets. And it will not force western banks to provide venture capital to the R&D sector itself, even if, through fundamental restructuring, real opportunities for profitable investment in that sector are finally created.

These simple microeconomic facts of life do, indeed, correspond to what we perceive at the macroeconomic level. Thus Verspagen (1999) distinguishes between countries not only in terms of whether they are leading, catching up or falling behind. He also identifies a *clamping-on* group of countries with relatively high levels of GDP per head, but which nevertheless continue to lag behind the leading countries, and show no signs of quickly closing the gap. In his formal analysis Verspagen (1999, p. 39) confirms the status of the post-socialist countries as catch-up countries, on the basis of their relatively low levels of GDP per head, relatively high investment ratios and low ratios of R&D expenditure (compared to the leading industrial countries). But he also identifies (p. 35) five out of a total of seventeen clamping-on countries for the period 1973–89 which had been catching up in the previous period, 1960–73. Thus today's catch-up country may well turn into tomorrow's clamping-on country. Is that the fate that awaits the post-socialist countries? Or could a worse fate be in store for them? Before trying to answer these questions, we have to look more closely at differences in levels of performance between different transition countries.

THE PROBLEM OF VARIANCE AMONG THE POST-SOCIALIST COUNTRIES

In the opening paragraphs of this paper we noted that aggregate economic performance has been extremely variable among the post-socialist countries — that while it may be reasonable to classify them all as catch-up countries in terms of situation and potential, the reality for many of them over the first decade of transition has been stagnation. And this problem of variability shows up in terms of other indicators as well. Table 2, Chapter 11, for instance, illustrates the enormous divergences between individual post-socialist countries in relation to performance on price stability. Over the first half of the 1990s there is a stark contrast between, on the one hand, countries like Poland, the Czech Republic and Slovenia, which establish and maintain a fair degree of price stability from an early stage, and, on the other hand, most of the countries of the former Soviet Union, which teetered on the brink of hyper-inflation throughout that sub-period. In the second half of the 1990s most countries managed a degree of stabilisation, but 1998 witnessed significant slippage in the former Soviet Union, most strikingly in Russia.[5] Since then, the majority of transition countries have managed to reduce their rates of inflation again, but rates remain high in Romania, Yugoslavia (Serbia-Montenegro) and Belarus, to mention only the most serious cases. Behind these statistical trends lies a story of social capability and deficiency thereof. In the case of Poland, where the Solidarity government that took power at the end of 1989 inherited a serious problem of open inflation from the previous communist regime, a happy combination of able and decisive economic policy-makers within the Polish government and well-directed advice from abroad, backed up by significant levels of international financial support, produced a rapid solution to the inflationary problem through an incisive package of fiscal, monetary and exchange rate regime policies. In Russia, the government struggled to come to terms with the fiscal implications of anti-inflation policies, and remained weak in the face of merciless lobbying from sectional interests intent on maintaining flows of "soft" credits in their direction. Russia's relatively good performance on inflation in 1996 and 1997 was largely based on two expedients, one dishonest, the other extremely dangerous: delaying payments of wages and salaries to public sector employees and pensions, and borrowing heavily on international money markets. The Russian financial crisis of August 1998 was in part due to the Asian crisis of the year before, but stemmed more fundamentally from the continued failure of the Russian government to assimilate the principles of good macroeconomic management, and to impose an adequate regime of supervision on a professionally and ethically weak commercial banking system. In stark contrast to the Polish case, foreign and international organisations seemed powerless to make much impact on these basic failures, suggesting a *sui generis*

---

[5]There are cyclical elements in transition economy inflation patterns too, but these are of minor significance compared to inter-country differences and medium-term time trends.

kind of technological congruence problem. Thus the Russian crisis of 1998 provides an outstanding illustration of how a fundamental deficiency of social capability (manifesting itself in this case primarily in the public sector) can perpetuate itself by perpetuating technological incongruence and blocking the diffusion of key technology or know-how (in this case financial and economic) from abroad.

The list of policy variables affected by differences in social capability could be extended — the story of monopoly and competition policy, policy on small and medium-sized enterprises (SMEs), policy on foreign direct investment (FDI) is similar, and the pecking order of countries is much the same in each case as well. What is the origin of these differences? There are obvious elements of serendipity, of "happy chance" in the Polish case, but this will hardly do as a complete explanation. A simple econometric analysis of the early period of transition (Kekic, 1996) suggests that differences in initial conditions can explain a substantial measure of the differences in aggregate performance among the post-socialist countries in that period. Thus the outstanding performers in the region over the period 1990–95 had pre-transition experience of some kind of market socialist (Slovenia, Hungary, and to a lesser degree Poland and Estonia), and/or already had relatively high levels of GDP per head at the beginning of transition (Slovenia, Czechoslovakia and Hungary) and/or were already to a degree open to the West in trading and financial terms in the pre-transition period (Slovenia, Hungary, and to a lesser degree Poland). The first and last of these factors have obviously had major implications in terms of capabilities and the capacity to learn, and the operation of the last meant that pressures for increased technological congruence were already present before the end of communism.

CONCLUSIONS

Introduction of the initial conditions dimension into the argument about differences in performance confirms some basic truths which are well known in the science policy literature. What you get depends on what you have got, the more you know the easier it is to learn, and the more you know the easier it is to identify what you do not know and need to learn from others. It also suggests a downside scenario which needs to be introduced into our analytical framework. The possibility that some of the post-socialist countries may face total blockages, largely inherited, in certain areas of social capability means that we may have to introduce a fifth category of countries in terms of Verspagen's taxonomy — of a special group of falling-behind countries which look, in terms of a current "snapshot", more like catch-up countries. That, certainly, was the reality for most of the countries of the former Soviet Union and some of the Balkan countries over the first ten years of transition. The picture over the early years of the 21st century has certainly been brighter, but it is too early to say whether this represents a change in trend. The fact, however, that these are the countries most isolated from the capability-building influence of the EU and the technological impact of international investment suggests that a degree of pessimism may be in order, and that the darker implications of the social capital approach may, indeed, be relevant to some transition economies. For all the post-socialist countries, the continued dysfunctionality of *S&T* systems, in the narrow institutional sense, is a major obstacle to wholly successful catch-up. Again, however, the impact of this dysfunctionality will be greater in the countries in which the countervailing pressures are weaker. The most likely scenario for the transition region as a whole over the next few decades, therefore, is of a group of Central-East European countries clamping on at a level of economic development that is fairly high, but still below the EU average; while the countries of the former Soviet Union and some of the Balkan countries will continue to fall behind, as they have done over the past decade, or at best establish a trajectory of weak catch-up. Within a generally disfavoured group of countries, the CEECs will clearly emerge as the most favoured subgroup. But within the expanded EU of the future they will be disfavoured, and assimilation of the *acquis communautaire* will do nothing to change that in the short-to-medium term. The implications of all this for international economic policy-making, at world and European levels, are serious indeed.

REFERENCES

Abramovitz, MA (1979). Rapid growth potential and its realization: The experience of the capitalist countries in the postwar period. In *Economic Growth and Resources*, Vol. I, E Malinvaud (ed.). London and New York: Macmillan Press.
———— (1994). The origins of the postwar catch-up and convergence boom. In *The Dynamics of Technology, Trade and Growth*, J Fagerberg *et al.* (eds.). Aldershot: Edward Elgar.
Arundel, A, G van der Paal and L Soete (1995). *PACE Report: Innovation Strategies of Europe's Largest Industrial Firms: Results of the PACE Survey for Information Sources, Public Research, Protection of Innovations, and Government Programmes.* Final Report, MERIT, Limburg University, Maastricht.
Balázs, K (1996). *Academic Entrepreneurs and Their Role in Knowledge Transfer.* STEEP Discussion Paper No. 37, SPRU, University of Sussex.
Brooks, H (1994). The relationship between science and technology. *Research Policy*, 23, 477–86.
Coleman, J (1988). Social capital in the creation of human capital. *American Journal of Sociology.* 94, S95–S120.
Department of Trade and Industry: Office of Science and Technology (1996). *Forward Look of Government-Funded Science, Engineering and Technology 1996.* HMSO, London, Cm.32571.
Dyker, DA and S Kubielas (2000). Technology and structure in the Polish economy under transition. *Economic Systems*, 24(1), March.
EBRD (2002). *Transition Report 2002.* London.
Fine, B (2001). *Social Capital Versus Social Theory.* London: Routledge.
Gokhberg, L (1999). The transformation of R&D in the post-socialist countries. In *Innovation and Structural Change in Post-Socialist Countries: A Quantitative Approach*, DA Dyker and S Radošević (eds.). Dordrecht: Kluwer.
Gower, P (1997). *Banking Development in the Czech Republic — An Analysis of Credit Allocation.* D. Phil. thesis, University of Sussex.
Hansen, W (1997). Developing indicators for a knowledge-based society: Human capital. Paper presented to *NATO Advanced Research Workshop Quantitative Studies for S&T Policy in Economies in Transition*, Moscow, 23–25 October.
Havas, A (1999). *Changing Patterns of Inter- and Intra-Regional Division of Labour: Central Europe's Long and Winding Road.* Budapest, mimeo.
Jasinski, A (1997). *Academy-Industry Relations for Innovation in Poland.* STEEP Discussion Paper No. 41, SPRU, University of Sussex, August.
Kekic, L (1996). *Assessing and Measuring Progress in the Transition.* Paper presented at Reading University, September 18.
Klevorick, AK, R Levin, R Nelson and S Winter (1995). On the sources and significance of inter-industry differences in technological opportunities. *Research Policy*, 24, 185–205.

Kubielas, S (1999). Transformation of technology patterns of trade in the post-socialist economies. In *Innovation and Structural Change in Post-Socialist Countries: A Quantitative Approach*, DA Dyker and S Radošević (eds.), pp. 385–407. Dordrecht: Kluwer.

Landes, D (1998). *The Wealth and Poverty of Nations — Why Some are so Rich and Some are so Poor*. New York and London: W. W. Norton.

Putnam, R (1993). *Making Democracy Work — Civic Traditions in Modern Italy*. New York: Princeton University Press.

Rosenberg, N (1992). Scientific instrumentation and university research. *Research Policy*, 21, 381–90.

Senker, J (1995). Tacit knowledge and model of innovation. *Industrial and Corporate Change*, 4, 425–47.

Verspagen, B (1999). A global perspective on technology and economic performance, and the implications for the post-socialist countries. In *Innovation and Structural Change in Post-Socialist Countries: A Quantitative Approach*, DA Dyker and S Radošević (eds.), pp. 29–44. Dordrecht: Kluwer.

World Bank (2003). *World Development Report 2003*. Washington.

Part VII

By Way of Conclusion

Chapter 13

What Transition Has Learned from Economics — and What Economics Has Learned from Transition

INTRODUCTION

When Soviet-style communism collapsed in the late 1980s and early 1990s, and the countries of Eastern Europe and the (former) Soviet Union proclaimed, one after another, their intention of reestablishing market-oriented economic systems based on private property, a watershed was reached, not just in world history but also in the development of economics as a policy science. Economists had argued for decades over whether Soviet-style centralised planning was irrational, or merely inefficient (Nove, 1965; McAuley, 1967; Dyker, 1970), but no one disputed its essential dysfunctionality, which had been demonstrated time and time again on the basis of simple growth accounting procedures (Bergson, 1978). While centralised socialist planning might not break the laws of economics in a Newtonian sense, it certainly did in a biological sense (Berliner, 1966), and this seemed to suggest that the organism would eventually die. That conjecture was eventually proved correct, and it is worth emphasising that central planning did, indeed, die rather than being killed. By the late 1980s, for instance, in the heyday of Gorbachev's *perestroika*, the institutional mechanisms of the planning system in the Soviet Union itself were already breaking down.[1]

No less striking in the late 1980s was the breakdown in the alternative form of socialist planning — the market socialist systems of Yugoslavia and Hungary. In the Yugoslav case the ultimate collapse of the system of socialist self-management was precipitated by the outbreak of civil strife. And in Hungary, there was, in truth, no collapse as such at all, but rather a well-managed shift from market socialism to full-flooded capitalism, orchestrated in its early stages by the communist party itself. Where Yugoslavia and Hungary showed a revealing similarity to the Soviet Union and the other countries in which central planning remained in force was in respect of the patterns of economic development that preceded the breakdown. In both cases, those patterns were dominated by the same tendency to inexorable slowdown in rates of growth and stagnation in levels of total productivity that characterised the countries of central planning in the 1970s and 1980s (Dyker, 1990; Csaba, 1989). Since the market socialist countries did have more or less normally functioning markets for final goods, the similarity in development paths between centralised and decentralised planning systems pointed to the labour and capital markets — which remained essentially non-marketised in Hungary and Yugoslavia (Smith, Alan, 1983, pp. 140–6; Dyker, 1982; 1990). Once again, then, economists were vindicated in their stress on the efficient operation of factor markets as the key to stable economic growth, and some went further to insist that the efficient operation of the capital market in particular was dependent on the preeminence of the principle of private property (Pejovich, 1972).

But predicting what had already happened was, in truth, no great service to the policy-makers who inherited the task of engineering a fundamental systemic revolution in the area of the old Soviet bloc in the early 1990s, and it is perhaps significant that the economists who dominated the early debates on transition policy as such were in the main economists from the region itself who had become involved in policy-making under the new regimes, or Western economists who

---

[1]Interviews conducted by the author with plant directors in the former Soviet Union.

were specialists in economic restructuring, rather than specialists in the (former) communist economies *per se*. The immediate problem that faced all the countries of the region as they moved into transition were the macroeconomic imbalances inherited from the communist period, and the early policy packages were very much focused on finding solutions for that problem.

"SHOCK THERAPY" IN HISTORICAL PERSPECTIVE

The problem of fiscal imbalances was a direct consequence of the underlying dysfunctionalities of the socialist planning systems of Eastern Europe. As rates of growth of national income and productivity fell, and as increasingly beleaguered communist governments strove to maintain at least the appearance of rising living standards through wage increases and increases in welfare expenditures, so budgets inevitably started to slip into the red. As Table 1 shows, budgets in the region were generally in deficit by anything up to 8–9 per cent of GDP by the late 1980s. And because socialist countries by definition have no money markets, and because in most cases the socialist countries had exhausted their foreign credit by this time, these deficits had to be largely monetised. What kind of inflationary impact that had depended on the extent of price control. In the Soviet Union, where price control remained almost universal right to

Table 1.   Budget surpluses and deficits (−) as percentage of GDP, 1989–92.

	1989	1990	1991	1992
Bulgaria	—	−4.9	−3.6	−3.1
Czechoslovakia	−0.9	0.5	−1.8	−1.8
GDR	—	−8.0	na	na
Hungary	−3.2	−0.1	−4.9	−7.4
Poland	−3.0	0.4	−3.8	−6.0
Romania	7.5	1.0	1.9	−2.0
Slovenia	na	−0.3	2.6	1.6
Soviet Union/Russia	−8.6	−5.9	−10.0	−4.9
Yugoslavia (Serbia/Montenegro)	na	−5.7	−9.6	—

Source: ECE, 1991, p. 58; 1993, p. 144.

the end of the old system, it took the form of repressed inflation, which manifested itself in the form of lengthening queues and flight into the second economy. In Poland, where prices had already been substantially liberalised by the late 1980s, it took the form of open inflation, with annual rates of increase in the retail price index averaging 69.7 per cent 1986–89 (ECE, 1990, p. 136).

The macroeconomic policy package implemented initially in Poland, and subsequently imitated to a greater or lesser extent in a number of other transition countries, was based on the following key principles:

1. Given the institutional constraints of an early transition country, where money markets still have not had time to develop, closing the inflationary gap means closing the fiscal gap. To all intents and purposes, fiscal policy and monetary policy are one and the same.
2. The price structures inherited from the communist period were distorted, especially with regard to fuel prices and rents, even in the countries where there had been substantial price liberalisation. Thus the initial phase of macro stabilisation would have to involve a degree of "corrective" inflation. The best way to ensure that the corrective inflation did not set off a new inflationary spiral would be to reestablish fiscal balance in short order, even at the cost of some "shock" to the population.
3. The "shock" element should probably be seen as a positive virtue of the package, rather than a necessary evil. To kill inflation you have to kill inflationary expectations, and this cannot be done in a gradualist way. In Poland the rate of inflation was reduced from 584.7 per cent in 1990 to 70.3 per cent in 1991 (ECE, 1992, p. 93). This was dramatic enough to shock Poles out of the inflationary mentality that had developed in the last years of socialism, and to reestablish trust in the price system as a system of signals through which individuals could orient their work efforts in a spirit of enlightened self-interest.

In the event, budget deficits quickly reappeared in Poland, as Table 1 illustrates. And victory over inflation did not extend to getting inflation down to zero. Indeed annual inflation in Poland was still averaging 10 per cent in 2000. But the shock elements in the package had changed certain key parameters irreversibly. It is salutary to compare the Polish experience in this connection with that of Russia. In that country, repressed inflation burst out into open inflation after the price liberalisation of 1992, with the year-end rate of inflation for that year reaching more than 2,000 per cent. The subsequent process of getting inflation down was painfully slow, and the year-end inflation rate did not drop below 100 per cent in Russia until 1996. By 1997 it was actually below the rate of inflation in Poland. But when economic crisis struck Russia in August–September 1998 and the rouble was devalued, prices of key foodstuffs doubled or tripled in a matter of days as Russians reverted to the "Soviet" mentality of queuing and hoarding. It would be foolish to suggest that if the Russian authorities had managed to get inflation down to under 100 per cent by 1993, all the problems of Russia's transition would have been solved. The fact remains that while the original (partly corrective) inflation of 1992 was certainly a shock, the slowness of the subsequent process of price stabilisation meant that there was little therapy to go with the shock, little immediate pressure to change mentality, in a country which, in truth, needed such a change much more badly than Poland.

One looks in vain for a clear-cut correlation between macroeconomic shock therapy and general success in transition in terms of rates of growth of GDP and productivity. Not all countries needed the full package of shock therapy. Czechoslovakia inherited a more or less balanced budget from the communist period (see Table 1), so was in little need of shock, though some therapy after the stultifying centralisation of the period after the Prague Spring of 1968 was clearly in order. Hungary and Slovenia both inherited a slight degree of fiscal imbalance from the old systems. (In the former case the fiscal situation deteriorated sharply in the early years of transition — see Table 1.) But they both had 20–30 years of experience of market socialism behind them, so that their need for mentality-changing therapy was that much less. On *a priori* grounds we would in any case expect macro stabilisation to be a necessary rather than a sufficient condition for successful restructuring at the micro level. What is clear is that the countries (mostly successor states to the former

Soviet Union) which needed shock therapy and did not get it, even in the attenuated Russian form, have achieved least with respect to restructuring. The father of shock therapy has a simple enough explanation for this.

> A preoccupation with structural factors and the corresponding neglect of macroeconomic ones freezes the poor economic structure which is seen as the principal engine of high inflation in the first place. Under this sort of policy there are no incentives for people (and other resources) to move to other sectors — they are being paid simply for coming to work. Tough stabilisation and comprehensive liberalisation seem to be the necessary conditions for any meaningful structural change, and in this role they are probably more important than microeconomic reforms in the state sector (Balcerowicz, 1993, p. 21).

Balcerowicz's dicta on necessary conditions for structural change and the role of microeconomic reform within the state sector itself can hardly be challenged. If, however, we want to reach a full understanding of the *sufficient* conditions for effective transition, and when we start to look beyond the inherited state sector, we must surely look at policies which explicitly address the micro side.

PRIVATISATION AND THE REVOLUTION IN PROPERTY RIGHTS

The transition from socialism is, in a sense, defined by privatisation, and Table 4, Chapter 11 shows how dramatic the rate of progress in privatisation has been over a wide spectrum of transition countries. But while everybody privatises, there are, it seems, no prizes for those who privatise most and fastest. Mass privatisation through vouchers has certainly not visibly held economic performance in the Czech Republic back, but it has not lifted that country above the pack of Visegrad countries in line for accession to the European Union. It is rather Poland, where progress on privatisation has been quite cautious, that reported growth rates of GDP and productivity distinctly superior to the other countries of Central-East Europe, at least until

2001 (Slovenia is similar to Poland in terms of a combination of slow progress on privatisation and impressive general economic performance). And mass privatisation in Russia has had no visible positive impact on performance whatsoever, while privatisation laggards like Moldova and Ukraine (not in the table) have done even worse than Russia in terms of the general impetus of transition.

Why is rate and level of privatisation such a poor indicator of restructuring performance? Not, of course, because privatisation does not matter, but rather because privatisation *per se* defines neither the extent and nature of the private sector, nor the manner in which that sector is organised and managed. The really striking indicator in Poland is not the slow rate of privatisation, but rather the extraordinarily high contribution of small and medium-sized enterprises (SMEs), mostly newly formed since transition began, to the private sector as a whole. In that country, at the end of 1997, some 60 per cent of the non-farm workforce were employed in SMEs, generating around one-third of total GDP (Bobinski, 1998). Slovenia is again similar in this respect to Poland (Rems *et al.*, 1997; OECD, 1997). In Russia, by contrast, SMEs employ only 10 per cent of the labour force. But they generate 12 per cent of Russian GDP and account for a third of total profits in the Russian economy (Pripisnov, 1996). The pattern is similar elsewhere in the transition region. Whether the SME sector is big or small, it is always more productive and more profitable than the large enterprise sector. But only where the SME sector is big can it make a perceptible contribution to overall economic performance.

What matters, then, is not privatisation, but rather private enterprise. And it is perhaps hardly surprising that newly created, nimble-footed SMEs should be more efficient than large enterprises which, privatised or not, continue to struggle with the legacy of the communist period in terms of the way that they are run, the kind of things they produce, and the way that they network with other enterprises. The bigger the enterprise, the more important does they dimension of *corporate governance* become. In a post-communist environment, the bigger the enterprise, the more likely it is that corporate governance will pose real problems. None of this is problematic or even surprising for an economic science that is used to considering the problems of large organisations in terms of managerial economies and diseconomies of scale. But changes in property relationships *per se* have demonstrably not been a decisive factor in processes of transformation in Eastern Europe. Have they at least been a necessary condition? We examine this question in the next section.

CORPORATE GOVERNANCE, MANAGEMENT AND TECHNICAL CHANGE

The old communist systems were, indeed, inefficient. But despite the ideologically-inspired rejection of the price mechanism as a system of parameters of governance under the old system, the economies of "real" socialism were not strikingly inefficient in terms of allocating resources. Even the Soviet Union, with its vast military-industrial complex and locational/regional complexity, by and large managed to allocate labour and capital to their best uses (in terms, of course, of a set of goals determined by the plan) (Whitesell, 1990). And it is worth bearing in mind, in this connection, that communist economic planners, Marxist or not, did have at their disposal perfectly functional and fully approved procedures for the evaluation of alternative investment projects which did not differ in essentials from standard Present Value/Internal Rate of Return procedures (Dyker, 1983; Bergson, 1964).

Where the old systems were increasingly and ultimately hopelessly inefficient was in terms of *organisation and management*, including the *organisation and management of technical change*. Perhaps the best example of this phenomenon is that of Hungary under market socialism. As noted earlier, the greatest weakness of the Hungarian New Economic Mechanism (NEM) was in relation to the application of factors of production. But these weaknesses were not primarily allocational. Rather the problem was that typical X-efficiency problems of the investment process manifested themselves as seriously under Hungarian market socialism as under Soviet centralised planning. Thus, for example, lead-times on investment projects were typically 2.5–3 times the norm in developed capitalist countries (Dyker, 1982). In relation to the labour force, too, the problem lay not in the distribution of the work force by sector, but in the fact that, even under this quasi-market system, over-manning was universal and post-Taylorist notions of efficient organisation of labour largely unheard of.

Why did the situation become worse, as evinced by the record of falling rates of productivity growth, rather than just remaining (statically) unsatisfactory? Care has to be taken in interpreting the falling rates of productivity growth. Increasing costs of extraction of natural resources, notably the Siberian oil and gas which largely powered the whole CMEA area, represented an important factor here which can only partly be explained in organisational terms. There is certainly evidence of declining effectiveness of R&D activity in the CMEA area in the early 1980s (cf. the figures in Table 2 on patenting by individuals and organisations from those countries in the United States). But Hungary is, in fact, the exception here. The striking thing in the Hungarian case is that, even as international patenting activity is maintained, rates of implementation of new technologies at the enterprise level continue to fall. The problem, clearly, was not R&D in itself, but rather the management of innovation and technology transfer at enterprise level.

How has improved corporate governance helped to resolve these problems in the context of transition? The pattern here is so mixed that it is best to proceed through examples. The *Szczecin Shipyard* in Poland is a particularly good illustration because it comes from a "sunset" sector, a sector prioritised by the communist regime in Poland, but now facing a global market with limited aggregate

Table 2. Number of Patents Registered in the US by Selected East European Countries 1975–93.

	1975	1980	1985	1989	1990	1991	1992	1993
Bulgaria	24	24	21	15	26	10	5	4
Czechoslovakia	120	55	54	34	38	28	18	12
Hungary	52	87	108	131	94	86	86	52
Poland	37	38	10	17	19	11	7	8
Romania	17	14	3	0	1	1	0	3
USSR	421	463	148	161	176	178	69	59

Source: Computer Horizon Inc.

growth potential, and up against fierce competition from low-wage countries like China (Bitzer & von Hirschhausen, 1998a,b).

The key factors in the successful turning round of the Szczecin Shipyard were listed in Chapter 4. Thus the Szczecin Shipyard has become profitable again by reorganising its activities into a market-oriented assembly operation, organised through contemporary computerised management systems, sourced from all over the world (not excluding Poland), and manned by a relatively small number of workers in Szczecin itself.

Does that mean that the Szczecin Shipyard is essentially an "off-shore" screwdriver factory, assembling imported kits on the basis of imported designs, and maintaining profitability purely on the basis of a combination of work-force cut-backs and low wages? There are, certainly, plenty of such screwdriver factories in the transition countries, notably (though the screwdriver epithet is purely metaphorical in this case) in textiles, where under the rubric of *outward processing*, Western companies "put out" raw materials to factories in Eastern Europe, usually on a custom-free basis, for reexport, after processing, to the West. But in the shipbuilding case, the story is more complex and interesting. Wage costs are an important variable for the Szczecin Shipyard, and it is significant that the yard employs Russian welders, because they are cheaper for a given quality of work. The fact remains that there are huge differences in real wages between Poland and its competitors in the industry. Polish shipyards can, nevertheless, compete against Chinese, just as Korean and Japanese can against Polish. So the key to success in shipbuilding does not seem to be cheap labour. Rather it seems to be efficient general organisation (including organisation of the work-force and the supply network) and a flexible approach to the development of specific in-house capabilities, relating (in this case) to the construction of container ships, which lower-cost competitors do not (yet) possess. Thus the Szczecin Shipyard has its own design department, but that department works mainly on the basis of standard designs from abroad. "[In the Polish shipbuilding industry as a whole] the yards tried to enhance their design capacities, through in-house development and/or by purchasing foreign equipment and knowledge. Expanding design capacities turned out to be a critical factor for product diversification" (Bitzer & von Hirschhausen, 1998a, p. 2). Thus management in the Polish shipbuilding industry has understood clearly that *there is no efficient technology transfer without in-house technological capabilities*

In terms of its pattern of equity holding, the Szczecin Shipyard epitomises the pragmatic Polish approach to privatisation. It is 30 per cent owned by two big Polish banks, while the state remains a significant shareholder. Divestment is a strategic option for the future, but the government has made no firm commitments. Comparison with the typical Russian enterprise — privatised but unrestructured — might incline one to surmise an inverse relationship between privatisation and organisational efficiency. But the inclination would not survive even the most perfunctory glance at the overall picture. There are plenty of cases of badly managed, publicly-owned organisations in Poland, and in Central-East Europe in general. And in Russia, too, privatisation can still make a difference, if not necessarily a critical difference. Thus in relation to the TsOT laser firm (a Russian-Bulgarian joint venture):

> Both the main shareholders of TsOT are state enterprises. Maybe that is the reason why those shareholders do not seem to be very interested in the managerial problems of TsOT. Optics Technology [the Bulgarian partner] does not really take any part in the management of the JV. As to the Russian partner, it does not seem to be very interested in the JV's activities either. The director of TsOT, Sergei Smirnov, states that in the early 1990s TsNIIM [the Russian partner, an Academy of Sciences research institute] did get involved in looking for orders for the JV. But at 1996 this was no longer the case (Bzhilianskaya, 1999, p. 73).

Thus the key, in the TsOT case, as in that of the Szczecin Shipyard, is good management; but privatisation can never guarantee that.

Not surprisingly, then, the formula for effective restructuring in conditions of transition is a mirror image of the factors of ineffectuality under socialist planning. X-inefficiency was the road to perdition for the old system, increases in X-efficiency are the key to good performance under the new system. And while the economics profession must be given credit for providing the back-up analysis that under-pins both those conclusions (it was, after all, an economist who invented the concept of X-efficiency — see Leibenstein, 1966), and enables us to move safely from case studies to generalisation, eco-nomics finds itself, at the end of the millennium, facing a challenge. If X-efficiency issues are really so much more important than issues of allocative efficiency, is there much more for the economist to do after the initial diagnosis? Can they leave the rest to the management spe-cialists and the engineers? We return to this question later on. At this point we pick up the issue of privatisation again. We have seen that privatisation is no very good indicator of success in transition. We have seen that being in the private sector is a much better indicator, because it pulls in newly created enterprises. Are there other special categories of private enterprise that might play a key role in the process of dynamic corporate governance that we have pin-pointed as the key vehicle for the solution of X-inefficiency problems? The most obvious such special category is the *foreign-owned private sector*.

FOREIGN DIRECT INVESTMENT, EFFICIENCY ENHANCEMENT AND TECHNOLOGY TRANSFER

In-depth case studies of FDI in the transition countries (Havas, 1997; Barz, 1999; Estrin *et al.*, 1997; Martin, 1998) support the following generalisations:

1. FDI always brings with it a transfer of "soft" technology, i.e., of organisational, managerial, marketing and office technology.
2. While in many cases it is possible to marry up Western soft tech-nology, as key firm-specific advantage (in Dunning's sense — see Dunning, 1988), with local "hard" technology (the technology of process and product), key elements of hard technology often have to be transferred to guarantee the success of the project.[2]

---

[2]The distinction between soft and hard technology is, of course, a blurred one. Integrated software and computer systems to support in-house e-mail systems and the like partake of both. Management and control of production processes, a key area of technology transfer, occupies a similarly ambivalent position.

3. As a result of points 1 and 2 above, productivity levels in firms hosting FDI are almost invariably enhanced.
4. FDI sometimes facilitates significant transfers of hard technology from East to West.
5. FDI sometimes reinforces the building of supply networks in host countries, thus producing ramified productivity impacts.

Of course there may be negative elements in the impact of FDI on host economies in the transition region. Foreign investors may be restrictive in their policies on hard technology transfer to the host enterprise (it is not really possible to be restrictive in relation to the transfer of soft technology). They may be exploitative, on the "Bangalore" model, in relation to East-to-West technology transfer. They may, indeed, be both those things at the same time. The record on supply networking is very patchy, and even where there is net-working there are doubts about how much ramified productivity impact there is in the case of lower-tier suppliers from host countries, where the relationship between the investing firm and the supplier has no R&D or design component. More generally, there are worries about the extent to which FDI will automatically lead to "deep" integration, leading to convergence to Western standards of productivity, as opposed to "shallow" integration, which tends to result in limited productivity enhancement and to institutionalise the technological lag *vis-à-vis* the West (Ellingstad, 1997; Radošević & Dyker, 1997; Inzelt, 1999).

None of this is to dispute the basically positive impact of FDI on the transition process. And it is, of course, the economics profession that has largely been responsible for charting and analysing FDI flows. But in doing so, they have encountered phenomena which are not easily explained in terms of traditional economic analysis. The transition region is a region of low real wages — very low in relation to the average levels of education and qualification that prevail. Yet in virtually no instances, except those coming under the Bangalore rubric, has the availability of cheap labour been a major factor in decision-taking by Western companies on FDI. Indeed accessing of Russian, Kazakh and Azerbaijani hydrocarbons and Uzbek gold has provided the only major examples of resource-seeking FDI in the transition region. Generally speaking, foreign investors have been more concerned to access markets than factors of production, and have clearly been keenly aware that low wages are no advantage at all if they are matched, or more than matched, by low productivity. Thus the Heckscher-Ohlin theorem provides few insights into patterns of FDI in the transition countries (though patterns of arms' length trade can largely be explained in terms of it). The key for foreign investors is effective control over productivity, and that means control over production process through the marshalling of soft technology. Traditional trade theory largely fails to consider the productivity variable, so that it is hardly surprising that it fails to explain pattern of FDI in the given context. It should, of course, be stressed that is again economists who, in their analysis of the notion of "competitiveness", have brought out the key importance of productivity differences in international economic relations (Porter, 1985; 1990). But in doing so they have pointed, once again, to the preeminence of X-efficiency considerations over those of resource allocation in the context of fundamental restructuring, and implicitly the predominance of management issues over strictly economic issues in the transition business.

More generally, FDI points up a conclusion that was already beginning to emerge from material cited earlier. Privatisation and private ownership are important, but are important in particular, not in general. In the end, it is the individual firm, whether it is a precocious SME from the region itself, a dynamic subsidiary of an MNC, or a successfully commercialised enterprise still in a degree of public ownership, that matters, and it is extremely difficult to generalise across the board about what makes a good firm in the transition region: active contact with foreign business (if not necessarily FDI) certainly, possession of some in-house R&D or design capacity almost certainly, a willingness to spend money on upgrading human capital very probably. But for a discipline like economics which likes to think deductively rather than inductively, to proceed from the general to the particular, this is all a bit awkward.

REGULATION AND INSTITUTION-BUILDING

One of the great underlying failures of socialist planning, in both its centralised and market-socialist variants, was the failure to establish systems of parameters, i.e., systems based on coefficients which are "constant in the case under consideration but which may vary from case to case" (Bullock & Stallybrass, 1977, p. 455). The most obvious illustration of this, as noted earlier, is in relation to price systems. But the problem was more general than that, and it was in the realm of budget constraints that centralised and decentralised systems showed the highest degree of similarity, with the principle of *soft budget constraints* universally applied. So economic actors never really knew where they were, but did understand very clearly that if you get into trouble the name of game is to change the "parameter" rather than to change the way that you react to the parameter on a day-to-day basis. It is not difficult, in that context, to understand why productivity was such a problem under socialism! Again, the collapse of the old system was a triumph for an economics profession which had always, explicitly or implicitly, based its analysis of economic efficiency on the concept of parameters. To refer back to some of the earlier analysis, it is, indeed, clear that the *microeconomic* dimension of shock therapy is largely about rerooting the notion of parameters in the minds of economic actors (whether those actors are familiar with the term as such is, of course, immaterial).

But the realities of on-going transition brought problems, practical and conceptual. It soon became clear that, in order to work efficiently, markets would have to be buttressed by appropriate institutions as well as systems of parameters. No economist familiar with the work of Friedrich Hayek (1983) should have been surprised by this. But again the transition from *a priori* analysis to practical policy-making caused some difficulty. To change parameters, or to change the way parameters impact on economic actors, governments need only resort to regulatory instruments of the conventional kind, such as taxes, interest rates, exchange rates, etc. or to legal requirements, e.g. in relation to the breaking-up of a monopoly.

Changing institutions is not so easy. Building institutions from the ground upwards is extremely difficult.

The key importance of institution-building in relation to markets soon become evident in connection with systems of foreign trade. All of the former socialist countries, not least the countries of the FSU, wanted to be rid of the old CMEA (Council for Mutual Economic Assistance), under which they had, in communist times, traded with each other on an essentially barter basis. They all welcomed the transition to settlements in hard currency (Flemming & Rollo, 1992). But the institutional vacuum left by the liquidation of the CMEA created serious problems in trade between erstwhile fraternal countries, some of which have not been resolved to this day. Settlements in hard currency should not mean that every import has to be paid in cash, but in the absence of satisfactory clearing systems this is the only way that hard-currency foreign trade can be carried on. Differences between countries in relation to customs procedures, domestic product regulations, etc. mean that normal trade cannot proceed without an efficient system of trade facilitation, which in the modern world involves participation in dedicated, computerised, international networks which can only be extended through active institution-building (Dyker, 1994).

A more deep-seated institutional problem is that of the banking system. One of the dominant institutional features of centralised socialist planning was the *monobank*, which combined the roles of central bank and "commercial" bank, in a setting where money was allowed to be "active" only in the consumer sector. The market socialist systems had banking structures similar to those of the advanced capitalist countries, with a clear distinction drawn between central and commercial banks, at least in principle. In practice, in the context of generalised soft budget constraints, the distinction was often blurred. But money was active in Yugoslavia and Hungary.

As transition began, the countries which had practised central planning were faced with the task of creating a commercial banking network *ab initio*. The market socialist countries had a foundation to build on, but they had to redefine the relationship between central and commercial banks, and the status of the latter in property terms.

In both cases, serious problems arose from the very start. The creation of privately-owned banks, far from proving the innate strengths of the market mechanism, tended rather to highlight problems of "the incentive to cheat" which are, indeed, familiar enough from Western experience and from economic research done on Western banking systems (Stiglitz & Weiss, 1981; 1986; Gertler, 1988; Akerlof & Romer, 1993; Norton, 1994). The essence of the problem is the vulnerability of banking systems to dishonest or foolhardy borrowers, and to "looting", where bankers misappropriate depositors' funds in the knowledge that some kind of banking insurance system will ensure that the lenders would not lose their money, and that the losses would, in fact, be "socialized". East European banking systems are particularly vulnerable to problems like these, partly because "new" central banks are still on a learning curve in relation to supervision, and the commercial bankers themselves in relation to credit allocation. More fundamentally, however, the stubborn survival of the mentality, and sometimes the reality, of soft budget constraints means that there is a sense in which bank deposit guarantee in the transition countries is universal, or at least believed to be universal. In the extreme case of the "zero" or "pocket" bank, individuals, usually members of the old *nomenklatura*, create banks to lend to themselves or to enterprises they control, in the belief that any losses thus incurred will eventually be covered by the central bank or the government. In the countries of mass, voucher-based privatisation, notably the Czech Republic and Russia, the problem of the incentive to cheat in the banking system has been compounded by the difficulty of regulating relations between banks and the investment funds which quickly sprung up to capitalise on the desire of most ordinary people to cash in their vouchers (Gower, 1997).

What is the solution to these problems? Credit rationing can provide defences against crooked or silly borrowers, but not against dishonest bankers. Credit rationing is in any case perhaps a little too like the old system in Eastern Europe to figure as a credible policy option. If credit rationing is excluded, we are left with two variables to work on — the soft budget constraints mentality and the competence of bankers. On the first count we are basically back with macroeconomic discipline, with the economists once again to the fore as policy advisers. But in countries like the Czech Republic where inherited fiscal strength has allowed the soft budget constraint to survive without causing headlong inflation, the policy recipe is less clear. What is clear is that formal deposit insurance is not a good idea in transition conditions. As far as the competence of bankers is concerned, the economics profession has a good deal to offer the central bankers. But commercial banking, credit allocation in particular, has little to do with economics as such. Here bankers have to be trained by bankers, preferably bankers conscious of the considerable problems that Western banking systems have had with incentive to cheat and credit allocation issues in recent years.

In other areas, too, economics has been able to set the agenda, without always being able to find answers to specific problems. In the area of *monopoly and competition policy*, the basic recommendation was clear enough — in building a market economy, make sure you build a competitive one, within which producers will be rewarded for addressing the demands of the masses, and for responding to innovative impulses, and where rent-seeking will not be allowed to distort the pattern of resource allocation and produce socially unacceptable inequalities in distribution of income. But real life is more complex. As with banking, the civil servants in the transition countries are still at a low point on the regulatory learning curve, and in the early days of transition attempts to curb monopoly were often manipulated by the very monopolists they sought to control (Dyker & Barrow, 1994). More stubborn problems have occurred on the interface between monopoly/competition policy and FDI policy. What should the policy of transition countries be towards Western tobacco companies which seek to buy up former state monopolies in the transition countries? Abuse of monopoly position apart, ethical and public health considerations should surely counsel against any accommodation of such initiatives. Yet the fact is that Western tobacco companies have been a major vehicle for the transfer of soft technology to the transition countries (Yegorov, 1999). Here is a classic static/dynamic dilemma, with serious moral complications thrown in for good measure. It would be too much to expect economics to solve all these problems by itself.

The issue of accession to the European Union has further complicated the issue of regulation. The general principle which guides EU policy on enlargement is that countries seeking accession must come into line with the *acquis communautaire* — the established framework of EU law, including in relation to regulation of the economy. A number of awkward problems have arisen in this connection. Going back to the monopoly/competition issue, should a general commitment to free, open markets necessarily involve wholesale extension of an EU competition law that is very much oriented to the requirements of advanced, West European economies? Is it, for instance, proper to enforce a severe regime in relation to restrictive practices in distribution in countries where distribution is one of the weakest sectors, and where practices such as retail price maintenance may help distributors to build networks? (Smith, Alasdair, 1999). And what about environmental standards and the protection of workers? Here again economic analysis is generally unsupportive of rigid convergence requirements.

It is possible to argue that there is simply no economic case for harmonisation of environmental and social policy at any stage of European integration, and that opt-outs should be permanently permitted. Within an integrated Europe, there is nothing unfair or unnatural about competition between the citizens of areas with differing climates, languages, educational systems. Where such differences confer competitive advantages on particular groups of workers, the advantaged workers can enjoy higher real wages than the less fortunate. Some groups of European citizens could choose to create competitive advantages for themselves by accepting lower environmental quality or poorer social protection. Forcing higher standards on them will force them to accept lower wages in order to compete. They should be free to choose the balance of cash and non-cash rewards they receive (Smith, Alasdair, 1999).

But in the real world, where policy-making on issues like enlargement and regulatory convergence are strongly influenced by sectoral lobbying and bureaucratic departmentalism on the EU side, and where the realities of monopoly and competition, pollution, safety at work, employment of children, etc. in the transition economies are determined to an even higher degree by the perceived self-interest of sectoral lobbies, what can economics do apart from simply "unmasking" the special pleaders? It can deliver good pieces of advice on specific issues. Thus Alasdair Smith (1999), for instance, argues that worries that an environmental free-for-all might lead to "environmental and social dumping" in relation to FDI are best addressed by international agreements on investment incentives, rather than rigid environmental convergence requirements. But what if the special pleaders in favour of enforced convergence are simply too strong for the champions of economic common sense? At that point the problem has to be handed over to the politicians, perhaps the political scientists. Once again, economics proves adept at diagnosis; the surgery, however, has to be left to others.

SUMMARY CONCLUSIONS

What Transition Has Learned from Economics

- Appropriate transition policies must be based on a clear understanding of the nature of the crisis out of which transition is sought. Only with the help of economics are we able to go beyond the purely rhetorical and ideological level in our analysis of the breakdown of socialism, and see how crucial microeconomic weaknesses affected aggregate production functions and ultimately macroeconomic equilibrium.
- Against that background, economics has been able to identify key macroeconomic priorities for first-stage transition, based on a clear understanding of how these priorities relate to underlying microeconomic goals.
- Economics has provided sharp diagnoses of the problems affecting ultimate implementation of these microeconomic goals, but without always being able to follow up the diagnoses with clear-cut policy-making recommendations.

What Economics Has Learned from Transition

- Professional humility: Further to the last bullet point of the previous sub-section, we can only pass from the stage of diagnosis to that of operational policy advice by working jointly with other social scientists, with management specialists, and with practitioners.

- Analytical pragmatism: We need neo-classical economics to identify and analyse the main quantitative variables involved and we need a good dose of old-fashioned industrial economics to help us to understand the microeconomic agenda; the evolutionary approach to economics helps in very general terms, but not on specifics, because ultimately transition (perhaps transformation is a better word[3]) has to mean some kind of clean break with the old system, rather than evolution out of it.

- Who owns what is important, but not as important as who runs what, and how they run it.

- The importance of being dynamic: X-efficiency is more important than allocative efficiency, long-term is more important than short-term, and learning processes, especially in relation to technology, ultimately dominate the prospects for individual transition countries: none of this is a problem for economics, but it is a challenge, a challenge that has to be met, day after day, by any economist working in the transition area.

REFERENCES

Akerlof, GA and PM Romer (1993). Looting: The economic underworld of bankruptcy for profit. *Brookings Papers on Economic Activity*, 2, 1–73.

Balcerowicz, L (1993). *Common Fallacies in the Debate on the Economic Transition in Central and Eastern Europe*. EBRD Working Paper No. 11, London, October.

---

[3]Some transition specialists of a markedly pragmatic bent refuse to use the word "transition" on the grounds that "transition" involves some notion of gradualism, which, they argue, is quite inappropriate in the given context. See von Hirschhausen, 1998.

Barz, M (1999). British and German MNCs in Russia and the FSU — evidence from the Western side. In *Foreign Direct Investment and Technology Transfer in the Former Soviet Union*, DA Dyker (ed.). Cheltenham: Edward Elgar.

Bergson, A (1964). *The Economics of Soviet Planning*. New Haven: Yale University Press.

———— (1978). *Productivity and the Social System — The USSR and the West*. Cambridge, Mass.: Harvard University Press.

Berliner, J (1966). Marxism and the Soviet economy. In *The Soviet Economy: A Book of Readings*, 2nd Ed., M Bornstein and DR Fusfeld (eds.). Homewood, Illinois: Irwin.

Bitzer, J and C von Hirschhausen (1998a). Case study Poland — Restructuring and integration in international networks: The case of the Szczecin shipyard, 1990–98. TSER programme "Restructuring and Reintegration of Science and Technology Systems in Economies in Transition", draft, Berlin, DIW, June.

———— (1998b). *The Shipbuilding Industry in Eastern Europe: A Sector Survey*. TSER programme "Restructuring and Reintegration of Science and Technology Systems in Economies in Transition", draft, Berlin, DIW, June.

Bobinski, C (1998). Polish business. Small enterprises optimistic. *Financial Times*, 8, January.

Bullock, A and O Stallybrass (1977). *The Fontana Dictionary of Modern Thought*. London: Collins.

Bzhilianskaya, L (1999). Foreign direct investment in the science-based industries in Russia. In *Foreign Direct Investment and Technology Transfer in the Former Soviet Union*, DA Dyker (ed.). Cheltenham: Edward Elgar.

Csaba, L (1989). The recent past and the future of the Hungarian reform: An overview and assessment. In *Hungary. The Second Decade of Economic Reform*, RA Clarke (ed.). London: Longman.

Dunning, JH (1988). *Multinationals, Technology and Competitiveness*. London: Unwin Hyman.

Dyker, DA (1970). Industrial location in the Tadzhik republic. *Soviet Studies*, xxi(4).

———— (1983). *The Process of Investment in the Soviet Union*. CUP.

———— (1990). *Yugoslavia: Socialism, Development and Debt*. London: Routledge.

———— (1982). Planned and unplanned investment patterns in the 1980s. In *The CMEA Five-Year Plans in a New Perspective*. Brussels: NATO, Economics and Information Directorates.

———— (1994). *Establishing Conditions Conducive to Expanding Trade among Economics in Transition*. STEEP Discussion Paper No. 12, SPRU, University of Sussex, March.

Dyker, DA and M Barrow (1994). *Monopoly and Competition Policy in Russia*. Post-Soviet Business Forum, Royal Institute of International Affairs.

Economic Commission for Europe (ECE) (1990). *Economic Survey of Europe in 1989–1990*. New York: United Nations.

Economic Commission for Europe (ECE) (1991). *Economic Survey of Europe in 1990–1991.* New York: United Nations.

———— (1992). *Economic Survey of Europe in 1991–1992.* New York: United Nations.

———— (1993). *Economic Survey of Europe in 1992–1993.* New York: United Nations.

Ellingstad, M (1997). The Maquiladora syndrome: Central European prospects. *Europe-Asia Studies,* 49(1), 7–21.

Estrin, S, K Hughes and S Todd (1997). *Foreign Direct Investment in Central and Eastern Europe.* London: Pinter and RIIA.

Flemming, J and J Rollo (eds.) (1992). *Trade, Payments and Adjustment in Central and Eastern Europe.* London: Royal Institute of International Affairs, European Bank for Reconstruction and Development.

Gertler, M (1988). Financial structure and aggregate economic activity: An overview. *Journal of Money, Credit and Banking,* 20(3), 559–96.

Gower, P (1997). *Banking Development in the Czech Republic: An Analysis of Credit Allocation.* D. Phil thesis, University of Sussex.

Havas, A (1997). Foreign direct investment and intra-industry trade: The case of the automotive industry in Central Europe. In *The Technology of Transition. Science and Technology Policy for Transition Countries,* DA Dyker (ed.). Budapest: Central European University Press.

Hayek, F (1983). *Knowledge, Evolution and Society.* London: ASI.

Hirschhausen, C von (1998). Industrial restructuring in post-socialist Eastern Europe and the Baltic countries: Privatisation, enterprization and new enterprise networks. In *New Neighbours in Eastern Europe: Economic and Industrial Reform in Lithuania, Latvia and Estonia,* C von Hirschhausen (ed.). Paris: Les Presses de l'École des Mines.

Inzelt, A-M (1999). The transformation role of FDI in R&D: Analysis based on material from a databank. In *Quantitative Studies for Science and Technology Policy in the Countries of Central and East Europe,* DA Dyker and S Radošević (eds.). NATO: Kluwer.

Leibenstein, H (1966). Allocative efficiency vs. X-efficiency. *American Economic Review,* vi(3).

Martin, R (1998). Central and Eastern Europe and the international economy: The limits to globalisation. *Europe-Asia Studies,* 50(1), 7–26.

McAuley, AND (1967). Rationality and central Planning. In *Soviet Studies,* xviii(3).

Norton, JJ (1994). *Banks, Fraud and Crime.* London: Lloyds of London Press.

OECD (1997). *Economic Surveys — Slovenia 1997: Special Feature, Economic and Financial Restructuring.* Centre for Cooperation with the Economies in Transition.

Pejovich, S (1972). Towards an economic theory of the creation and specification of property rights. *Review of Social Economy,* 30(3).

Porter, ME (1985). *Competitive Advantage.* New York: Free Press.

———— (1990). *The Competitive Advantage of Nations.* London and Basingstoke: Macmillan Press.

Pripisnov, V (1996). *The Development of Small and Medium-Sized Enterprises (SMEs) in Russia 1993–95*. STEEP Discussion Paper No. 35, SPRU, University of Sussex.

Radošević, S and DA Dyker (1997). Technological integration and global marginalization of Central and East European economies: The role of FDI and alliances. In *Restructuring Eastern Europe: The Microeconomics of the Transition Process*, S Sharma (ed.). Cheltenham: Edward Elgar.

Rems, M, M Rojec and M Simoneti (1997). *Ownership Structure and Performance of Slovenian Non-Financial Corporate Sector*. Ljubljana: Institute of Macroeconomic Analysis and Development.

Smith, Alan (1983). *The Planned Economies of Eastern Europe*. London: Croom Helm.

Smith, Alasdair (1999). The European Union and the challenge of enlargement: Integration into the Single Market. In *The European Economy*, 2nd Ed., DA Dyker (ed.). Harlow: Longman.

Stiglitz, J and A Weiss (1981). Credit rationing in markets with imperfect information. *American Economic Review*, 71, 393–410.

——— (1986). Credit rationing and collateral. In *Recent Developments in Corporate Finance*, J Edwards, J Franks, C Mayer and S Shaefer (eds.). New York: Cambridge University Press, pp. 101–35.

Whitesell, R (1990). Why does the Soviet economy appear to be allocatively efficient? *Soviet Studies*, 42(2), 259–68.

Yegorov, I (1999). FDI in Ukraine: First results, tendencies and prospects. In *Foreign Direct Investment and Technology Transfer in the Former Soviet Union*, DA Dyker (ed.). Cheltenham: Edward Elgar.

Index

372   *Index*

distribution 11, 56, 77, 116, 146, 226,
227, 257, 262, 264, 272, 310, 326,
352, 362, 363
Drnovšek, J. 39
dual economy 265
dual-purpose technology 64
Dunning, J. 11, 88, 171, 219, 356
J. Dunning 88

East Asia 105, 167, 172, 192, 203, 218
East Germany 264
East Prussia 17
economic learning 253, 254, 257, 272,
274, 281, 282
Economics 9, 122, 345, 355, 362, 365
economies of scale 139, 140, 144, 172,
195, 213
education 9, 161, 188, 195, 265, 266,
325, 328, 333, 334, 357
EKTA 280
elasticity of substitution 95
Elbrus-2 supercomputer 233
Elcibey, A. 41
electro-welding 125
electronics 174, 180, 182, 232, 280,
330, 332
Elsag-Bailey 234
Energiya 244, 245
Energomash 236, 244
energy 16–18, 57, 58, 80, 118, 130,
232, 317
Energy Charter 130
engineering 10, 11, 111, 123–125,
152, 227, 231, 240, 241, 243, 253,
273, 302, 330, 332–334, 346
English 14, 81, 217
enlargement 15–19, 120, 140,
194, 363
environment 3, 7, 47, 69, 71, 72, 154,
162, 172, 205, 213, 239, 247, 258,
271, 274, 275, 305, 308, 351
environmental and social dumping 364
Estonia 28, 121, 141, 145, 148,
160–162, 165, 259, 292, 293, 296,
297, 300–302, 308, 315, 316, 318,
323, 325, 338

ethnic sectarianism 40, 41, 46, 48
Europe 3, 12, 13, 25, 79, 87, 130,
158, 160, 186, 207, 221, 279,
291–297, 300, 323, 345, 361
Europe Agreements 141, 143
European Coal and Steel
Community 140
European Commission 17, 18, 61, 73,
122, 127, 128, 134, 142, 223, 236
European Economic Area
(EEA) 132
European Union (EU) 6, 15, 139, 154,
163, 189, 294, 350, 363
Eurostat 93, 95, 96, 100, 101,
145, 323
exclusion 4, 15, 16, 19, 76
export 60–62, 74, 109, 117, 128, 133
expropriation 47, 78
extensive development 324
external economies 19, 172
external economy of scale 267, 279
extra-hard metals 232

factor incongruity 92
factor price equalisation 103
Farsi 41
Fergana Valley 116
feudal 5, 39, 44, 47, 56, 75, 77, 79–81
feudalism 26, 75, 78, 79
Fiat 109
financial sector 53, 277
Finland 13, 235
firms 7, 12, 47, 89, 107, 144, 157,
171, 178, 183, 191, 205, 217, 253,
307, 333, 357
First-order economic learning 253, 274
First-tier suppliers 12, 164–166,
179–182, 194, 220, 334
fishing rights 36
food industry 58, 59, 226, 227
footwear 157, 183, 224
Ford 109, 159, 235, 307
foreign debt 51
foreign direct investment (FDI) 8, 11,
69, 80, 159, 171, 207, 217, 218,
268, 306, 338, 356

Printed in the United States
By Bookmasters